Christian Political Theory and Church Politics in the Mid-Twelfth Century

Published under the auspices of the
CENTER FOR MEDIEVAL AND RENAISSANCE STUDIES
University of California, Los Angeles

Publications of the
CENTER FOR MEDIEVAL AND RENAISSANCE STUDIES, UCLA

1. Jeffrey Burton Russell: Dissent and Reform in the Early Middle Ages
2. C. D. O'Malley: Leonardo's Legacy
3. Richard H. Rouse: Serial Bibliographies for Medieval Studies
4. Speros Vryonis, Jr.: The Decline of Medieval Hellenism in Asia Minor and the Process of Islamization from the Eleventh through the Fifteenth Century
5. Stanley Chodorow: Christian Political Theory and Church Politics in the Mid-Twelfth Century

Christian Political Theory and Church Politics in the Mid-Twelfth Century

The Ecclesiology of Gratian's Decretum

Stanley Chodorow

Berkeley   Los Angeles   London
UNIVERSITY OF CALIFORNIA PRESS
1972

BV
761
·A65
C5

University of California Press
Berkeley and Los Angeles, California
University of California Press, Ltd.
London, England
Copyright © 1972 by The Regents of the University of California
ISBN: 0–520–01850–8
Library of Congress Catalog Card Number: 71–138512
Designed by Jorn B. Jorgensen
Printed in the United States of America

FOR MY PARENTS
Doris and Julius Chodorow

Preface

When I started working on the Decretum Gratiani, I intended to study the Magister's ecclesiology and to compare his ideas with those of his contemporaries. As the study progressed, I began to see striking similarities between Gratian's work and other works I was reading. When I delved into the political history of the period in which the Decretum was written, I saw the connections between Gratian and his contemporaries more clearly than I had before. My studies on the Decretum have shown that his generation of intellectuals—including Saint Bernard of Clairvaux, Peter the Venerable, Gerhoh of Reichersberg, and other well-known writers—was deeply involved in ecclesiastical politics and that the political situation had a profound effect on their thought.

The result of this development of my original theme is that two normally separate areas of medieval historical scholarship have been brought together in this book. The intellectual history of the twelfth century, especially that part of it dealing with political and legal thought, has been united with the political history of the period. The contribution that I have tried to make to political history demonstrates clearly what all historians should always keep in mind: Politics and political thought are often intimately connected and study of both subjects is necessary if a satisfactory picture of political history is to be constructed.

As in all projects like this one, I owe thanks to many people for aid and encouragement, and it gives me great pleasure to mention at least some of them here. First, I want to thank Professor Brian Tierney of Cornell University who first interested me in medieval history and then took on the task of making me a historian. He has seen many drafts of this work and offered innumerable suggestions for its improvement. His help is deeply appreciated. Second, much of the research that went into this book was done during the fourteen months I spent at the University of Tübingen, Germany. I want to thank the Alexander von Humboldt Stiftung for enabling me to go to Tübingen through a generous fellowship. While at Tübingen, I worked with Professor Horst Fuhrmann who gave me a great deal of help in the course of my research. He also read and commented upon a part of the original draft of my work, and his comments were very helpful. Third, Professor Donald Kagan of Yale University and Professor Steven Muller of Cornell, who were on my doctoral committee, have made suggestions for which I am grateful. Fourth, I want to thank two typists, Mrs. Louise Massicci and Mrs. Eunice Konold, who did excellent work notwithstanding the obstacles presented by a text and footnotes in several languages. Finally, in mentioning my wife, Peggy, I can only indicate the enormous debt that I owe her. She has been not only my steady support while I labored with Gratian and his friends but also my best critic and editor.

I have undertaken a broad subject touching on several branches of medieval intellectual and political history. There are bound to be lacunae and errors in such a work, and I of course take full responsibility for them.

Contents

Abbreviations xi

I. Introduction 1

II. Gratian and Church Politics 17
   Reforming the Reform Papacy 27
   The Policy Positions of the Two Parties 39
   Gratian and the Reform Party 47

III. The Church as a Juridical Community 65
   The Foundation of the Church 68
   Membership in the Church According to Gratian's Con-
   temporaries 76
   Membership in the Church According to Gratian . . 87

IV. Human Authority and the Hierarchy of Law . . . 96
   Gratian's Argument in the Tractatus de Legibus . . 99

V. Human Authority and the Divine Law 112
   The Theory of Obedience 114
   The Sacrament of Penitence 124

VI. Human Authority and Its Own Law: The Theory of Legis-
lative Power 133
   The Tractatus de Legibus 135
   Causa 25 141
   The Historical Importance of the Theory of Legislative
   Power 148

VII. Sacerdotal Power and the Hierarchy of the Church . . . 154
   The Problem of Sacerdotal Power 155

Sacerdotal Power According to the Schools of Laon, Saint Victor, and Peter Abelard 159

Sacerdotal Power According to Gratian 164

The Ordo Episcopalis *and the Position of the Pope* . . 178

VIII. The Source of Legitimate Authority in the Church . . . 187

The Election: Choice of God or the Community? . . . 189

The Ordination: The Priest's Reception of Power and Authority 195

The Theory of the Electorate: Its Historical and Constitutional Importance 199

IX. The Division of Governmental Responsibilities Between *Regnum* and *Sacerdotium*: The Ecclesiastical Community and Other Communities 211

The Division of Judicial and Legislative Power . . . 215

The Use of Force by the Church 223

X. Conclusions 247

The Decretum in the Twelfth Century 247

The Place of the Decretum in Medieval Political Theory 250

Appendix I: The Date of the Decretum 255

Appendix II: Saint Bernard and the Law 260

Bibliography 267

Index 293

Abbreviations

AKKR   Archiv für katholisches Kirchenrecht
Bernard de Clairvaux   Commission d'histoire de l'Ordre de Citeaux, III, *Bernard de Clairvaux,* Paris, 1953.
CSEL   Corpus Scriptorum Ecclesiasticorum Latinorum
DA   Deutsches Archiv für Erforschung des Mittelalters
DDC   Dictionnaire de droit canonique
DTC   Dictionnaire de Théologie catholique
Études Le Bras   Études d'histoire du droit canonique dediées à Gabriel Le Bras. 2 vols., Paris, 1965.
JL   Regesta Pontificum Romanorum, ed. P. Jaffé; 2d ed., 2 vols., ed. S. Loewenfeld, 1885–1888.
Mansi   Mansi, J. D., *Sacrorum Conciliorum Collectio*
MGH   Monumenta Germaniae Historica
PL   J. P. Migne, *Patrologiae cursus completus,* series latina
RHD   Revue historique de droit français et étranger
RHE   Revue d'histoire ecclesiastique
SG   Studia Gratiana
SMGBOZ   Studien und Mitteilungen zur Geschichte des Benediktiner-ordens und seine Zeige
ZRG, Kan. Abt.   *Zeitschrift der Savigny-Stiftung für Rechtsgeschichte,* Kanonistische Abteilung
All English quotations of the Bible are from the Douay version.

I. Introduction

Shortly after 1139 the Bolognese monk Gratian completed and circulated a great collection of the ancient canons of the Church, the Decretum Gratiani as it was to be called. This work became the foundation of a new science of canon law separate from the study of theology. A school of canon law arose in Bologna very soon after the appearance of the Decretum, and a few years later, schools were founded in cities north of the Alps.[1] During the 1140's and 1150's, the leading canonists of these schools, the decretists who commented on the Decretum, were students of Gratian; among them was Rolandus Bandinelli who, in 1159, was to become Pope Alexander III, the first

1. There are several general histories of canon law which give the reader a sense of the importance of Gratian's collection and explain briefly the development of the schools. Alfons Van Hove, *Prolegomena ad Codicem Juris Canonici,* 2d ed. (Rome, 1945). Alfons M. Stickler, *Historia Iuris Canonici Latini* (Turin, 1950). In English, see R. C. Mortimer, *Western Canon Law* (London, 1953). The work of J. F. von Schulte is still standard for the history of canonical jurisprudence after the appearance of the Decretum. Schulte, "Zur Geschichte der Literatur über das Dekret Gratians," I, *Sitzungsberichte der kaiserlichen Akademie der Wissenschaften in Wien,* Phil.-Hist. Kl., vol. 63 (1869); II, vol. 64 (1870); III, vol. 65 (1870). Schulte, "Die Glosse zur Dekret Gratians von ihren Anfängen bis auf die jüngsten Ausgaben," *Denkschriften der kaiserlichen Akademie der Wissenschaften,* Phil.-Hist. Kl., vol. 21 (1872). Schulte, *Die Geschichte der Quellen und Literatur des canonischen Rechts von Gratian bis auf die Gegenwart,* 3 vols. (Stuttgart, 1875–1880). Recently, the work of the Anglo-Norman school has been investigated by Stephan Kuttner and E. Rathbone, "Anglo-Norman Canonists of the Twelfth Century," *Traditio,* 7 (1949–1951), 279–358. See also Kuttner's article, "Les débuts de l'école canoniste française," *Studia et documenta historiae et iuris,* 4 (1938), 1–14. The most essential work on the output of the canon law schools is Kuttner's *Repertorium der Kanonistik,* Prodomus corporis glossarium, *Studi e Testi,* vol. 71 (Vatican City, 1937).

1

of the great lawyer popes of the Middle Ages. Gratian holds the preeminent position in the history of canonical jurisprudence not only because he was the teacher of the first generation of canon law specialists but also because he provided the basic textbook of that law for future generations of student lawyers and the basic legal sourcebook for judges and practicing lawyers in the canon law system. Medieval canonists looked upon Gratian as the Magister; they valued his work both for its content and its methodological innovations.

More than anything else it is his method of treating the canons which has earned Gratian the title of "father of the science of canon law." [2] The Decretum is a massive collection of the ancient law of the Church which goes beyond any of the numerous previous collections of the eleventh and twelfth centuries, but it is a presentation of the old law with a new twist. The Magister applied to the law new methods first employed by the early scholastic theologians in their treatment of patristic texts. He gave later ecclesiastical lawyers a means by which the contradictions found in the canons could be brought to light and then eliminated. Arranging the law into an effective order according to subject, he tried to reconcile the different doctrines that it often produced. In his dicta, he made distinctions, exceptions, and sometimes excuses in order to resolve difficulties raised by the canons. His position in the history of canonical jurisprudence is therefore similar to Peter Abelard's position in the development of scholastic theology, and several scholars have argued that he took his method from Abelard.[3]

2. Van Hove, "Quae Gratianus contulerit methodo scientiae canonicae," *Apollinaris*, 21 (1948), 12–24. Kuttner, "The Father of the Science of Canon Law," *The Jurist*, 1 (1941), 2–19.

3. It has proven very difficult for scholars to answer the question: What were the sources of Gratian's method? Ivo of Chartres, whose collections served as the most important source of canons for the Decretum, wrote a *prologus* for either his Decretum or his Panormia in which he suggested rules for dealing with contradictions found in the canons. The canonist ought to consider the original purpose of the text because admonitions should yield to statements of law and indulgences should not be given the force of general law. Also, the canonist should ask whether the provisions of the canon were meant to be revocable or irrevocable and whether a dispensation could be granted in certain circumstances. Rules for reconciling contradictions were also briefly expounded by Bernold of Constance in the treatise, *De excommunicatis vitandis, de reconciliatione lapsorum et de fontibus iuris canonici* (edited in *MGH*, Libelli de lite II). The most

Gratian's work remained in use, while Abelard's did not, because Gratian expounded legal doctrines that were seminal in the history of law, and because he incorporated the greater part of the ancient law of the Church into his work. The *Decretum* is at once a model of method and of the comprehensive presentation of the vast legal tradition. Theologians had to wait for Peter Lombard's *Sentences* before they possessed a similar model.

Gratian's work and the legal system that arose from it are of interest not only to those concerned with the history of the Church and its institutions but also to those who study the history of secular legal systems in the West. During the past few decades, scholars have shown that many of the lawyers who were responsible for the development of governmental and legal institutions in the secular kingdoms of medieval Europe were trained in canon law. Through the agency of these men, the doctrine of Gratian, and that of the decretists, holds an important place in the history of constitutional government. At the same time, canon law doctrines justified the international political activity of the popes of the eleventh through fourteenth centuries. Canonical theories of world order therefore hold a prominent place in the history of the disputes between *regnum* and *sacerdotium*. Historians have come to recognize that canon law and its practitioners played a very

---

extensive use of the rules outlined by Ivo and Bernold, before Gratian's work appeared, was found in Alger of Liège's *Liber de misericordia et iustitia*. Gratian utilized Alger's work in his own dicta. Stickler, *op. cit.*, pp. 188–193. Gabriel Le Bras, "Alger de Liège et Gratien," *Revue des sciences philosophiques et théologiques*, 20 (1931), 5–26.

The influence of the development of scholastic theology on Gratian's method is also recognized by scholars. Kuttner argued that Gratian's method derived from Abelard's treatment of patristic texts in *Sic et Non* and most scholars have accepted his view. Bliemetzrider, however, has argued for the importance of the school of Laon as the chief source of the Magister's method. Kuttner, "Zur Frage der theologischen Vorlagen Gratians," *ZRG*, Kan. Abt., 24 (1934), 243–268. *Idem*, "The Father of the Science of Canon Law," pp. 10 ff. Van Hove, "Quae Gratianus contulerit methodo scientiae canonicae," pp. 23 f. Stickler, *op. cit.*, pp. 193–194. Kuttner supported Thaner's position that Gratian was theologically closer to Abelard and especially Hugh of Saint Victor than to anyone else. Friedrich Thaner, *Abaelard und das kanonische Recht* (Graz, 1900). For Bliemetzrieder's argument, see Franz Bliemetzrieder, "Gratian und die Schule Anselms von Laon," *AKKR*, 112 (1932), 37–63. Most recently, D. E. Luscombe, *The School of Abelard* (Cambridge, 1969).

significant role in the political as well as legal history of the West.[4] Gratian, as the father of canonical jurisprudence, is a preeminent figure in the history of Western law and government as well as in the history of ecclesiastical institutions.

Ironically, awareness of Gratian's importance has had an unfortunate effect upon those who have studied his work. They have looked at the Decretum as the beginning of something new and exciting in the history of the Middle Ages; it has been treated as part of the legal system based upon it. The problem with this approach is that it limits our appreciation of Gratian's achievement. The tendency of historians to fix upon elements of ancient times which can be linked with present-day or at least later institutions, ideas, or events has been carried to the extreme in Gratian scholarship. In the corpus of that scholarship, there are many articles that present excellent analyses of the Magister's doctrines on one point or another,[5] but there is no attempt, with only one exception to be discussed shortly, to study the work as a whole and to determine its general orientation. From studies of Gratian's doctrines, nothing is learned about the importance of the Decretum at the time it was written or about the Magister's purposes in undertaking his enormous task. The aim of this book is to assess the historical significance of the Decretum in the year 1140 or thereabouts. The basic question to be answered is: What was Gratian trying to do in the Decretum?

It is important to note that an understanding of or at least a concern for the original purpose of the work seems to have been lost very early in its history. The different names given to the work by Gratian and his successors provide a hint of the different views of the work held by him and the schools. The decretists called the work the Decretum or

4. Brian Tierney, "Medieval Canon Law and Western Constitutionalism," *Catholic Historical Review,* 52 (1966), 1–17. Gaines Post, *Studies in Medieval Legal Thought* (Princeton, 1964), Frederick W. Maitland, *Roman Canon Law in the Church of England* (London, 1898).

5. In 1948, to celebrate the eighth centennial of the Decretum, the journal *Apollinaris* devoted a volume to it in which the leading scholars were represented —S. Kuttner, A. Van Hove, A. M. Stickler, A. Vetulani, among others. Since 1953, many articles on Gratian have been published in the series *Studia Gratiana* edited by A. M. Stickler and J. Forchielli. A large number of articles on Gratian and his collection have appeared in other journals as well as in Festschriften.

Decreta and thereby emphasized that for them it was a canonical collection—in fact, it was the canonical collection. Gratian called his work the *Concordia discordantium canonum,* the Concordance of Discordant Canons, and thus emphasized the methodological innovations that he made in it.[6] Gratian's title implies that he was conscious of his role as a reformer of the legal tradition of the Church. Why did he undertake to reform the law? There are two possible answers to that question. First, he may have been a part of the intellectual movement associated with Abelard and the early scholastic theologians. In this case, his effort would have to be understood as purely intellectual, one might say academic, in character. Second, he may have had other motives for his reform of Church law, motives that would become clear only when one studies the historical context in which he wrote the work.

During the years when he compiled the Decretum and taught law at Bologna, Gratian lived in the Camaldulese monastery of Saints Felix and Nabor.[7] It is therefore easy to assume that he was not a man of this world and that his work is indeed the product of the new emphasis on logic and reason in understanding the teaching of Christ and the Fathers. In fact, all studies of Gratian's work have been based on this assumption, and making this assumption has freed scholars from considering what effect, if any, the events of Gratian's times had on his ideas and interests. Yet, it is true that medieval canon lawyers, both before and after Gratian, played an active role in the politics of their times or at least that their collections were profoundly affected by events and political ideas.[8] It is also true that the Magister did not

6. Friedrich Heyer, "Der Titel der Kanonessammlung Gratians," *ZRG,* Kan. Abt., 2 (1912), 336–342. *Idem,* "Namen und Titel des Gratianischen Dekretes," *AKKR,* 94 (1914), 501–517. Rudolf Köstler, "Zum Titel des Gratianischen Dekrets," *ZRG,* Kan. Abt., 21 (1932), 370–373. *Idem,* "Noch einmal: Zum Titel des Gratianischen Dekrets," 23 (1934), 378–380.

7. Very little is known about Gratian's life. What is known has been presented by Kuttner in "The Father of the Science of Canon Law." See chap. ii, n. 33.

8. Paul Fournier, probably the leading modern scholar of pre-Gratian collections, has pointed out that those collections are divided into two groups, Roman and French. The groups are distinguished by their content and sources. The Roman collections dwell on papal primacy and questions dear to the reformers who won control of the Curia in the eleventh century. Roman collectors did a considerable amount of original archival research in their hunt for canons that

5

simply offer to his contemporaries and successors a comprehensive treatment of ecclesiastical law. He left much of importance out of account and later canonists made extensive additions to his work. Also, historians take for granted the worldliness and activity of Saint Bernard of Clairvaux and Peter the Venerable of Cluny, and they know that other monastic leaders of the twelfth century were deeply involved in the affairs of both the Church and the secular kingdoms. They have assumed, however, that the monk Gratian was a man buried away in a monastery in Bologna teaching and writing about the law—a study traditionally connected with things worldly—but supposedly unaffected by the world around him. Scholars have therefore concluded that the first answer to the question about Gratian's purpose in the Decretum is correct; they have assumed that the Magister sought only to reform the law of the Church according to methods established by Abelard and others in the study of theology. Gratian was a monastic intellectual apart from the world and oblivious to its goings-on.

Looking at the history of canon law and of the mid-twelfth century, one can make a strong argument supporting the view that Gratian was affected by the political events and movements of his day and that his work exhibits an interest in the issues raised during his times. The thesis of this book is that the purpose, structure, and orientation—ultimately, the meaning—of the Decretum can only be understood if its connection with the developments within the Church at the time it was written is grasped. This is not to deny that the Magister was concerned with methodology or that he saw his work as a decisive step forward in the treatment of canon law. No one can deny that he had a profound intellectual motivation in undertaking his work. But con-

---

would support their political position, but most of the collections are based on the Collection in 74 Titles and the collection of Anselm of Lucca, both of which were closely associated with the reformers. The French collectors based their works on the Decretum of Burchard of Worms (1002–1008). The content of these collections is not limited to the problems of the reform, but range widely over the areas of canon law jurisdiction. This group culminated in the large and well-known collections of Ivo of Chartres, the most important canonist before Gratian. Paul Fournier, "Une collection canonique italienne du commencement du XIIe siècle," *Annales de l'Enseignement superieur de Grenoble*, 6 (1894), 115. Fournier and Le Bras, *Histoire des collections canoniques en Occident* (Paris, 1932), 2:115.

centrating attention on his use of the dialectical method will not help in understanding the substance of his teaching. For a complete understanding of the Magister's aims and the character of his thought, the Decretum must be looked at from the perspective of the 1120's and 1130's, the period when he was compiling it. In addition, the ideas set forth in the Decretum must be compared with those expounded in contemporary works. Such a study will show that Gratian sought to develop a Christian theory of the structure of society, and that his work is one of the most significant works of political theory written in the mid-twelfth century. Concern with the relationship between the Decretum and the politics of the period in which it was written makes it necessary to involve oneself in the historiography of twelfth-century political history. But before turning to a consideration of Gratian's times and to an exposition of his ideas, the most important views presented in earlier studies of his work must be reviewed.

From a historiographical point of view, the most important work of modern scholarship concerning the Decretum is Rudolph Sohm's *Das altkatholische Kirchenrecht und das Dekret Gratians,* published posthumously in 1918.[9] Basically, Sohm argued that scholars who had found a theory of the ecclesiastical constitution in the Decretum had only imposed their own suppositions and ideas on the Magister's work. The truth of the matter was, he said, that historians could learn nothing

9. This work appeared in the Festschrift der Leipziger Juristenfakultät für Adolf Wach (Munich-Leipzig, 1918). It almost seems as if Sohm planned the piece as a time bomb that would go off when he was well out of the way. The reaction to the book has been vehement and long lasting; attacks on it have been made on a wide range of subjects.

Among the works that consider Sohm's opinions, see H. Barion, *Rudolph Sohm und die Grundlegung des Kirchenrechts,* Recht und Staat in Geschichte und Gegenwart (Tübingen, 1931). *Idem,* "Der Rechtsbegriff Rudolph Sohms," *Deutsche Rechtswissenschaft,* 7 (1942), 47–51. Ernst Kohlmeyer, "Charisma oder Recht? Vom Wesen des ältesten Kirchenrechts," *ZRG,* Kan. Abt., 38 (1952), 1–26. G. Kuhlmann, "Rudolph Sohm und unsere gegenwärtigen kirchenrechtlichen Situation," *Archiv für Kirchenrecht,* 5 (1941), 155–172. Max Reischle, *Sohms Kirchenrecht und der Streit über das Verhältnis von Recht und Kirche* (Giessen, 1895). Joseph de Ghellinck, *Le mouvement théologique du XIIe siècle* (Paris-Brussels, 1948), pp. 523–532. For a complete bibliography, Dieter Stoodt, *Wort und Recht, Rudolph Sohm und das theologische Problem des Kirchenrechts* (Munich, 1962).

whatever about the constitutional law of the medieval Church from the Decretum. Gratian actually sought only to expound the sacramental law of the Church. A review of Sohm's interpretation will clarify the present state of scholarship concerning the Decretum.

Sohm's treatment of Gratian's collection was part of his overall theory of the history of ecclesiastical law.[10] He divided the history of that law into three periods, which developed as the emphasis shifted within the Church from spiritual to material concerns. The first stage was the charismatic period, which lasted only up to the end of the first century. The charismatic Church law was unformulated and existed only in the spirit of the early Christian community. Already during the pontificate of Clement I, this primitive law of the spirit had begun to develop by defining the sacraments and by expressing the spirit of the religion in ceremonial. This was the beginning of the second stage in the history of Church law, the sacramental stage. All Church law during this period was sacramental law, according to Sohm, and at least *de jure,* the ecclesiastical power was wholly devoted to sacramental functions.

The transitional period between this stage and the third stage is the period that is of most interest, because Sohm thought that the change took place in the late twelfth century, *after* the appearance of the De-cretum Gratiani. During this time, ecclesiastical lawyers introduced the idea of jurisdictional power, and the law began to define the power of the priesthood as divided into the powers of orders and jurisdiction. Not until this period did the ecclesiastical hierarchy actually become a governmental authority. The transition in the view of the Church hierarchy's function led to development of ecclesiastical constitutional law and definition of the power of ecclesiastical officers.[11]

The changes in Church law accompanied a new conception of the Church. Sohm argued that the electoral decree of Alexander III, sanctioned by the Third Lateran Council in 1179, was the first official expression of the corporational view of the Ecclesia. The decree refined

10. Besides the work on Gratian, see Sohm's general history of Church law, *Kirchenrecht 1* (Munich-Leipzig, 1892); *Kirchenrecht 2,* ed. E. Jacobi and O. Mayer (Munich-Leipzig, 1923).

11. Sohm, *Das altkatholische Kirchenrecht,* pp. 536–674.

the electoral procedure for choosing a new pope by making a two-thirds majority of the college of cardinals necessary for a valid election. According to Sohm, this provision was crucial in the history of ecclesiastical law because it codified the new conception of the Church and ensured that the governing power would be a juridically legitimate authority. In the 1170's the law of the Church took on a new guise and became the law of governmental power as well as of sacraments.[12]

Gratian's work, according to Sohm, fits into the second phase of ecclesiastical law. The decretists and historians of law had always considered the Decretum as the beginning of the new and independent science of canon law. Sohm argued that Gratian was actually the last of the great theologians to treat canon law and that the work was wholly concerned with sacramental law. Gratian, wrote Sohm, saw every act of the ecclesiastical hierarchy as a sacrament and recognized no limit on the number of sacraments. Only when the Church was redefined, about two decades after the Magister's death, did there develop a definite list of sacraments that corresponded with the new understanding of the Church's place in the world. When traditional hierarchical functions were redefined as acts of a juridical power, sacramental functions had to be circumscribed and defined as well.[13]

12. *Ibid.*, pp. 57–58, 614. *passim.* One of the most important pieces of evidence used by Sohm in developing his theory that the character of Church law changed in the 1170's was a decree issued by the general chapter of the Cistercians in 1188. This decree prohibited the study of law by monks of the order, and Sohm argued that the prohibition stemmed from a recognition of the change in emphasis in ecclesiastical law. This argument has been rejected by Stutz in an article devoted to the Cistercians' attitude toward legal studies. Ulrich Stutz, "Die Cistercienser wider Gratians Dekret," *ZRG*, Kan. Abt., 9 (1919), 63–98.

13. *Sohm, Das altkatholische Kirchenrecht,* pp. 81, 583–584. On the development of early scholastic theology of the sacraments, see Damien Van den Eynde, "La définition des sacrements pendant la première periode de la théologie scolastique (1050–1235)," Antonianum, 24 (1949), 183–228, 439–488 (reprinted as *Les définitions des sacrements* [Louvain, 1950]). Ghellinck, "Un chapitre dans l'histoire de la définition des sacrements au XIIe siècle," *Mélanges Mandonnet,* II, Bibliothèque thomiste. 14 (Paris, 1930), 79–96. Nicholas M. Häring, "Character, Signum und Signaculum. Die Einführung in die Sakramententheologie des 12. Jahrhunderts," *Scholastik,* 31 (1956), 182–212. On the treatment of the sacraments by the canonists, see Franz Gillmann, "Die Siebenzahl der Sakramente bei den Glossatoren des Gratianischen Dekrets," *Der Katholik,* 89 (1909), 182–214. Ghellinck, "La 'Species quadriformis Sacramentorum' des canonistes du

Nearly all the scholarship concerning the Decretum, published both before and after Sohm's work, has been in some way a refutation of his interpretation. On the whole, scholars working on the doctrine of the Magister have not taken up Sohm's contentions with a view to refuting them, but the rejection of his ideas has been implicit in their work. These studies of Gratian's doctrine are not strictly relevant to the present discussion of Sohm's interpretation, but one part of the corpus of Gratian scholarship must be considered. Because Sohm based his views on an analysis of the division of the Decretum, the principal reaction to his work has occurred in articles dealing with the many textual problems raised by the Magister's opus. The amount of work done on these problems is not all the result of Sohm's challenge, however. As medievalists who specialized in fields other than canon law became aware of Gratian's importance, they also became interested in the textual difficulties. It is clear that the meaning of the work cannot be understood without arriving at a clear conception of how the work looked when it left the Magister's workroom.

Modern editions and most manuscripts of the Decretum present it as a work in three parts, the *Distinctiones,* the *Causae,* and the *Tractatus de consecratione.* Sohm argued that the standard divisions were not accurate and that a proper conception of the divisions made by Gratian would show that scholars had misconstrued the Magister's ideas and interests.[14] Scholars now agree with Sohm about the inadequacy of the

---

XIIe siècle et Hugues de Saint-Victor," *Revue des sciences philosophiques et théologiques,* 6 (1912), 527–537. Arthur Landgraf, *Dogmengeschichte der Frühscholastik,* vol. 3 (Regensburg, 1954–1955).

14. Sohm proposed that the division of Gratian's work be understood according to the subject matter. Part one in his scheme consisted of Dist. 1–20, the *Tractatus de legibus,* which treats the sources of law—that is to say, the sources of sacramental law. As will be seen, Gratian considered not only the sources of law in the *de legibus* but also the relationship between the various kinds of law. His main purpose was to examine the hierarchy of law from the standpoint of the ecclesiastical authority. Sohm ignored this theme in the *Tractatus.*

Part two extended from Dist. 21 to Causa 26 and treats the sacrament of orders. Part three consisted of the last *Causae* and the *de consecratione,* treating the sacrament of marriage and the other sacraments. This division seems strange when one considers the format of the Decretum; the reader naturally expects the *Distinctiones, Causae,* and *de consecratione* to make up three integral parts. And Sohm's distinctions between parts appear even more curious when we consider

modern editions,[15] but they can show that his assertions about the original state of the work are wrong. The conclusions of research on the text of the Decretum done after Sohm made his views known are pertinent to my thesis.[16]

The most difficult questions about the original state of Gratian's text concern the additions made by members of the school. The most common kind of addition was the single canon or short series of canons intended to fill gaps in Gratian's discussions of specific issues and given the name *paleae* from the Latin word for chaff.[17] These canons

his division of the second part into two sections. In order to maintain his argument at this point, he argues that Gratian changed course in the middle of a Causa.

The division of part two in Sohm's system is made at C. 1, q. 6. Thus, the first section of part two extends from Dist. 21 to C. 1, q. 6 and the second section from C. 1, q. 7 to C. 26. Sohm, *op. cit.*, pp. 19–36. For the traditional division of the Decretum, see Schulte, *Die Geschichte der Quellen*, I:62.

15. Kuttner, "De Gratiani opere noviter edendo," *Apollinaris*, 21 (1948), 118–128.

16. Franz Gillmann wrote the classic refutation of Sohm's interpretation. In an article published in 1926, he focused his attack on Sohm's views concerning the division of the work. Gillmann noted that all the early decretists recognized three parts in the Decretum corresponding to the *Distinctiones, Causae,* and *de consecratione* and that Gratian's own pupil Paucapalea thought the work treated dignities, causes, and orders, not sacraments. Gillmann, "Einleitung und System des Gratianischen Dekrets nach den alten Dekretglossatoren bis Johannes Teutonicus," *AKKR*, 106 (1926), 472–574. Gratian himself gave certain indications about the division and content of his work. At six places in the Decretum, the Magister referred to the first part, now the *Distinctiones*, as the *Tractatus ordimandorum* or the *Tractatus de promotionibus clericorum.* He referred to the first twenty *Distinctiones* as the *principium or initium*, and to Dist. 19 as the *Tractatus decretalium epistolarum.* The section now called *Causae* was normally called by that name in the Decretum. Gillmann, "Rührt die Distinktioneneinteilung des ersten und dritten Dekretteils von Gratian selbst her?" *AKKR*, 112 (1932), 504–533.

17. See Gillmann, "Paucapalea et paleae bei Huguccio," *AKKR*, 88 (1908), 466–479. Adam Vetulani, "Gratien et le Droit romain," *RHD*, 4th *ser.*, 24 (1946–1947), 11–48. *Idem*, "Une suite d'études pour servir à l'histoire du Décret de Gratien avec une préface de G. Le Bras, I. Les manuscrits du Décret de Gratien conservés dans les bibliothèques polonaises," *RHD*, 4th ser., 15 (1936), 343–358. René Metz, "A propos des travaux de M. Adam Vetulani. La date et la composition du Décret de Gratien," *Revue de Droit canonique*, 7 (1957), 67–69. Jacqueline Rambaud [-Buhot], "L'Étude des manuscrits du Décret de Gratien," *Congrès de Droit canonique mediévale* (Louvain-Bruxelles, 1958), Bibliothèque

are identified through the comparison of manuscripts since their order is inconsistent, and they are sometimes left out altogether. Because of the Decretum's importance during the Middle Ages, there are hundreds of manuscripts of the work, and as the study of these continues, the list of paleae is constantly revised.[18] But the schools were responsible for additions to the Decretum which were much more important than the incorporation of individual paleae. The *Tractatus de consecratione,* normally considered the third part of the work, now appears to have been a later addition.[19] This conclusion is important because of all the parts of the Decretum, the *de consecratione* is the most theological in character. It concerns the sacraments, and its deletion from the work profoundly affects the interpretation offered by Sohm.

---

de la Revue d'histoire ecclesiastique, vol. 33 (1959). Ullmann suggested that the term *palea* came from the Greek for double and argued that originally *paleae* were texts that appeared twice in the Decretum. Walter Ullmann, "The paleae in Cambridge Manuscripts of the Decretum," *SG,* 1 (1953), 156–216. This view has been rejected by Madame Rambaud. Rambaud [Buhot], "Les paleae dans le Décret de Gratien," *Proceedings of the Second International Congress of Medieval Canon Law,* Boston College, 1963, ed. S. Kuttner and J. J. Ryan (Rome, 1965), pp. 23–44. Marguerite Boulet-Saltet, "Les 'paleae' empruntées au Droit romain dans quelques manuscrits du Décret conservés en France," *SG,* 1 (1953), 149–158. As Kuttner says, the paleae are evidence of the critical attitude that members of the schools took toward the Decretum. They did not hesitate to add material that they thought completed the collection. Kuttner, "New Studies in the Roman Law in Gratian's Decretum," *Seminar* (special number of *The Jurist*), 11 (1953), 14.

18. Madame Rambaud of the Bibliothèque Nationale in Paris has the widest knowledge of the manuscripts and has published a new list of paleae in: *L'Âge Classique, Histoire du Droit et des Institutions de l'Église en Occident,* ed. G. Le Bras (Paris, 1965), 7:52–129. Students interested in the textual problems of the Decretum ought to begin with Madame Rambaud's studies here.

19. In some early manuscripts, the *de consecratione* was part of the last Causa and in some early summaries of the Decretum, it was not mentioned. Also, though the *auctoritates* in the treatise were contained in the same collections that served as the main source for other sections of the Decretum and though they are cited in the same way as other auctoritates, there are no dicta in the *de consecratione* giving the treatise a look different from the rest of the work. Taking all the evidence into account, Madame Rambaud has concluded that the text of the *de consecratione* was an addition to the Decretum and that Gratian wrote a work in two parts instead of three. Rambaud, *L'Âge Classique,* pp. 90–97. *Idem,* "L'Étude des manuscrits," pp. 32–33. Vetulani, "Le Décret de Gratien et les premiers Décrétistes à la lumière d'une source nouvelle," *SG,* 7 (1959), 345.

Another part of the edited Decretum now seen as an addition is the *Tractatus de penitencia,* which makes up *Causa* 33, *quaestio* 3. Scholars think that most of this treatise is palea, though some of it constituted the original quaestio 3 of the Causa. The evidence for this view is primarily based on manuscript studies, but there is another strong argument for excluding the treatise from the original Decretum. It is too theological to be considered the work of Gratian. As Wjotyla pointed out, large parts of the *de penitencia* do not conform to the Magister's interests as they are exhibited throughout his work.[20] When stripped of the *Tractati de consecratione* and *de penitencia,* the Decretum becomes very much a work concerned chiefly with the theory and practice of ecclesiastical government.[21] Sohm's position has be-

20. The *Tractatus de penitencia* presents several problems for the student of the Decretum. The treatise was interpolated into a discussion concerning the crime of adultery, and though one would expect treatment of the problems of penitence for such a crime, the *de penitencia* gives considerably more space to the problem than necessary in the context of the Causa. Also, the treatise carries on its discussion in terms of the crime of homicide and does not mention adultery. The auctoritates used in the work do not derive from the earlier collections commonly used by the Magister and do not possess rubrics, as do all the other canons in the Decretum. Often, the citations differ from Gratian's typical way of citing passages. Finally, the auctoritates and dicta are not well separated in the manuscripts and their order, as well as the divisions of the treatise, did not become regular until the later Middle Ages. Rambaud, *L'Âge Classique,* pp. 82–90. *Idem,* "L'Étude des manuscrits," pp. 33–34.

These textual observations are corroborated by the researches of Wojtyla who showed that Dist. 2 through 4 of the treatise concerned aspects of penitence which were often discussed in speculative writings of contemporary theologians. Based on the manuscript evidence, these *Distinctiones* ought to be deleted from the edition of the Decretum. Madame Rambaud has confirmed Wojtyla's findings and suggests that the original quaestio 3 of Causa 33 contained only part of what is now the *de penitencia.*

Karol Wojtyla, "Le traité 'de Penitentia' de Gratien dans l'abrégé de Gdansk Mar. F. 275," *SG,* 7 (1959), 355–390. Rambaud *L'Âge Classique,* pp. 85–86. Madame Rambaud thinks that the original version of C. 33, q. 3, contained what is now *de penitentia,* Dist. 1 (less cc. 6–30); Dist. 5, dict. ante c. 1 and c. 1; Dist. 6 and 7. On penitence in Gratian's period, see P. Anciaux, *La Théologie du sacrement de pénitence au XIIe siècle* (Louvain, 1949).

21. The treatise on marriage, cc. 26–36, might be construed to be outside the unity of purpose and theme which I see in the Decretum. At the same time, this part of the work is more theologically oriented than other parts. Of course, the argument that the work is a unit of thought and aims can be taken too far, but it does not seem to me that the last ten Causae should be considered separate

come untenable, even if it could, at one time, have been taken seriously.

There is one other aspect of the palea problem which should be briefly mentioned here. Many of the texts of the *de penitencia* which have been rejected as paleae, were taken from the Roman law collection of Justinian.[22] Scholars now think that none of the Roman law texts from the *Corpus Iuris Civilis* were incorporated by the Magister when he compiled his work. The evidence for this view has been built up through the detailed manuscript studies of Vetulani, Kuttner, and Rambaud, and it is very convincing.[23] It has become clear that Gratian

---

from the main body of the work either in subject or character. As will be seen in the next chapter, the treatise on marriage does contain discussions that are of great importance to an understanding of Gratian's ecclesiology. It can therefore be argued that the ecclesiological theme of the work is not abandoned in the section dealing with marriage. That is not to say that much in the treatise does not concern the great questions of constitutional law, though a discussion of marriage law is certainly part of any consideration of the structure of society, if not of the structure of government. A reading of the Decretum would in fact show that in every part there are discussions that do not directly concern the main questions of political theory, though they are derived from those questions. The inclusion of these points of detail in the Decretum, its richness, is one of its most important characteristics and one of the things responsible for its lasting significance. Without very much difficulty, Gratian's series of canonical treatises could become a great canonical collection.

The distinction between "legalistic" and "theologically oriented" which Wjotyla has made in his discussion of the *de penitencia* should also not be accepted without some comment and reservations. It is, of course, very difficult to distinguish between theological orientation and the lack of it in a canon law treatise, and this difficulty is greatest when the work in question is the first bona fide work of canonical jurisprudence, the first work in which the distinction can be made at all. Where to draw the line between theological and nontheological in the Decretum will always be a matter of judgment on which scholars will differ. Yet, the character of Gratian's treatment of subjects that were of interest to contemporary theologians, such as the topic in Causa 33 (see chap. v) or Dist. 20 (see chap. vii), should be recognized. As will be seen later, Gratian's treatment of these subjects differed significantly in emphasis and focus from the treatment of the theological schools. Moreover, this difference in orientation should be recognized even though some areas of the canon law, like the law of marriage, never can be completely or even, for the purposes of discussion, artificially separated from theological speculation on the same subject. A canon law doctrine that has no counterpart in the theological literature is inconceivable.

22. For example, Dist. 1 *de pen.*, cc. 6–30. The avoidance of Roman law in the treatise on marriage is also striking. See C. 29, q. 1.

23. Vetulani, "Gratien et le Droit romain." *Idem,* "Encore un mot sur le Droit

consciously avoided the inclusion of Roman law texts in the Decretum. He even took care to delete extracts from that law which were embedded in series of canonical texts that he borrowed from earlier collections; one of the most striking differences getween the Magister and his predecessors is this attitude toward the law of Justinian. No one has been able to suggest a satisfactory explanation for Gratian's attitude,[24] and I shall attempt to do so in the next chapter.

One last part of the textual scholarship on the Decretum is relevant to my thesis about the work's general orientation. In 1933 two scholars, Franz Gillmann and Adam Vetulani, concluded independently that Gratian himself did not introduce the divisions of the *Distinctiones* into the first part of the Decretum. They attributed the division to the members of the schools, suggesting that Paucapalea, the first decretist, may have made it. Gillmann went further and suggested that the Magister had organized his book into *tractati* and that the *tractati* were subdivided into paragraphs. It is also probable that the division between *dicta* and *capitula,* which one finds in the modern editions and in most manuscripts, was not so sharp in the original work.[25] Separation between these two elements of the work emphasizes its character as a collection of the canons, among which is interspersed commentary by the collector. The separation also made the work easier to use as a source book for the ancient law of the Church. In its original form,

romain dans le Décret de Gratien," *Apollinaris,* 21 (1948), 129–134. Kuttner, "New Studies in the Roman Law in Gratian's Decretum," *Seminar,* 11 (1953), 12–50. *Idem,* "Additional Notes on the Roman Law in Gratian," *Seminar,* 12 (1954), 68–74. Rambaud [-Buhot], "Le 'Corpus Juris Civilis' dans le Décret de Gratien," *Bibliothèque de l'École des Chartes,* 111 (1953), 54–64. *Idem,* "Le Décret de Gratien el le Droit romain," *RHD,* 4th ser., 35 (1957), 290–300. Boulet-Saltet, "Les 'paleae' empruntées." Most recently, Jean Gaudemet, "Das römische Recht in Gratians Dekret," *Österreichisches Archiv für Kirchenrecht,* 12 (1961), 177–191.

24. The only attempt to explain Gratian's attitude toward Roman law is that of Vetulani, "Le Décret de Gratien et les premiers Décrétistes."

25. Gillmann, "Rührt die Distinktioneneinteilung." Vetulani, "Über die Distinktioneneinteilung und die Paleae im Dekret Gratians," *ZRG,* Kan. Abt., 23 (1933), 346–370. *Idem,* "Études sur la division en distinctions et sur les paleae dans le Décret de Gratien," *Bulletin international de l'Academie polonaise des sciences et des lettres,* Cl. philologie, histoire, philosophie, 1932 (Cracow, 1933), pp. 110–114.

however, the Decretum would have had the appearance of a series of canonical treatises dealing with the structure of ecclesiastical society.[26]

Gillmann once said that if Rudolph Sohm was correct in his reading of the Decretum, he was the only one to have ever understood it.[27] I am in the slightly uncomfortable position of joining Sohm in this stance. In effect, I am arguing that within a few years after the work appeared, the members of the schools changed its character with the result that its original purpose was lost. I do not suggest that the early decretists did not know what Gratian was trying to do in his work, but that they did not have any interest in his original purpose. They remade the collection according to their own view of its significance. What Gratian's view of his work was will become clear in the next chapter and in the study of his theme in subsequent chapters.

26. See n. 16 above.
27. Gillmann, "Rührt die Distinktioneneinteilung."

II. Gratian and Church Politics

Gratian and his generation participated in the beginnings of the twelfth-century renaissance and witnessed the end of the Investiture Contest, the first great dispute between regnum and sacerdotium. It was a period supremely important in the history of the High Middle Ages. The papacy now stood independent of the secular authority of the German kings, and it began to develop the intricate machinery of international ecclesiastical government for which it has become famous. Schools flourished in cathedral centers all over Europe, and the number of students steadily increased. England was now ruled by the dukes of Normandy, and the Capetians in France were consolidating their power within the Ile-de-France in preparation for extending their authority over their vassals. In Germany, things were not so stable. The Investiture Contest left the king in a severely weakened position and enabled the magnates, both secular and ecclesiastical, to assert their independence. The proof of the magnates' power came in 1125 when, under the leadership of Archbishop Adalbert of Mainz, the Germans elected Lothar of Supplinburg king. Lothar was duke of Saxony and was not related to the Salian family. He was chosen over Frederick of Swabia, Henry V's brother-in-law. In 1137 the magnates again changed dynasties when they elected Conrad of Hohenstaufen, Frederick's younger brother, to be king in place of Lothar's son-in-law Henry the Proud of Bavaria and Saxony. The principle on which the electors acted in these elections was simple: The weaker candidate should be chosen king so that the king would be unable to establish himself as a strong central authority. To the generation of ecclesiastical leaders growing up in the early decades of the twelfth century, then, the German king did not appear as formidable as he had appeared to the clerical reformers of the eleventh century.

The Church was also deeply affected by the Investiture Contest, and the effects became noticeable during the reign of Pope Pascal II (1099–1118). The question of who would invest bishops with their office and authority became, in the early years of Pascal's pontificate, almost the sole concern of those involved in the struggle between pope and emperor. Earlier, the dispute had been much broader, touching on all the issues of regnum-sacerdotium relations. Now the issue between pope and emperor was almost petty and certainly not significant enough to justify their great dispute. Men on both sides of the dispute began to seek a way out of it. But finding a way out was not easy. The distrust of one side for the other was deeply seated, and both sides had legitimate claims that had to be satisfied in the solution. It was only after several abortive attempts at agreement that a compromise was finally reached in the Concordat of Worms in 1122.

Each of the failures to resolve the contest left in its wake some residue of enmity among leaders within the Church. It is not surprising, then, to find that the final compromise solution itself created a controversy in the Roman Curia and in the general European Church. This led ultimately to a papal schism in 1130. It was in the midst of this controversy that Gratian wrote the Decretum. Also during this period, Saint Bernard of Clairvaux emerged as a leader of the Western Church, and Peter the Venerable obtained authority over the vast Cluniac movement. The new orders of monks and canons regular began to play a major part in the life of the Church, and a host of important figures in medieval intellectual history—Hugh of Saint Victor and Peter Abelard among others—did their work. The situation in the Church in the 1120's and 1130's involved most of these men and movements, and induced the writers of the period to think about the nature of the ecclesiastical community. An account of the dispute within the Ecclesia at the time is therefore crucial to an understanding of how Gratian and his contemporaries looked at the Church.

The election of two popes in 1130 and the schism that followed are the focal points for the history of the reform movement of the 1120's and 1130's. The desire for reform among the spiritual leaders of France is a well-known feature of the period's history, but for a long time scholars did not see the connection between the reforming spirit and the political events within the Church of Rome. This failure to recognize the connection was caused by a misunderstanding of the true origins of the double election. Zöpffel and Mühlbacher, who supplied historians with the standard account of the events and their meaning, thought that the election difficulties of 1130 stemmed from a technical dispute over the place in the electoral process held by the three ranks or *ordines* in the Sacred College.[1] Mühlbacher noted that the electoral decree of 1059 gave no guidance concerning how to determine the outcome of elections, especially close elections. This lacuna in the decree is understandable, since there existed no established principle for deciding elections in the electoral law of that period. The majority principle was introduced into electoral theory only in 1179, when Alexander III promulgated it in the Third Lateran Council. In 1130 there was only the vague and, as it proved, wholly inadequate notion that the *maior et sanior pars* ought to prevail. The definition of this phrase could vary, but as Mühlbacher shows, rank was an important consideration in the 1120's and 1130's.[2] Since there were three ranks

1. Richard Zöpffel, *Die Doppelwahl des Jahres 1130* (Göttingen, 1872). Emil Mühlbacher, *Die streitige Papstwahl des Jahres 1130* (Innsbrück, 1876). P. F. Palumbo, *Lo Scismo del MCXXX,* Miscellanea della R. Deputazione romana di Storia patria (Rome, 1942). *Idem,* "La cancellaria di Anacleto," *Scritti di paleografia e diplomatica in onore di Vincenzo Frederici* (Florence, 1944). Much attention has been paid to the role of Saint Bernard of Clairvaux in the schism. E. Amelineau, "St. Bernard et le schisme d'Anaclet II," *Revue des questions historiques,* 30 (1881), 47–112 (a pro-Innocent account). E. Vacandard, "Saint Bernard et le schisme d'Anaclet II en France," *Revue des questions historiques,* 43 (1888), 61–123. H. Ochier, "Saint Bernard et la fin du schisme d'Occident," *Bulletin de la Société historique et archéologique,* Les amis des antiquités de Parthenay, 1 (1952), 6–10. H. Claude, "Autour du schisme d'Anaclet: Saint Bernard et Girard d'Angoulême," *Mélanges Saint Bernard* (Dijon, 1954), pp. 80–94. Bernard Jacqueline, "Bernard et le schisme d'Anaclet," *Bernard de Clairvaux,* pp. 349–354.

2. Mühlbacher, *op. cit.,* pp. 65–67, 149–172. For a recent treatment of this question of *ordines* within the Sacred College, see Franz-Josef Schmale, *Studien zum Schisma des Jahres 1130* (Cologne-Graz, 1961), pp. 82–90. On the majority principle in ecclesiastical elections, see K. Ganzer, "Das Mehrheitsprinzip bei den

19

of cardinals, the problem of determining the *sanior pars* was especially difficult. In 1130 Petrus Pierleoni, cardinal priest of Santa Maria in Trastevere, won support from only two cardinal bishops, while the great majority of his electors were cardinal priests. He took the name Anaclet II. The other party elected Gregory, cardinal deacon of Sant' Angelo, who took the name Innocent II. Innocent's supporters were mostly cardinal deacons, but he also counted five cardinal bishops among his electors. Apportioning the wisdom between these two parties was bound to be difficult, and, in fact, considerable space was devoted to the problem in the polemical writings that arose after the election.

Mühlbacher emphasized another aspect of the dispute besides the problem of electoral law. He brought out the effect of the factionalism of Roman city politics on the schism. City politics in this period centered on the rivalry of two powerful families, the Frangipani and the Pierleoni, and Mühlbacher thought that the curial dispute which led to the schism was founded on this rivalry. The papal chancellor Haimeric, prominent in the Curia as a supporter of Innocent, appears, in Mühlbacher's study, as the close ally and sometimes as the instrument of the Frangipani.[3] There is no doubt that the political activities of the Roman nobles were a significant factor in the situation that led

---

kirchlichen Wählen des Mittelalters," *Tübinger theologische Quartalschrift*, 147 (1967), 60–87.

3. Mühlbacher, in making his argument about the importance of the question of rank, says that in 1124 at the election of Honorius II the cardinal priests sided with the Pierleoni and the cardinal bishops with the Frangipani (Mühlbacher, *op. cit.*, p. 67). By 1130, according to Mühlbacher, the leadership of the Frangipani party had passed to the papal chancellor Haimeric and a third party, which Mühlbacher calls the Rechtspartei, had come into existence led by Peter of Pisa and the cardinal bishop of Porto, also named Peter (Mühlbacher, *op. cit.*, p. 69). Zöpffel had already indicated the existence of this party calling it the Vermittelungspartei—a title that Mühlbacher rejects because it does not show that these men were primarily interested in preserving legal form in the election of the new pope (Zöpffel, *op. cit.*, pp. 341, 379). Peter of Porto, like Peter of Pisa, sided with Anaclet and a letter from him to four cardinal bishops of the other party exhibits some concern for the relationship of the *ordines* in the Sacred College. (See *Epistola Petri Portuensis, MGH,* Scriptores, X, 484–485.) On the factional struggles in Rome between the two chief families, see Pietro Fedele, "Pierleoni e Frangipani nella Storia medievale di Roma," *Roma,* 15

to the double election of 1130 and the schism, but Mühlbacher misunderstood its place in the conflict. The present view of the affair is based on the brilliant work of the German scholar Hans Klewitz. His interpretation has been developed by Franz-Joseph Schmale.[4]

Zöpffel had already recognized that there were policy differences between the two parties that grew up in the 1120's. He called the party of Haimeric and Honorius II the pro-imperial party. But neither Zöpffel nor Mülhbacher followed the interpretative possibilities to which this recognition pointed.[5] For them, the question of rank was the predominant problem involved in the double election. Klewitz did pick up the idea of general policy differences between the two parties and demonstrated that they were one of the major causes of the double election. Klewitz's insight was that the politics of the 1120's and 1130's represented the end of the reform papacy of the eleventh century. He studied in detail the developments within the college of cardinals from Pascal II's reign onward and showed that Haimeric, closely associated with the French reformers led by Saint Bernard, played an important

(1937), 1–12. *Idem*, "Le famiglie di Anacleto II e di Gelasio II," *Archivio della R. Societa Romana di Storia patria*, 27 (1904), 399–433. More recently, Demetrius Zema, "The House of Tuscany and of Pierleoni in the Crisis of Rome in the Eleventh Century," *Traditio*, 2 (1944), 155–175.

4. Klewitz died as a soldier on March 15, 1943. His best work has been reprinted in a volume dedicated to his memory, *Reformpapsttum und Kardinalkolleg* (Darmstadt, 1957). See "Das Ende des Reformpapsttum," *Deutsches Archiv*, 3 (1939), 372–412 (*Reformpapsttum*, pp. 207–259). Also "Die Entstehung des Kardinalkollegiums," *ZRG*, Kan. Abt., 25 (1936), 115–221 (*Reformpapsttum*, pp. 9–134). Schmale, *op. cit. Idem*, "Die Bemühungen Innocenz II. um seine Anerkennung in Deutschland," *Zeitschrift für Kirchengeschichte*, 65 (1954), 240–296. Palumbo has reviewed recent work on the schism, "Nuovi studi (1942–1962) sulla scisma di Anacleto II," *Bullettino dell'Istituto storico italiano per il medio evo e Archivio Muratoriano*, 75 (1963), 71–103.

5. Zöpffel, *op. cit.*, pp. 289, 328, 377, 390. Mühlbacher, *op. cit.*, p. 73. Pandulphus says that Innocent II was originally a Wibertine. That would mean that the future pope had begun his career as a pro-imperial cleric in the train of Henry IV's antipope Clement III (Wibert of Ravenna). In 1106, at the Council of Guastalla, Pascal received the Wibertine clerics into the Church so long as they were sincerely reconciled with the true hierarchy. *Liber Pontificalis prout exstat in codice Dertusensi*, Ed. I. M. March (Barcelona, 1925), p. 207. Schmale points out that there were many stories about the origins of Innocent and that Pandulphus's is one of the least acceptable among them (Schmale, *Studien zum Schisma*,

role in the curial politics of the period after 1123.[6] Schmale has taken over the conclusions reached by Klewitz and expanded them.

Not everyone is prepared to accept the Klewitz-Schmale interpretation of early twelfth-century politics. Recently, scholars have challenged some of the factual points on which the interpretation rests, and Gerd Tellenbach has attacked some of its most important conclusions. Tellenbach's reservations are expressed in an important article on the fall of Abbot Pontius of Cluny in 1121[7] and a consideration of them makes the best possible introduction to this study of the connection between Gratian and the party dispute.

Tellenbach accepts the basic conclusion of Klewitz's studies, that the double election of 1130 was the result of a curial party dispute that arose after the promulgation of the Concordat of Worms. What he will not accept is that this party dispute was European-wide, that it involved nearly all the great ecclesiastical leaders of the period, and that it was the cause of schisms and troubles within many of Europe's greatest ecclesiastical institutions. The troubles in Cluny in the early 1120's had been ascribed to the party dispute,[8] and it is that ascription that attracted Tellenbach's attention to the general interpretation of ecclesiastical politics in the period.

Tellenbach rejects the view that the troubles at Cluny were connected with the curial party dispute. According to this view, Pontius was allied with the curial establishment represented by Petrus Pierleoni while the opposition to the abbot was allied with the party of Haimeric.[9] Tellenbach sees the fall of the abbot as the culmination of a

---

p. 39). But the passage from Pandulphus's work shows that the Anacletians considered the party of Innocent to be pro-imperial.

6. Haller had already emphasized the importance of Haimeric and the French clique, but as Klewitz points out, he did not see the effects of the developing college of cardinals. Johannes Haller, *Das Papsttum. Idee und Wirklichkeit* (Munich, 1965), 3:29 ff. Hans Walter Klewitz, "Das Ende," p. 210 n. 1.

7. Gerd Tellenbach, "Der Sturz des Abtes Pontius von Cluny und seine geschichtliche Bedeutung," *Quellen und Forschungen aus italienischen Archiven und Bibliotheken*, 42/43 (1963), 13–55. Mario da Bergamo, "Osservazioni sulle fonte per la duplice elezione papale del 1130," *Aevum*, 39 (1965), 45–65.

8. See the article of Hayden V. White cited in the next note.

9. This view was expounded by White, "Pontius of Cluny, the Curia Romana and the End of Gregorianism in Rome," *Church History*, 27 (1958), 195–219. It

long dispute between Cluny on the one side and the new monastic orders and the episcopate on the other. But this dispute by itself would not have brought about Pontius's demise. The crucial change in the great monastery's political environment was a shift in papal attitude. With the election of Calixtus II in 1119, the papacy sided with the monastery's opponents, making the pressure on the abbot of Cluny unbearable.

This view of the affair of Cluny would seem to be consistent with the idea that it was connected with the curial party dispute, but Tellenbach does not see it that way. His hesitancy in making the connection between the two affairs stems from his belief that there was no significant political difference between Pontius and his successor Peter the Venerable. Peter continued to work for all the goals that Pontius had worked for, and he worked for them in the same way as his predecessor.[10] If, Tellenbach asks, the party dispute cannot be found at Cluny, did it ever become a European-wide affair involving other figures who, it has been claimed, were members of one party or the other?

Tellenbach does not think that the evidence supports the conclusion that the curial parties were of great significance before the double election of 1130. While he admits that Calixtus II and his successor Honorius II sided with the new monastic groups against the traditional Benedictinism represented by Cluny and Montecassino, he does not think these popes and their chancellor Haimeric can be said to have been more spiritualistic than those who supported the ancient mon-

---

is based on the account of the Pontian schism given by Peter the Venerable in the second book of his *de miraculis*. Tellenbach subjects Peter's story, written after 1146, to a searching criticism and prefers to rely on Ordericus Vitalis who relates Pontius's troubles with the episcopate. The chief element in Peter's version of the events is a secret schism within the monastery which he says lasted ten years before coming out into the open in 1121. Tellenbach does not believe that the schism ever existed and points out that Pontius appeared as the rightful and fully honored abbot of Cluny even after his supposed abdication. This is not the place to discuss Tellenbach's interpretation of the affair, but it seems to me that he has erred in his judgment of Peter the Venerable's value as a witness. It is possible that both Peter and Ordericus are telling the truth. Tellenbach, *op. cit.*, pp. 13–30, 38–40, 45–46.

10. Tellenbach, *op. cit.*, pp. 36–37, 52–55.

asteries. The attack on Cluny and Montecassino, he says, had nothing to do with the growth of spiritualism, and, in fact, it is hard to grasp the character of the much-discussed spiritualism. What, he asks, is the spirit of Saint Bernard to which the new curial party is supposed to have adhered? The great Cistercian's mysticism had nothing to do with papal elections, and his important participation in the papal schism had nothing to do with his mysticism. Furthermore, it is very difficult to assess the character of the relationship between Bernard and the party of Haimeric before the double election. Klewitz and Schmale used Bernard's letters to the chancellor as evidence of their political alliance during the 1120's, but Tellenbach does not consider this evidence very conclusive. He points out that the letters always concern specific cases and that Haimeric's replies are not extant. The correspondence may simply be evidence, he suggests, that two such important men in the Church could not avoid consulting each other from time to time.[11]

The basic element in Tellenbach's objections is his refusal to accept as established, or even probable, the connection between the monastic reformers and the curial party of Haimeric. The views of Saint Bernard and others do not, he thinks, have the political importance implied by the Klewitz-Schmale view of the ecclesiastical parties, and, conversely, the parties were not so widespread as those scholars assert. Their interpretation cannot be accepted, he says, because they have failed to discover the differences between the two great parties that they think existed. His study of the situation at Cluny shows that there was no great difference in outlook or policy between Pontius and Peter the Venerable, and he goes further by arguing that there is no firm evidence that Europe was divided by competing world

11. *Ibid.,* pp. 40–44. On the change in the papal attitude toward Cluny and Montecassino, see *ibid.,* pp. 35–38. The shift had already been noted by A. Hessel, "Cluny und Mâcon. Ein Beitrag zur Geschichte der päpstlichen Exemptionsprivilegien," *Zeitschrift für Kirchengeschichte,* 22 (1901), 524. H. Diener, "Das Verhältnis Clunys zu den Bischöfen, vor allem in der Zeit seines Abtes Hugo (1049–1109)," *Neue Forschungen über Cluny und die Cluniacenser,* ed. G. Tellenbach (Freiburg i. Br., 1959), pp. 219–252. Georg Schreiber, *Kurie und Kloster im 12. Jahrhundert* (Stuttgart, 110), 1:176–177. See also Schmale, *op. cit.,* pp. 43–45, 99–100.

views.[12] There is a great deal wrong with this critique of the Klewitz-Schmale interpretation.

Tellenbach may be substantially correct in his assessment of the situation at Cluny in the early 1120's, but his doubts about the connection between the affair and the party dispute in the Church do not necessarily put the existence of the European-wide party dispute in question. His interpretation of events at Cluny and Klewitz's interpretation of events in the Church-at-large are not mutually exclusive. In addition, Tellenbach has not proven that Peter the Venerable, an important figure in Schmale's account of the party dispute, was unconnected with Haimeric's group in the Curia. One would expect Peter and Pontius to agree on the matters that Tellenbach has shown they agreed—the place of Cluny in the Church and its justification vis-à-vis the episcopate. Agreement on some important issues is not a bar to political enmity as all students of the Tweedledee and Tweedledum politics so common in modern democracies are well aware. Moreover, Peter and Pontius did differ on some important matters. Peter did become a reform abbot who leaned toward the views of the new monastic groups and his defense of Cluniac monasticism must be seen in that context.[13] Also, he was associated with Haimeric and Honorius II during the late 1120's and was an early adherent of Innocent II after the double election of 1130.

It is difficult to understand why Tellenbach draws the line where he does in his acceptance of parts of the Klewitz-Schmale thesis. He argues that there was a shift in the allegiance of the papacy from Cluny and Montecassino to the new monastic orders and the episcopate. This shift took place under Calixtus II, who was responsible for Haimeric's rise to power. Tellenbach does not, however, want to see the shift as a result of the party dispute associated with the rise of Haimeric or as a sign of the connection between the Curia and views of the new monastic leaders. Yet, when one considers the origins of

12. Tellenbach, *op. cit.,* pp. 40–42.

13. Tellenbach (*ibid.,* pp. 46–48, 54–55) recognizes Peter's leanings toward the new monasticism though he correctly emphasizes that Peter was a great defender of the Cluniac way of life and did not want to turn the Cluniacs into Cistercians or Carthusians. *Ibid.,* pp. 48–51.

Calixtus's pontificate, it is not at all farfetched to argue that there existed a connection between him and the French church. Calixtus had been one of the most influential prelates of France and was elected at Cluny in the presence of many French bishops. And Haimeric was French also. The shift in the papal attitude toward Cluny was, as Tellenbach himself says, partially the result of the Curia's new enthusiasm for the recently established monastic movement born out of criticism of traditional Cluniac monasticism. It is certainly possible that there existed further agreement between the papacy and these new movements, and the changes of personnel in the cardinalate during the pontificates of Calixtus and Honorius confirm this possibility.[14]

The spiritualism of Bernard of Clairvaux and his confreres was much broader than Tellenbach is willing to admit. Mysticism aside, Bernard's views of the Church and his approach to politics were more spiritual than that of many of his contemporaries. His political goals cannot be separated from his theological conception of things, as Tellenbach implies they can, even though he did not always use means that were as righteous as his goals. And we need not suppose that Haimeric was as spiritual as Bernard in his outlook to argue that the two men were political allies. It is clear from the studies of Klewitz and Schmale that political support for these men came from the same sources, and this fact makes it probable that they were political allies. Their extant correspondence may not be conclusive evidence, but it does corroborate the other findings.

Thus, Tellenbach's objections do not make the interpretation of Klewitz and Schmale improbable. Except with respect to the affair of Cluny, he has not tried to disprove the conclusions of these writers by a detailed study of the evidence. He only questions those conclusions per se and argues that they go beyond the evidence on which they are based. His doubts are not well founded because they are based on an assumption that cannot be accepted. The Klewitz-Schmale interpretation fails, he says, because they have not been able to expose the differences between the two parties. He assumes, therefore, that these scholars have brought forth all the evidence for the dispute, and since he thinks that evidence is insufficient, he concludes that the interpretation

14. On all this, see below.

must be set aside. But it is exactly to this problem of what separated the two parties that much of this book is devoted. Building on the studies of Klewitz, Schmale, and others, I shall describe the intellectual content of the party dispute. The victorious party, the party of Haimeric, left a remarkably rich account of its political views; the political significance of many major mid-twelfth-century works has not been recognized. Tellenbach has detected the major lacuna in the Klewitz-Schmale interpretation, and to fill that lacuna is one of my main purposes.

What follows, then, is a brief account of the reform movement of the 1120's and 1130's based on the work of Klewitz and Schmale.

Reforming the reform papacy.

The chief political aim of the reformers who obtained control of the Roman Curia in the middle of the eleventh century was to create a strong papacy. As the ideas of Humbert of Silva-Candida gained acceptance in the Curia, it became common to view political independence as the necessary precondition for moral reform of the Church. The main obstacle to autonomy was the German emperor, and in order to achieve independence from that monarchy, the reform papacy needed allies. In fact, it needed two kinds of allies. The Norman conquerors of southern Italy supplied the necessary armed troops that would be used to meet any German army the emperor might lead south to Rome. But the popes also needed allies in the city itself. Local factions were numerous and unruly, and in the past they had brought the papacy to the nadir of its existence while trying to make it into a hereditary office. It was clear to the reformers that the exigencies of day to day life in the city demanded that they win some strong allies among the city's factions. They could do this because the reemergence of the papacy as a powerful institution helped to ameliorate the chaotic conditions of Roman politics.

As the factions in the city lined up for and against the new holders of papal power, a pattern emerged which was to last until the middle of the twelfth century. The focal points of this pattern were the great families of the Frangipani and Pierleoni, while the other lesser factions shifted allegiance back and forth according to the dictates of their own interests. The Pierleoni had already, apparently, associated themselves with reform efforts undertaken in Rome before the events of Sutri in 1046.[15] It is commonly believed that Gregory VI, the reform-minded pope of 1046 who was deposed with the others by Henry III, was a member of this family—perhaps a brother of its leader. The new papacy that developed under the leadership of Leo IX and his advisers preserved the thin thread of reform tradition in Rome. Hildebrand, a close associate of Gregory VI and, some historians think, a member of the same family, became a leading power in the Curia before becoming Gregory VII.[16] The Pierleoni retained their special position with respect to the Curia. The Frangipani were for a long time also allied with the reform papacy. But as the competition between them and the Pierleoni increased in the later stages of the Investiture Contest, they aligned themselves with the antipapal interests and then with

15. The Pierleoni were originally Jewish and had made a fortune, apparently as moneylenders. In the early eleventh century, Baruch, the head of the family, converted, and almost immediately the Pierleoni became one of the leading factions in the city. The center of their power seems to have remained the ghetto and its environs. Their name derived from Anaclet's father, Petrus Leonis. Schmale, *Studien zum Schisma*, pp. 15–28. Zema, *op. cit.*, pp. 169–175, with the other works cited in n. 3 above.

16. Fedele thought that John Gratian, who became Gregory VI, was the son of Baruch (Benedictus Christianus was his Christian name). He would, therefore, be the brother of Leo, Baruch's eldest son, who took over the leadership of the family in 1051. This view of Gregory VI's parentage is now generally accepted. The family background of Hildebrand is less certain. Fedele thought that Hildebrand's mother, Bertha, was Leo's daughter and that he was therefore the nephew of Gregory VI. Tangl strongly dissented from this view of the pope's familial connection. Poole thought that Bertha was only the gentile sister of Leo's wife and that Hildebrand was therefore only related by marriage to Leo and hardly at all connected with John Gratian. Hildebrand's Jewish ancestry remains possible but not probable. Hugh of Cluny remarks that Hildebrand had Semitic looks (*Ex Willelmi gestis regum anglorum, MGH*, Scriptores, X, 474). Also, Hildebrand did inherit the fortune of John Gratian. Fedele, "Le famiglie di Anacleto II e di Gelasio II." Reginald Lane Poole, *Benedict IX and Gregory VI*, Proceedings of the British Academy, VIII (London, 1917), 22 ff. F. Zazzera, *Della nobilità dell'Italia*, pt. II (Naples, 1628), unpaged (Zazzera even tried to show that the Hapsburgs derived from the Pierleoni). Michael Tangl, "Gregor VII, judischer Herkunft?" *Neues Archiv*, 31 (1906), 159 ff. Zema (*op. cit.*, pp. 170–171) reviews this literature.

the imperial party, when the definitive split between Henry V and Pascal II occurred.[17] City politics became only one part of the enlarged political horizon of the papacy created by the reform movement.

But city politics remained an important factor in the history of the reform papacy. The struggle between pope and emperor forced papal authorities to rely on the support of the Pierleoni more heavily than they had in the early years of the reform. The importance of the Pierleoni therefore grew apace. From being a relatively insignificant faction that had had the temerity to buy the papal throne for one of its own, it became, by the time of Pascal II, the most powerful family in the city and one of the chief supports of the reform papacy. But in the course of Pascal's reign, the position of the Pierleoni was changed from chief supporter of the papacy to effective power behind the throne; the end of the reform movement of the eleventh century began. The rise of the family in the Curia led to the renewed involvement of the papacy in Roman politics. Likewise, the expanded importance of the papacy in the Church which resulted from the reform effort gave the factional politics of Rome a wider effect than it had

---

17. The Frangipani rose to power within the city in the early eleventh century. From the beginning, the family was associated with the imperial power—occurring for the first time in a 1014 charter for the great imperial monstery of Farfa (*Regestrum Farfensis,* ed. U. Balzani, 3:201). They were even called *de Imperatore* on occasion. See Fedele, ed., "Tabularium S. Mariae Novae" *Archivio della Società Romana di storia patria,* 23 (1910), 37–38, Charter of 1039, "Nobilissimi viri Leo, Bernardus et Bona, filii quondam Petri Frajapane de Imperatore sponte donaverunt d. Paulo archipresbitero venerabilis ecclesiae S. Mariae Novae terram vacuam juxta arcum majorem templi quod domus Nova appellatur." The family lived in the area mentioned by the document, apparently near the Basilica of Constantine next to the monastery of Santa Maria Nova. Fedele, "Pierleoni e Frangipani nella Storia medievale di Roma," pp. 1–12. *Idem,* "Sull'origine dei Frangipane (a proposito di un recente lavoro)," *Archivio della Società Romana di storia patria,* 33 (1910), 493–506. The work to which Fedele refers in the title to this article is F. Ehrle, "Die Frangipani und der Untergang des Archivs und der Bibliothek der Päpste am Anfang des 13. Jahrhunderts," *Mélanges Chatelain* (Paris, 1910). See also, Palumbo, *Lo Scismo del MCXXX.* pp. 87–91. Pascal left Leo Frangipani and Petrus Leonis in charge of the city when he went to France in 1107, but Palumbo (p. 110) thinks that the Frangipani may have already acted against the pope in fomenting the schism of Maginulf. There is no evidence, so far as I know, to support this contention. The definitive break between the pope and the Frangipani occurred in 1116.

ever had before, and at the same time led to the growth of an awareness of its evils in all the corners of the Church.

Schmale sees the origins of the schism of 1130, the major event in
the decline and fall of the reform papacy, as stemming from the political conflict created by the Concordat of Worms. During the reading
of the Concordat at the First Lateran Council in 1123, the Pierleoni
group caused such a commotion against the agreement that the whole
council nearly broke up over that issue.[18] Pope Calixtus II and members of the Curia who were in favor of the compromise began from
that point on to seek to counter the power of Pierleoni. The party dispute had begun.[19]

The year 1122–1123 and the Concordat of Worms was indeed a
turning point in papal and curial politics, as Schmale says, but the
origins of the dispute actually go back to the period just after the
abortive agreement of Sutri in 1111. The Pierleoni had been deeply involved in the negotiations that led to the agreement and in the arrange-
ments made for carrying out its terms. When the compromise collapsed
and Pascal had capitulated to Henry V on the matter of investiture, it
was Petrus Pierleoni who emerged as the leader of the most powerful faction within the Curia. Sometime between the capitulation of
Pascal in April, 1111, and the Lateran Council in March, 1112, when
the coerced agreement was repudiated, Pascal raised Petrus Pierleoni
to the cardinalate. In the council of March, 1112, Petrus and his supporters took the predominant role.[20]

18. Gerhoh of Reichersberg, who was an eyewitness, reports on the reception
of the Concordat at the council: Gerhoh, *de ord. don. Sancti Spiritus, MGH,
Libelli de lite* III:279 f. Other writers do not mention it.

19. Schmale, *Studien zum Schisma*, p. 24, *passim.*

20. The importance of 1111 for the later political history of the Church in the
twelfth century has been only partially recognized by scholars. Thirteen of
twenty-one cardinals who sided with Anaclet in 1130 owed their promotion to
Pascal, and most of them received the cardinal's hat after 1111. Petrus Leonis,
the future pope's father, delivered the promise of the pope to the emperor in the
agreement of Sutri concluded in February, 1111. He also gave hostages from his
own family to the emperor as a guarantee for carrying out the contract. (See
Zema, *op. cit.*, p. 174; Schmale, *Studien zum Schisma*, p. 18.) Petrus himself was
required to take an oath on the occasion. (All the documents for the agreements
of February and of April, 1111, are edited in Angelo Mercati, *Raccolta di concordati su materie ecclesiastiche tra la Santa Sede e le auctorita civili* [Rome,

Petrus stood by Pascal when Henry V set up an antipope, Mauritius of Braga, in 1116. It seems clear, in fact, that curial policy was made and carried out by Petrus and his associates in this period. The most important legateships and political tasks went to this group. In 1118 Petrus was active in the election of John of Gaeta as Gelasius II, and he followed the new pope into exile in France shortly afterward. When Gelasius died at Cluny in 1119, the cardinals present chose the Burgundian Guy of Vienne as the new pope and he took the name Calixtus II. Again, Petrus Pierleoni appears to have played an important role in the election. Until 1121–1122, when the arrangement for peace between pope and emperor was accomplished through the Concordat of Worms, Curia and pope were solidly in the hands of Petrus, his family, and his supporters.[21]

Calixtus was related to Henry V, and historians have assumed that he was elected because of this connection.[22] It was obviously hoped,

---

1919], pp. 10–16.) At the Lenten Council of March, 1112, Girard, bishop of Angoulême and legate of the Holy See in France, read the repudiation of the April, 1111, concessions for Pascal. Girard later became Anaclet's chief supporter in France and the most formidable enemy of Saint Bernard there. (Mercati, *op. cit.,* pp. 16–18; Klewitz, "Das Ende," p. 214.) Bernheim has shown that the later negotiations between pope and emperor, in 1119 and 1122, were based on the agreement of Sutri. Ernst Bernheim, *Das Wormser Konkordat und seine Vorurkunden* (Breslau, 1906).

21. On Pierleoni's position in the Curia between 1111–1112 and 1119, see Schmale, *Studien zum Schisma,* pp. 15–28. Schmale notes that Guy of Vienne had been one of the outstanding opponents of Pascal in 1111, but remarks that in 1119, Guy was elected pope with the "massgeblichen Unterstützung" of Pierleoni (*ibid.,* p. 20). The history of this election needs further investigation, however, since Calixtus later became the staunch enemy of Pierleoni representing all the elements in the Church opposed to the Roman faction's policies and outlook.

22. Calixtus was in fact exceedingly well connected. He was the sixth son of William the Great, count of Burgundy; brother-in-law of Eudes I, duke of Burgundy; brother-in-law also of Humbert II, count of Savoy; and of Robert II, count of Flanders; first cousin of Henry of Burgundy, count of Portugal; uncle of Adelaide, wife of Louis VI of France; and, finally, nephew of the emperor Henry V. He may have been raised as a monk at Cluny. U. Robert, *Histoire de Calixte II* (Paris, 1891). M. Maurer, *Papst Calixt II* (pt. 1–2, Munich, 1886–1889). J. H. Pignot, *Histoire de l'Ordre de Cluny,* 3 (Paris, 1868), 22. P. Freçon, "Calixte II et la querelle des Investitures," *Bulletin de la Societe des Amis de Vienne 1967,* 63 (1968), 43–54. Stanley Chodorow, "Ecclesiastical Politics and the Ending of the Investiture Contest," *Speculum,* vol. 46 (1971).

they say, that the new pope would settle the differences between the two powers and the conflict would come to an end. If this view is accepted, then it is difficult to ascertain the attitude Petrus and his supporters held toward a settlement at the time of Calixtus's election. While it is clear to us that settlement of the Investiture Contest could only be accomplished through a broad compromise agreement, settling the issues that separated pope and emperor, the faction of Pierleoni does not seem to have looked at the situation in this way. Taking into account the reaction of the Pierleoni group at the First Lateran Council of 1123, the faction apparently had thought that Calixtus would be able to win the fight over investitures without compromising with the emperor. In 1119, at least, Calixtus must have appeared as a strong anti-imperialist.[23] It can be assumed that Petrus and his supporters opposed the arrangement from the moment that its provisions became known in the Curia, and that the actions of the party at the council were designed to bring about a general repudiation of the Concordat. Petrus probably hoped to bring about a repetition of the events that led to the repudiation of the agreement of Sutri in 1111.

The dispute over the Concordat created a clear issue on which the cardinals could split into factions, and it was the basis of what was to become a general power struggle in the Curia. Calixtus, seeking to preserve the Concordat, attempted to counter the power of Pierleoni's party by doing two things. The first step was to bring the Frangipani, in eclipse because of the relationship between the papacy and the Pierleoni, back into Roman city government by making Leo Frangipani commandant of the forces in the city.[24] This action reestablished an

23. Calixtus had been one of the most extreme critics of Pascal II's capitulation to Henry in 1111 and had called a council at which he excommunicated Henry. One of his first official acts as pope was to renew the excommunication. When one sees also that Petrus Pierleoni supported the election of the new pope, it becomes clear that the usual reasons given for the election are not satisfactory. The traditional view is set forth by Karl Jordan. See Bruno Gebhardt, *Handbuch der Deutschen Geschichte,* ed. Herbert Grundmann, vol. 1 (Stuttgart, 1954), p. 278. See also, Pignot, *op cit.,* p. 22. I am now working on a reevaluation of the narrative of the first two decades of the twelfth century.

24. Schmale, *Studien zum Schisma,* pp. 25–27. Previously, the Pierleoni faction had been left in charge of the city when the popes went on their journeys as Gelasius II had done in 1118 when he went to France. Zema, *op. cit.,* p. 174. The

effective balance of power in the city, but it constituted only one part of the campaign that the pope now waged against Pierleoni. With Petrus Pierleoni holding a leading position within the Curia, the threat of his faction could not be completely suppressed by changes in the structure of power within the city. The Curia still showed the effects of city politics in Calixtus's time, but it was no longer a part of the general arena in which those politics were played out. Only one faction held effective power in the Curia, and this situation had resulted from the choice made by a greater power, not from the free-for-all struggle characteristic of the city's political life. The Curia had become an independent political forum even though it retained its connections with city politics until the election of 1130. The Concordat of Worms had introduced the change into the situation that created the necessity for political action on the part of the pope. If Calixtus wanted to save his agreement with the emperor, he would have to undermine and ultimately defeat the dominance of Pierleoni within the Curia.

Calixtus did not simply introduce a Frangipani into the Sacred College in order to balance the power in the Curia. This move would have created impossible conditions of dissension and political division in that body. To add a member of the Frangipani family to the cardinalate would also be a step backward, since it would nullify the progress that the papacy had made away from total involvement in the struggles of the local nobility. Calixtus seems to have possessed a view of the Curia more elevated than that probably held by the local and Italian churchmen. As a Burgundian, he saw the Curia as an international body, the center of the universal Church. For him, the dispute over the Concordat of Worms was one between himself, as the representative of the Church in general, and Pierleoni, as the representative of the local power that had always had so pernicious an effect on the Church of Rome. Calixtus saw the need to counter Pierleoni power within the city—which was in any case the proper arena for the conflicts of local factions—but he determined to win control of the Curia himself. This was the second action that he took shortly after the First

---

Frangipani came over to the papal side when Calixtus II entered Rome in 1120. Ferdinand Gregorovius, *History of the City of Rome in the Middle Ages,* trans. A. Hamilton, vol. 4, pt. 2 (London, 1905), pp. 391–393.

Lateran Council where the split between himself and the party of Petrus Pierleoni had been brought to light.

As the first step in gaining control over the Curia, Calixtus raised the exceptionally capable Haimeric to the cardinalate and made him chancellor of the papal see. For the next seven years, Haimeric led the anti-Pierleoni party in the Curia and through Calixtus and Honorius created a large number of cardinals. As Klewiz showed, the electors of Innocent II in 1130 were cardinals, the great majority of whom were raised to the Curia in the 1123 to 1130 period, while those who sided with Anaclet II were mostly men who had become cardinals before 1123.[25] Thus, of twenty cardinals who sided with Innocent in 1130, fifteen owed their cardinal's hat to Calixtus (in his last two years) or Honorius. Among the Anacletians, only seven of twenty-two were promoted during this period, and one of these transferred his allegiance to Innocent shortly after the election. There was a significant generation gap as well as a political one between the two groups, and this difference explains the term of abuse used by those who sided with Anaclet that the electors of Innocent were *cardinales novitii.*[26]

The battle for control of the papacy and papal policy was, therefore, fought in the Curia. Haimeric carefully created a group of cardinals who would challenge the power of the Pierleoni within that central administrative body. When Calixtus died in 1124, Haimeric's plans were far from being realized, and he had to use the military might of the Frangipani in order to install Lambert of Ostia as Pope Honorius II. It is important to understand that it was Haimeric who took the initiative at the election of 1124 and not Leo Frangipani and to

25. Klewitz, "Das Ende," pp. 211–229. Schmale, *Studien zum Schisma,* pp. 29–82. Klewitz presents a list of the cardinals during the years of Pascal II (1099–1118) in "Die Enstehung des Kardinalkollegiums," pp. 119–34. This list complements that given by J. M. Brixius, *Die Mitglieder des Kardinalkollegiums von 1130–1181* (Berlin, 1912). Brixius thought that there were forty-four cardinals in 1130. Klewitz corrected this number to forty-two. (Klewitz, "Die Enstehung," p. 211 n. 3.)

26. *Epistola Petri Portuensis* (1130), *MGH,* Scriptores, X:485. Klewitz points out that many of Innocent's supporters in the election had been promoted in the years 1127 and 1128. Compared with Petrus, cardinal bishop of Porto, who was probably the oldest member of the college, these men were indeed *novitii.* Klewitz, "Das Ende," p. 218.

see the event as resulting from Haimeric's political situation.[27] He could not afford to lose the papacy at that critical juncture, and he resorted to using local military force to surprise and upset the much larger party of Pierleoni. The trick worked in 1124 but could not be expected to succeed again, and the creation of twelve cardinals during the reign of Honorius shows that Haimeric wanted to elect his man constitutionally the next time. Of those twelve, ten sided with Innocent in 1130.

The curial parties differed in geographical origin as well as age. The party of Innocent, led by the Frenchman Haimeric, was almost exclusively from northern Italy and France, while the supporters of Anaclet came from Rome and its environs.[28] The difference reflected the change in the Curia's international position, which resulted from the election of Calixtus and the dispute over the Concordat. From being the creature of the local Roman forces of the Pierleoni in the

27. Klewitz remarks, "die Frangipani als die Werkzeuge Aimerichs angesprochen werden müssen." "Das Ende," p. 245. Schmale, *Studien zum Schisma,* p. 27. As Schmale points out (pp. 145-146), Haimeric was not ready when Honorius II died in 1130 either. Had the pope lived a few years longer, the older party would have been seriously weakened by the deaths of its members, and the schism would probably have been avoided. In 1130 there was strength on both sides.

28. Of the Anacletian cardinals whose origins we can trace, only two stem from northern Italy or France, Peter of Pisa, cardinal priest of Santa Susanna, and Aegidius, cardinal bishop of Tusculum who was from the region of Auxerre and who had entered Cluny in 1119. All the other Anacletians about whom something is known came from Rome or its surrounding area. The Innocentians counted few Romans among them. Conrad of Sabina, the oldest cardinal in that party, was from Rome, but he was also a canon regular and thus supported the party of the canons regular (see p. 42 below). Nearly all the other members of the party came from northern Italy. Matthew of Albano was born at Reims. Schmale, *Studien zum Schisma,* pp. 31-81. It should also be noted that the lesser Roman clergy, the career civil servants of the papal see, sided with Anaclet. During the period before 1130, the subdeaconate was a stepping-stone to the cardinalate. This *cursus honorum* continued to operate in Anaclet's Curia after 1130, but not in Innocent's. Of the seventeen cardinals promoted by Anaclet, all of the six whose origins can be traced had been subdeacons. None of Innocent's new cardinals, fifty-two in number, appear to have had this status. These statistics underscore the lines of division between the two parties. Anaclet found support among the careerists of the Curia, while Innocent drew upon the churchmen of northern Europe who had never had anything to do with the Curia. R. Elze, "Die päpstliche Kapelle im 12. und 13. Jahrhundert," ZRG, Kan. Abt., 36 (1950), 165-166.

early part of the century, it became the focal point of the whole Church in the 1120's and 1130's. The twenty cardinals who sided with Innocent were outnumbered in the college, but they represented the views and aspirations of the European Church much more satisfactorily than their opponents.

The geographical differences of the parties led to differences in their relations with the city of Rome and with Europe. The party of Innocent, coming from the north, concerned itself with the general community of the Church from which it stemmed and in which it held an overwhelming advantage. Haimeric busied himself with creating European-wide support for his group in the Curia. In this work, he used to the fullest extent his connections with his compatriots Bernard of Clairvaux, Peter the Venerable, and Guigo of Chartreuse, as well as the German Norbert of Xanten.[29] During the schism, these

29. Saint Bernard corresponded often with Haimeric. *Epp.* 15, 20, 48, 51–54, 157, 160, 163, 181, 311, 316, 338. In *Ep.* 144, Bernard wrote to his monks at Clairvaux, "Orate pro domino cancellario, qui mihi pro matre est." Bernard speaks of the importance of the chancellor's office in *Ep.* 31, "nullum ferme fiat in orbe bonum, quod per manum quodammodo Romani cancellarii transire non habeat, ut vel vix bonum iudicetur, quod eius prius non fuerit examinatum iudicio, moderatum consilio, studio roboratum et confirmatum adiutorio, cui iustius erit quam ipsi deputandum, quidquid iustis in negotiis vel infectum vel minus perfectum fuerit deprehensum sicut et aeque omne quod invenietur utiliter atque laudabiliter consummatum." Peter the Venerable wrote only two letters to Haimeric, *Epp.* 3, 34, ed. Giles Constable, *The Letters of Peter the Venerable,* 2 vols. (Cambridge, Mass., 1967). He mentioned the chancellor, however, in a letter to Roger II of Sicily dated by Constable 1139/41. The passage demonstrates the important position of the chancellor who is set next to the pope as an *auctoritas. Ep.* 90, ed. G. Constable. On the friendship between Haimeric and Peter, see Schmale, *Studien zum Schisma,* pp. 96, 168, 188–189. Guigo considered Haimeric a special friend of himself and his order. *Ep.* 3 to Haimeric. PL 153, col. 595 ff. Schmale, *Studien zum Schisma,* pp. 165 n. 14, 188–189. As Schmale notes, Norbert's active promotion of Innocent's cause in Germany earned him the reputation of being the German Saint Bernard. (So A. Fliche, *Histoire de l'Église,* 9:58). In 1126 Norbert had given up his wandering apostolate for the archbishopric of Magdeburg at the behest of Honorius. Also, Norbert's foundation at Prémontré and the order of canons regular which grew out of it were aided by the Curia. Anaclet indicates that Norbert and Haimeric were in personal contact and that the chancellor had informed him of happenings in Rome. JL 8409, to Norbert, "Quae quidem mendosa figmenta ab Haimerico . . . hausisti et serenissimo regi Lothario ebibenda propinasti." Schmale, *Studien zum Schisma,* pp. 244–245, 277–279. *Idem,* "Bemühungen." When some of this correspondence

men played an important role in Innocent's victory. Haimeric and his fellow *cardinales novitii* also had extensive connections among the burgeoning orders of canons regular. But in all this activity of party-building, it must be remembered that Haimeric held the initiative and the central position in the movement. Neither Bernard nor any of the other well-known personages ruled the party. Haimeric kept close control himself and could at times dispense with the aid of influential individuals who disagreed with his policy or interfered with his methods of achieving it.[30]

The party of Anaclet, in contrast, was cut off from the general European community and was forced to rely on its power in Rome. After the election of Honorius, the members of Pierleoni's faction ceased to receive important political jobs and were removed from the channels of legitimate exercise of authority even in Rome itself. The family of the future Anaclet therefore sought to win control of the city, its only hope in maintaining its power, by extragovernmental means. They involved themselves in the nascent commune movement in the city, made famous by the participation of Arnold of Brescia, and when the Republic of Rome was proclaimed in 1144, Jordan Pierleoni,

---

is read, Tellenbach's reservations about using it as evidence of a political connection between the chancellor and the northern monastic leaders seem unfounded. There is no doubt, however, that the schism cemented the relationship between the Curia and these men.

30. Bernard wrote to Haimeric in 1129 to defend himself against complaints about his meddling in affairs which had apparently been brought forth by other cardinals. Bernard says that his activities were undertaken because Haimeric ordered him to act in the interests of the Church. Schmale (*Studien zum Schisma*, p. 133) believes that Bernard's words, in *Ep.* 52, imply that the saint considered the criticism to have come from the chancellor, even though not directly. Schmale also points out that Haimeric's treatment of Bernard at this juncture was determined by the situation within the Church and Curia. Affairs stood at a point where Bernard's enthusiasm and eagerness were an obstacle instead of a help to Haimeric's plans. Klewitz thought that Bernard held the central position in the party (Klewitz, "Das Ende," p. 228). Schmale's studies show that Jacqueline has missed the point in his article on Bernard and the Curia, "Saint Bernard et la Curia romaine," *Rivista di storia della chiesa in Italia*, 7 (1953), 27–44.

Haimeric's control of papal policy and curial politics can also be seen, according to Schmale, in the *arenga* of papal documents dating from his period. A specific type of *arenga* came into use when he became chancellor and disappeared after his death in 1141. Schmale, *Studien zum Schisma*, pp. 105–119.

nephew of the antipope, was elected the first *patricius*.[31] This policy was all but hopeless. In fact, Haimeric had driven the powerful Pierleoni into a position directly opposed to the policy of the reform papacy they were supposed to represent. Since the middle of the eleventh century, the reformers had sought to bring the government of the city under papal control.

The result of the struggle between the two parties was the destruction of Pierleoni's party and with it the end of the Gregorian papacy. Only a very few of the Anacletians were able to maintain a political career in the Church after the end of the schism in 1138.[32] But the struggle effected a change in the political ideology as well as in the political leadership of the Church. There existed in the 1120's and 1130's two positions regarding the direction of the Church. The enumeration of these policy differences is difficult because the sources for the period rarely discuss them explicitly and because most of the history of the Pierleoni party was carefully expunged by their victorious opponents.[33]

31. Schmale, *Studien zum Schisma,* pp. 79–81. G. W. Greenaway, *Arnold of Brescia* (Cambridge, 1931), p. 104. Pierleoni's party was excluded from papal affairs in the 1120's. Schmale notes that use of Comes, cardinal priest of Saint Sabina, in 1125 as legate to Genoa and Pisa was exceptional. Schmale, *Studien zum Schisma,* p. 59. The activities of the family in the second half of the twelfth century demands further study.

32. When Victor IV, Anaclet's successor in 1138, submitted at the end of May in that year, Innocent received into his Curia all those cardinals from Anaclet's party who had been promoted before 1130. Nine cardinals with these qualifications still remained in the opposition party at the end of the schism. At the Second Lateran Council, held in 1139 to celebrate the victory of the Innocentians and to cement the renewed unity of the Church, all those cardinals who had supported Anaclet were deposed. Peter of Pisa, well known as a canonist, was reinstated by Innocent's successor, Celestine II. Brixius, *op. cit.,* pp. 20–22.

33. An excellent example of the way in which the victorious party destroyed the vestiges of the Anacletian viewpoint is the *Liber Pontificalis.* The lives of Gelasius II, Calixtus II, and Honorius II (and perhaps of Pascal II) were written by Pandulphus who favored Anaclet in the schism; he was promoted to the cardinalate by that pope. Peter William, who compiled the *Liber,* edited the biographies written by Pandulphus so that remarks hostile to Honorius were removed. Fortunately, one copy of the original by cardinal Pandulphus survived in a Spanish manuscript, and it has been edited by March, *Liber Pont. Dertus.* This work was used by Herbert Bloch in an excellent article relating to the schism, "The Schism of Anacletus II and the Glanfeuil Forgeries of Peter the Deacon," *Traditio,* 8 (1952), 159–264. Bloch attacked the traditional account of the events

But some conclusions on this subject can be drawn from the extant sources. In the next section, an attempt will be made to reconstruct the platforms, if they may be called that, of the two parties.

The policy positions of the two parties.

It appears that until the double election of 1130, the dispute continued to relate to the issue raised by the opposition of Pierleoni's faction to the Concordat of Worms. Schmale describes the members of that faction as being hard-nosed opponents of the emperor, unwilling to settle the old dispute over lay control of bishops through the compromise contained in the agreement. The party of Haimeric had already been described as pro-imperial by Zöpffel.[34] The central point of opposition between the two parties during the 1120's was the policy of friendship or enmity toward the emperor—in other words, the continuation or resolution of the Investiture Contest.

The basic disagreement had ramifications in other matters of policy.

---

and significance of the schism passed down by Zöpffel and Mühlbacher and also demonstrated how widespread the effects of the schism were.

Bloch points to another example of the Innocentians' suppression of the traces of the Anacletains which is very instructive. Calixtus had built a chapel in the lateran dedicated to Saint Nicholas of Bari to celebrate the end of the Investiture Contest. In the apse of the chapel, there was painted a mural depicting Calixtus and other of the reform popes together with ancient popes who had served as their models. Among the popes appears Anastasius IV (1153–1154), and Duchesne showed that the name originally attached to this figure was Anaclet II. (Louis Duchesne, "Le nom d'Anaclet II au palais de Latran," *Memoires de la Société des Antiquaires de France*, 5th ser., 9 [1888], 197–206.) The fresco was well known in the twelfth century; it was mentioned by the Abbot Suger, Otto of Freising, Arnulf of Lisieux, and John of Salisbury. It was obviously done under the direction of Anaclet, and it is striking in that Honorius II is left out. (Bloch notes that the unabridged version of Pandulphus's life of Honorius shows that the cardinals in Pierleoni's faction saw the origins of the schism in the elevation of Honorius, Bloch, *op. cit.*, p. 174.) As Bloch says, the mural is an impressive monument to Anaclet's consciousness of being the end of an era. Bloch, *op. cit.*, pp. 178–180. Gerhard Ladner, "I mosaici e gli affreschi ecclesiastico-politici nell'antico palazzo Lateranense," *Rivista di archeologia Cristiana*, 12 (1935), 265–292.

34. Schmale, *Studien zum Schisma*, p. 64. He also characterizes Anaclet's party as conservative (*ibid.*, pp. 57–58). On Zöpffel's characterization of Innocent's party, see n. 5 above.

One of the most important of these was the attitude of the papacy toward the Normans in Sicily and southern Italy. Having solved the problem of papal-imperial relations, the party of Haimeric saw no need to continue the alliance between the pope and the Norman king. In fact, it looked upon the increasing royal ambitions of Roger of Sicily with distrust and hostility. The supporters of Anaclet, believing that there was still a battle to be fought on the imperial front, sought to maintain the alliance with the Normans which had been a part of the foreign policy of the reform papacy since 1058–1059. When the tide turned in Innocent's favor during the schism, Anaclet and his followers found refuge in Roger's territories, and it was Anaclet who first granted the royal dignity to Roger. After the schism, the party of Innocent only reluctantly accepted the Sicilian ruler's new status.[35]

The disputes over the agreement of Worms and over the related policy toward the Normans were only the surface signs of a deeper disagreement between the parties. The party of Anaclet sought to continue the old struggle against the emperor and to win, according to their own definition, the battle over investitures. In their minds, the gains of the reform period had to be consolidated and firmly established; the reform was over. The party of Haimeric represented a growing number of Church leaders, outside of Rome and the Curia, who were campaigning for a general reform of ecclesiastical society. Many of the leading members of the party have left a considerable corpus of writing, and their works present the basic ideas and political outlook of the Innocentians. For all of them, Haimeric stood as the chief architect of reform in the Church of Rome. While the chancellor's party appears to historians as a political faction, it appeared to its supporters, especially in the new monastic orders, as a reform party.

35. On the policy of Haimeric's party during the pontificate of Honorius, see Schmale, *Studien zum Schisma,* pp. 82, 137–138. On Anaclet's attitude toward the Normans and on his relations with Roger of Sicily, see Bloch, *op. cit.,* p. 181. Also Paul Kehr, "Diploma purpureo di re Roggero II per la casa Pierleoni," *Archivio della R. Società Romana di storia patria,* 24 (1901), 253–259. *Idem,* "Die Belehnungen der Süditalienische Normannenfürsten durch die Päpste 1059–1192," *Abhandlungen der preussischen Akademie der Wissenschaften,* Phil.-Hist. Kl. (Berlin, 1934), n. 1. Roger was a symbol of tyranny for those sympathetic with the reform. Helen Wieruszowski, "Roger II of Sicily, Rex-Tyrannus, in Twelfth Century Political Thought," *Speculum,* 38 (1963), 46–78.

Writers of this reform party put great emphasis on the moral regeneration of the clergy. Saint Bernard's long letter to Henry the archbishop of Sens entitled *De moribus et obligationibus episcopi* and his *Vita Sancti Malachi* are perhaps the most outstanding examples of that interest as it was expressed during the years of the struggle. The chief work in this genre, however, was Bernard's *De Consideratione* which was composed over a period of years during the pontificate of his monastic son, Eugene III. At the same time, members of Haimeric's party were deeply involved in efforts to uproot the worsening problem of heresy in the Western Church. Peter the Venerable in particular wrote several tracts against Jews, Moslems, and Petrobrusians, a group that later merged into the Cathars.[36] Of course, the members of the party of Anaclet may also have been concerned with reforming the prelature and defeating the heretics; all medieval Christians advocated these goals. Yet, there is no evidence that the supporters of Anaclet actively sought these goals. There are no treatises nor historical records extant which would demonstrate that the party of the old guard was involved in the activities of the new guard. It can be concluded, therefore, that while the Anacletians probably thought reasonably well of the stands taken by the reform party, they did not participate in its activities. Active reform was not part of the life-style of the Anacletians.

36. The Petrobrusians received their name from the leader of the group, Peter of Bruis. Peter the Venerable's tracts are edited in PL 180. The abbot of Cluny was of course not the only member of the party active against the heretics. Norbert of Xanten devoted most of his life to preaching the faith in northern France and Germany while Saint Bernard preached against the heretics in southern France in 1145. Bernard wrote the *Tractatus de baptismo* at the request of Hugh of Saint Victor, and he may have traveled to Cologne after Evervinus, provost of the Premonstratensian house of Steinfeld, had described the activities of the heretics in that city. See *Ep.* 472 *inter Bernardinas*. On these activities of Bernard, see Vacandard, *Vie de Saint Bernard* (Paris, 1895), 2:202–234. The saint was also active against Arnold of Brescia's heretical movement in Rome. Vacandard, *Vie de Saint Bernard*, pp. 235–258. On the heretical movements in the twelfth century, see Herbert Grundmann, *Religiöse Bewegungen im Mittelalter* (Hildesheim, 1961), pp. 13–69. Arno Borst, *Die Katharer* (Stuttgart, 1953). *Idem*, "Neue Funde und Forschungen zur Geschichte der Katharer," *Historische Zeitschrift*, 174 (1952), 17–30. Jeffrey Burton Russell, *Dissent and Reform in the Early Middle Ages* (Berkeley and Los Angeles, 1965).

As has been already noted in the discussion of Tellenbach's views, the members of Haimeric's party represented the new monastic movements in the Church. This was especially true in France where the personality of Saint Bernard dominated. The new reform effort within Cluny, led by Peter the Venerable, was also associated with Haimeric, though as Tellenbach has shown, it is difficult to tell whether the older monks sided with the opposing party.[37] Petrus Pierleoni had been a monk of Cluny before the abbacy of Peter the Venerable. Within the Curia, however, the Cistercians and other reform Benedictines played a subordinate role. When one looks into the backgrounds of the *cardinales novitii* who voted for Innocent in 1130, he finds that many of them were canons regular. Popes Honorius and Innocent and the chancellor Haimeric were canons.[38] It was the canons who led the

37. Until the work of Tellenbach (see n. 7 above), it was thought that the affair at Cluny in 1121–1122 was connected with the party disputes in the Curia. Bloch, *op. cit.,* pp. 166, 175. Tellenbach thinks the affair was part of the old rivalry between Cluny and the episcopate as well as the rivalry, more recent, between the great monastery and the new monastic orders. See the comments in n. 9 above.

Honorius II supported the new abbot, Peter the Venerable, and had Pontius imprisoned when he sought to regain his abbacy in 1126. For a fuller account of the events, see White, *op. cit.* Tellenbach, *op. cit.*

Bloch's article was devoted to investigating the connection between affairs at Montecassino and the schism. Honorius attacked the established authority at Montecassino in 1125. In 1126 he deposed and excommunicated Oderisius II, who had voted against him in the election of 1124. In 1127 two legates, Conrad of Santa Prudentia (later Pope Anastasius IV) and Matthew of Albano, went to Montecassino and brought about the election of Seniorectus, a supporter of the pope, as the new abbot. Bloch and Schmale have pointed to a large number of local disputes which were drawn into and exacerbated by the struggle in the Curia.

38. Schmale, *Studien zum Schisma,* pp. 31–79, 98, 139–141. In Innocent's party, Conrad of Sabina, Gerhard of San Croce, and Hubert of San Clemente were canons besides Haimeric and Innocent himself. John of Crema, another important member of the cardinalate, apparently had close connections with the canons even though he may not have been one himself. He established the canons in his title church of San Crisogono. For twelve of the cardinals who supported Innocent in 1130, we have no information about whether they belonged to any order. Three of the cardinals in the party belonged to the new orders or to the anti-Pontian party in Cluny. Matthew of Albano was a Cluniac of Saint Martin des Champs and an ally of Peter the Venerable (see Ursmer Berlière, "Le cardinal Matthieu d'Albano," *Revue Bénédictine,* 18 [1901], 113–140, 280–303). Peter

party in the Curia, and it was the general community of canons who formed the basis for the success of the movement. The suddenness of the entrance of this recently developed religious order into political influence in the Church can be seen from a look at the numbers of privileges given to them after Haimeric became chancellor. In the period before 1123, the Benedictines, including the new orders, received four times as many papal privileges as the canons regular. In the last two years of Calixtus's reign, the ratio fell to 3 to 1 in favor of the Benedictines, and during the reign of Honorius there were 49 privileges granted to Benedictine houses and 30 to canons, a ratio of 1.6 to 1. The troubled reign of Innocent II produced an even more striking increase in the importance of the canons. There were 277 privileges granted to Benedictines and 255 to canons.[39]

These figures, compiled by Schmale, reflect the results not only of the rivalry between the canons and the monks but also of the contro-

---

of San Anastasius was another Cluniac who appears to have been in the same group as Matthew. John of Ostia was former prior of Camaldoli, Gratian's order. From Schmale's researches, it appears that none of Anaclet's supporters were canons. This impression is confirmed by Gerhoh of Reichersberg who tells Innocent that all the canons are on his side. See *Ep. ad Inn., MGH,* Libelli de lite III:227. The canons were a recent development and it was Urban II who laid the foundations for their continued growth by regulating their legal position within the Church. See JL 5459, 5763. Charles Dereine, "L'elaboration du statut canonique des chanoines reguliers specialment sous Urbain II," *RHE,* 46 (1951), 534–565. *Idem,* "Les origines de Prémontré," *RHE,* 42 (1947), 352–378. During the mid-twelfth century Urban II, instead of Gregory VII, stood out as the foremost reform pope of the eleventh century. This popularity may be because of his association with the canons. Hofmeister noted that up to 1118, about 25 percent of the cardinals came from the Benedictine order while there were almost no canons regular in the cardinalate. This discovery makes the development of the 1120's and 1130's very striking. Philipp Hofmeister, "Kardinäle aus dem Ordensstände," *SMGBOZ,* 72 (1961), 158–159.

39. Schmale, *Studien zum Schisma,* pp. 139–140. These figures demonstrate the rapid growth of the canons regular in this period and their connection with the new powers in the Curia, but they do not tell the whole story. First, there are grants to houses where it is unclear to what order the house belongs. In Germany the heads of houses of canons regular were called provosts (witness Gerhoh, provost of Reichersberg and Evervinus, provost of Steinfeld) while the heads of monastic communities were called abbots. It is more difficult to tell the French and Italian houses apart. Second, the figures do not show how important the new reform Benedictine orders were.

versy between the orders and the bishops. The canons and new orders of monks were the most important agents for carrying out the program of reform. Increasingly in this period, monks were becoming priests and houses were sending out their own members to perform the cure of souls in churches under their jurisdiction. In the early twelfth century, there was a strong reaction against this activity among the canons regular, who were by definition priests, and among the bishops who saw parishes being removed from their jurisdiction by exempt monasteries. While the canons were arguing that monks ought to stay in the monastery and that the cure of souls was incompatible with the monastic profession, they were themselves expanding into new parishes and thus threatening the authority of the bishops and the position of the secular clergy. The bishops looked with displeasure on both types of intruders.[40]

40. On the history of monastic participation in the *cura animarum* during this period, see Berlière, "L'exercice du ministère paroissial par les moines dans le haut moyen-âge," *Revue Benedictine*, 39 (1927), 227–250. *Idem*, "L'exercice du ministère paroissial par les moines du XIIe au XVIIIe siècles," *Revue Benedictine*, pp. 340–364, Jean Leclercq and Raymonde Foreville, "Un débat sur le sacerdoce des moines au XIIe siècle," *Analecta Monastica*, 4th ser. (Rome, 1957) (=*Studia Anselmia*, vol. 41), pp. 8–118. Marjorie Chibnall, "Monks and Pastoral Work: A Problem in Anglo-Norman History," *Journal of Ecclesiastical History*, 18 (1967), 165–172. J. Winandy, "Les moines et le Sacerdoce," *La vie spirituelle*, 80 (1949), 23–36. Hofmeister, "Mönchtum und Seelsorge bis zum 13. Jahrhundert," *SMGBOZ*, 65 (1953–1954), 209–273.

As Constable has pointed out, the dispute over the exercise of the *cura animarum* by monks was closely connected with the dispute over the monastic possession of tithes. If monks could hold a pastoral care, they could, like other pastors, receive the ecclesiastical revenue that was attached to their benefice. Those who denied the right of receiving tithes to monks also denied that the *cura* was compatible with the monastic profession. Constable, *Monastic Tithes* (Cambridge, 1964), pp. 145–165, where there is also an extensive bibliography on this problem. Gerhoh of Reichersberg, *de aed. Dei*, p. 162, "Neque enim vel monachi vel claustrales canonici sine periculo utuntur decimis plebium, nisi, habeant curam earum. Cum enim apostolica confirmet auctoritas, ut qui pascit gregem de lacte gregis manducet, et qui plantat vineam de fructu eius participet." See also Paul Remy Oliger, *Les évêques reguliers* (Paris, 1958).

As Bloch and Schmale have shown, many of the local disputes concerning elections to abbacies and bishoprics were connected with the struggle in the Roman Curia. In most cases, the reform party in a diocese won out, and its candidate supported the movement of canons and new monks. But that many bishops remained opposed to the new orders and their activities is demonstrated

The main argument brought forth in favor of parochial activity of the canons and monks was tied to the reform movement. Writers pointed to the poor character of parish priests and to the high quality of their monastic or canonical replacements. The chief principle in the cure of souls, they argued, ought to be that good men be entrusted with this important work. Monks and canons were good men, well trained and living a morally pure life.[41] The relationship between the

by the often repeated complaints of Gerhoh of Reichersberg who sought to bring all priests into canonical communities. Gerhoh, *de aed. Dei*, pp. 51–52, *passim*. *Ep. ad Inn.* (Dialogus inter clericum saecularem et regularem), *MGH*, Libelli de lite III:204, 205, 208, 210, *passim*. *Comm. in Ps. 64* (de ecclesiasticis negotiis), pp. 35–36, 43–50, 123–133, 150 ff. *De novitatibus*, passim. *De invest. Anti christi*, pp. 41, 45. To say that Gerhoh was preoccupied with this matter is no exaggeration. Several authors report that there were bishops who refused to allow canons to exercise the ministry. See Peter Damien, *Opusculum* 27 (de communi vita canonicorum), PL 145, col. 503–512. Ivo of Chartres, *Epp.* 69; 213. Gerhoh of Reicherberg, *Ep. ad Inn.*, cited above. Arno of Reichersberg, *Scutum canonicorum*, PL 195, col. 1493–1528. Berlière, "L'exercice . . . dans le haut moyen-âge," p. 246.

41. See Theobald of Étampes, *Improperium cuiusdam in monachos*, Leclercq and Foreville, *op. cit.*, pp. 52–53, "Ecclesia namque est convocatio fidelium, monasterium vero locus et carcer damnatorum, id est monachorum qui se ipsos damnaverunt ut damnationem evitarent perpetuam; fructuosius tamen damnantur a se ipsis quam ab alio. Nullus autem monachus dignitatem habet clericalem; quod enim habent capicia in transverso posita, significatio est quia ipsi, clerum exuentes, iam perdiderunt capita, quia non licet eis populo predicare, vel baptizare, vel penitentem ligare vel solvere, sive cetera talia que dicuntur ad ecclesiam pertinere. . . . Locus [monastery] enim penarum, qui tantum propter corporum afflictionem et peccatorum deplorationem eligitur, claves ecclesie prorsus habere denegatur, quia nimirum qui monasticum habitum eligendo et numdum postponendo se ipsum damnavit, se ipsum damnando dignitate ecclesiastica indignum iudicavit." An anonymous monk answers Theobald, *Rescriptum cuiusdam pro monachis*, Leclercq and Foreville, *op. cit.*, pp. 55–56, "Videmus tamen vel audimus monachos ubique terrarum ab episcopis, cum res et tempus exposcit, ad sacerdotium canonice promoveri et consecrari, vec alias vel plures, immo nec meliores orationes in ordinatione clericorum quam in ordinatione monachorum recitari." Leclercq and Foreville, *op. cit.*, pp. 60–61, "verum inter tot Christi dispensatores, quem imitari vivendo possint et secure debeant, a monachis sollicite requiritur, et, quod cum lacrimis dicendum est, vix aut raro reperitur. . . . Sciendum etiam quia monachi per Paulos et Antonios apostolorum doctrinam perceperunt, quia, testante Gregorio, secundum apostolorum regulam viventes eosdem patres habere meruerunt. Insistant igitur clerici potius ut mores et vitam in melius convertere studeant, quam ut monachis aliquatenus, presertim iuxta regulam sancti Benedicti et sanctorum patrum instituta victitantibus, in monasteriis derogent." Gerhoh of Reichersberg uses the

45

reform papacy and the canons in the 1120's and 1130's, which is reflected in the statistics concerning the number of privileges granted to the new order, demonstrates that Haimeric and his party agreed with the argument of the religious orders.

The general outlines of the reform program appear obvious from the interests and activities of its leading members. Saint Bernard was the model member—and its most important beside the chancellor—of Haimeric's party, even though the abbot of Clairvaux was often made uneasy by the political maneuvering of the curial group. Haimeric was a politician, but that did not mean he was unaffected by the prevailing views and interests of his supporters. It is clear from statements about him found in letters of the monastic reformers that he preserved his image as a reformer himself. Had he not put the maintenance of power over ideals, the party would have been easily defeated by Pierleoni and his group, and the split between Curia and the Church at large would have been widened.

Where does Gratian fit in this picture of political activity and re-

---

same reasoning to defend the parochial activity of the canons themselves. See *de novitatibus, MGH,* Libelli de lite III:294, "Ipsi vero religiosi viri suas ecclesias aut per semetipsos regant, sobrie, iuste, pie vivendo et populum sibi commissum in idipsum fideliter erudiendo, aut secundum canones obedientiae stabilitatem exigant ab his, quos in adiutorium sui ad regendum populum volunt assumere." See also Damien, *Opusculum* 27; Ivo of Chartres, *Epp.* 69, 213; Peter Abelard, *Ep.* 12; Rupert of Deutz, *Altercatio monachi et clerici,* PL 170, col. 537–542; Wibald of Stablo, *Epp.* 372, 373. Hugh of Saint Victor, who was a canon, gave only limited support to the exercise of the *cura animarum* by monks. See *de Sac.,* II:3, 4, "Propterea quod in illis [monks] est sacri signaculi, ad indulgentiam est, non pro potestate praelationis in populo Dei, sed ne in ipso quoque habitu poenitentiae quo se sponte propter Deum sequestraverunt, sacrosanctam corporis et sanguinis Christi communionem. . . . Ut ergo intrinsecus quietius vivant, ordines ministerii divini per indulgentiam ipsis conceduntur."

Saint Bernard spoke against the exercise of parochial duties by monks (*S. de diversis,* 93), but it should be pointed out that many from his order and even from his abbey entered holy orders. Eugene III (Bernard of Parma) was a monk of Clairvaux. Bernard even actively sought the episcopacy for some of his monks. Vacandard, *Vie de s. Bernard,* 2 vols. (Paris, 1897), *passim.* On Bernard's attitude toward monastic exemption and the *cura,* see Jean de la Croix Bouton, "Bernard et l'Ordre de Cluny," *Bernard de Clairvaux,* pp. 203–204. *Idem,* "Bernard et les Chanoines Reguliers," *Bernard de Clairvaux,* pp. 263–288. Jacqueline, "A propos de l'exemption monastique," *Bernard de Clairvaux,* pp. 339–343.

form? Because the party was primarily interested in the reform of the Church, the exposition of its ideas concerned the nature of the ecclesiastical community. But the writings of the reformers, even those of Saint Bernard, set forth the ideology of reform in a very fragmentary manner. Gratian, while he did not stand out as an active member of the party, expounded its ideas more fully than any other writer. The connection between him and the party of Haimeric and Bernard is not proven by any piece of direct evidence, but when one looks at his work and at those of his contemporaries, and when one considers the circumstantial evidence for the connection, its existence cannot be doubted. The Decretum must be looked at as product of Haimeric's movement.

Gratian and the reform party.

Almost nothing is known about Gratian's life. Though he is mentioned often in the works of the decretists, they say little that enlightens us about his career.[42] There is a medieval tradition, however, almost unnoticed by modern students, which connects Gratian with the reform party. The tradition is contained in a poem written at the abbey of Bec in Normandy during the pontificate of Alexander III but after 1168. It is the *Draco Normanicus* of Stephen of Rouen. According to Stephen, Gratian, the *Fons Decretorum,* was an essential member of Pope Innocent's entourage in 1131 at the Council of Reims. The pope, he says, could have done nothing concerning the law without the advice of the Magister.[43] This tradition appears to be con-

42. See chap. 1 n. 7. He was probably born at the end of the eleventh century in Italy; Kuttner suggests Carraria-Ficulle, near Chiusi, as the place of his birth. When he wrote the Decretum, Gratian was a Camaldulese monk in the house of Saints Felix and Nabor in Bologna, and he was a master of theology. In 1143 he was a consultant judge in a case before an ecclesiastical court. He died in the 1150's. Stephan Kuttner, "The Father of the Science of Canon Law," *The Jurist,* 1 (1941), 2–19.

43. The poem was discussed by Paul Fournier in "Deux controverses sur les origines du Décret de Gratien," *Revue d'histoire et de litterature religieuse,* 3 (1898), 266–267. It is edited in *MGH,* Scriptores, XXVI:163. It reads:

> Hinc fluvius torrens Gratianus ad alta redundat
> Quo sine nil leges, nil ibi jura valent;

firmed by no less a figure than Dante, who mentioned Gratian in the *Paradiso*. Dante notes that Gratian served the two courts well, presumably referring to the papal and the imperial court.[44] It was the party of Haimeric which reconciled the two powers.

There exists another bit of evidence concerning the Magister's activities and connections. It stems from the chronicles of Croatia and is thus more significant than the poetic tradition. Nonetheless, the infor-

---

Fons Decretorum, totius juris abyssus
  Luminis ecclesiae splendida stella micat.
Affluit, exornat, distinguit, terminat, arcet
  Verbis, flore, locis, sensibus, epulogis.
Ut jus jure docet, pro causa quisque laborat,
  Partem nempe suam firmat, adauget, init.
Haec pater Innocuus componit, judicat, urget,
  Lites, facta, modum foidere, jure, fide.
Hujus apostolici manibus rex inde sacratur
  Ludovicus, honor maximus iste troni.

See further, n. 49 below.

44. Dante, *Paradiso*, 10.103–105. Dante places the Magister third in the circle of luminaries representing twelve of the wisest men of the Church.

Quell'altro fiammeggiare esce del riso
  di Grazian, che l'uno e l'altro foro
  aiuto si che piace in Paradiso.

Italian historians of law have used this passage to argue that Gratian sought to reconcile the two laws, secular and ecclesiastical. Gaudenzi (*Lo Studio di Bologna nei primi due secoli della sua esistanza*) took this argument a step farther by suggesting that in reconciling the two laws, Gratian was continuing the work of Lambert of Fagnano who had been one of the chief papal negotiators at Worms and who became Pope Honorius II in 1124. Gaudenzi even suggests that Lambert may have urged the work of reconciliation on Gratian. Calcaterra cites the relevant passage from Gaudenzi in *Alma Mater Studiorum* (Bologna, 1948), p. 29. Other Italian scholars have since rejected the idea that Gratian was trying to reconcile the secular and ecclesiastical law and pointed out that he was almost exclusively interested in the Church's legal tradition (Calcaterra, *op. cit.,* pp. 30–32). Whatever the truth is about Gratian's motive, Gaudenzi's interpretation of the medieval tradition preserved by Dante appears to be correct. The poet does seem to say that Gratian was connected with the solution of the Investiture Contest and with the party of men who brought about that solution and supported it afterward against opposition from the Pierleoni faction in the Curia. Dante therefore confirms the tradition found in the *Draco Normanicus*. Gratian's connection with the party of Honorius II and his chancellor Haimeric led him to distinguish and separate the two laws rather than to reconcile them.

mation received from the Croatians is not certain enough to settle the issue.

Two sixteenth- and seventeenth-century writers from Dubrovnik (Ragusa), James Lukarevíc (Luccari) and Junius Rastíc (Resti), state that Gratian was a *legatus a latere* to Croatia in 1151. They claim to base their report of the legateship and what it accomplished on medieval, presumably twelfth and thirteenth century, accounts that are now lost. In fact, their story can be corroborated from other sources. At the Council of Dubrovnik, the legate Gratian deposed, they said, Gaudius, archbishop of Split (Spalato), and regulated the affairs of the Croatian church.[45] The deposition of the archbishop is confirmed by a letter of Alexander III, and the story told by Rastíc is found also in the *Historia Salonitana* of Thomas the Archdeacon, canon of Split (1201–1268).[46] The only part of the story that cannot be confirmed

45. I learned of this material and its story from the work of I. Omrčanin, *Graziano e la Croazia* (Chicago, 1958). This work has apparently gone unnoticed by scholars. Giacomo Luccari, *Copioso ristretto degli Annali di Rausa* (Venice, 1605), p. 19, "Ma nel 1153 il Papa Eugenio Secondo [sic], ch'era succeduto a Lucio di Bologna, per rimediare a' disordini di Slavonia, mando in Rausa Gratiano Legato a latere, il quale raunati i Vescovi d' intorno, celebro un Concilio Provinciale, nel quale depose Glauculo Arcivescovo di Spalato." D. Farlati, *Illyricum Sacrum*, 3:179. Lukarevíc appears to have used anonymous annals of the city as the source of his story of the period up to the end of the fifteenth century. See Omračanin, *op. cit.*, p. 11. The date given by Lukarevíc is mistaken. A. Rastíc wrote after Lukarevíc and seems to have used the same sources, but he was more accurate on the date and Eugene's number. The language of the two accounts is very similar. *Chronica ragusina Junii Restii (ab origine urbis usque ad annum 1451)*, ed. S. Nodilo, *Monumenta spectantia historiam Slavorum Meridionalium* (Zagreb, 1893), 25:51, "In questo tempo (a. 1151) trovo alcune croniche avere scritto, che Eugenio papa III mandasse un suo legato, a nome Graziano, a Ragusa per porger qualche rimedio ai disordini della Slavonia, con ordine che dovesse far a Ragusa un concilio provinciale . . . [Gratian], avendo nel mese di settembre congregato, oltre i vescovi di Dalmazia superiore ed inferiore, tutti quelli a chi toccava d'intervenire nella chiesa metropolitana, tra gli altri buoni ordini e costituzioni, avesse privato della dignita arcivescovile Glacciolo, arcivescovo di Spalato." Rastíc notes that he has good sources for this information. Nodilo, *op. cit.*, p. 52. Nodilo says that Rastíc is considered to be the most authoritative chronicler of Dubrovnik. Rastíc is really, he says, the third redactor of the "Chronicle of Ragusa" which is known under his name. Nodilo, *op. cit.*, p. vii.

46. Alexander III, letter of 1161, T. Smičiklas, ed., *Codex Diplomaticus Regni Croatiae, Dalmatiae et Slavoniae* (Zagreb, 1904), 2:92, writing to Peter, the new

is that it was Gratian who was the legate. The weight of the evidence leads to the assumption that Lukarevíc's and Rastíc's identification is correct, and the only Gratian historians know during the mid-twelfth century is the author of the Decretum.

The actions of the legate in 1151 are relevant to Gratian's position in the 1120's and 1130's because of the circumstances of Gaudius's deposition. The sources say that the archbishop was deposed because he performed an illegal consecration of one of his suffragan bishops.[47] That being the complaint against the archbishop, the pope would be expected to chastise him or perhaps even to go so far as to suspend him until he did penance, but deposition is unexpectedly harsh. Furthermore, the consecration was performed between 1124 and 1130. Pardon for something done so long ago might have been expected in 1151. What seems clear, however, is that the unfortunate Gaudius was an

---

archbishop of Split, "Pater et predecessor noster pie recordationis Eugenius papa . . . in V. quondam Chroatensem episcopum, pro eo, quod cum uno solo archiepiscopo, nullo alio presente episcopo, contra sacros canones alium presumpsit non dicimus consecrare sed potius execrare, et in eum, qui ab eis est consecratus, depositionis sententiam promulgavit . . ." The cause of the deposition is reported by Rastíc in Nodilo, *op. cit.,* p. 51, "La cagione di questa deposizione dicono essere stata avere esso spalatrense, senza riguardo alle sacre constituzioni, consecrato il vescovo di Trau [Trogir], assistente solamente il vescovo dulcinense, ed in luogo del terzo vescovo avesse fatto servire una mitra, posta sopra un altare; e fossero deposti, per questa causa, il dulcinense ed il consecrato." Thomas the Archdeacon reports essentially the same, see *Historia Salonitana* [Split], ed. F. Rački, *Monumenta spectantia historiam Slavorum Meridionalium* (Zagreb, 1894), 26:45, "Factum est autem, ut Dessa Macarelli traguriensi foret ecclesie in episcopum consecrationem celebrandam secum dumtaxat episcopum chroatensem. Qui veniens et videns processum archiepiscopi contra canonicas institiones fieri, prohibuit eum, dicens: 'Non debet archiepiscopus cum uno episcopo solummodo electo consecrationis munus impendere.' Gaudius vero tante simplicitatis, immo temeritatis erat, ut diceret: 'quia pallium michi est loco alterius episcopi.' Tunc episcopus chroatensis, utpote vir discretus et cautus, volens honoris sui evitare periculum, ascendit in ambonem, et coram omni populo protestatus est, quod non voluntarius, sed invitus et coactus metropolitano suo in hac parte parebat. Tandem consecratione huiusmodi celebrata, protinus apud sedem apostolicam factum Gaudii archiepiscopi divulgatum est. Summus vero pontifex, misso apochrisario suo iussit tam archiepiscopum, qui ordinaverat; quam episcopum qui ordinatus fuerat, ab administratione suorum ordinum perpetuo amoveri; episcopum vero, qui protestationem fecerat, decrevit a culpa fuisse immunem."

47. See n. 46.

old opponent of Haimeric and that the victorious party, now led by Saint Bernard and Eugene III, still wreaked vengeance on old enemies in outlying provinces of the Church in the late 1140's and early 1150's.[48] When looked at this way, the choice of Gratian as legate becomes more significant. The successors of Haimeric in the papal leadership sent an old associate to carry out a political assignment. Considering the technical nature of Gaudius's case, the great canonist was the logical choice. Other evidence, from the period of Gratian's writing activity, also suggests that there was a link between the Magister and the supporters of Innocent.

Haimeric himself may have had a personal connection with Gratian. Haimeric was, as stated, born in France, the center of the new reform monasticism. He had close relations with the spiritual leaders of Europe. When he entered the Church as a young man, the future papal chancellor did not do so in his native land. Instead, he traveled to Bologna and joined the canons regular in the house of Santa Maria in Rheno. This happened about 1115.[49]

48. Innocent II had dealings with Gaudius in 1139, and it is clear that the pope reluctantly tolerated his exercise of authority only because he had the support of Bela, king of Hungary. Innocent II, letter of May 24, 1139, (JL 8035) PL 179, col. 476, "Sicut beati Gregorii testatus auctoritas, et tam veterum quam modernorum gestorum monumenta declarant, examinatio et consecratio Salonitani archiepiscopi ex antiqua institutione ad romanum pontificem specialiter pertinet. Quocirca in sanctam romanam ecclesiam graviter deliquisse, et claves beati Petri ausu temerario evacuare voluisse dinosceris, dum spreta dignitate sedis apostolice, ad aliam provinciam convolasti, et contra veterum consuetudinem, a Strigoniensi archiepiscopo consecrationem suscipere attemptasti. Licet ergo vehementer excesseris, licet contra stimulum calcitrare molitus sis; quia tamen dilectus filius noster Bela Hungarie rex pro te multoties apud sedem apostolicam per litteras et nuncios intercessit, ipsius tandem precibus condescendimus, et per dilectum filium nostrum Hubaldum diaconum cardinalem . . . fraternitati tue palleum pontificale officii plentitudinem, signum humanitatis et iustitie destinamus." This letter was sent shortly after the Second Lateran Council where Innocent and his party dealt with those who had supported Anaclet. They were all removed from office. See n. 32 above.

49. Schmale, Studien zum Schisma, pp. 93–104. Schmale states that Haimeric was a Burgundian, but as Classen has pointed out, there is no evidence to prove this assertion. In fact, it seems to be based only on the connection between Haimeric and Calixtus II who was a Burgundian. Classen points to the relationship between the chancellor and Peter of La Châtre who came from Berry and argues that the relationship is evidence that Haimeric did not come from Burgundy.

ment spread and gained control of an increasing number of bishoprics, Gratian's doctrine was one of the bases for the expanding em-
ployment of monks and canons as parochial priests.

Another striking characteristic of Gratian's work may be viewed as
the result of his connection with the party of Haimeric—the disinterest
of the party members and of Gratian in the problem of Church and
State. The canonists of the later schools, and modern scholars as well,
mined the Decretum for its teaching on the subject of regnum and
sacerdotium. There is much material in the work which touches upon
this important problem and much which, with a little imagination, can
be used as the basis for elaborate commentary on it, but Gratian did
not, in fact, deal with the subject. He is always interested exclusively
in some aspect of the ecclesiastical constitution. In Dist. 10, where
there seems to be a discussion concerning the relationship between
secular and ecclesiastical law, Gratian is actually interested in the conditions under which secular laws may be used in Church courts.[53] In

---

allowed to hold property. C. 12, q. 1, dict. post c. 25, "De rebus vero ecclesiae
queritur, an liceat eas per prebendas dividi, ut annuos redditur quisque sibi
specialiter vendicet? Hoc non posse fieri, argumento et auctoritate probatur.
Clerici successores sunt eorum, de quibus dicitur: 'Multitudinis autem credentium
erat cor unum et anima una.' Necesse est ergo, ut eorum consequantur vitam,
quorum in ecclesia gradum administrant. Non ergo aliquid proprium sibi ven-
dicabunt, sed erunt eis omnia communia."

53. The argument in these paragraphs is much more fully developed in an
article by the author, Chodorow, "Magister Gratian and the Problem of *Regnum*
and *Sacerdotium*," Traditio, 26 (1970), 364–381. The dictum ante c. 1 in Dist. 10
is misleading: "Constitutiones vero principum ecclesiasticis constitutionibus non
preminent, sed obsecutur." But the Magister shows almost immediately that he
is concerned with use of the secular law by ecclesiastical judges. Dist. 10, c. 1,
"Lege imperatorum non in omnibus ecclesiasticis controversiis utendum est,
presertim cum inveniantur evangelicae ac canonicae sanctioni aliquotiens obviare."
Dist. 10, c. 3 (rubric), "In ecclesiasticis causis regia voluntas sacerdotibus non
est preferenda." The dictum post c. 6 is ambiguous like the first dictum: "Ecce
quod constitutiones principum ecclesiasticis legibus postponendae sunt. Ubi
autem evangelicis atque canonicis decretis non obviaverint, omni reverentia dignae
habeantur." The following rubric again shows the Magister's meaning, c. 7
(rubric), "Leges imperatorum in adiutorium ecclesiae licet assumi." Albert
Hauck and Franz Arnold have argued, largely on the basis of Dist. 10, that
Gratian supported a hierocratic view of regnum and sacerdotium. Hauck, *Der
Gedanke der päpstlichen Weltherrschaft bis auf Bonifaz VIII* (Leipzig, 1904), p.
33. Arnold, "Die Rechtslehre des Magisters Gratians," SG, 1 (1953), 476. See also

Dist. 22, the passage that was later expanded on by the decretist Rufinus so that it seemed to justify the superior authority of the pope in
temporal as well as spiritual affairs, actually refers only to the position
of the pope within the Church hierarchy.[54] In Dist. 96, which later
became the most important basis for decretist commentary on the relationship of the two powers, Gratian actually did not consider anything
more than the right of secular powers to act on ecclesiastical property
and in ecclesiastical affairs.[55] The capitula contained in this *Distinctio*

the comments of Charles Munier, "Droit canonique et droit romain d'après
Gratien et les Décrétistes," *Études Le Bras,* 2:943–954. Alfons M. Stickler has
treated the problems raised by the *Distinctio* in "Magistri Gratiani sententia de
potestate ecclesiae in statum," *Apollinaris,* 21 (1948), 86. See also F. Marchesi,
"De rationibus quae intercedunt inter ecclesiam et res publicas in Gratiani Decreto," *SG,* 3 (1954), 181–191.

54. Rufinus, *Summa decretorum,* ed. H. Singer (Paderborn, 1902), pp. 47–48.
Rufinus was commenting on Dist. 22, c. 1, "Illam [The Roman Church] vero
solus ipse fundavit, et super petram fidei mox nascentis erexit, qui beato eternae
vitae clavigero terreni simul et celestis imperii iura commisit." The rubric of the
capitulum indicates the Magister's interest in citing the canon: "Romana ecclesia
ceterarum primatum obtinuit." The canon stems from a letter of Nicholas II to
the clergy of Milan. The text of the letter was transmitted by Damien, *op. cit.,*
col. 91.

55. Stickler (*op. cit.,* p. 48) emphasizes the importance of Dist. 96 for the study
of Gratian's ideas on Church and State. But the Magister begins Dist. 96, dict. ante
c. 1, "non solum de ordinibus, sed nec etiam de rebus ecclesiasticis laicis legatur
aliquando attributa disponendi facultas." See also Dist. 97, dict. ante c. 1 (which
actually should be part of Dis. 96), "Hoc capitulo [Dist. 96, c. 16] patenter
ostenditur, quod nec inperatori, nec cuilibet laico licet decernere vel de electione
Pontificis, vel de rebus ecclesiasticis. Quecumque autem ab eis constituta fuerint,
pro infectis habenda sunt, nisi subscriptione Romani Pontificis fuerint roborata."
The last line emphasizes Gratian's interest in defining and supporting the authority
of the ecclesiastical power over Church affairs. Capitulum 10 in Dist. 96 later
took on special importance, along with the paleae added by the school, as a basis
for commentary dealing with the problem of regnum and sacerdotium. The
passage derives from Gregory VII's famous letter to Hermann of Metz and the
Magister seems to have gotten it from Ivo of Chartres' *Panormia,* V, 109 (cf. text
of the c. 9–10 in Dist. 96 with *Panormia,* V, 108–109 and cf. the rubrics used by
both canonists). The passage is indeed ambiguous and could be construed as
referring to the relationship between the two powers, but Gratian did not use all
the text found in the *Panormia.* He deleted the part of the letter dealing with the
deposition of Childeric III and thereby removed the most striking reference to
regnum-sacerdotium relations in the original text. As it stands, c. 10 fits into the
discussion of the *Distinctio* by asserting the power of the hierarchy over ec-

which do refer to the regnum-sacerdotium question are those that derived from the Donation of Constantine. They are paleae.

In the *Causae,* there are two places where Gratian refers to the two powers. Of these, the one contained in Causa 2 is embedded in a long discussion concerning the admissibility of accusations of inferiors against their ecclesiastical superiors. The dictum in question is very rich in possible interpretations for those interested in the relationship of the two powers, but Gratian is not to be included among them. The passage does not expound a clear theory of the juridical relationship between the priesthood and the royal power, but concerns the question of accusations. In support of the doctrine that inferiors may accuse their superiors, Gratian proposes the example of Nathan's reproval of King David. The Magister's imaginary opponents in the quaestio then point out that there is more than one hierarchy in the world and that in the ecclesiastical hierarchy, Nathan the prophet is superior to David the king. It is significant that the statement about the relationship between the two powers makes up part of the argument that Gratian ultimately rejects in the quaestio, but that is not the only problem. The passage also leaves the reader with a confusing idea of regnum-sacerdotium relations. It is only clear on the matter of accusations; the example of Nathan and David does not prove that subjects can accuse their superiors.[56]

---

clesiastical affairs. Gratian asserts the same doctrine in Dist. 97, dict. ante c. 1 cited above. Later in the Decretum, at C. 15, q. 6, c. 3, Gratian does cite the deleted portion of the letter while discussing the pope's authority over oaths. At that place, however, the Magister is more interested in the power to dissolve oaths than to depose.

56. C. 2, q. 7, dict. post c. 41, "§2. Item cum David adulterium et homicidium commisisset, missus est a Deo Nathan propheta, ut eum redargueret. Ecce, quod prelati sunt arguendi et reprehendendi a subditis. §3. Sed notandum est, quod duae sunt personae, quibus mundus iste regitur, regalis videlicet et sacerdotialis. Sicut reges presunt in causis seculi, ita sacerdotes in causis Dei . . . David ergo, etsi ex regali unctione sacerdotibus et prophetis preerat in causis seculi, tamen suberat eis in causis Dei."

Stickler has argued that while the Magister rejects other parts of his opponents' argument, he accepts this statement on the separation of the two powers (*op. cit.,* pp. 69–71). That may be the case since Gratian does not stop to consider and refute the points made by his opponents. He continues the discussion by bringing up another example showing that prelates may be accused by their inferiors.

Finally, Causa 23 would seem to be the place where the Magister did consider the problem of regnum and sacerdotium. Here, the discussion concerns the use of the material sword, a subject traditionally associated with secular power. Yet, as Stickler has shown, Gratian's treatment of the two swords did not involve him in the question of the two powers. For the magister and his contemporaries, the swords represented only the two forms of coercion which existed, the spiritual and physical. Gratian argued in Causa 23 that the Church possessed both of these swords and that while priests were forbidden by the canons from exercising the material sword, they still had, as Rufinus later said, a *jus auctoritatis* to it. Prelates could seek the aid of any layman when they deemed it necessary to raise the material sword in the interests of the Church.[57]

Yet, the Magister's treatment of the passage and its place in the general argument of the Causa shows that he was not particularly interested in its ideas. He is preoccupied with the problem of accusations and, in fact, with which accusations are admissible in *ecclesiastical* courts.

Furthermore, the doctrine of the passage on the matter of regnum and sacerdotium is ambiguous. It is shown conclusively that the existence of two hierarchies makes the example of David and Nathan ineffective as a weapon against the argument that inferiors may not accuse their superiors, but there is no consideration of how Nathan can judge David without injuring his majesty. Also, the passage makes questionable the independence and equality of the two powers. While David is obviously within the jurisdiction of the priesthood in criminal matters, Causa 11, quaestio 1 demonstrates that priests are never to be judged by civil courts. The *privilegium fori* gives a juridical advantage to the priesthood in its dealings with the civil power. The Magister has therefore not given his followers any clear guidelines on the problem of the two powers in this dictum.

57. This claim to possession of both swords was new with the Investiture Contest period. It shows that the Church was now considered to be a juridical community. Stickler has devoted a series of studies to the history of the theory of the two swords. See, for example, Stickler, "De ecclesiastica potestate coactiva materialis apud magistrum Gratianum," *Salesianum*, 4 (1942), 2–23, 96–119. *Idem*, "Il 'gladius' negli atti dei concili e dei RR. Pontefici sino a Graziano e Bernardo di Clairvaux," *Salesianum*, 13 (1951), 414–445. *Idem*, "De potestate gladii materialis ecclesiae secundum 'Quaestiones Bambergenses ineditas,'" *Salesianum*, 6 (1944), 113–140. *Idem*, "Il 'gladius' nel Registro di Gregorio VII," *Studi Gregoriani*, 3 (1948), 89–103. *Idem*, "Der Schwerterbegriff bei Huguccio," *Ephemerides Juris Canonici*, 3 (1947), 1–44. The traditional view of the two swords image as representing the two powers can be found in Joseph Lecler, "L'argument des deux glaives dans les controverses politiques du moyen-âge," *Recherches de science religieuse*, 21 (1931), 299–339. Wilhelm Levison, "Die

Such is Gratian's supposed treatment of the regnum-sacerdotium problem. He did not leave his successors any guidelines on this issue, and when they sought his teaching on it, they were left to their own devices and to their imagination. As is well known, the decretists produced two opposing theories about the relationship between the two powers, and both sides looked to the Decretum for support of their position. When the Decretum is studied with respect to this matter, it must be concluded that neither group of decretists was justified in claiming that the Decretum supported its argument.

Gratian's lack of interest in the relationship of the two powers stemmed from his connection with Haimeric's party. In the 1120's and 1130's, interest in the problem of regnum and sacerdotium became a political issue. The party of Pierleoni took a stand in favor of continued concern with the relations of the civil and ecclesiastical powers because it looked upon the Concordat of Worms as unsatisfactory. The members of Haimeric's party swung to the other extreme and hardly considered the problem at all. Gratian is not the only member of the party whose work indicates the attitude of the group. Saint Bernard only referred to Church and State when he was concerned with the protection of the Church, that is, when he wished the secular power to act so that the Church hierarchy would be able to carry on its work. When the Roman republic founded by Arnold of Brescia threatened the papacy, Bernard wrote to the German king Conrad urging him to act in the interests of the Church. He expounded the idea that the two powers, established by Christ, ought to cooperate to convince Conrad to act, but his emphasis here is on bringing order to the Church, and he does not delve into the nature of the relationship between the secular and ecclesiastical authorities. The famous passage of the *De Consideratione* in which Bernard says that both the ma-

---

mittelalterliche Lehre von den beiden Schwerten," *DA,* 9 (1951), 14–42. This problem will be examined in a later chapter, but see C. 23, q. 8, dict. post c. 18, "sacerdotes, etsi propria manu arma arripere non debeant, tamen vel his, quibus huiusmodi offitia conmissa sunt, persuadere, vel quibuslibet, ut ea arripiant, sua auctoritate valeant inperare." Rufinus makes the distinction between the *jus auctoritatis* and *jus administrationis* in his commentary to Dist. 22, c. 1. See Rufinus, *op. cit.,* pp. 47–48. See also Hartmut Hoffmann, "Die beiden Schwerter im hohen Mittelalter," *DA,* 20 (1965), 78–114.

terial and spiritual swords belong to the Church was meant, as Stickler has also shown, in the same sense as Gratian's Causa 23. That the passage later became the basis of much theorizing by both canonists and theologians on the relations of the two powers does not reflect on Bernard's original purpose.[58] Likewise, Hugh of Saint Victor, whose house had close relations with Haimeric, wrote very little about regnum and sacerdotium. The passages that touched upon the question in the *De Sacramentis* have left scholars puzzling.[59] When the subject of the two powers did come up in the writings of the members

58. See Saint Bernard, *Ep.* 244. See also *Ep.* 139 to Lothar. Idem, *De Consid.,* IV:3, 7, "Quid denuo usurpare gladium tentes, quem semel jussus es reponere in vaginam? Quem tamen qui tuum negat, non satis mihi videtur attendere verbum Domini dicentis sic: 'Converte gladium tuum in vaginam.' Tuus ergo et ipse, tuo forsitan nutu, etsi non tua manu, evaginandus." Stickler, "Il 'gladius' negli atti dei concili," *passim.* A. Depoorter, "De argumento duorum gladiorum apud S. Bernardum," *Collationes Brugenses,* 48 (1952), 22–26, 95–99. Recently, Elizabeth Kennan has reviewed the scholarship on this point and supported Stickler's interpretation. Kennan, "The 'De Consideratione' of St. Bernard and the Papacy in the Mid-Twelfth Century," *Traditio,* 23 (1967), 73–115. Kennan, like others who have worked on Bernard's political thought, does not seem to recognize that the saint did not consider the matter of regnum and sacerdotium. Scholars have noted that Bernard had little to say about political theory and they have attributed the cryptic and ambiguous character of passages touching on regnum and sacerdotium to this general lack of interest in the theory of social structure. In fact, as will be seen, Bernard has some interesting and important things to say about social organization; in particular, about the characteristics of good prelates (as was noted earlier), about canonical election, and about the theory of obedience. His lack of concern for the problem of the two powers seems to stem from his association with Haimeric's party.

59. Hugh of Saint Victor, *De Sac.,* II:2, 4, "Quanto autem vita spiritualis dignior est quam terrena, et spiritus quam corpus, tanto spiritualis potestas terrenam sive saecularem potestatem honore, ac dignitate praecedit. Nam spiritualis potestas terrenam potestatem et instituere habet, ut sit, et judicare habet si bona non fuerit." Note also, Hugh, *De Sac.,* II:2, 3, "Clericis vero spiritualia tantum committuntur." As Tierney has pointed out, it is difficult to extract a political theory from the writings of Saint Bernard and Hugh of Saint Victor. This is especially true of their theory of regnum and sacerdotium (see Brian Tierney, *The Crisis of Church and State* [Englewood Cliffs, N.J., 1964], p. 88). Hugh, in these passages, speaks of the greater dignity of the spiritual power over the secular power, but is ambiguous about the juridical effect of this difference in dignity. It remains unclear whether he thinks that the spiritual power may judge the secular in all or only in spiritual matters. Haimeric gave some gifts to the house of Saint Victor. Schmale, *Studien zum Schisma,* p. 104.

59

of the reform party, therefore, the ideas expressed were ambiguous. All that can be said is that the authors seem to accept the independent existence of the two powers. The fundamental issues raised by the Investiture Controversy receive little attention.

There is one more general characteristic of Gratian's work which indicates his connection with Haimeric's party. This is his careful deletion of Roman law from his presentation of the legal tradition of the Church. Adam Vetulani sees the rejection of Roman law as a reflection of Gratian's ideological sympathies. Based on his argument that the Magister compiled his work between 1105 and 1120, he thinks that the avoidance of the law of Justinian stemmed from Gratian's agreement with the principles of the ill-fated settlement of 1111. Gratian would have deleted Roman law from the corpus of canons, according to Vetulani, because he believed in the radical separation of the secular and ecclesiastical spheres.[60] But it was his allegiance with the reformers of the 1120's and 1130's rather than with the supporters of the agreement of 1111 which determined his attitude toward Roman law. The compromise solution of the Investiture Contest which Haimeric and his followers supported in the Concordat of Worms was based on a distinction between the secular and ecclesiastical aspects of the episcopal office. This compromise preserved, at least in theory, the separation between the two spheres which had been at the basis of earlier attempts to resolve the dispute. Legendre has noted that from the pontificate of Pascal until about 1160, canonists stopped adding Roman law to the corpus of canon law.[61] This attitude—and Gratian was the most

---

60. A. Vetulani, "Le Décret de Gratien et les premiers Décrétistes dans la lumière d'une nouvelle source," SG, 7 (1959), 273–353. Vetulani's argument about the date of the Decretum has been universally rejected. See app. i.

61. Pierre Legendre, La pénétration du droit romain dans le droit canonique classique de Gratien à Innocent IV (1140–1254) (Paris, 1964), pp. 25–26, 99–100. Legendre notes that the attitude of the canonists in this period did not mean that they were unlearned in the Roman law, but their use of Roman law was very restricted. Gratian borrowed the idea of ius condendi legem (C. 25, q. 1, dict. post c. 16 and C. 11, q. 1, dict. post c. 30) and the doctrine concerning the distinction between judges and arbitrators (C. 2, q. 6, dict. post c. 33) from Justinian's collection or from commentaries on it. See Codex, 1.14.12. Legendre's work shows again that there was a connection between the period of Pascal and that of Haimeric (see remarks in app. i). The addition of texts from the

extreme of the canonists on this matter—may show that on the whole the canonists were attracted by theories that made a clear distinction between the temporal and spiritual spheres.[62] Gratian, in any case, seems to have purged secular law from his collection in response to the idea that the two spheres ought to be kept distinct and separate. Furthermore, this idea appears occasionally to have been in the minds of others of the reform party.

There is a famous passage from Saint Bernard's *De Consideratione* which indicates that the saint had the same attitude as Gratian toward Roman law. Bernard complained to Eugene III, "Daily the laws resound in the palace, but they are laws of Justinian, not of the Lord." [63] The context in which this sentence occurs shows that the saint is actu-

---

Corpus Juris Civilis to the Decretum probably began before 1160, however, since even the earliest manuscripts contain some Roman law paleae (see the studies cited in chap. i, n. 22). Professor Tierney has suggested to me that the changed attitude toward Roman law among the canonists which took place around 1160, at the time when the second great battle between regnum and sacerdotium began, may reflect a new confidence in the sovereign status of the Church. The canonists may have thought, in 1160, that use of the Roman law in no way damaged the sovereignty of the ecclesiastical hierarchy which had been energetically promoted by the party of Haimeric and by Gratian in the Decretum. This question goes beyond this study, but certainly the interpretation of the outlook and interests of the reform party offered here suggests that Professor Tierney's notion is close to the truth. A study of the influence of politics on the introduction of Roman law into the Corpus Juris Canonici is needed.

The idea that the two laws ought to be separated may have derived from a tradition of the Gregorian papacy itself. Fournier and Le Bras have noted here and there pre-Gratian collections that do not contain any Roman law. One example of these is the Collection in Five Books completed during the later years of Gregory VII's reign. Paul Fournier and Gabriel Le Bras, *Histoire des collections canoniques en Occident* (Paris, 1932), 2:131–135. On the history of the relations between the two laws see C. G. Mor, "La recezione del diritto romano nelle collezioni canoniche dei secoli IX–XI in Italia e oltr'Alpe," *Acta di Congresso Jur. internazionale* (Rome, 1935), 2:281–302. *Idem,* "Diritto romano e canonico pregraziano," *Europa e il diritto romano; studi in memoria di Paolo Koschaker* (Milan, 1954), 2:15–32.

62. See the comment made relative to C. 23, q. 8, dict. post c. 20 on p. 243 below.

63. Saint Bernard, *De Consid.,* I:4, 5, "Et quidem quotidie perstrepunt in palatio leges, sed Iustiniani, non Domini. Iustene etiam istud?" This passage is one of the main points of reference for an extensive scholarly debate over Bernard's attitude toward the law and legalism. For a review of the debate, see app. ii.

ally unhappy with the amount of time and energy the pope expends hearing cases. But why did Bernard pick out the law of Justinian for particular disapprobation? He certainly did not confuse the law of the Corpus Iuris Civilis with canon law, but rather he is exhibiting the attitude that Roman law does not belong in the Church courts. In fact, he is implying that it is the introduction of Roman law cases into canonical jurisprudence which has caused the unacceptable growth of legal activities at the Curia. Gratian took effective action against this abuse when he deleted secular law texts from series of canons that he borrowed from earlier collections. His work embodies the ideas of Saint Bernard on this as on so many other points.

The members of the reform group did not often express themselves about the place Roman law ought to have in the Church. Only Gerhoh of Reichersberg, in a work written around 1126, formulated a complaint against the presence of Roman law in the Church almost identical with Bernard's later one to Eugene.[64] It cannot be expected that

64. Gerhoh, *de novitatibus, MGH*, Libelli de lite III:301–302, "Possunt quoque haut absurde surdis ad legem Dei auribus et ad leges Iustiniani patulis ac pruritu magno estuantibus in aures, quas amant quasque decenter in forensi conventu ostentant, in domo Iacob denegari, ubi decentius iudicatur secundum legem Dei quam secundum legem Iustiniani vel Theodosii, quorum tamen leges non inprobamus, nisi forte alicubi discordent a divinae legis constitutionibus, verum in domo Iacob simplex narratio et sincerum iudicium secundum consuetudines antiquorum pontificum Romanorum perornat ipsam domum, si lex Domini inreprehensibilis presideat in ea, tamquam domina gentium princeps provinciarum, qua dominante et regnante in domo Iacob lex forensis iudicii vel ancilla subserviat per contemptibiles ad maiora minus idoneos amministrata, sicut apostolus consulit, ne maiores qui orationi et ministerio verbi cum apostolis vacare debent, nimium secularibus negociis implicentur et per hec utiliora suffocentur." Bernard's cryptic comment on this subject and Dist. 10 in the Decretum contain the same doctrine expounded here by Gerhoh.

There is no question that Gerhoh was part of the reform party led by Haimeric. As Classen, Gerhoh's biographer points out, the provost had close relations with the papal chancellor, and he declared for Innocent almost immediately after the double election. Classen, *Gerhoch von Reichersberg* (Wiesbaden, 1960), p. 54. But Gerhoh was certainly in the conservative wing of the party. He looked upon the Concordat of Worms as a hopeful beginning in the process of depriving the secular powers of all their authority in ecclesiastical elections (Classen, *op. cit.,* 41 ff). The opposition to the Concordat as too favorable to the emperor was very strong in the diocese of Salzburg where Reichersberg is situated and where Gerhoh was very active. Gerhoh hoped to make the Church wholly spiritual and this point would be a major one in the writings of the party. The reformers were against the law of Justinian and did not concern themselves with it unless they were confronted with its effect on ecclesiastical affairs; then, they could be eloquent in their denunciations. Gratian's treatment of the collection of Justinian was the most direct indication of their attitude, and it was part of the most extensive and most profound exposition of the party's theory of ecclesiastical society.

It is now apparent that scholarship on the general characteristics of Gratian's work strongly supports the thesis that the Decretum had a

---

warned priests and bishops not to accept gifts or *regalia*. He was of the opinion that all property held by the Church ought to be wholly in its power—all of it ought to be considered *ecclesiastica*. It is probable that other members of the reform party hoped to improve upon the compromise contained in the Concordat, but Gerhoh definitely sought this goal more actively and more vocally than the others. In the political situation of the 1120's and 1130's, he is a hybrid. Gerhoh, *de aed. Dei,* 13-15. Idem, *Comm. in Ps. 64,* 27 "spiritualiter electo et constituto episcopo deinde accedat laicorum assensio et illa regalium donatio, de qua constitutum iam episcopum rex vel imperator investire habet, quando [iam] in electione vel promotione prorsus non est contradictio. [28] Nam, si electionis patet dissonantia, iure in talibus expectatur iudicum spiritualium sententia, ut electo iam confirmato fiat regalium donatio; quanquam eadem iam aecclesiis olim donata in possessione sint aecclesiastica censenda, sed obsequio decenti apud regem deservienda, non ad nutum eius aecclesiis quasi ex novo conferenda vel auferenda." See *de quarta vigilia noctis,* 17. Cf. text of the agreement of 1122. Concordat, Mercati, *op. cit.,* p. 19, "electiones episcoporum et abbatum Teutonici regni, qui ad regnum pertinent, in praesentia tua fieri, absque simonia et aliqua violentia; ut si qua inter partes discordia emerserit, metropolitani et conprovincialium consilio vel iudicio, saniori parti assensum et auxilium praebeas. Electus autem regalia absque omni exactione per sceptrum a te recipiat et quae ex his iure tibi debet faciat." Gerhoh expressed the view that the Church ought to work in order to preserve its spirituality in *de aed. Dei,* 45, "Infelix ille, qui implet desiderium suum contra ipsos [the precepts of Isa. 23:14 and Ps. 126:4] munera suscipiendo; beatus ille, qui implet desiderium suum ex ipsis manus suas ab omni munere excutiendo." *De aed. Dei,* 46, "Omnia enim licent, sed non omnia expediunt. Licet episcopo post consecrationem aecclesiarum munus sponte oblatum suscipere; sed puto cursum predicationis per hoc magis impediri, quam expediri." Note here the similarity between the phrase "Omnia enim licet, sed non omnia expediunt" and the famous phrase of Saint Bernard, "Facitis hoc, quia potestis: sed utrum et debeatis, quaestio est." (*De Consid.,* III:4, 14.). See also Gerhoh, *Ep. ad Inn., MGH,* Libelli de lite III:208-209. Irene Ott, "Der Regalienbegriff im 12. Jahrhundert," *ZRG,* Kan. Abt., 35 (1948), 234-304. M. Schützeichel, "Beiträge zur Geschichte des Säkularisationsgedankens im Mittelalter" (Ph.D. diss., Münster, 1939), p. 14.

great political significance when it appeared around 1140. Textual studies have shown that in its original state, the work was not simply a collection of ancient law of the Church, as it appears in the form given to it in later manuscripts and in modern editions. Rather, it was a series of treatises on legal subjects in which a great proportion of ancient legal tradition was cited. Gratian had a purpose that went beyond his desire to reassemble the canons into a useful topical arrangement and to treat them according to dialectical method. Other studies on the text of the Decretum permit us to say more about the purposes and views of the author. It has been shown that he is not responsible for the theologically oriented parts of the Decretum or for a large number of paleae some of which make it difficult to discern his aims in the work. In addition, he deleted Roman law extracts from his presentation of the Church's legal tradition and avoided direct discussion of the issues of regnum and sacerdotium. Furthermore, these attitudes were not peculiar to the Magister and should be seen in the light of his general interests. His exposition in the *Tractatus ordinandorum* provided the legal foundation on which the reforming efforts of Saint Bernard and others could rest. Study of Gratian's constitutional theory will expose not only the doctrines that became the basis of later canonical theorizing but also the ecclesiological views that won out in the mid-twelfth century, when the party of Haimeric ousted the old guard of the Gregorian papacy from the Curia. That ecclesiology amounted to a Christian theory of political society.

III. The Church as a Juridical Community

Most writers connected with the party of Haimeric stressed the mystical nature of the Church. This emphasis on spiritual values was part of the reaction of the party's members to the worldliness of the Gregorian papacy as it had developed during the later stages of the Investiture Contest. The ecclesiology of the mid-twelfth century differed from that which prevailed during the Investiture period primarily in its emphasis, but that emphasis, renewed spirituality, brought out the inherent duality of the conception of the Church. It thus hindered Gratian's attempt to develop a constitutional theory of the Church. Saint Bernard, among others, did not deny that the Church on earth was ruled by a juridical authority and that therefore the Church was a juridical community. The new reformers accepted this legacy of the eleventh-century reform movement. Yet in keeping with the rest of their theology, they brought the mystical aspect of the Church to the fore in their ecclesiology. For them, the Church was a mystical entity that had a special relationship with God; it was the *corpus Christi,* the Bride of Christ, the city of the good.[1] In their writings, the two ideas

---

1. The image of the Church as the Bride of Christ was Bernard's favorite. Here are some citations: *Epp.* 172, 330, 331, 341, 348, 395, 467, 468. *Apologia,* 3, n. 6. *In Cant.,* 1, n. 8; 14; 22, n. 5–6; 27, n. 7; 49, n. 2; 57, n. 3; 69, n. 1; 76, n. 8; 78; 79, n. 4. To which add 55 doxologies in variations of "ad laudem et gloriam Sponsi Ecclesiae Domini nostri . . ." The saint used other images as well. The Church was the *corpus Christi* in *in Cant.,* 71, n. 11. It was a *tunica inconsutilis* in *Epp.* 219, n. 2; 334. There are many other images. Yves Congar, "L'écclesiologie de s. Bernard," *Saint Bernard Théologien,* pp. 136–190. (This article was pub-

of the Church, as an earthly community and as a mystical body, inter-
mingled so that the image of the Ecclesia necessarily remained vague.

The duality of the Church's image was useful for the mystical theologians associated with Haimeric's faction, and it created no particu-

lished also in German in *Bernhard von Clairvaux: Mönch und Mystiker,* ed.
Joseph Lortz [Wiesbaden, 1955], pp. 76–119.) See also Klemens Kilga, *Der
Kirchenbegriff des hl. Bernard von Clairvaux,* Sonderdruck: *Cistercienser Chro-
nik* (1947–1948).

Hugh of Saint Victor called the Church a city of the good which he opposed
to a city of the evil. *De duabus civitatibus,* Misc. I, 48, PL 177, col. 496A–497A.
De Sac., I:8, 11. See n. 2 below. On Hugh's ecclesiology, Jean Châtillon, "L'idée
de l'Église dans la théologie de l'école de Saint-Victor au XIIe siècle," *Irenikon,* 22
(1949), 115–138, 394–411. Only one scholar has studied the ecclesiology of the
early scholastics in general. Johannes Beumer has concluded that theologians of
the period neglected the juridical aspect of the Church—the problems concerned
with the tangible ecclesiastical community and its constitution. He thinks further
that theologians purposefully neglected this side of the Church because they
considered it to be the special province of the canonists. This interpretation may
be correct for theologians of the late twelfth century, but it cannot explain the
point of view of Gratian's contemporaries. At that time, canonical jurisprudence
was not a discipline independent from theology. In fact, Peter Lombard, who
completed his *Sententiae* around 1158, apparently did not see a radical separation
between the two fields. He borrowed a great many texts and arguments from
the Decretum. The character of ecclesiological theory in Gratian's time seems to
have resulted from the inclination to mysticism of the chief writers, and there
is also the element of reaction against the worldliness of the Gregorian Church.
Beumer, "Zur Ekklesiologie der Frühscholastik," *Scholastik,* 26 (1951), 364–389.
Idem, "Ekklesiologische Probleme der Frühscholastik," *Scholastik,* 27 (1952), 183–
209.

Beumer points out that the juridical conception of the Church was expressed
by some early scholastic theologians, in particular Hildebert of Lavardin, Peter
Abelard, and Anselm of Havelberg. See Hildebert of Lavardin, *Sermo 98 (de
div.* 12), "Non sunt, inquit [St. Paul], contemnendae potestates, sive mundi,
sive Ecclesiae, quia omnes ordinatae sunt a Deo, . . . Hi [priests] autem positi
sunt in Ecclesia ad humilitatem [one ms. has *utilitatem*] nostram, ut nobis
provideant." The sermon is a commentary on Rom. 13:1, "Non est potestas nisi
a Deo." Certainly, *utilitatem* is to be preferred in the last quoted sentence. Peter
Abelard, *Sermo 23 (de sancto Petro).* Abelard concentrates, in this sermon, on
Peter's principate in the Church and the powers that he received from Christ.
Anselm of Havelberg, *Dialogi,* 3:12, "caput Ecclesiae Christus, ascendens in al-
tum, vicem suam in terris Petro apostolorum principi commisit." The *Dialogi*
report on negotiations between the Roman and Greek churches in which Anselm
participated. Chap. 12 of Bk. 3 concerns the primacy of the Roman See. Beumer,
"Ekklesiologische Probleme," pp. 203–205.

It should be pointed out that Beumer's articles suffer from a lack of attention

lar difficulty for them. But the all-embracing vagueness of mysticism could not be preserved when one sought to examine the structure of the earthly Church. Only Gratian, among the writers who supported Haimeric, recognized and dealt with the implications of reemphasizing the spiritual aspect of the Church. The duality in ecclesiological theory prevailing in writings by members of his party and by those sympathetic with its goals became for him the most important problem in the exposition of a theory of Church structure. The Church was at once spiritual and temporal, and there was an essential unity in it which could not be destroyed. But these two aspects of the Church are contradictory: because the Church is a spiritual body, it must be perfect both in its organization and in its operation; because the Church is a temporal body, it cannot be perfect and must be organized and must operate according to the imperfect rules of social life. Gratian was in a dilemma created by his own political and theological views. He had to expound a constitutional theory that preserved the union of the spiritual and worldly qualities of the Church, but under these circumstances, it was very difficult to expound a constitutional theory at all. He deemphasized, of necessity, the views that his contemporaries and political confreres were presenting, and yet he tried to make his doctrine of ecclesiastical organization reflect the essential spiritual nature of the Church. This attempt caused him much trouble in expounding some of the central doctrines in his theory.

What follows is a brief comparison between the views of Gratian and of his contemporaries about the Church—the nature of its origins and its membership. This discussion of the foundation of the Church is focused on Saint Bernard and Gratian. Bernard was representative of other writers of the age including early scholastic theologians like Hugh of Saint Victor. He had much to say about the nature of the Church, but in general he made only passing reference to it using his characteristic images to convey his meaning. In particular, he calls it

---

to chronology and do not treat all the important writers of the period. There is little consideration of the nonscholastic theologians such as Saint Bernard and none of the canon lawyers. Bernard and the early scholastic theologians like Hugh of Saint Victor did not differ significantly in their view of the Church. Beumer's studies are therefore misleading or at least incomplete.

the Bride of Christ. But it is at the point where he discusses the origins of the Church and its relationship with the institutions of the previous age of man that he gives us the fullest understanding of his idea of the Church. In these passages, he expresses his ideas through his favorite images, but he uses them in a context that makes it easier to comprehend his notion of the union of temporal and spiritual in the Church. Likewise, Gratian's basic approach to the Church is most clearly presented in passages that refer to its foundation. Bernard and Gratian therefore have a common point of reference for looking at the Church; they express very different notions, nonetheless.

The difference between the two men becomes clear when their theory of Church membership is examined. In dealing with this problem, the theologians and canonists clarified their conception of the Church by envisioning the community through the definition of its membership. The contemporary works used in this discussion are varied because many twelfth-century writers touched on the problem of membership. They treat the conditions for being a member in the Church community when they consider the reception of the sacraments, and their treatment of this issue brings out the ambiguity of their notions of the Church.

The foundation of the Church.

Bernard considered the Jewish community to be a *figura* of the earthly Church, and he approached it, as he did the Church, with a particular concern for its spiritual nature. His views on the transition from the Synagogue to the Church were connected with his ideas about man's spiritual progress through history, and in these views, he was representative of most of his contemporaries. The history of man was divided into three ages, and writers of Bernard's period saw the transition from one age to another as taking place in a brief historical moment through a revolutionary mystical event. For Bernard as for all Christians, the coming of Christ was one of these events, and Christ's work was not seen as creating a bond between man and God, but rather as a reformation of that bond. Man had always been in relation to God, but that relationship changed from age to age. God's concern for man was symbolized in His sacraments, for in each age there were sacraments that were suitable for the quality of man's spiritual condition in that age.[2] Bernard exposed his views of the Church when he considered the sacrament by which one entered the

2. Saint Bernard, *in Oct. Epiph.*, nn. 1–2, "Nihil ergo mirum, si pro diversitate temporum mutata sint sacramenta, ut daretur utrisque quod eis congruum erat. Ipse vero Christus utrumque suscepit, ut tanquam lapis angularis utrique parieti cohaereret, ac si duarum capita corrigiarum consuendo connecteret, sicut ei Pascha figuratum ipse complevit, et verum protinus inchoavit." Idem, *Vigilia Nat. Dom.*, 4, n. 3. Hugh of Saint Victor expressed this view of human history more fully than Bernard. Each age had not only a set of sacraments that were particularly suited to it, but also a type of man to which the majority of the population conformed. Hugh of Amiens, *Dialogi*, V:7. Hugh of Saint Victor, *de Sac.*, I:8, 11, "Tria sunt tempora per quae praesentis saeculi spatium decurrit. Primum est tempus naturalis legis; secundum tempus scriptate legis; tertium tempus gratiae. Primum ab Adam usque ad Moysen. Secundum a Moyse usque ad Christum. Tertium a Christo usque ad finem saeculi. Similiter tria sunt genera hominum; . . . homines naturalis legis sunt aperte mali, homines scriptae legis ficte boni, homines gratiae vere boni. . . . Ista tria genera hominum ab initio nunquam ullo tempore defuerunt. Tempus tamen naturalis legis ad aperte malos pertinet, quia illi tunc et numero plures et statu excellentiores fuerunt." See Hugh of Saint Victor, *de Sac.* I:11, 1, "Sacramenta ab initio ad restaurationem et curationem hominis instituta sunt; alia sub naturali lege, alia sub scripta lege, alia sub gratia." See also idem, *de Arca Noe Mystica*, 5. Heinrich Weisweiler, *Die Wirksamkeit der Sakramente nach Hugo von St. Viktor* (Freiburg i. Br., 1932), pp. 23–43. The authenticity of many of the works attributed to Hugh in the manuscripts and by medieval writers has caused some difficulty. D. Van den Eynde provided an extensive study of Hugh's writings and their dates, and I have based my use of the Victorine's works on his account. Damien Van den Eynde, *Essai sur la succession et la date des écrits de Hugues de Saint-Victor* (Rome, 1960).

The idea of the continuous development of man's spiritual capacity was connected in the works of Hugh of Saint Victor and others with the idea that the Church was a great *civitas*. City of the good was not the Church per se, but it was a community that had existed since the earliest days of man's existence. In the minds of these writers, the city of the good, Jerusalem, was opposed by the city of the evil, Babylon. Hugh of Saint Victor, *De duabus civitatibus*, Misc. I:48, col. 496A–497A, "Duo sunt civitates, Jerusalem et Babylon, et duo populi, amatores Dei cives Jerusalem et amatores mundi cives Babylonis. Et duo reges, Christus rex Jerusalem, et diabolus rex Babylonis. . . . Hi duo populi duas civitates ab initio suo aedificaverunt, Babylonem quae a Cain initium cepit et Jerusalem, quae ab Abel." See *de Sac.*, I:8, 11, after the Fall of Adam, "coepit ergo genus hominum mox in partes contrarias dividi." Beumer points out that this idea was common during the early scholastic period. See Gerhoh of Reichersberg, *Comm. in Ps. 64*, 3. Hildebert of Lavardin, *S. de sanctis*, 73:1. Peter Lombard, *Comm. in Ps.*,

religious community in the age of the Jews and in that of Christ. It is his comparison of circumcision and baptism, found in his work *In circumcisione Domini,* which is of interest here.

Bernard considered circumcision to be the sacrament that prefigured baptism. It was a sign of the faith that the Jews had in God and a sign of the grace that God extended to the Jewish people. But circumcision was an imperfect sacrament because it was restricted to a single people and to a single sex within that people. When Christ congregated the dispersed sons of God into the one true Church, he introduced a new sacrament that was perfect both in its internal and external aspects. Baptism signified more clearly than circumcision that God cleanses the soul in the sacrament. It also symbolized the essence of Christ's work, the bringing of divine grace to all men of whatever nation and of either sex. The new sacrament symbolized that the new religious community was supranational, a congregation of all the faithful.[3]

118:8. Beumer, "Zur Ekklesiologie," pp. 379–382. Bernard also referred to the Church as the *civitas Domini virtutum.* See *in Conv. S. Pauli,* n. 7, "Domine, quid me vis facere? Et Dominus ad illum: Surge, et ingredere civitatem, ibi dicetur tibi, quid te oporteat facere [Acts 9:6–7]. . . . Eum cui tu loqueris, erudiendum de voluntate tua mittis ad hominem, ut socialis vitae commendetur utilitas, et edoctus per hominem, discat et ipse secundem datam sibi gratiam hominibus subvenire. Ingredere civitatem. Videtis, fratres, non sine divino consilio factum esse, ut hanc civitatem Domini virtutum ingrederemini, divinam discere voluntatem." Karl Wisser, "Individuum und Gemeinschaft in dem Anschauungen des hl. Bernhard von Clairvaux," *Cistercienser Chronik,* 49 (1937), 257–263. Leopold Grill, "Saint Bernard et la question sociale," *Mélanges Saint Bernard* (Dijon, 1953), pp. 194–211. As Jacqueline points out, Bernard sustains this theme in other parts of his work. See *in Conv. S. Paul,* n. 3; *in festo S. Michaelis,* 1, n. 5; *in dedicatione eccles.,* 5, n. 10. Bernard Jacqueline, *Papauté et épiscopat selon s. Bernard* (Saint-Lô, 1963), pp. 2–6. See also, Étienne Gilson, "La cité de Dieu de s. Bernard," *S. Bernard homme d'église* (1953), pp. 101–105.

3. Saint Benard, *in circum. Dom.,* 1, n. 1, "Ad quid enim tibi circumcisio necessaria, qui peccatum non commisisti nec contraxisti?" Saint Bernard, *op. cit.,* n. 2, "Circumcisio nempe salvandi potius, quam Salvatoris esse videtur, et Salvatorem circumcidere decet, quam circumcidi." On the difference between the two sacraments, see Saint Bernard, *op. cit.,* n. 3, "Et nos enim, fratres, circumcidi necesse est, et sic nomen salutis accipere; circumcidi sane non littera, sed spiritu et veritate; circumcidi non uno membro, sed toto corpore simul. Licet enim magis in ea parte, in qua mandata est Judeis circumcisio, regnet additamentum Leviathan, quod a malo est et amputari debet, universam tamen occupat carnem. . . . Propterea sicut parvulus adhuc in fide et dilectione populus congruum sibi

These historical ideas about the foundation of the new Church reflect Bernard's conception of the congregation. He emphasizes the new spiritual condition of man, but does not see that condition as being only the result of a deepened spiritual sense and heightened spiritual capacity. It is also an extension of divine grace to all men. For the saint, the reception of baptism made one a member of a community of the faithful similar to but more extensive than the Synagogue. It is a temporal community with a spiritual significance for its members.

Our attention is again focused on the ecclesiological result of Christ's coming when Bernard's comparison of Synagogue and Church is considered. Both communities are the Bride of God, but the Jewish Church had been an imperfect Bride. The imperfection derived from its restrictiveness, and Christ perfected his Bride by extending the possibility of salvation to all men.[4] This view demonstrates that Bernard thought there was essential unity of spiritual and temporal aspects of

---

mandatum exiguae circumcisionis accepit: sic ubi crevit in virum perfectiorem, toto jubetur corpore baptizari, quae totius est hominis integra circumcisio." Bernard says that Christ congregated the sons of God into one in *in Oct. Pasch.*, 1, n. 5. J. C. Didier, "La question du baptême des enfants chez s. Bernard et ses contemporains," *Saint Bernard Théologien*, pp. 191–201. Artur M. Landgraf, "Kindertaufe und Glaube in der Frühscholastik," *Gregorianum*, 9 (1928), 337–373. Beumer, "Ekklesiologische Probleme," pp. 185–187. Congar, *op. cit.*, pp. 180–181. The same ideas about baptism and circumcision are expressed by other writers of the period, many of them associated with the party of Haimeric. Peter the Venerable, *Contra Petrobr.*, PL 180, col. 758. Hugh of Saint Victor, *De sac. leg. nat.*, PL 176, col. 38D. Hugh of Amiens, *Contra Haer.*, I:17 (PL 192, col. 1255–1298). Ekbert of Schönau, *S. contra Catharos*, 7, n. 4–5 (PL 195, col. 11–98). Peter Lombard, *Sent.*, IV, *Dist.* 3, 10. See also *Ysagoge in Theologiam*, II:182. *Sententie Parisenses*, II, pp. 37–38. These works are from Peter Abelard's school and are edited by Landgraf in *Écrits théologiques de l'école d'Abélard*, *Textes inedits* (Louvain, 1934). The editor dates the *Ysagoge* 1148–1152 and the *Sententie*, which he thinks are notes from the master's lectures, 1139–1141. On the school of Abelard and its influence, see the recent work of D. E. Luscombe, *The School of Abelard* (Cambridge, 1969). On the foundation of the Church according to the early scholastic theologians, Beumer, "Zur Ekklesiologie," pp. 378–379.

4. Saint Bernard, *in Cant.*, 67, n. 11, "O fatuam sponsam Synagogam, quae contemnens Dei iustitiam, id est gratiam sponsi sui, et suam volens constituere, iustitiae Dei non est subiecta. Ob hoc misera repudiata est, et iam non est sponsa, sed Ecclesia, cui dicitur: Desponsavi te mihi in fide." See also *in Cant.*, 14, n. 2; 30, n. 5.

the Church. The image of the Bride, like that of the corpus Christi, conveys an idea of the Ecclesia which emphasizes its mystical personality; it is one, and it is intimately associated with Christ. But it remains clear that the Church is also the congregation of the faithful on earth. Christ remade the Church of God both by infusing it with the true spirit and by redefining its community. For Bernard, temporality is part of the Church's spirituality.

Gratian's treatment of the transition from Synagogue to Church presents a view of the Church which brings its temporality to the fore. The Magister recognizes the spiritual change that took place, but he emphasizes the institutional change. He is very conscious that one's view of the Church constitutes the basis for his ecclesiological theory, and thus he writes of the Church's foundation when he begins his consideration of the ecclesiastical hierarchy. In the first dictum of the *Tractatus ordinandorum,* he says that the priesthood of God had been first instituted in Old Testament times: "The highest pontiffs and the lesser priests were instituted by God through Moses. . . ." This priesthood of the Synagogue was consummated and perfected by Christ who gave to the new priesthood the power of the keys.[5] By focusing on the priesthood, Gratian stresses the temporal nature of the Church while recognizing its essentially spiritual task. The power of the keys, which is the basic power of the priests, is the power of binding and loosing

---

5. Dist. 21, dict. ante c. 1, "Ministri vero sacrorum canonum et decretorum pontificum sunt summi Pontifices et infra presules atque reliqui sacerdotes, quorum institutio in veteri testamento est inchoata, et in novo plenius consummata. §1. Summi enim Pontifices et minores sacerdotes a Deo sunt instituti per Moysen, qui ex precepto Domini Aaron in summum pontificem, filios vero eius unxit in minores sacerdotes. Postea David, cum ministeria domus Domini ampliaret, ianitores et cantores instituti. Porro Salomon quendam modum exorzizandi invenit, quo demones adiurati ex obsessis corporibus pellebantur; huic offitio mancipati exorcistae vocati sunt, . . . Hec omnia in novo testamento ecclesia imitata habet suos ianitores, quos hostiarios appellamus. Pro cantoribus lectores simul et cantores instituit. Exorcistas autem nomine antiquo et offitio permanente recepit. Pro filiis vero Aaron omnes infra summum pontificem sacerdotium administrantes sunt consecrati. . . . Simpliciter vero maiorum et minorum sacerdotum discretio in novo testamento ab ipso Christo sumpsit, qui XII. apostolos tanquam maiores sacerdotes, et LXXII. discipulos quasi minores sacerdotes instituit. Petrum vero quasi in summum sacerdotem elegit, dum ei pre omnibus et pro omnibus claves regni celorum tribuit."

granted to them by Christ in Matthew 16:19. It is a spiritual power to give penitence and to remit sins. It is also a juridical power that justifies judicial and legislative authority exercised by the hierarchy. Which of these aspects of the power interests Gratian is very clear in the passage. The Magister refers not only to the action of Christ in founding the Church but also to that of the early Church community. He points to two determining factors in the history of the ecclesiastical hierarchy.

There is no doubt that Gratian saw Christ as the founder of the Church on earth. The Savior, he says, instituted the priests and gave them their power, but He only distinguished between the greater and lesser priests, the episcopate and the presbyterate. The further distinctions of rank within these orders were established by the early Church and were founded on the priestly offices of the gentiles. Thus, priests, archpriests, bishops, archbishops and other ecclesiastical offices derived from the *flamines, archiflamines, protoflamines,* and other pagan priestly offices.[6] This view of the role played by the Church itself in the establishment of the ecclesiastical constitution demonstrates that Gratian thought Christ had founded a juridical community when He instituted the new priesthood. The Church had control over its own destiny and development so that when its members recognized the need for a complex organization, they could act on their recognition. Christ had given the community its divine purpose and power necessary for carrying out that purpose, but he had provided little guidance for its organization. For Gratian, Christ gave the Church the legal foundation on which its further development rested, and the Decretum recorded and explained the theoretical support for that development in accord with the views of the reform party.

Bernard saw the earthly Church as an extension of the Synagogue, and this conception of the religious community concentrated attention

6. Dist. 21, dict. ante c. 1, "§2. Inter eos quedam discretio servata est, ut alii appellentur simpliciter 'sacerdotes,' alii 'archipresbiteri,' alii "corespiscopi,' alii 'episcopi,' alii 'archiepiscopi' seu 'metropolitae,' alii 'primates,' alii 'patriarchae,' alii 'summi Pontifices.' §3. Horum discretio a gentilibus maxime introducta est, qui suos flamines alios simpliciter flamines, alios archiflamines, alios protoflamines appellabant. Simpliciter vero maiorum et minorum sacerdotum discretio in novo testamento ab ipso Christo sumpsit exordium, qui XII. apostolos tanquam maiores sacerdotes, et LXXII. discipulos quasi minores sacerdotes instituit."

on the people of God, the congregation of the faithful. Gratian, too, looked at the transformation of the religious community from the perspective of the congregation. He approached the Church from this standpoint when he considered the law of marriage and recognized that the canonical doctrines on this subject had implications for the definition of the community. They reflected the relationship between members of the Church and outsiders. Thus, the Magister discussed the problems raised by intermarriage between Christians and non-Christians.[7] But he became most explicit about the nature of the new Church community when he considered the canonical prohibition of consanguinous marriage. It was his dialectical method that caused him to compare the Jewish and Christian churches.

The canons were very clear in their prohibition of marriage between relatives, and Gratian notes that this prohibition had its origin at the very beginning of human life. But Abraham, Isaac, Jacob, and others of the Hebrews who took wives from among their relatives, made it seem that the prohibition was not so ancient. The Magister explains that the Hebrews were excused from the law. In fact, God commanded the Hebrews to intermarry because the salvation of man was realized in the pure Jewish race. The Synagogue was a prefiguration of the Church, because it was the congregation of the saved, and the Magister actually called the Synagogue the *primitiva ecclesia* in the passage. From this ancient people, he continued, Christ elected his apostles and made them the basis of a new Church that was not to be limited to one nation. Already elsewhere in his work Gratian had said that Christ changed the nature of God's people by spreading the faith beyond the bounds of the Hebrews. Faith, not blood, was to be the criterion for membership in the chosen people. Again, in his discussion of consanguinous marriages, he argued that such marriages were no longer permitted because purity of blood no longer served as the foundation of the community.[8]

---

7. C. 28 and C. 32, q. 8.

8. C. 35, q. 1, dict. post c. 1, "§1. Est etiam alia causa, quare coniunctiones consanguineorum in populo Dei permissae primum, vel potius inperatae fuerint. Deus sic ab inicio salutem humani generis dispensavit, ut primitivam ecclesiam in populo illo institueret, qui sibi carnis consanguinitate erat propinquus. Unde de

As he did in the earlier passage concerning the establishment of the hierarchy, Gratian shows in this passage that he was looking at the Church primarily as a juridical community. Christ, he says in effect, founded a community in which intermarriage had no place, but He left it to the community itself to actually prohibit these marriages in law.[9] The Magister sees the coming of Christ from the standpoint of its juridical outcome. He occasionally employed such phrases as *mater ecclesia* or *corpus Christi* to designate the Church,[10] but he did so only

---

plebe Judaica primum Apostolos elegit, quos quasi fundamentum ecclesiae instituit, quorum predicatione de eadem plebe multi ad Deum conversi, in se ipsis originem ecclesiae prestiterunt. . . . Et quia non in una tantum familia, sed in omni multitudine gentium fidelium populus invenitur, non de propria cognatione, sed de qualibet alia cuique uxorem ducere conceditur." Very recently, G. Olsen has interpreted this passage differently from the way I have. Studying the history of the conception of the primitive church, Olsen concludes that Gratian uses the phrase here to designate the early Christian church. I think that the Magister used the term in an unusual way in the passage to designate the Synagogue. This interpretation is based on the context in which the phrase occurs and the connection between the ideas expressed in the dictum and those expounded in contemporary works which consider the relationship between Synagogue and Church. See, for example, Saint Bernard, *In Cant.*, 67 n. 11. Glenn Olsen, "The Idea of the Ecclesia Primitiva in the Writings of the Twelfth Century Canonists," *Traditio*, 25 (1969), 79–80, *passim*. See also C. 32, q. 4, dict. post c. 2, "Pro varietate temporum varia invenitur dispensatio conditoris. . . . Cum ergo, ceteris in idolatria relictis, Abraham et filios eius in peculiarem populum sibi Dominus elegisset, rite multarum fecunditate mulierum populi Dei multiplicatio querebatur, quia in successione sanguinis erat successio fidei. . . . Quia vero per incarnationem Christi gratia fidei ubique dilatata est, nec iam dicitur: 'Dic domui Iudae, et domui Israel;' sed: 'Euntes docete omnes gentes.'" This passage refers to the problem raised by Abraham's relations with Agar his servant and by Jacob's relations with a servant. Note the similarity between the first line in this dictum and the ideas of Saint Bernard, Hugh of Saint Victor, and others about the historical progress of man's spiritual condition.

9. C. 35, q. 1, dict. post c. 1, "§2. Consanguineorum ergo coniunctiones, quamvis evangelicis et apostolicis preceptis non inveniantur prohibitae sunt tamen fugiendae, quia ecclesiasticis institutionibus inveniuntur terminatae."

10. Gratian used the image of *mater ecclesia* three times: Dist. 51, dict. ante c. 1; Dist. 63, dict. post c. 28; and C. 1, q. 7, dict. post c. 23. He used the phrase *corpus Christi* twice, C. 1, q. 1, dict. post c. 16; and C. 3, q. 4, dict. post c. 12. The Magister nowhere called the Church *sponsa Christi*, but several capitula came close to the idea by calling it the bride of priests, C. 7, q. 1, cc. 11, 39; and C. 27, q. 1, c. 10. There is also a long discussion in the Decretum concerning the symbolic marriage between the bishop and his church. The image was used in order

as a manner of speaking and not in a conscious effort to explore the conceptions of the Church reflected in these images. On the whole, he ignored the mystical qualities of the Ecclesia so important to Bernard and others of the new reform party.

The difference between Gratian and Bernard on this matter does not affect the argument that they were political allies. Gratian did use the same framework as Bernard in exposing his ideas. He did recognize the spiritual character of the Church, and he never denied the intimate connection between the earthly ecclesiastical community and the spiritual sphere. This recognition was necessitated by the view of the origins of the Church as part of Christ's work on earth. The difference between the Magister and the abbot of Clairvaux was only one of emphasis, and it stemmed from their different purposes. Bernard never focused his attention on the constitutional structure of the Ecclesia and thus could always put emphasis on its essentially spiritual nature. Gratian sought to expound a constitutional theory for the Church which would reflect its spirituality and therefore embody the reemphasis of the mystical aspect of the Church among the members of the reform party. It is paradoxical that he had to ignore the mystical conceptions of the Church in order to accomplish this task, and as the ecclesiology of the Decretum is studied, it becomes increasingly clear that constitutional theory can, only with great difficulty, reflect the spirituality of the Church.

Membership in the Church according to Gratian's contemporaries.

Just as they emphasized the spiritual nature of the Church and did not make a clear distinction between that spirituality and the temporality of the Ecclesia, Gratian's contemporaries expounded a theory of Church membership which did not delineate between membership in the heavenly and earthly congregation. Every juridical act affecting membership in the earthly Church was, because of the divine nature of the community, also a spiritual act affecting the relation of the individual to the heavenly Church. Membership in the Church was based

---

to clarify the problems raised when a bishop was transferred from one see to another. C. 7, q. 1.

on the reception of three sacraments, and this fact alone meant that the social life of man in the Church was part of his spiritual life. The spiritual life, of course, took precedence. When attention is focused on the earthly ecclesiastical community, therefore, the theory of membership found in the works of the Magister's contemporaries produces the same sort of ambiguity and confusion as that found in their views of the Church. The problem that Gratian confronted on this matter can be understood if the ideas these men expressed are studied.

During the twelfth century the problems inherent in the traditional understanding of Church membership were brought to the fore through challenge, offered by a variety of heretical sects, to the theology of baptism.[11] The dispute arose from a contradiction in the parallel Gospel

11. The reforming spirit that infused the party of Haimeric also infused a large number of small groups of men whose fervor led them into heresy. These groups went through the countryside preaching against the wealth of the Church and the evil clergy. Gradually, influenced by the Manichaean Bogomils from the Eastern empire, they began to deny the value of the sacraments. The Cathars, a group first mentioned in the 1140's, were the most numerous group. (See the works cited in chap. ii, n. 2 to which add those of Landgraf and Didier cited in n. 3 above.)

The antiheretical writings of Peter the Venerable and Saint Bernard, in particular Peter's *Contra Petrobrusianos* and Bernard's *De baptismo* have already been mentioned. See also the work by Hugh of Amiens, *Contra haereticos sui temporis* (PL 192, col. 1255–1298). Hugh was also connected with the party of Haimeric. He was allied to the family of the counts of Amiens and a relative of Matthew, cardinal bishop of Albano and one of Haimeric's closest allies. Hugh had been a pupil of Anselm of Laon, then a monk at Cluny before becoming prior, first of Saint Martial at Limoges and then of Saint Pancratius at Lewes in England. When Pontius of Cluny joined with Henry I to found a new Cluniac house at Reading, Hugh was chosen to be abbot. In 1123 he was elected archbishop of Rouen, and when he refused to accept the position, Honorius II intervened to oblige him to accept it. The see of Rouen was too important to permit anyone but a friend to occupy it. Besides his tract against the heretics, Hugh wrote a long compendium of all the theological questions of his time called the *Dialogi*. J. H. Pignot, *Histoire de l'Ordre de Cluny,* (Paris, 1868), 3 35–36.

Another work against the heretics is that of Ekbert, abbot of Schönau, *Sermones contra Catharos* (PL 195, cols. 11–98; Sermon 7 is most important). Ekbert became abbot in 1166–1167 by which time the Cathars had become the dominant group among the heretics. *DTC*, vol. 5, col. 1911.

The victorious party of Haimeric enacted legislation against the heretics at the Second Lateran Council in 1139 (c. 23), but the questions raised by the sects were of interest not only to the ecclesiastical leaders and to some who wrote

texts that referred to the sacrament. The traditional teaching was based on a passage from Matthew, "Going therefore, teach ye all nations: baptizing them in the name of the Father, and of the Son, and of the Holy Ghost" (Matt. 28:19). This text emphasized that Christ promised salvation to all men,[12] and as we have seen, it was also bound up with the ideas concerning the transition between Synagogue and Church. The heretics brought forth the parallel passage from the Gospel of Mark. In that place, the Savior was reported to have said, "He that believeth and is baptized shall be saved; but he that believeth not shall be condemned" (Mark 16:16). This text, according to the heretics, meant that belief in Christ and his sacraments was an essential element in the performance of an effective baptism. Since only adults could have the faith of their own volition, only adults could receive the sacrament with the desired effect. Membership in the Church was limited to those who had reached the age of reason.[13]

---

antiheretical tracts but also to theologians not directly involved in the anti-heretical movement. In particular, reference will be made to the works of Hugh of Saint Victor, who was very aware of the views of the heretics and for whom Saint Bernard undertook his *Tractatus de baptismo,* of Peter Lombard, and of the school of Abelard (the *Ysagoge in Theologiam* and the *Sententie Parisenses* to which I have already referred in n. 3 above).

12. See, for example, Alcuin, *Epp.* 110, 111, 113 (ed. E. Duemmler, *MGH,* Epistolae Karolini Aevi, II [Berlin, 1895]). Smaragdus, *Collectiones in epistolas et evangelia,* PL 102, col. 265. Haimo, *Homiliae de tempore,* 96, PL 118, col. 544. *Glossa Ordinaria,* PL 114, col. 176. Anselm of Laon or one of his school, *Sententie divine pagine,* ed. Franz Bliemetzrieder, *Anselms von Laon systematische Sentenzen* (Münster, 1919), pp. 44 f. Ekbert of Schönau, *S. contra Catharos,* 7, PL 195, col. 41 f. Landgraf, "Kindertaufe und Glaube," pp. 337–338.

13. Landgraf (*op. cit.,* p. 338) says that this text was first explained by Hugh of Saint Victor (*de Sac.,* II:1, 7) and that afterward it was considered by Rolandus Bandinelli (*Sententiae,* ed. A. Gietl, *Die Sentenzen Rolands nachmals Papstes Alexander III* [Freiburg i. Br., 1891], p. 1), Innocent III (*Sermones de tempore,* 7, PL 217, col. 343), and Roland of Cremona (*Summa,* Cod. Paris. Mazar. lat. 795, fol. 87 which Landgraf quotes, p. 338 n. 19). Actually, it seems that the heretics were the first ones to use the text from Mark as the basis of a theology of baptism. The orthodox writers probably took it up because of the challenge from these groups.

The heretical charge is summarized by Peter the Venerable, *Contra Petrobr.,* PL 180, cols. 722, 728–729. Evervinus of Steinfeld, *Ep.* 472 *inter Bernardinas,* n. 4. Hugh of Amiens, *Contra Haer.,* I:11 Ekbert of Schönau, *S. contra Catharos,* 7:1. Saint Bernard, *Ep.* 241 n. 1. On an appearance of this heresy early in the

The importance of this argument was that it exposed the difficulties caused by the dual nature of the sacraments. Church writers had always recognized that the faith or motive of the recipient played an important role in making baptism and other sacraments effective. A passage from the first letter of Peter supported this doctrine. But they had also always seen the sacraments, and especially the baptismal sacrament, as a gift of grace from God. Thus, they argued that the passage from Matthew 28:19 demonstrated that Christ would grant grace to all men of whatever age.[14] The heretical interpretation of the sacrament ignored this aspect and focused on the role of the recipient in making himself a member of the congregation of the faithful. On the one hand, then, their argument put Christ's promise of salvation in question. On the other hand, it forced an alteration in the conception of the Church.

The ecclesiological aspect of the heretical position was very important to the orthodox writers of the period.[15] By denying that children could

eleventh century, see Jeffrey Burton Russell, *Dissent and Reform in the Early Middle Ages* (Berkeley and Los Angeles, 1965), pp. 23–24.

14. I Peter, 3:21, "whereunto baptism being of the like form, now saveth you also: not the putting away of the filth of the flesh, but the examination of a good conscience towards God by the resurrection of Jesus Christ." Lanfranc, *Liber de corpore et sanguine Domini adversus Berengarium Turonensem*, PL 150, col. 424. Landgraf, *op. cit.*, p. 339. Augustine had commented on the text in *In Joannis evangelium*, PL 35, col. 1840 and *Ep.* 98, nn. 9–10, *CSEL*, 33:531.

On the role of Christ in the sacrament and the universality of his promise of salvation, see Peter the Venerable, *Contra Petrobr.*, col. 759, "Quod si ita est, sicut per unius delictum omnes homines condemnati, ita et parvuli homines condemnati. Et sicut per unius justitiam omnes homines justificati, ita et parvuli homines justificati." Idem, *Contra Petrobr.*, col. 758, "Sacramento baptismi, et salvatur per Christi gratiam Christianus." Hugh of Amiens, *Contra Haer.*, I:11, "In parvuli quidem homo potuit, sed peccatum peccator suum dimittere sibi non potuit. Quapropter omnis eget gloria Dei, qui peccata dimittit homo factus pro nobis; ut quod non potuit homo solus, efficiat homo Deus." Saint Bernard, *in Cant.*, 66, n. 9, "non relinquit Dominus plebem suam, quae est sicut arena maris, nec contentus erit paucitate haereticorum, qui omnes redemit. Neque enim parva, sed plane copiosa apud eum redemptio." Idem, *De baptismo*, 1:4. Ekbert of Schönau, *S. contra Catharos*, 7, 4; 11. Hugh of Saint Victor, *de sac. leg. nat.*, PL 176, col. 38D.

15. The ecclesiological aspect of baptism was brought out by many writers. Peter the Venerable shows that his interest in this aspect of the sacrament was aroused by the heretics. *Contra Petrobr.*, PL 180, col. 729B, "Et, O dicti homines

be members of the Church, the heretics were saying that the Ecclesia was not a community or society, but only a congregation. The heretical theology of baptism made it impossible to draw an analogy between the Church on earth and other human communities. But to establish that the Church was independent and juridically equal to the secular state had been one of the chief goals of the Gregorian papacy, and

---

[the heretics], insipientibus et indoctis nunc tandem quod intelligere hactenus non potuerant exponentes, itane desipuere praeterita saecula, ut tot millibus parvulorum per mille et eo amplius annos illusorium baptisma tribuerent, et a Christi temporibus usque ad vos, non veros et christianos, sed phantastiscos crearent?" *Contra Petrobr.,* col. 729C, "Nam qui Christi baptismate baptizatus non fuit, Christianus non fuit. Si Christianus non fuit, nec de clero nec de populo, nec de Ecclesia esse potuit." Gerhoh of Reichersberg, *Epistola ad Inn., MGH,* Libelli de lite III:223–224. Idem, *de aedificio Dei,* p. 132, "post baptisma . . . ut, si nec his [the laws of penitence] vellet subiacere, privaretur ecclesiastica societate." *Ysagoge in Theologiam,* II:195. Hugh of Saint Victor, *de Sac.,* I:2, 1, "Per baptismum efficimur membra corporis." Hugh of Saint Victor, *de Sac.,* II:11, 13. *Sent. Paris.,* 11:47. Arnulf of Lisieux, *Invectiva in Girardum Engolismensem Episcopum, MGH,* Libelli de lite III:3, "Susceptis ita que fidei sacramentis, urbi novus civis insitus est factus [Petrus Pierleoni]." Ivo of Chartres, *Sermones,* PL 162, col. 512, "His omnibus supra memoratis [baptismal ceremonies] novus homo in utero Ecclesiae inchoatur, provehitur, consummatur et unitati Ecclesiae aggregatur." Richard of Saint Victor, *de pot. ligandi et solvendi,* 20, "concorporatione quando ille per corporis ablutionem, iste per sacerdotis absolutionem Ecclesiae Christi consociatur." Wolbero of Saint Pantaleon, *in Cant.,* 1, 9, "Per fidem et baptismi gratiam Ecclesiae incorporantur." See Beumer, "Ekklesiologische Probleme," p. 187. It should be pointed out that the idea baptism saved only within the Church was current at the time. A pseudo-Augustinian work, now attributed to Fulgentius and called the *Liber de fide,* made this argument. Gratian incorporated the text in the Decretum at C. 1, q. 1, c. 55. He took the capitulum from Alger of Liège, *Liber de misericordia et iustitia,* III:16, and he even included one of Alger's own sentences in the text of the canon as he reported it. Much of C. 1, q. 1 comes from Alger's work. See n. 33 below. The text of the capitulum is quoted in n. 34 below.

Twelfth-century theologians did recognize the possibility of being saved without ever becoming a member of the Church, however. The vehicle of salvation in this case was the *sacramentum in voto,* a conversion to Christ, which because of circumstances beyond the control of the individual, could not be completed through the actual reception of baptism. The person saved through a *sacramentum in voto* always died before he could be baptized and thus never entered the earthly Church. This doctrine again shows that theologians were conscious of the ecclesiological effect of the sacrament. Landgraf, "Das sacramentum in voto in der Frühscholastik," *Mélanges Mandonnet,* II, Bibliothèque Thomiste, 14:97–144.

the compromise solution of the Investiture Controversy, worked out and supported by the new reformers, preserved the equality and sovereignty of the two communities at least in theory. Thus, writers of the period, including those of Haimeric's party, did not want to accept a view of the Church which denied its communal nature.

The orthodox theologians who concerned themselves with the heretical position proposed to solve the difficulties it raised through an ecclesiological argument that emphasized the role played by the earthly ecclesiastical community in the baptism of children. The child who could not have faith himself was baptized, they said, in the faith of the Church.[16] The prescription of the passage from Mark was satisfied, therefore, because not only would consent by the individual suffice as an act of faith but also consent for him. This argument did not totally reject the view of the heretics but only modified it. The act of faith was recognized to be an essential element in the effective performance of the sacrament; it made God's grant of grace possible. At the same time, it is the Church itself which performs that act of faith in carrying out the baptism of children, making them members of the community and protecting them against death without divine grace. By postulating this act of the Church, these writers reconciled the two

16. This view was to be found in the writings of Augustine, *De baptismo libri VII*, IV:24, n. 31, "pro eis [infants] alii respondent, ut impleatur erga eos celebratio sacramenti, valet utique ad eorum consecrationem, quia ipsi respondere non possunt." Idem, *De libero arbitrio*, 23, "Quo loco etiam illud perscrutari homines solent, sacramentum baptismi Christi quid parvulis prosit, cum eo accepto plerumque moriuntur, priusquam ex se quidquam cognoscere potuerint. Qua in re satis pie recteque creditur prodesse parvulo eorum fidem, a quibus consecrandus offertur. Et hoc ecclesiae commendat saluberrima auctoritas, ut ex eo quisque sentiat, quid sibi prosit fides sua, quando in aliorum quoque beneficium, qui propriam nondum habent, potest aliena commodari." Peter the Venerable, *Contra Petrobr.*, PL 180, col. 730A, "Discite parvulis nostris nullatenus fidem, quo salventur, deesse, quia non possunt dici filii infideles, pro quibus intervenit matris ecclesiae fides." Hugh of Amiens, *Contra Haer.*, I:12. Ekbert of Schönau, *S. contra Catharos*, 7, 11; 14. Gerhoh of Reichersberg, *Epistola ad Inn.*, MGH, Libelli de lite III:224. Saint Bernard, *De baptismo*, 1, 4; 2, 9. Idem, *in Cant.*, 66, n. 9–10. *Ysagoge in Theologiam*, II:189. Peter Lombard, *Sententiae*, IV, Dist. 6, c. 6. Several of these authors argue that the faith of the parent who brings the child to be baptized suffices for the requirement of Mark 16:16. See especially, *Ysagoge*, II:193 and *Sent. Paris.*, II:39. This view did not solve the problem caused when the parents were heretics or negligent in their religious duties.

aspects of their idea of baptism as a grant of grace by God and as an entrance into the community of the Church.

Baptism was not the only sacrament affecting a man's relationship with God and His Church. Theologians of Gratian's period recognized that a child who attained the age of discretion had to participate in further sacramental acts if he was to keep the grace he had received in baptism and to preserve his membership in the Church.[17] The new Church of God was based on faith, as Gratian had so clearly stated, and by receiving the sacraments, members of the Church exhibited their faith. The two sacraments bound up with membership in the Church and the renewal of grace were confirmation and the Eucharist.

As was pointed out in a previous chapter, the twelfth century was the period when theologians began to define the sacraments and to debate their significance with more precision than before.[18] It was a period of transition in the practice as well as the theory of the sacraments. It appears that in the twelfth century ecclesiastical custom began to mark the age of discretion by the sacrament of confirmation,[19] and there was also an apparent change in the theological conception of the sacrament. Traditionally, confirmation had signified the

17. Hugh of Amiens, *Contra Haer.*, I:5, "Ut igitur perfectum teneas Christianum, primo eum ex aqua et Spiritu renatum, dehinc charismatum gratia, pontificis manu perornatum, mox ad mensae Dominicae sacrosanctum intromitte convivium." Hugh of Amiens, *Contra Haer.*, I:14, "Talibus [Christians] dum in praesentis vivitur, necesse est ut vitalis refectio praeparetur, panis vivae, cali benedictionis aeternae, corpus et sanguis . . . Christi. Hoc autem omnino necesse est, nec alicui Christiano a participatione tanti mysterii abstinere licitum est." Gerhoh of Reichersberg, *Epistola ad Inn., MGH*, Libelli de lite III:224, "Quod bona fides parentum [for children] prosit, habemus. . . . Qui tamen si ad annos etatis legitimae perveniunt, perdunt acceptam in baptismo gratiam, nisi deserentes ac detestantes eresim diligant catholicam ecclesiam." Peter Lombard, *Sententiae*, IV, *Dist.* 4, c. 7. See also the passage from the Porretain commentary on Saint Paul cited in n. 23 below.

18. See chap. i, p. 9.

19. N. Iung, "Confirmation dans l'église occidentale," *DDC*, IV:99–103. Before the twelfth century, confirmation was given shortly after baptism. By the late thirteenth century, the new practice of confirming children when they reached the age of discretion was incorporated into conciliar legislation. At the time of the Fourth Lateran Council (1215), the age of discretion was considered to be fourteen.

corroboration of the grace received in baptism. Twelfth-century theologians preserved this understanding of confirmation,[20] but now, challenged by the heretical argument, they began to emphasize the individual's role in the performance of an effective sacrament. A treatise of Peter Abelard's school, the *Sententie Parisenses,* expresses this concern very clearly: Confirmation is given to young people so that they feel the virtues of the Holy Spirit as they come to the age of discretion.[21] At the same time, writers looked upon confirmation as one of the three sacraments, along with baptism and the Eucharist, necessary for the perfect Christian.[22] This idea, in conjunction with that expressed by the *Sententie Parisenses,* implies that confirmation was the act in which, for the first time, the child affirmed his faith and expressed his consent to membership in the Church.

The third necessary sacrament was the Eucharist, the only one that could be received repeatedly. Twelfth-century theologians recognized the ecclesiological aspect of this sacrament explicitly. It was, for them,

20. See, for example, Hugh of Saint Victor, *de Sac.,* II:7, 3 and 5. *Sent. Paris.,* II:40; II:47. *Ysagoge in Theologiam,* II:196. Peter Lombard, *Sententiae,* IV, Dist. 7, c. 1.

21. *Sent. Paris.,* II:40, "Sicut in consecratione episcoporum quantumcumque fuerit malus, tamen virtus ei datur aliqua, quam prius non habebat, ita et hic pueris. Et tunc eas virtutes sentiunt, cum ad annos discretionis veniunt."

22. Hugh of Amiens, *Contra Haer.,* I:5, "Si vero post baptismum supervixerit, qui sanctificatus per gratiam Christi a baptismo surrexit . . . nisi indutus virtute ex alto stare non peterit." Hugh of Saint Victor also implies that the confirmation is given some time after the baptism. *de Sac.,* II:7, 4, "haec duo ita coniuncta sunt in operatione salutis, ut nisi morte interveniente omnino separari non possunt." Hugh of Saint Victor, *de Sac.,* II:7, 5, "filii qui accipiunt perfectae aetatis fuerint, ut mundi donum Spiritus sancti accipiant."

On the place of confirmation, along with baptism and the Eucharist, as necessary for the perfect Christian, see Hugh of Amiens, *Contra Haer.,* "Tria ista sacramenta, baptismus scilicet . . . confirmatio . . . et [the Eucharist] civitatem Dei constituunt." (See also the passage from the same place quoted in n. 17 above.) *Sent. Paris.,* II:37, "Sacramentorum alia sunt necessaria ad salutem, ut baptismus, confirmatio et corpus et sanguis Christi." Hugh of Saint Victor says that confirmation is important, but does not stress its place so much as Hugh of Amiens. Hugh of Saint Victor, *de Sac.* II:7, 3, "Quid autem prodest si a lapsu erigeris, nisi etiam ad standum confirmeris? Propterea timendum est iis qui per negligentiam amittunt episcopi praesentium, et non suscipiunt manus impositionem."

the sacrament of unity and by receiving it, Christians reaffirmed their union with the body of Christ, which is the Church.[23] But the sacrament not only effected the union of the individual to the Church, it also symbolized the unity of the faithful in a single body. Another Abelardian treatise, the *Ysagoge in Theologiam,* pointed out that the bread and wine were two things made from many grains and many grapes. Likewise, the Church was a body consisting of many men.[24]

23. See, for example, the text of a Porretain commentary on the letters of Paul contained in Cod. Paris. Nat. lat. 686, fol. 73 (quoted by Landgraf, *Dogmengeschichte der Frühscholastik,* III/2, 198 n. 19), "Baptismus namque ideo non repetitur, quia veritas huius sacramenti est fiendi membrum Christi. Quod quia non potest contingere nisi semel, idcirco hoc sacramentum non repetitur. Eucharistia vero videtur repeti, quoniam non designat veritatem fiere membrum Christi. Eucharistia illud ostendit, quod, qui communicat corpori Christi, iam sit factus membrum Christi in baptismate, et idcirco multotiens communicari non prohibetur, quia multotiens possumus ostendare nos esse membrum Christi, quod demonstrat eucharistie sacramentum." See also Hugh of Saint Victor, *de Sac.,* II:11, 13, "Ita ergo verum Christi corpus non est quod conficit schismaticus, quia, cum corpus Christi sacramentum sit unitatis, in ipso utique schismaticus sibi unitatem non conficit qui se ab ipsa unitate dividit." *Sent. Paris.,* II:41, "in sacramento altaris sacramentum ipsum corpus Christi, res sacramenti corpus Ecclesiae." *Sent. Paris.,* II:47, "in sumptione corporis non membrum efficitur, sed signum est eum iam esse de corpore Christi." Hugh of Amiens, *Dialogorum libri septem,* V:7. Gerhoh of Reichersberg, *de Simoniacos, MGH,* Libelli de lite III:261, "Unitas enim ecclesie res sacra est . . ." On the connection between the Eucharist and the body of Christ, see F. Holböck, *Der Eucharistische und der mystische Leib Christi in ihrem Beziehungen zueinander nach der Lehre der Frühscholastik* (Rome, 1941). Weisweiler, review of Holböck, *Scholastik,* 18 (1943), 267–273. Beumer, "Ekklesiologische Probleme," pp. 186 ff. Landgraf, *Dogmengeschichte der Frühscholastik,* III/2, 192–206. Henri de Lubac, *Corpus Mysticum* (Paris, 1949). Giving penitence and last rites were also sometimes included in the number of necessary sacraments. See, for example, C. 1, q. 1, dict. post c. 42 in the Decretum.

24. *Ysagoge in Theologiam,* II:205, "Illius quoque corporis Christi, quod est Ecclesia, panis et vinum sacramenta dicuntur. Nam et ex multis granis unus panis et multi botri in unum confluunt vinum. Sic et ex multis membris una coadunatur Ecclesia." Gerhoh of Reichersberg, *de Simoniacos, MGH,* Libelli de lite III:261. *Sent. Paris.,* II:41.

The twelfth century was a period of transition for the Eucharist as well as confirmation. Practice during this time ruled that the Eucharist should be received at least once a year by every Christian adult. At the same time, the practice of giving communion to children disappeared. In the Fourth Lateran Council, held by Innocent III in 1215, the yearly communion for all who had achieved the age of discretion (fourteen years old) was incorporated in the canon

It can be seen that the Eucharist was a focal point for community self-consciousness and cohesion in the Church.

The theory of Church membership embedded in the theology of baptism, confirmation, and the Eucharist exposes very clearly the difficulties created by the dual nature of the Church. The writers thus far mentioned did not distinguish between the ecclesiological and spiritual aspects of the sacraments, and their theory of membership was therefore ambiguous. It is clear that participation in the sacraments made one a member of the Church, but it is also clear that these writers were thinking of the Church as a spiritual rather than as a temporal entity. In their argument against the heretics, the orthodox theologians admitted that consent of or for the individual was an essential part of becoming a member of the Church. Their discussions of confirmation and the Eucharist only emphasized this point. But if consent based on faith was necessary, then the Church, and the earthly Church, too, was a consensual society. The logical consequence of this view is that if the members lose their faith and withdraw their consent, the community ceases to exist. This is a conclusion that medieval writers did not accept, for it contradicted the basic conceptions of their ecclesiology. The Church did not originate in the consent of the earliest members, in a kind of social contract; Christ founded the Church. Also, the Church would not disintegrate if its members ceased to believe, because Christ had promised that his Church would not perish: "The gates of Hell shall not prevail against it" (Matt. 16:18). Thus, for all these writers, the permanency of the community was independent of the consent of its members.

Twelfth-century theologians would have argued that the preservation of the Church was no problem because there would always be men who believed in Christ. Yet, while this argument might be valid for the mystical Church, it could not suffice as the basis for the con-

---

law. Peter Browe, *Die Pflichtkommunion im Mittelalter* (Regensburg, 1940). *Idem,* "Die Kinderkommunion im Mittelalter," *Scholastik,* 5 (1930), 8. See IV Lat. Conc., c. 21, "Omnis utriusque sexus fidelis, postquam ad annos discretionis pervenerit . . . suscipiens reverenter ad minus in pascha eucharistiae sacramentum" (*Conciliorum Oecumenicorum Decreta,* 221). Franz Gillmann, *Die 'anni discretionis' im Kanon Omnis utriusque sexus (c. 21, Conc. Lat. IV)* (Mainz, 1929).

stitutional theory of the earthly community. There was needed some justification of coercive action by the hierarchy when the community was threatened by the recalcitrancy of some of its members. The theory of membership expounded by Gratian's contemporaries did not justify such action, but the Magister had to find a theory that did. He founded his theory on a conceptual distinction between the spiritual and temporal natures of the Church.

Membership in the Church according to Gratian.

Gratian, like his contemporaries, recognized the place of the recipient's consent in the performance of a valid sacrament, but there is an added dimension to his doctrine which makes it differ significantly from theirs. In a section devoted to the doctrine that prelates ought not to use force, the Magister notes several uses of force that are legitimate. Jews ought not to be forced to receive the faith, but if they have received it unwillingly, they should be forced to retain it. The capitulum that follows this dictum explains that they ought to be forced to remain Christians lest the name of God be blasphemed and the faith be made to seem vile and contemptible.[25] Faith is the foundation of the *com-*

25. Dist. 45, dict. post c. 4, "Iudei non sunt cogendi ad fidem quam tamen si inviti susceperint, cogendi sunt retinere." Dist. 45, c. 5, "fidem, quam vi vel necessitate susceperint, tenere cogantur, ne nomen Domini blasphemetur, et fides . . . vilis ac contemptibilis, habeatur." The Magister gives several other examples of the legitimate use of force and concludes, Dist. 45, dict. post c. 13, "Ex his omnibus apparet, quod nec lenitas mansuetudinis sine rectitudine severitatis, nec zelus rectitudinis sine mansuetudine in prelatis debet inveniri. Percussores ergo, qui premissis auctoritatibus ab episcopali offitio removentur, non quilibet corporaliter flagellantes, sed pretermissa mansuetudine ad verbera semper parati intelligendi sunt, qui per flagella non vicia corrigere, sed timeri appetunt."
That Gratian considered baptism to be an entrance into the earthly community of the Church in a juridical sense is shown by another passage found in C. 23, q. 4. Those who are not baptized and therefore not Christians are not within the jurisdiction of the ecclesiastical hierarchy. The power to bind and loose only affects those within the Church. See C. 23, q. 4, dict. post c. 16, "eorum vindicta divino examini tantem est reservanda, quando in delinquentes disciplinam videlicet exercere non possumus, vel quia non sunt nostri iuris . . . §1. De his, qui non sunt nostri iuris, ait Apostolus in epistola prima ad Corinthios: 'Quid enim michi attinet de his, qui foris sunt, iudicare? de his enim Dominus iudicabit.'" See also C. 23, q. 4, dict. post c. 17.

munitas ecclesiae, and thus the prelate's coercive action is necessary in order to preserve the integrity of the community.

The implications of this doctrine contain the most important elements of Gratian's view of what membership in the Church means. His concern with those who have received baptism unwillingly shows he was conscious of the distinction between the earthly community and the mystical body of the Church. He affirms the view that consent of the recipient of baptism is desired, but he shows that in the context of the earthly community, willing consent is not essential. What is essential is the satisfaction of all formal requirements for the performance of the sacrament. The rite must be the same as that accepted by the Church; consent must be given even if it is unwilling consent. Gratian exposes, in this dictum, the difficulty raised by the two natures of the Church, when one concentrates on the juridical aspect of baptism. He also shows that he will solve this difficulty by insisting on only the formal, juridical requirements for a valid sacramental act.

Gratian's concern for the juridical structure of the earthly community and for conditions of membership in that community is demonstrated further by his treatment of the doctrine of excommunication and anathema. Again, a comparison between the views of Gratian and his contemporaries exposes the sophistication of the Magister in his discussion of the problem. F. Russo and A. M. Landgraf have studied the views of twelfth-century writers on the penalty of excommunication and have argued that the meaning of excommunication was very unclear in the writings of these men. The chief difficulty, they think, was the failure to distinguish between the spiritual and earthly effects of the sentence.[26]

26. F. Russo, "Pénitence et excommunication. Étude historique sur les rapports entre la théologie et le droit canonique dans le domaine pénitentiel du XIIe au XIIIe siècle," *Recherches de science religieuse,* 33 (1946), 257–279, 431–459. Landgraf, "Sünde und Trennung von der Kirche in der Frühscholastik," *Schoastik,* 5 (1930), 210–247. Both Russo and Landgraf assume that medieval writers confused the penalties of excommunication and anathema. This assumption is incorrect when one is considering Gratian's doctrine. The Magister distinguishes clearly between the two sentences saying that while excommunication removes one from the society of the faithful, anathema removes him from the body of Christ. This distinction shows that Gratian considered excommunication to be an essentially juridical penalty. It does not remove one from the spiritual Church

Landgraf studied the twelfth-century notion that the act of sinning itself entailed an automatic separation from the Church. He concluded that until the end of the twelfth century, writers thought the sinner was separated from both the earthly community of the Church and the heavenly congregation of God.[27] Gratian was no exception to this general trend in the thought of the mid-twelfth century, according to Landgraf. The scholar pointed to a capitulum in Causa 24 in order to show that the Magister considered the sinner separated from the *castra ecclesiae,* even if his bishop did not formally pronounce a sentence of excommunication. The doctrine was confirmed by the further statement that an unjust sentence had no effect whatever. Thus, said Landgraf, Gratian's theory of excommunication is very difficult to understand because the sentence of excommunication could only be

---

but only from the earthly society. Anathema was, for him, a more direct use of the power of binding and loosing. It goes beyond juridical action and in itself expresses the unity of spiritual and temporal in the Church.

C. 11, q. 3, dict. post c. 24, "Hec sententia excommunicatio vocatur quia a communione corporis et sanguinis Christi notatum prohibet." No one ought to communicate with an excommunicate, C. 11, q. 3, cc. 2–5, 7, 9, 16–19 on the condition of the excommunicate. To be an excommunicate is even worse, in some ways, than to be a pagan. C. 11, q. 3, c. 24, "Ad mensam quippe paganorum si volueris ire, sine ulla prohibitione permittimus . . . §2 . . . 'si quis [St. John Chrysostomus] inquit, 'nominatus fuerit frater fornicator, aut avarus, aut ebriosus, cum huiusmodi neque cibum sumere.'" C. 11, q. 3, dict. post c. 24, "Qua sententia [excommunication] non separatur quis a consortio fidelium. Est et alia sententia, que anathema vocatur, qua quisque separatur a consortio fidelium." C. 3, q. 4, dict. post c. 11, "Notandum vero est, quod aliud sit excommunicatio, et aliud anathematizatio." C. 3, q. 4, dict. post c. 12, "Unde datur intelligi, quod anathematizati intelligendi sunt non simpliciter a fraterna societate omnino separati, sed a corpore Christi (quod est ecclesia)." Only the pope can reconcile an anathematized person to the Church. C. 11, q. 3, dict. post c. 24, "qui [anathematized] a nullo episcoporum absolui, id est more penitentium reconciliari, poterit, nisi primum apostolico conspectui se representare curaverit." Notwithstanding the distinction that Gratian himself makes between the two penalties, some of the capitula are less definite about the character of excommunication and justify the contention of Landgraf and Russo that some, at least, confused the two penalties. C. 11, q, 3, c. 32, "Omnis Christianus, dilectissimi, qui sacerdotibus excommunicatur, sathanae traditur: quomodo? scilicet, quia extra ecclesiam est diabolus, sicut in ecclesia Christus." C. 11, q. 3, c. 21 (rubric), "Duobus modis aliquis sathanae traditur."

27. Landgraf, "Sünde und Trennung," pp. 234–236.

judged as irrelevant.[28] Either the sentence was just, in which case the sinner had already separated himself from the Ecclesia, or it was unjust, in which case it had no force. Landgraf concluded that the difficulty in this theory stemmed from a failure to distinguish between the two spheres of the Church. Gratian and his contemporaries would have expounded a clearer theory of excommunication, he said, if they had seen that sin separated one from the heavenly Church, while excommunication separated one from the earthly community. A juridical act was necessary for expelling the sinner from the community of the faithful.

Landgraf's interpretation of Gratian's theory is based on a false understanding of his idea of excommunication; a clear understanding of Gratian's doctrine is not always received from the capitula. Gratian understood that no separation from the society of the faithful was possible without a publicly read sentence of excommunication and that though an unjust sentence could be appealed, the sentence was effective until overturned by a higher court.[29] The unjust sentence was honored on earth though Gratian recognized that it was not honored in

28. C. 24, q. 3, c. 7, "Cum aliquis exiit a veritate, a timore Dei, a fide, a karitate, exit de castris ecclesiae, etiamsi per episcopi vocem minime abiciatur; sicut e contrario, aliquis non recto iudicio foras mittitur, sed si ante non exieret, id est non egerit ut mereretur exire nichil leditur." Landgraf ("Sünde und Trennung," pp. 234–236) reports that later in the twelfth century, heretics used this text to prove that the excommunication of the prelate had no effect whatever. This argument led to the conclusion that the ecclesiastical hierarchy possessed no power.

29. C. 11, q. 3, dict. post c. 21, "Cum ergo per sententiam quis nominatus fuerit, cum eo communicare non debemus. Cum autem solo reatu occulte excommunicationis contraxerit penam, non est ab eius communione cessandum." C. 11, q. 3, dict. post c. 24, "Evidenter itaque ex premissis apparet, quod eorum communionem vitare non cogimur, qui sententia, notati non sunt." C. 11, q. 3, c. 26 (rubric), "Nullus clericorum vel laicorum ad domum excommunicati accedat." C. 11, q. 3, dict. post c. 26, "Sed hoc specialiter in his, qui nominatim excommunicatis communicant." The sentence stands until overturned by a higher court. C. 22, q. 3, dict., "Cum ergo, ut ratione et exemplo monstratum est, episcopus reus periurii non esse [when he swears to a falsehood that he believes is true], consueta obedientia ab archidiacono sibi denegari non debuit, cum etiamsi criminosum illum esse constaret, ante definitivam tamen sententiam, . . . nulli suorum clericorum ab eo liceret discedere." See also C. 11, q. 3, dict. ante c. 1. C. 11, q. 3, dict. post c. 64. C. 16, q. 6, dict. ante c. 1. C. 3, q. 1, dict. post c. 6.

heaven.[30] It must be admitted that Gratian recognized the juridical nature of the sentence of excommunication and its significance for a man's membership in the earthly Church. When a mortal sinner escaped the eyes of human justice, he said, in effect, that his separation from the Church was only an *excommunicatio conscientiae*.[31] Thus, he made a distinction between real and apparent membership in the Church. When guilt is secret, he said, Church members continue to communicate with the sinner though in reality—spiritual reality—he is burdened by the penalty of excommunication.[32] The juridical understanding of the penalty is implicit in this statement as is the separation between the earthly and the heavenly Church.

There is something to be said for the interpretation offered by these scholars, however. Gratian does affirm that anathema separates one from the body of Christ, and separation from the *consortium fidelium,* which is the result of excommunication, does have a spiritual effect on the sentenced. Such a man cannot receive the Eucharist, which prevents him from reaffirming his union with the mystical body and re-

30. C. 11, q. 3, dict. post c. 64, "Ex his datur intelligi, quod iniusta sententia nullum alligat apud Deum, nec apud ecclesiam eius aliquis gravatur iniqua sententia, sicut ex Gelasio capitulo habetur." The latter part of this sentence is denied by Gratian in the subsequent part of the quaestio. The first part remains the accepted view, of course.

31. This term was used by the decretists. They delineated three types of excommunication while commenting on C. 11, q. 3, c. 24. Karl Mörsdorf, "Der Rechtscharakter der iurisdictio fori interni." *Münchener theologische Zeitschrift,* 8 (1957), 164. Gratian put forth a similar, though less distinct, view in C. 11, q. 3, dict. post c. 21. See also, Dist. 50, dict. post c. 32. The Magister certainly recognized the difference, for the legal institutions of the Church, between manifest and occult crimes. See also Stephan Kuttner, "Ecclesia de occultis non indicat," *Acta Congressus Iuridici Internationalis,* 3 (Rome, 1934), 225–246.

32. The same arguments used against Landgraf's interpretation can be turned against the view of Russo. Russo recognized that in the twelfth century excommunication was reserved for grave offenses and was accompanied by solemn ceremony and pronouncement. (Russo, *op. cit.,* pp. 262–263.) But, like Landgraf, he argued that Gratian did not have a clear idea of the juridical nature of the penalty, and that in Gratian's time too much spiritual importance was accorded to excommunication. Russo, like Landgraf, supports his interpretation of Gratian's doctrine on the capitula alone. Russo, *op. cit.,* pp. 265–266, 269. He cites C. 11, q. 3, cc. 9, 24, 33, 106.

90

newing the grant of divine grace. The hierarchy exercises its power of binding and loosing when it passes sentence on a member of the Church, and, thus, it acts in its capacity both as an agent of God and an earthly governor. This duality in the position of the priesthood is brought out further in passages treating the relationship between the validity of sacramental acts and the character of the performer. It is the problem raised by the question: how are the sacraments given by simoniacs to be treated? This question focuses attention on the relation of the priest's action to God's in the sacrament[33] as well as on the place of the sacrament itself in the constitutional framework of the earthly Church.

In considering this problem, Gratian divides the sacraments into two groups, the sacraments of dignity and those of necessity. A sacrament of dignity—for example, the sacrament of orders—must be performed "worthily by worthy priests." Thus, morally degenerate members of the hierarchy, even if they are tolerated by the Church, cannot perform these sacraments. The sacraments of necessity are too important to permit the condition of the agent to hinder their effectiveness.[34] In

33. Gratian expresses awareness of this problem in: C. 1, q. 1, dict. post c. 24 [quoting 1 Cor. 3:7], "Cum enim in sacramentis 'neque qui plantat, neque qui rigat, est aliquid, sed qui incrementum dat, Deus' quis operatur in eis, si Dominus qui incrementum dat, in eis non lucet, sed est otiosus?"

34. C. 1, q. 1, dict. post c. 39, "Sed notandum est, quod sacramentorum alia sunt dignitatis, alia necessitatis. Quia enim necessitas non habet legem, sed ipsa sibi facit legem, illa sacramenta, que saluti sunt necessaria, quia iterari possunt, cum sit vera, auferri vel amitti non debent, sed cum penitentia rata esse permittuntur. Illa vero sacramenta, que sunt dignitatis nisi digne fuerint administrata, ita ut digni digne a dignis provebantur, dignitates esse desinunt." C. 1, q. 1, dict. post c. 42, "Ecce si clericus vel ordinatione, vel quolibet sacramento hereticis communicat, cessans a promotione vix in suo ordine perseverat. Non est enim de hoc sacramento ut de ceteris; cetera enim vel ad culpas abluendas dantur, ut baptismus et penitentia, vel pro culpis non in eternum, sed ad horam negantur, ut eucharistia, que in articulo mortis penitenti etiam de nefariis peccatis conceditur: hoc solum non solum pro culpa, sed etiam infamia interdicitur, etiam pro inminuta mundiciae suae, vel extrinsecae, vel intrinsecae perfectionis prerogativa, ut bigamis, vel viduae maritis, vel illiteratis, vel corporis qualibet parte vitiatis denegatur, quibus tamen baptismus vel eucharistia non negatur. Potest etiam talis cuncta sacramenta administrare, qui istud solum non valet conferre." See also C. 1, q. 1, dict. post c. 43. The distinction between the two types of sacraments

baptism especially, anyone can baptize a person so long as the rite is the same as the one used in the Church and the recipient considers himself to be entering the true Church. Even one who receives the sacrament as a heretic can enter the Church when he repudiates his heresy and seeks reconciliation. His baptism is not repeated in this case, but through the ceremony of imposing the hands, it becomes entirely effective.[35]

Another sacrament of necessity is the Eucharist. It is not considered to be as essential as baptism, however, and therefore the condition of the performer is more significant in determining the validity of the Eucharist than baptism. No priest who has been expelled from the Church or suspended from his cure of souls can perform an effective Eucharist, but any priest who is tolerated by the Church, even if he is

---

was made by Alger of Liège, *Liber de misericordia et iustitia,* III:55. Gratian copied this chapter almost verbatim in C. 1, q. 1, dict. post c. 39. The dict. post c. 42 in the same place comes directly out of Alger's next chapter. Note also that about the same time as Gratian's work appeared, the author of the *Sententie Parisenses* made the same division between necessary and unnecessary sacraments. See n. 20 above.

Weitzel points out that Causa 1 is connected with the *Tractatus ordinandorum* since it is a continuation of the Magister's treatment of the impediments to ordination. J. Weitzel, *Begriff und Erscheinungsformen der Simonie bei Gratian und den Dekretisten* (Munich, 1967), pp. 22–57, *passim.*

35. On the special character of baptism, C. 1, q. 1, dict. post c. 45, "Patet ergo illud Augustini (sacramenta videlicet Christi per hereticos ministrata suo non carere effectu) non de omnibus intelligi generaliter, sed de sacramento baptismatis." C. 1, q. 1, dict. post c. 57, "Si cum fidei integritate et animi puritate de manu hereticorum aliquis in forma ecclesiae baptisma acceperit, tunc inpletur illud Augustini: 'Per lapidem canalem aqua transit ad ariolas.'" C. 1, q. 1, dict. post c. 74, "patet quod sacramenta ecclesiastica preter baptisma . . . hereticis ministrari non possunt." See also C. 1, q. 1, dict. post cc. 53, 97.

The Magister cites a passage from Augustine to show that those baptized outside the Church must return to the Church in order for their baptism to be effective. C. 1, q. 1, c. 55, "Firmissime tene et nullatenus dubites, extra ecclesiam baptizatis, si ad ecclesiam redierint, baptismo cumulari perniciem. Tantum enim valet ecclesiasticae societatis communio ad salutem, ut baptismo non saluetur cui ibi non datur, ubi oportet ut detur." But the baptism ought not to be repeated. C. 1, q. 1, c. 57. C. 1, q. 1, dict. post c. 57, "Ecce quando ab hereticis baptisma cum sua virtute accipitur, cuius tam necessaria amministracio est, ut nec etiam a paganis datum possit reiterari." On the imposition of hands, see C. 1, q. 1, dict. post c. 73. C. 1, q. 1, c. 74. See n. 39 below.

sinful, can give the sacrament.[36] This doctrine is the legal expression of the view that the Eucharist is the sacrament of unity. Only if it is received within the Church can it have meaning as the act that effects the union of the individual and the body of Christ. Likewise, the doctrine in these passages concerning both baptism and the Eucharist shows that Gratian too thought that the perfect Christian, as Hugh of Amiens said, must participate in certain of the sacraments.[37] But the Magister focuses on the role of the performer rather than on that of the recipient. He sought to define in law the power of the governors in the earthly Church so that it would be consistent with the Church as a juridical community on earth and as a spiritual congregation. Some of the sacraments, those of dignity, present little problem because they are obviously most significant as juridical acts within the earthly community. As the Magister says in one of his dicta, the creation of a new priest through the sacrament of orders must be accomplished with special concern for formal as well as moral perfection because it is an act affecting all the members of the Church. The sacraments of necessity, however, are most important as spiritual acts affecting the relationship between the recipient and God.[38] The valid performance of

36. C. 1, q. 1, c. 72 (rubric), "De manu hereticorum communio non est recipienda." C. 1, q. 1, dict. post c. 97, "Potestas dandi baptismum, et ius consecrandi dominicum corpus, et largiendi sacros ordines, plurimum inter se differunt. Suspenso enim vel deposito sacerdote, nulla ei relinquitur potestas sacrificandi. Sacramentum tamen baptismi non solum a sacerdote deposito vel laico catholico, verum etiam ab heretico vel pagano si ministratum fuerit, nulla reiteratione violabitur; nulla autem ratio sinit, ut inter sacerdotes habeantur, qui de manibus laici vel pagani oleum sacrae (imo execrandae) unctionis assumunt."
The doctrine expounded in this dictum is a refinement of one set forth at other places in the Decretum. See Dist. 23, dict. post c. 6, "Christi sacramenta neque in bono, neque in malo homine fugienda . . ." C. 1, q. 1, dict. post c. 95, "Quod vero sacerdos, etiamsi malus sit, tamen pro offitio suae dignitatis gratiam transfundat hominibus." C. 15, q. 8, c. 5 (rubric), "De manu sacerdotis, qui ab ecclesia tolleratur, licite sacramenta sumuntur." C. 15, q. 8, c. 5, in cap., "Non potest aliquis, quantumcumque pollutus sit, sacramenta divina polluere."
37. The Magister did not treat the confirmation in the Decretum, but the patristic and early medieval tradition of the baptism, confirmation, and the Eucharist was collected, almost without any *lacunae,* in Dist. 4, *de consecratione,* which was added to the work later. See chap. i, pp. 12–13.
38. C. 1, q. 1, dict. post c. 43, "sollicite notandum est, quod sacramentum sacerdotalis promotionis pre ceteris omnibus magis accurate et digne dandum vel

93

these sacraments must make one a member of the Church, or reaffirm that membership, but Gratian explicitly recognizes the action of God, the granting of grace, in them and shows that he can imagine cases in which the recipient of the sacrament only becomes a member of the mystical body of the Church and not of the earthly community. This is the meaning of the imposition of hands ceremony performed when an already baptized person presents himself to the Church. It is the sign that the earthly community recognizes his membership in it.[39]

Even the simple act of imposing the hands over the reconciled Christian presents a duality that prevents Gratian's doctrine from being free from ambiguity. The ceremony must be considered as more than a juridical act because it represents the priesthood's power to act as the agent of God. Is the baptized man a member of the mystical body the instant he reconciles himself to God or must he receive the imposition of hands from the bishop? If the imposition of hands is not necessary, but only a juridical act, what is the power of binding and loosing? These questions demonstrate the ramifications of the relationship between the spiritual and temporal Church, between the divine and earthly power of the hierarchy. Gratian thinks that there is a difference between being a member of the community of the Church on earth and the mystical body, but he cannot establish the distinction in legal doctrine without denying his theological understanding of the Church

---

accipiendum est, quia nisi ita collatum fuerit, eo desinet esse ratum, quo non fuerit rite perfectum. Cetera enim sacramenta unicuique propter se dantur, et unicuique talia fiunt quali corde vel conscientia accipiuntur. Istud solum non propter se solum, sed propter alios datur, et ideo necesse est, ut vero corde mundaque conscientia, quantum ad se, sumatur, quantum ad alios vero non solum sine omni culpa, sed etiam sine omni infamia, propter fratrum scandalum, ad quorum utilitatem, non solum ut presint, sed etiam ut prosint, sacerdotium datur." This passage exhibits as clearly as any in the work, Gratian's profound interest in the ecclesiastical polity.

39. The imposition of hands is not a sacrament and does not constitute a repetition of the sacrament. It is a simple prayer. Gratian is not at all explicit about its significance, but he implies that it is of concern only to the earthly Church. See C. 1, q. 1, dict. post c. 73, "Ex eo autem, quod manus inpositio iterari precipitur, sacramentum non esse ostenditur." C. 1, q. 1, c. 74, "Manus inpositio non, sicut baptismus, repeti non potest. Quid enim est aliud, nisi oratio super hominem?"

as a whole. This problem is reflected in his theory of membership in the Church and in his idea of the nature of the hierarchy's authority. The effect of this duality on Gratian's theory of constitutional structure will be exposed at several points in the course of this study.

IV. Human Authority and
the Hierarchy of Law

Gratian began the Decretum with a *Tractatus de legibus* that surpassed the earlier treatments of the hierarchy of laws. The few canonists who had brought forth canons dealing with the sources of the laws had not presented a systematic or complete consideration of the subject. They embedded these canons in the midst of their collections and often interspersed them with canons treating other, unrelated subjects. Gratian placed his *de legibus* at the beginning of his work and as one scholar has said, this section is better organized than any other in the Decretum.[1] The *de legibus,* like the rest of the Decretum, became the

1. Jean Gaudemet, "La doctrine des sources du droit dans le Décret de Gratien," *Revue de Droit canonique* 1 (1951), 6, *passim*. The inclusion of canons dealing with the sources of the laws was rare before Gratian. Abbo of Fleury was, as Gaudemet says, the modest precursor of the Magister. He incorporated five canons on the sources in his *Collectio canonum*. After him, Burchard of Worms cited ten canons concerning custom, written law, and the hierarchy of authorities—in the earlier collections, treatment of the sources of the laws was not separated from that of the hierarchy of *auctoritates*. The Polycarpus (1104–1106) followed Burchard and devoted five titles to the subject in Book III. Ivo of Chartres gave considerable space to the subject, however. In Part IV of his Decretum, Ivo included 174 canons on the sources, though among them are texts treating the relative authority of ecclesiastical and profane writers, and the sources of Frankish law. Ivo's treatment of the subject is therefore confused and disorganized like that of his predecessors, but it surpasses theirs by its completeness. Finally, the author of the *Caesaraugustana* (1110–1120), a collection based on Ivo's, took over the *de legibus* from his model and innovated by placing it at the beginning of his work. The whole of Book I and a good part of Book II in the collection are devoted to the sources. The most recent and most extensive treatment of natural law doctrine in this period is Rudolf Weigand, *Die Naturrechtslehre der Legisten*

basis of later canonical theorizing and was one of the principal sources for the theories of law expounded by the scholastic theologians.

The *Tractatus* has been studied because of its later importance, but little attention has been given to the relationship between it and the remainder of the Decretum. Gratian obviously thought the *de legibus* was of primary importance since he not only placed it first in his work but also took special care with the structure of its argument. As Gaudemet says, the Magister recognized the importance of a treatise on the sources of the laws as the basis for a comprehensive canonical collection.[2] For Gaudemet as well as other scholars, it was Gratian's insight as a legal scholar which led him to treat the *de legibus* as it should be treated. But just as I argue that the Decretum was much more than a collection of the canons, I also say that the *Tractatus de legibus* is more than a treatise on the sources of the laws. In fact, the *de legibus* provides some of the strongest internal evidence to support the thesis that Gratian's primary aim in the Decretum was to expound a theory of Church government in accord with the political outlook of the reform party.

Gratian looked at the hierarchy of laws from the standpoint of the political community, and he looked upon the Church as a community analogous to other juridical communities. The *de legibus* is therefore

---

und Dekretisten von Innerius bis Accursius und von Gratian bis Johannes Teutonicus (Munich, 1967). Weigand (pp. 121–132) treats the sources of the *Tractatus de legibus,* in particular that part of it dealing with the *ius naturale.* R. L. Cosme, "La teoria de las fuentes del derecho eclesiastico en la renascencia juridica de principios des siglo XII," *Rivista espanola de derecho canonico,* 15 (1960), 317–370.

2. Gaudemet, *op. cit.,* pp. 9–11. Gaudemet considers Gratian to be original in three ways. (1) He placed the *de legibus* at the beginning of his work, although he was probably influenced by the *Caesaraugustana* when he did so. (2) He saw the distinction between the questions: What were the sources of the laws? What was the relative authority of the Scriptures, ecclesiastical writers, and profane writers? He therefore did not treat the second question in the *de legibus* and avoided some of the confusion found in earlier collections. [Actually, Gratian did consider the question of which *auctoritates* were to be preferred in Dist. 20, but the discussion—dealing with the legal force of decisions by the pope and by learned theologians—does fit neatly into the *de legibus.*] (3) The Magister presented the best organized consideration of the sources in the history of canon law up to his time.

the foundation of the political theory of the ecclesiastical community and is an integral part of that theory. We want to know about the laws, Gratian says in effect, because, "The human race is ruled by two, namely natural law and customs."[3] But the *de legibus* is also justification for the remainder of the Decretum, in particular for the *Tractatus ordinandorum*. By examining the framework of laws in which ecclesiastical society exists, Gratian shows that concern for the quality of prelates, to which nearly all the *Tractatus ordinandorum* is devoted, is an essential part of constitutional theory and law. Medieval legal theory did not provide adequate protection for the community against the caprice of its governors. Thus, the *de legibus* must hold the first place in the Decretum. It justified the direction taken by Gratian in the rest of the work, and at the same time, it constituted the theoretical foundation for the reform program of the party with which the work was associated.

The *de legibus* is made up of the first twenty *Distinctiones* of the Decretum as the work now exists and, as was noted above, is the best organized part of the work. But if Gratian did take special care with the organization of the *de legibus,* he did not succeed in banishing the demon of ambiguity from its doctrine. There have been two main difficulties in the interpretation of the Magister's ideas. Did he equate natural law and divine law? What did he mean by the term *ius naturale*? The first of these problems is not a genuine one. It is based on a misunderstanding of the Magister's purpose in the *Tractatus,* which has led to a misreading of some of his dicta. The second question—what did Gratian mean by the term *ius naturale*—is a genuine problem arising from a shift in the Magister's use of the term. It was a problem that interested and perhaps even amused the earliest commentators on the Decretum. Stimulated by Gratian's apparent inability to give a single, comprehensive definition for *ius naturale,* the later canonists exercised their imaginations in order to list all the possible meanings of the term. One canonist found six such meanings.[4] Con-

3. This sentence is the very first in the Decretum. Dist. 1, dict. ante c. 1, "Humanum genus duobus regitur, naturali videlicet iure et moribus."
4. Brian Tierney, *Medieval Poor Law* (Berkeley and Los Angeles, 1959), pp.

sideration of both these problems is part of the study of the Magister's argument.

Gratian's argument in the Tractatus de legibus.

Gratian moves by degrees, in the *Tractatus,* from the broadest generality concerning human government to the topic that is at the center of his attention throughout the *Distinctiones,* the government of the Church. What he is doing, even in the first dicta, is demonstrating his commitment to the idea that the Church is a juridical community and as such must be equated with other, secular communities. The first sentence of the work, already quoted above, explains the relationship between governing authority and laws. There are two kinds of law, divine and human; one is beyond the control of the governor and the other is subject to his power.[5] The next dictum confirms this twofold distinction. At the same time, it raises the question whether the Magister identifies the divine and natural laws:

From the words of this authority [c. 1] it is given to be understood, how divine and human laws differ, since all that is right [*fas*], is called by the name of divine and [*vel*] natural law; by the name of human law are understood customs [*mores*] written and handed down in law.[6]

28–32. The canonist whose imagination was so fertile was Honorius. Stephen of Tournai, for example, listed four meanings of natural law, then said, "and if you do not shrink from yet another interpretation," and set down a fifth. *Ibid.,* p. 145 n. 12.

5. See n. 3 above. The relationship between the governor and the laws reflects that between the subjects and the laws. Gratian does not, in the *de legibus,* expound a theory of obedience, but does treat this subject in C. 11, q. 3. The problem of obedience is raised in regard to the question whether members of the Church ought to obey an unjust sentence of excommunication, and the doctrine expounded on this point is an elaboration of the ideas set forth in the *de legibus.* The Magister's theory of obedience will be considered in the next chapter, when study of his view of the relationship between the human authority and the higher law is continued.

6. Dist. 1, dict. post c. 1, "Ex verbis huius auctoritatis evidenter datur intelligi, in quo differant inter se lex divina at humana, cum omne quod fas est, nomine divinae vel naturalis legis accipiatur, nomine vero legis humanae mores iure

The great German scholar Martin Grabmann argued, primarily on the basis of this passage, that Gratian did not make a distinction between the divine and natural law. Most scholars have followed Grabmann's interpretation.[7] The problem seems to stem from the phrase, "all

conscripti et traditi intelligantur." For the text of Dist. 1, c. 1 (Isidore, *Etymologies*, V:2), see n. 8 below.

7. Martin Grabmann, "Das Naturrecht der Scholastik von Gratian bis Thomas von Aquin," *Archiv für Rechts-und Wirtschafts-Philosophie*, 16 (1922), 12–53. Odon Lottin, "Le droit naturel chez saint Thomas et ses prédécesseurs," *Ephemerides theologicae Lovanienses*, 1 (1924), 369–388; 2 (1925), 32–53, 345–366; 3 (1926), 155–176. Willibald Ploechl, *Das Eherecht des Magisters Gratian* (Vienna, 1935), pp. 23 f. Johannes Brys, *De dispensatione in iure canonico praesertim apud Decretistas et Decretalistas* (Bruges, 1925), p. 82. A. J. and R. W. Carlyle, *The History of Medieval Political Theory in the West* (1909), II: 102–142. Walter Ullmann, *Medieval Papalism* (London. 1949), pp. 38–49. Franz Arnold, "Die Rechtslehre des Magisters Gratians," *SG*, 1 (1953), 453–482. Michel Villey, "Le Droit naturel chez Gratien," *SG*, 3 (1955), 85–99. The traditional view of the hierarchy is expounded by Saint Thomas in *Summa Theologica*, q. 90–97.

Two scholars have challenged Grabmann's interpretation of Gratian's views. Arthur Wegner argued that Grabmann's reading of the *de legibus* led to the conclusion that the Magister was outside the medieval tradition on the hierarchy of laws. Grabmann was arguing, said Wegner, that the Magister was unorthodox. But the interpretation that had prevailed since Grabmann's work, according to Wegner, was too influenced by modern positivist ideas and demanded too definite a statement from the Magister on the division of the divine law. Arthur Wegner, "Über positives göttliches Recht und natürliches göttliches Recht bei Gratian," *SG*, 1 (1953), 502–518.

Dario Composta argued that though Gratian saw natural law as part of divine law, he recognized that natural law was not positive law. If the Magister had confused the two laws, said Composta, he would have seen natural law as deriving from divine legislation instead of from human nature. The scholar cited Dist. 1, c. 7 to support his argument. "Ius naturale est commune omnium nationum, eo quod ubique instinctu naturae, non constitutione aliqua habetur." Composta also pointed to a dictum in Dist. 6 (dict. post c. 3). Composta, "Il diritto naturale in Graziano," *SG*, 2 (1954), 153–210.

Weigand (*op. cit.*, pp. 137–139) reviews and comments upon the views of Villey and Composta, and he finds them one-sided. Villey's contention that for Gratian natural law was a moral principle to which the social order could not be contradictory but from which that order did not derive in the legal sense, misses the import of the Magister's teaching. Composta, Weigand points out, wants to show that there is a consistent conception of natural law expounded throughout the Decretum and that this conception is virtually identical with that of Saint Thomas. Most scholars would agree that Gratian cannot be accused of consistency on the meaning of the term *ius naturale*.

that is right, is called by the name of divine *vel* natural law." *Vel* can signify *or* as a disjunctive between two virtually interchangeable alternatives as in the example: "He is concerned with the foundations *or* origins of parliamentary government." But *vel* can also be used as a disjunctive between two mutually exclusive terms or things as in the statement: "I like borscht hot *or* cold."[8] Here, one might say, "hot *and* cold," in order to make certain there was no confusion and I have translated the word *and* in the passage for that reason. Grabmann's reading of the passage implies that he took *vel* in the first sense, as separating interchangeable alternatives. But a close look at the dictum and consideration of what Gratian was trying to say shows that he did not mean to equate the two types of divine law.

The two central conceptions in the dictum are *fas* and *mos*. They are the basic types of legal precepts contained in the law of the human community, which from the first sentence of the *Tractatus* is at the center of Gratian's attention. *Fas* is contained in natural and divine law, *mos* in customary and written law. The Magister does not seek here to establish even the general outlines of the hierarchy of laws, but only to examine further the types of law according to which the human race is ruled.[9]

What follows this dictum is a short digression on the types of *ius* that, like the material in the whole of the first *Distinctiones* up to

8. Lewis and Short, *A Latin Dictionary* (Oxford, 1879), pp. 1963–1964.

9. Gratian was careless in his use of the phrase *ius naturale* in the first dictum of the work; he should have perhaps used the word *fas* in the phrase, "naturali videlicet iure et moribus." But that he meant to distinguish between *fas* and *mos* is shown by the text of the first capitulum.

Dist. 1, c. 1 (rubric), "Divinae leges natura, humanae moribus constant." in cap. "Omnes leges aut divinae sunt, aut humanae. Divinae natura, humanae moribus constant, ideoque he discrepant, quonium aliae aliis gentibus placent. §1. Fas lex divina est: ius lex humana. Transire per agrum alienum, fas est, ius non est." Dist. 1, dict. post c. 1 clarifies the statement in the first dictum.

The argument offered here leads us to look upon the remainder of Dist. 1 as a digression. Gratian is led to consider the various kinds of *ius* by Isidore's use of the term in Dist, 1, c. 1, "Fas lex divina est: ius lex humana." Dist. 1, dict. post c. 1, "§1. Est autem ius generale nomen, multas sub se continens species." Capitula 2 through 5 confirm this point and cc. 6–12 enumerate, according to Isidore, the kinds of *ius*. In Dist. 2, Gratian returns to the analysis of human law. This discussion continues to Dist. 5, dict. ante c. 1.

4, c. 2, is taken from Isidore of Seville's *Etymologies,* book five. In fact, the course of Gratian's discussion is largely determined in this beginning section of the *de legibus* by the order of Isidore's treatment of the laws.[10] After the enumeration of the types of *ius,* the Magister treats the types and to some extent the character of human law. In Dist. 5, he returns to the distinction between the natural law, as the embodiment of *fas,* and other laws; this is the beginning of his treatise on the hierarchy of laws.

In these passages, Gratian again shows, but more specifically than he did earlier, that he does not equate natural law and divine law. He says that natural law holds primacy among the kinds of law in time and dignity, since it originated with the creation of rational creatures and remains immutable.[11] But earlier, in the first dictum of the work, the Magister had said that natural law was that contained *in lege et evangelio,* and this statement leads now to the first objection to his doctrine. "When it is said above that natural law is comprehended in the law [O.T.] and Gospel, it seems that natural law does not remain immutable [because] some things are found now which are contrary to those things established in the law." [12]

Gratian solves the contradiction raised in this passage by making a distinction, destined to have a long career in canonical commentaries, between two types of law found in the Old Testament, *moralia* and *mystica.* Moralia correspond to the natural law and lay down the immutable rules of human conduct. The Ten Commandments are moralia. Mystica govern the ceremonies and sacraments of the Jewish

10. On Gratian's use of Isidore and on the character and importance of Isidore's *de legibus,* see Gaudemet, *op. cit.,* pp. 11–27.

11. Dist. 5, dict. ante c. 1, "Nunc ad differentiam naturalis iuris et ceterorum revertamur. §1. Naturale ius inter omnia primatum obtinet et tempore et dignitate. Cepit enim ab exordio rationalis creaturae, nec variatur tempore, sed immutabile permanere."

12. Dist. 1, dict. ante c. 1, "Humanum genus duobus regitur, naturali videlicet iure et moribus. Ius naturale est, quod in lege et evangelio continetur, quo quisque iubetur alii facere, quod sibi vult fieri, et prohibetur alii inferre quod sibi nolit fieri." Dist. 5, dict, ante c. 1, "§2. Sed cum naturale ius lege et evangelio supra dicatur esse comprehensum, quedam autem contraria his, que in lege statuta sunt, nunc inveniantur concessa, non videtur ius naturale immutabile permanere."

religion and were changed by Christ.[13] Thus, the objection raised in the sentence quoted above is met by a distinction analogous to that later made between divine and natural law.

But Gratian complicates his simple doctrine by recognizing that mystica contain two levels. On the one hand, there is a superficial level that is not part of the natural law. On the other hand, there is the deeper meaning of the ceremony or festival, its significance for the work of man's salvation, which does not change. This part of the mystic command does pertain to the natural law.[14] There is, in this doctrine, an understanding of man's spiritual progress through history similar to that found in the writings of the Magister's contemporaries. The elements, sacramental and ceremonial, of Jewish religion were seen as *figurae* of the elements of Christian religion, and the essence of the prefiguration was not contained in the form of the Jewish sacrament, but in its meaning. Thus, circumcision meant, according to Saint Bernard and others, that God cleansed the soul of the Jew, and insofar as the act of circumcision was a sign of God's gift of grace, it was a moralium. The act itself, however, was a mysticum and as Bernard says, it was abolished by Christ when he instituted the new sacrament of baptism.[15]

The idea of mystica expounded by Gratian takes into account the Christian interpretation of the Old Testament as a prophecy of Christ and a prefiguration of the Christian religion. It does not, however, undermine the distinction between moralia and mystica which the Magister has made. There are both types of law in the Old Testament, according to Gratian, but distinguishing between them depends on the proper interpretation of the scriptural passages. With this con-

13. Dist. 6, dict. post c. 3 "In lege et evangelio naturale ius continetur, non tamen quecumque in lege et evangelio inveniuntur naturali iuri coherere probantur. Sunt enim in lege quedam moralia, ut: non occides et cetera, quedam mistica, utpote sacrifitiorum precepta et alia his similia."

14. *Ibid.,* "Moralia mandata ad naturale ius spectant atque ideo nullam mutabilitatem recepisse monstrantur. Mistica vero, quantum ad superficiem, a naturali iure probantur aliena, quantum ad moralem intelligentiam, inveniuntur sibi annexa; ac per hoc, etsi secundum superficiem videantur esse mutata, tamen secundum moralem intelligentiam mutabilitatem nescire probantur."

15. See chap. iii, pp. 69–70. For the contemporary views of man's spiritual progress through history, see chap. iii, n. 2.

clusion, Gratian completes the first step in his attempt to distinguish between natural law and other laws.

The significant distinction to be drawn between natural law and other laws is, the Magister said, according to their temporality and dignity. It is clear that moralia are distinguished from mystica according to their temporality since ius naturale began with the creation of man while mystica of the Old Testament were first revealed to Moses. As Hugh of Saint Victor had said, the period from Adam to Moses was the age of natural law, when man's life was regulated only by that law, and also his relationship with God depended on the dictates of his natural reason.[16] Mystica explained, better than man could learn from natural law, the way to please God and to improve one's spiritual life. Mystica, therefore, represented an advance over unaided natural reason, but the law to be learned from natural reason held a primacy over mystica in time.

The treatise on the difference between natural law and other laws according to their temporality continues after these passages, with comparison between natural law and human law. Custom arose when man first began to live in cities. The law of constitutions arose even later, when Moses gave the law to the Jews.[17] This latter comparison, between natural law and written human law, is completed in a dictum

16. Hugh of Saint Victor, *de Sac.,* I:8, 11, "Tria sunt tempora per quae praesentis saeculi spatium decurrit. Primum est naturalis legis; secundum tempus scriptae legis; tertium tempus gratiae. Primum ab Adam usque ad Moysen."

17. Dist. 6, dict. post c. 3, "§1. Naturale ergo ius ab exordio rationalis creaturae incipiens, ut supra dictum est, manet immobile. Ius vero consuetudinis post naturalem legem exordium habuit, ex quo homines convenientes in unum ceperunt simal habitare; quod ex eo tempore factum creditur, ex quo Cain civitatem edificasse legitur, quod cum diluvio propter hominum raritatem fere videature extinctum, postea postmodum a tempore Nemroth reparatum." Composta (*op. cit.,* p. 160) thinks that this passage refers to natural law and that it says natural law existed throughout human history even though it appears to have been extinguished after the Flood. But the passage clearly refers to custom that was first produced when men came to live together and that because of the rarity of men, seemed to disappear at the time of the Flood.

Dist. 7, dict., ante c. 1, "Ius autemn constitutionis cepit a iustificationibus, quas Dominus tradidit Moisi dicens: 'Si emeris servum ebreum etc.'" (Exod. 21:1). The capitula of Dist. 7 present the traditional history of written law.

that has caused many interpretative difficulties. It is the first dictum of Dist. 8, and the difficulties concern the meaning of the term *ius naturale*.

Gratian had explained the content of natural law in the first dictum of the Decretum. "The natural law is that contained in the law and Gospel by which one is ordered to do to another what he wishes to be done to himself, and is prohibited from doing to another what he does not wish to be done to himself." [18] Thus, natural law is the basic principle of social life. All other laws of the social community are based on it, but none of the specific precepts of those laws are actually part of natural law. In the first dictum of Dist. 8, the Magister did appear to attribute a specific precept to natural law. He says, "For by the law of nature all things are common to all." [19]

The problem created by the comparison of Gratian's statements about the content of natural law is exacerbated by the succession of ideas in Dist. 8 itself. In the last part of the first dictum of the *Distinctio,* the Magister states that property institutions, not based on natural law, are established by custom or written law. This argument

18. See n. 12 above.

19. The problem of what Gratian means by the term *ius naturale* is actually raised earlier in the *de legibus* by a passage from Saint Isidore's *Etymologies.* Dist. 1, c. 7, "Ius naturale est commune omnium nationum eo quod ubique instinctu naturae, non constitutione aliqua habetur, ut viri et feminae coniunctio, liberorum successio et educatio, communis omnium possessio et omnium una libertas, acquisitio eorum, quae celo, terra marique capiuntur; item depositae rei vel commendatae pecuniae restitutio, violentiae per vim repulsio. §1. Nam hoc, aut si quid huic simile est, numquam iniustum, sed naturale equumque habetur." It can be seen that the idea of natural law set forth in Dist. 8, dict. ante c. 1 reflects the text of Isidore's definition. In fact, the passage suggests several meanings for the term. It is the instincts of nature which man shares with other animals. The Roman jurist Ulpian had defined *ius naturale* in this way: "Quod natura omnia animalia docuit." It is also the law common to all nations, the *ius gentium* of Gaius's definition (I, 2, 1). Later, Saint Thomas delineated three meanings for natural law which reflect the content of Dist. 1, c. 7. For Thomas, it is first the inclination of all "substances" to seek their own preservation. Second, it is the instincts of nature represented by the sexual relationship, which man shares with other animals. Third, it is the inclination of man to know God and to do nothing that will offend those with whom he must live. *Summa Theol.,* q. 94, art. 2. Gaudemet, *op. cit.,* pp. 16–17.

105

is supported by a famous fragment from St. Augustine's commentary on the Gospel of John.[20] But in the very next dictum, Gratian continues by saying that anything contained in custom or included in the written law which is found to be contrary to natural law ought to be considered null and void.[21] As Brian Tierney has said, Gratian set up a logical ambush in these passages. The logical consequence of the second dictum is that the institutions of property contained in human law are null and void.[22]

Tierney has also pointed out, however, that the ambush is apparent rather than real, for it is predicated on the interpretation that Gratian thought natural law contained the precept, "All things are common to all." This interpretation of the Magister's meaning is incorrect. He has indeed offered a new definition of natural law in this passage, but he does not mean to say that it contains specific precepts. Rather, he now uses the term to describe the primitive state of man's life. Tierney supports this interpretation of the dictum by citing the view held by the author of the *Summa Parisiensis*. "Divine law is here to be interpreted strictly, namely as the natural law that existed in the beginning, that is to say, the primeval institution of things." [23]

20. Dist. 8, dict. ante c. 1, "Differt etiam ius naturae a consuetudine et constitutione. Nam iure naturae sunt omnia communia omnibus, quod non solum inter eos servatum creditur, de quibus legitur: 'Multitudinis autem credentium erat cor unum et anima una, etc.' verum etiam exprecedenti tempore a philosophis traditum invenitur. Unde apud Platonem illa civitas iustissime ordinata traditur, in qua quisque proprios nescit affectus. Iure vero consuetudinis vel constitutionis hoc meum est, illud vero alterius." Dist. 8, c. 1 which is from Augustine's *in Joannis evanglium, VI*, ad c. 1, 25.

21. Dist. 8, dict. post c. 1, "Dignitate vero ius naturale simpliciter prevalet consuetudini et constitutioni. Quaecumque enim vel moribus recepta sunt, vel scriptis comprehensa si naturali iuri fuerint adversa, vana et irrata sunt habenda."

22. Tierney, *op. cit.*, p. 30.

23. *Ibid.*, p. 31. *Summa Parisiensis*, ed. Terrence McLaughlin, p. 7, "Ius divinum multum stricte hic accipitur, scilicet illud ius naturale quod fuit in initio, scilicet primaeva institutio rerum."

Composta (*op. cit.*, pp. 177–178) has tried to solve the apparent contradiction between the two dicta by examining the Magister's doctrine of property law. He points to a rubric of a canon in Causa 23 to show that Gratian actually saw property rights as based on both divine and human law. C. 23, q. 7. c. 1 (rubric), "Res terrenae non nisi divino vel humano iure tenentur." On the basis of this text, Composta suggests that there are three ways of interpreting Gratian's view

There is no question that Gratian has presented more than one definition of *ius naturale* in the *de legibus,* but the apparent logical contradiction found in *Dist.* 8 results more from the efforts of the members of the canon law schools than from the work of the Magister himself. The canonist who divided part one of the Decretum into *Distinctiones*—after it had left the workroom of the Magister—made a problem of definition into one of contradiction. Studying the argument of Dist. 7 shows that it ends with Dist. 8, c. 1. The first dictum of the eighth *Distinctio,* and its first capitulum, continue the discussion of the difference between natural law and human law according to their temporality. Natural law made no provision for ownership of property, but human law, arising later, created property rights. Gratian clearly meant to say that the case of property laws demonstrates, in a substantive way, that natural law arose earlier than customary and written human law.

The dictum post c. 1 of Dist. 8 actually begins the second part of Gratian's distinction between the law of nature and other laws. It should have been the beginning of a new *Distinctio.*

By dignity natural law simply prevails over custom and constitution. For whatever things were either received in customs, or comprehended in

---

of the relationship between property institutions and natural law. First, the law of property according to natural law is communistic and all private property rights derive from human law. Second, the law of property is based on both natural and human law. Third, there is no law of property contained in natural law, only in human law. The rubric from Causa 23, he argues, shows that the third interpretation is impossible. The second reading seems to him to be the correct one.

But the rubric on which Composta so heavily relies is not Gratian's own and cannot be assumed to be a conscious representation of his thought. The same rubric is found in Ivo of Chartres, *Decretum* (III:179), from which Gratian apparently took the canon. Furthermore, the discussion in the place where that capitulum occurs concerns the dispossession of heretics by the ecclesiastical power. The point that the Magister is making is that property rights are not immutable or above the authority of the earthly governors. The rubric is even a bit out of place in its context. Ivo of Chartres, *Decretum,* III:179 (rubric), "Res terrenas a nullo recte possideri nisi vel jure divino, vel humano" (PL 161, col. 239). The third interpretation should not, then, be ignored in considering Gratian's theory of the relationship between natural law and property institutions. Tierney favored that interpretation when he studied the problem of property law in the Decretum.

107

writing if they will have been against natural law, they ought to be held null and void.[24]

This dictum sets forth the second way in which natural law differs from other laws, according to its dignity. While the differences according to the temporal quality were complex, those according to dignity are, by contrast, simple. In the remaining part of Dist. 8 and in Dist. 9, Gratian gives examples that illustrate the rule stated in the dictum. None of the capitula in these two *Distinctiones* refers to the problem of property law. For the Magister, there was no problem created by the relationship of property law and natural law.

The discussion concerning conflicts of natural and human law is completed in the final dictum of Dist. 9. Gratian expounds a complex argument in this passage and brings us back to the two interpretative difficulties raised earlier in the *de legibus:* Does he equate natural and divine law? and what does he mean by *ius naturale?*

When therefore by natural law it is commanded to do nothing other than what God wishes, and to avoid nothing other than what God prohibits; and also when nothing other is found in the canonical scriptures than what is in divine laws, divine laws indeed arise from nature: it is obvious that whatever things are proven to be contrary to divine will, or canonical scriptures, would also be found adverse to natural law. Whence whatever it is thought ought to be put after divine will, or canonical scriptures, or divine laws, also natural law ought to be preferred to it. Constitutions therefore, either ecclesiastical or secular, if they are proven to be contrary to natural law, ought to be excluded entirely.[25]

24. See n. 21 above.

25. Dist. 9, dict. post c. 11, "Cum ergo naturali iure nichil aliud precipiatur, quam quod Deus vult fieri, nichilque vetetur, quam quod Deus prohibit fieri; denique cum in canonica scriptura nichil aliud, quam in divinis legibus inveniatur, divine vero leges natura constant: patet, quod quecumque divinae voluntati, seu canonicae scripturae contraria probantur, eadem et naturali iuri inveniuntur adversa. Unde quecumque divinae voluntati, seu canonice scripture, seu divinis legibus postponenda censentur, eidem naturale ius preferri oportet. Constitutiones ergo vel ecclesiasticae vel seculares, si naturali iuri contrariae probantur, penitus sunt excludendae.' Note that the phrase "divine vero leges natura constant," comes from Dist. 1, c. 1. The verb *constare* can be translated in several ways. With the ablative, it can mean "to agree with something," "to rise from something," or "to consist in something." It seems to me that in the context of Dist. 1, c. 1 and Dist. 9, dict, post c. 11 either of the first two of these definitions fits best. In either case, the meaning conveyed is that divine law embodies *fas* or the law of nature,

Gratian begins the passage by giving natural law yet a third meaning; it orders us to do God's will. He then explains what this precept entails for a Christian, and thus he brings divine law into the discussion. He does not equate natural and divine law, but he shows that they are above both human law and the power of human governors. The governing authority of a Christian community must concern itself with transgressions of divine law as with other kinds of law, and the Magister here indicated in what capacity it judges concerning such transgressions.

Mystica agree with natural law in that they are based upon and imply a moral command. This doctrine is repeated in a cryptic form in the final dictum of Dist. 9. Obedience to divine law is enjoined, Gratian says, by natural law because natural law commands that we do God's will and God's will is contained in divine law. Thus, when Gratian said at the outset of the *de legibus* that the human race was ruled by *mores* and *ius naturale,* he meant that these two categories of law subsume the other types of law so far as the juridical community is concerned. By mores, he means customary and written human law, and by ius naturale, he means, principally, the basic social principle of doing unto others what you wish to be done unto yourself, and the precept that man should obey God's will. Men learn their obligation to obey divine law from natural law, and it is this problem of exposing the relationship between man and laws to which Gratian has devoted the *de legibus.*

By bringing divine law into the discussion in Dist. 9, the Magister focuses attention on the corpus of laws of a Christian community and in particular of the Church. This train of thought leads him into a brief but important digression on the use of secular law in Church courts. It can be seen that the last sentence of the dictum quoted above leads naturally into this discussion. The digression, however, does not end with the discussion in Dist. 10. Gratian continues to explicate the hierarchy of laws relative to the community by comparing the status of constitutions and customs. In Dist. 12, he returns to

---

and Gratian has explained that the mystica do indeed embody moralia because they have a spiritual significance. Dist. 6, dict. post c. 3.

the distinction between natural law and other laws according to their dignity with a consideration of dispensations. While dispensations from human law may be granted, natural law may not be transgressed under any circumstances.[26]

In the last five *Distinctiones,* Gratian treats the types and sources of ecclesiastical law,[27] but interspersed in the first fifteen *Distinctiones* are passages that show the Magister was, from the beginning, concerned with the Ecclesia. He divides the human law into secular and ecclesiastical and describes the types of written ecclesiastical law in Dist. 2 and 3.[28] He brings out the problems raised by the relationship between divine and natural law in Dist. 5 and 9. He treats the

26. The tendency of the discussion, begun at Dist. 8, dict. post c. 1, leads naturally into a consideration of the whole hierarchy of laws according to their dignity. Thus, Dist. 9 shows, "Quod autem constitutio naturali iuri cedat" (dict. ante c. 1). Dist. 10 that, "Constitutiones vero principum ecclesiasticis constitutionibus non preminent, sed obsecuntur" (dict. ante c. 1). Dist. 11, the final part of the digression, demonstrates, "Quod vero legibus consuetudo cedat" (dict. ante c. 1). In Dist. 12, the Magister returns to the problem of how natural law differs from human law in dignity. No dispensation from natural law is permitted, says the Magister, except in a single case: When a man is faced by two evil choices, he may choose the lesser evil thereby transgressing the natural law precept, "Never do evil." Dist. 13, dict. ante c. 1 and Dist. 14, dict. ante c. 1. The decretists did not recognize choice of the lesser of two evils as a dispensation from natural law, however. They pointed out that he who was faced with two evil choices could not be said to have free choice and that therefore the natural law rule did not apply to his case. Transgression of law could only occur when freedom of choice existed. Stephan Kuttner, *Kanonistische Schuldlehre* (Rome, 1935) pp. 257–266. The precept, "Never do evil" should not be considered different from, "Do God's will."

On dispensation from human law, see Dist. 14, dict. post c. 1.

27. Dist. 15, dict. ante c. 1, "De naturali iure et constitutione vel consuetudine hactenus disservimus, differentiam, qua ab invicem discernuntur, assignantes: nunc ad ecclesiasticas constitutiones stilum vertamus, earumque originem et auctoritatem, prout ex libris sanctorum Patrum colligere possumus, breviter assignantes."

28. Gratian first mentions ecclesiastical law in Dist. 3. He distinguishes there between the two types of human law, secular and ecclesiastical. Dist. 3, dict. ante c. 1, "Omnes he species [of the *ius Quiritum*] secularium legum partes sunt. Sed quia constitutio alia est civilis, alia ecclesiastica: civilis vero forense vel civile ius appellatur, quo nomine ecclesiastica constitutio appelletur, videamus. §1. Ecclesiastica constitutio nomine canonis censetur." Dist. 3, dict. post c. 1, "Porro canonum alii sunt decreta Pontificum alii statuta conciliorum."

110

relationship between secular and ecclesiastical law, within the jurisdiction of the Church, in Dist. 10. Gratian is led into these digressions
by the texts that he cites and by the trend of his argument. His willingness to digress, however, is caused by his overriding interest in the
ecclesiastical community.

Gratian did, then, have an overall plan for the *Tractatus de legibus*.
He started out with the basic questions concerning human government:
According to what laws does human authority govern and what is its
power relative to the types of law? He treated this topic first by dividing law into two basic categories—that superior to men and that subject
to men—and then by analyzing the differences between these categories. But throughout his discussion, he indicates that it is Church government that really interests him, and in Dist. 15 he comes to speak of
it *ex professo*. It is the distinction between higher law and human law,
the distinction according to their dignity, which is the more important
one for Gratian. This distinction permits him to construct a meaningful theory of conflicts of laws, which results in a hierarchy of laws
beginning at the top with natural law and ending with local customary
law.

The doctrine developed in the *de legibus* exposes the considerable
power of human governors with respect to laws. The law of God
is the immutable guide for the ruler, but nothing prevents him from
transgressing this law if he does not fear God. It is therefore necessary
to ensure that leaders of the ecclesiastical community fear God, and
the rest of the *Distinctiones* are devoted to this concern. The *Tractatus
de legibus* does not, however, contain the whole of Gratian's theory
concerning the relationship between ecclesiastical power and laws. The
Magister expands on his doctrine in the *Causae,* as he does with many
other doctrines expounded in the *Distinctiones*. The next two chapters
will consider his further treatment of this subject, and the exposition
is divided into two parts—the relation of the governing authority to
higher law and to human law.

111

V. Human Authority and
the Divine Law

In the *Tractatus de legibus,* Gratian set forth a theory of the relationship between human authority and laws. His purpose in examining the hierarchy of laws was to show that there are, as he said at the outset, two types of law—divine and human—according to which men are ruled. The two sections of his discussion which focus on the power of the ecclesiastical governor relative to these laws are in what are now Dist. 9 and 19. In the earlier *Distinctio,* the Magister was interested in the power of ecclesiastical hierarchy over divine law while in the later one, he considered its power over human laws. In this chapter, the theory expounded in Dist. 9 and in subsequent parts of the Decretum dealing with the same subject will be considered.

In Dist. 9, Gratian established only the general principle governing the relationship between authority and divine precepts: Whatever a power does contrary to the command of God is null and void. But the Magister's complete doctrine concerning this aspect of ecclesiastical authority can only be understood if Dist. 9 is read in conjunction with Causae 11 and 33, for in these sections of his work he clarifies and qualifies the theory developed earlier.

When Gratian treated the theory of power in the *Causae,* he looked at it from two points of view. First, he considered the way in which the relationship between Church authority and divine law affected the individual members of the community. By examining the limits of the obligation to obey one's superiors, he indicated the extent to which human power could hand down commands that were authoritative.

In effect, his discussion concerned the maintenance of authority when the governor transgressed the higher law, since only in such cases did the governor's power to command come into question. It will be seen that Gratian's theory of obedience implies a scale of values that is an important element in his ecclesiology. The first place in the scale is occupied by the sanctification of the individual, the highest good in Christian cosmology and the fundamental justification for the existence of the Church. In second place, the Magister valued the stability of the ecclesiastical community. Only in third place did he put the conformity of the ecclesiastical governor's judgments with higher law. Thus, the theory of obedience alters the doctrine that Gratian enunciated in the *de legibus* and makes the relationship between human power and divine law seem very tenuous. At the same time, the Magister's theory of obedience makes the need for ensuring that the prelates are good men more imperative than did the doctrine expounded in the early *Distinctiones*.

But while approaching the theory of power from the standpoint of the subject's obligation to obey leads to the conclusion that the ecclesiastical authority is virtually independent of divine power, the second point of view from which Gratian approaches the problem of power produces the opposite conclusion. When he expounded his theory of penitence, he focused on the position of the prelature and showed that he valued the connection between earthly Church authority and divine power very highly. One of the disputed questions in the schools of Gratian's period concerned the necessity of confession and penitential satisfaction for the remission of sins. The question involved the relationship between God and his agent in the performance of sacraments because the theologians of the mid-twelfth century, following the teaching of the Fathers, connected the remission of sins with the power of the keys held by priests. Thus, if confession and satisfaction were not necessary for the remission of sins, the priests would receive no power through the keys. But it was not only sacramental power of the priesthood which was in question. The power of binding the sinner and loosing the penitent, which was represented by the image of the keys, also affected the earthly community of the Church because it involved the punishment of crime. If sinners could

113

win pardon from God for their transgressions, how could canon lawyers justify the law enforcement and judicial activities of the earthly ecclesiastical authority? They could, of course, argue that the earthly community was one thing and the spiritual Church, ruled by God himself, another. Then forgiveness for sins would be sought after separately, and in different ways, in each of these communities to which Christians belonged. But belonging to the earthly Church was part of one's membership in the spiritual body and to separate the two communities would be to deny a basic principle of Christian ecclesiology. Gratian refused to make a radical separation of the two spheres of the Church in order to solve the difficulties raised by the sacrament of penitence. He preserved the connection between earth and heaven— at the cost of clarity in his constitutional theory—in order to preserve the central mystery of Christian ecclesiology.

The theory of obedience.

Gratian treated the obligation of obedience differently from his contemporaries, but his doctrine conformed largely to theirs. His discussion will be easier to understand, therefore, if the views of Saint Bernard, which represent the main current of twelfth-century thought about the problem, are reviewed. Bernard dealt with obedience in a letter to a renegade monk named Adam. The monk had left his abbey, and when Bernard had admonished him for this, he had answered that his action was justified because he was only following the order of his abbot. Bernard rejected this excuse and undertook to explain to him the limits of his obligation to obey. The saint did not think that the doctrine that he expounded for Adam applied only to those who had taken the monastic vows, however. In a later treatise, he showed that the theory defined all Christians' obligation to obey their superiors.[1]

Bernard divided commands into three categories. In the first group are commands that repeat provisions of divine law. These orders concern actions that God has already commanded to be done, and according to the saint, they are not really commands. No one ought to await an order from his superior to perform those acts that are

1. Saint Bernard, *Ep.* 7 and *De praecepto et dispensatione,* V:11; IX:19 and 21.

commanded by God. Obedience in the case of such orders applies therefore to divine precepts and not to human command. The second category includes commands of a superior which contradict divine law and are ipso facto null and void. The Christian ought never to obey evil orders no matter how high the earthly authority from which they emanate. The third category, then, includes all commands that do not simply repeat or contradict the divine precepts. Christians must obey these orders, according to Bernard.[2]

The obligation of obedience is thus strictly limited by Bernard to those commands that are morally indifferent. No act that contradicts divine precepts ought to be obeyed and those commands that simply corroborate the precepts are unnecessary repetitions. It is clear that for Bernard as for Gratian, divine law is part of the legal institutions of the Christian community. It is one of the laws according to which men are ruled. Yet, Bernard makes an addition to this theory, which indicates that the way in which he looks at the problem of obedience is different from the way in which Gratian looked at it. The abbot of Clairvaux recommends that men obey evil commands as far as possible in order to achieve a perfect obedience. Such obedience demonstrates the humility of the individual and the excellence of his soul.[3] Bernard demonstrates, with this doctrine, that his main interest is the preserva-

2. St. Bernard, *Ep.* 7 n. 4, "Sane hoc advertendum, quod quaedam sunt pura bona: quaedam pura mala, et in his nullam degeri hominibus obedientiam: quoniam nec illa omittenda sunt, etiam cum prohibentur; nec ista, vel cum jubentur, committenda. Porro inter haec sunt media quaedam, quae pro modo, loco tempore vel persona, et mala possunt esse, et bona: et in his lex posita est obedientiae." Idem, *De praecepto ed dispensatione*, V:11; IX:19 and 21. Hugh of Saint Victor, *de Sac.*, I:11, 7, "Tria sunt genera operum; quaedam ita bona sunt, ut nunquam licite praeteriri possint: quaedam autem ita mala, ut nunquam licite possint committi: quaedam autem media sunt." Idem, *De oboedientia quibus sit praestanda*, Miscellanea, I:185, PL 177, col. 581–582. Idem, *Institutiones in Decalogum*, 1, PL 176, col. 9–12. Gerhoh of Reichersberg, *De invest. AntiChristi*, 57. Peter Lombard, *Sententiae*, II, Dist., 3. Stanislas Giet, "Saint Bernard et le troisième degré d'obéissance ou la soumission du jugement," *L'année théologique*, 7 (1946), 192–221.

3. Saint Bernard, *De praecepto et dispensatione*. VI:12, "Nam perfecta oboedientia legam nescit, terminis non arctatur; . . . Haec iusti illius, cui lex posita non est, propria est; non quod vel ille perfectus vivere debeat sine lege sed quia non sit sub lege, minime quippe contentus voto suae cuiuscumque professionis, quam superat animi devotione."

115

tion of the individual's sanctity. He limits the obligation of obedience so that a man can conform as closely as possible with the dictates of God, but he shows also that he hopes the best men will be able to go beyond the acceptable to achieve something higher through the practice of humility, which he considered the chief virtue.

The ideas of Bernard were incorporated, by implication, into the passages of the *Tractatus de legibus* in the Decretum, when the Magister said that those human laws that contradicted divine law were to be considered null and void. Natural law commands us to obey the divine precepts.[4] Through this idea, Gratian implied that subjects of ecclesiastical hierarchy ought not to obey evil commands of their superiors and that they ought not to await an order to perform those things that God commanded himself. But the doctrine of obedience was much more fully developed in Causa 11 where the Magister dealt with an unjust sentence of excommunication. Quaestio 3 of this case concerned whether an unjust sentence of excommunication pronounced by a bishop ought to be obeyed.[5]

The circumstances created a problem concerning limits of obedience that was more difficult than the one created for Bernard by the actions of the renegade monk. A sentence is not the same as a command. Commands can be easily classified into the three categories established by Bernard, but sentences do not fit into these groups. The theory of obedience to sentences is much subtler than the theory of obedience to commands, and, likewise, the doctrines of ecclesiastical authority based on these theories of obedience differ significantly. When a prelate commands a subject to perform an action that is clearly against divine law, there is no difficulty showing that the prelate has overstepped the limits of his authority. Since an unjust sentence does not force members of

---

4. Dist. 9, dict. post c. 11, "Constitutiones ergo vel ecclesiasticae vel seculares, si naturali iuri contrariae probantur, penitus sunt excludendae." See also, Dist. 8, dict. post c. 1.

5. The quaestio ostensibly asks, "queritur, utrum sit deponendus qui offitium contra prohibitionem episcopi celebrare ausus est?" but Gratian immediately connects this issue with the question of whether an unjust command ought to be obeyed. He continues. "Sed quod sententia episcopi, sine iusta sive iniusta fuerit, timenda sit, Gregorious testatur." C. 11, q. 3, dict. ante c. 1.

the Church to do evil and also does not have a spiritual effect,[6] it does not hinder men's progress toward salvation or violate the basic purpose of the Ecclesia. The problem whether or not to obey a sentence is thus one of whether obedience is justified by the need to preserve the authority of the governing power and through that the stability of the community. The cause of justice must be weighed against the value of the community, which at times can act unjustly. Gratian looked at the problem of obedience with the stability of the community in mind, and the quaestio in which he developed his doctrine is one of the best organized parts of the whole work. By following the Magister's argument, the considerations on which he founded his theory of political obedience can be observed.

Gratian developed his doctrine by solving two related problems in the canonical tradition. The ancient texts were contradictory about whether an unjust sentence ought to be obeyed or ignored by the members of the Church. Gratian solved this contradiction in favor of disobedience and therefore created another difficulty. The Church Fathers had decreed in council that no sentence ought to be disobeyed until it was overturned by a higher court. If an unjust sentence ought to be disobeyed, how was this rule to be preserved?

The first question arose because of a text from the *Homilies* of Saint Gregory the Great. Gregory said, "The sentence of the pastor, whether it will have been just or unjust, ought to be feared." [7] From this passage and from a Pseudo-Isidorian Decretal attributed to Pope Urban I, Gratian concluded that all sentences of prelates ought to be humbly obeyed by ecclesiastical subjects.[8] Against this view, he then put twenty-

---

6. C. 11, q. 3, dict. post c. 64. See the studies of Russo and Landgraf cited in chap. iii, n. 26.

7. C. 11, q. 3, c. 1, "Sententia pastoris sive iusta sive iniusta fuerit, timenda est."

8. The Pseudo-Urban text is C. 11, q. 3, c. 27, "Quibus episcopi non communicant non communicetis, et quos eiecerint non recipiatis. Valde enim timenda est sententia episcopi, licet iniuste liget." This and other *capitula* lead to the conclusion that the sentence of the bishop ought to be obeyed until it is examined further in the courts. Gratian does not take up the problem of an unjust sentence which is upheld by the higher courts. He seems to assume that an injustice

117

four canons that expounded the opposite doctrine, and on the basis of these texts, he reinterpreted the passages from Gregory and Pseudo-Urban. They say, he argues, that the sentence of pastors ought to be feared, not obeyed.[9]

At this point in the discussion, Gratian introduces the conciliar decrees that set down that no one ought to presume to disobey a sentence of a prelate until a higher court has ruled. The Magister sets up the contradiction between his earlier doctrine and this provision in this way:

From these [cc. 44–64] it is understood that an unjust sentence binds no one before God, nor is anyone weighed down by an iniquitous sentence in the Church, just as is held from the *capitulum* of Gelasius. We ought not to abstain from communion with him who has been unjustly sentenced nor should he be expelled from office. Why then do the canons of Carthage and Africa, and of other councils, prohibit the unjustly damned to be received in communion before the examination of the judge? [10]

The reconciliation of these doctrines leads Gratian into a lengthy dis-

---

will be corrected when it is reviewed. See C. 11, q. 3, dict. post c. 40, cited in the next note.

9. C. 11, p. 3, dict. post c. 40, "Premissis auctoritatibus, quibus iniustae sententiae usque ad examinationem utriusque partis parere iubemur, ita respondetur: Gregorius non dicit sententiam iniuste latam esse servandam, sed timendam. Sic et Urbanus. Timenda ergo est, id est non ex superbia contempnenda. Reliquae vero auctoritates de excommunicatis locuntur, qui vel vocati ad sinodum venire contempserunt, vel calliditatibus adversantium occurrere nescientes iniustam sententiam a iudice reportaverunt, vel qui neglectu suae vitae sinistram de se opinionem nasci permittentes, sententiam in se exceperunt. Hos siquidem solos excommunicationis sententia ferire licet." C. 11, q. 3, dict. post c. 43, "De his, inquam, et huiusmodi premissae auctoritates locuntur, non de iniuste suspensis. Quod autem iniustae sententiae parendum non sit, multis auctoritatibus probatur." Capitula 44–64 support this contention.

10. C. 11, q. 3, dict. post c. 64, "Ex his datur intelligi, quod iniusta sententia nullum alligat apud Deum, nec apud ecclesiam eius aliquis gravatur iniqua sententia, sicut ex Gelasii capitulo habetur. Non ergo ab eius communione abstinendum est, nec ei ab offitio cessandum, in quem cognoscitur iniqua sententia prolata. Cur ergo capitula Cartaginensis et Affricani, atque aliorum conciliorum prohibent iniuste dampnatum in communione recipi ante iudicii examinationem." The capitulum from Gelasius is C. 11, q. 3, c. 46 and reads: "Cui est illata sententia deponat errorem, et vacua est; si iniusta est, tanta curare eam non debet, quanto apud Deum et eius ecclesiam neminem potest gravare iniqua sententia. Ita ergo ea se non absolui desideret, qua se nullatenus perspicit obligatum."

cussion concerning the ways in which a judgment can be unjust. He seeks to explain the decrees of the council fathers by showing that the justice or injustice of a sentence depends on legal technicalities that must be judged by competent jurisprudents. In the course of this discussion, he shows that he is vitally concerned about the state of the community.

There are three ways, according to the Magister, in which a sentence of excommunication may be unjust—*ex causa, ex animo,* and *ex ordine.* An injustice is committed *ex causa* when the condemned individual has not committed any crime worthy of the penalty given to him or when the individual is condemned for the wrong crime. An injustice is committed *ex animo* when the judge acts through hate or anger or for favor in condemning the criminal. Finally, an injustice is committed *ex ordine* when a sentence is passed without following the correct judicial procedure.[11] In each of these cases, Gratian advises Christians to obey the sentence humbly.[12] He bases his conclusion on the argument that the actual facts of the case are more important than its legal technicalities.

Thus, he says, those sentences that are unjust *ex ordine* or *ex animo,* but just *ex causa,* ought to be obeyed because the condemned man deserved the penalty anyway. Likewise, when a man is convicted of the

11. C. 11, q. 3, dict. post c. 65, "sententia aliquando est iniusta ex animo proferentis, iusta vero ex ordine et causa; aliquando est iusta ex animo et causa, sed non ex ordine; aliquando est iusta ex animo et ex ordine, sed non ex causa. Cum autem ex causa iniusta fuerit, aliquando nullum in eo omnino delictum est, quod sit dampnatione dignum: aliquando non est in eo illud, super quod fertur sententia, sed ex alio nominandus est. Ex animo est iniusta, cum aliquis servata integritate iudiciarii ordinis in adulterium vel in quemlibet criminosum non amore iustitiae, sed livore odii, vel precio, aut favore adversariorum inductus sententia profert." C. 11, q. 3, dict. post c. 73, "Item sententia est iniusta ex ordine, quando non servato iudiciali ordine quilibet pro culpa sua dampnatur."

12. C. 11, q. 3, dict. post c. 72, "Huic itaque sententiae, que non amore iustitiae, sed ex alia qualibet causa fertur in quemquam, humiliter obediendum est." C 11, q. 3, dict. post c. 77, "Cum ergo sententia ex ordine iniusta est, nec tunc ab ea recedendum est, quia etiam ante, quam sententia daretur in eum, pro qualitate sui reatus ligatus apud Deum tenebatur. Contingit aliquando, ut adulter sententiam pro sacrilegio reportet, cuius reatum in conscientia non habet. Hec sententia, etsi iniusta sit, quia non est in eo crimen, super quod lata est sententia, tamen ab eo iuste reportata est, qui ex reatu adulterii iamdiu Deum excommunicatus fuerat."

wrong crime, but deserves the same penalty for a crime that he did commit, the sentence ought to be obeyed because it is still deserved. Gratian is not saying that the criminal is automatically excommunicated by his act of sinning; a sentence of excommunication has been pronounced against him. But it is clear that the legitimacy of the sentence, and the obligation of Christians to obey it, is founded more on the guilt or innocence of the condemned than on the legal technicalities of how the sentence was passed. This view implies that the description of the legal technicalities to which Gratian has treated us was gratuitous; they were of no special importance in any case.

This conclusion is premature, however, because Gratian deals next with the obligation to obey a sentence brought against an individual who has committed no crime whatever, and in this part of the discussion, he reveals the purpose of his earlier speculations. The Magister strongly advises Christians to obey a sentence against a completely innocent person and to submit to the sentence if it is brought against themselves. The passage from Gregory the Great is cited again and is quoted more fully than earlier in the quaestio:

"Whether the pastor binds justly or unjustly, nevertheless the sentence of the pastor ought to be feared by the flock," [and] he added afterward: "Lest he who is subject and is by chance unjustly bound, should merit the sentence from another guilt. The pastor should therefore fear to absolve or bind indiscretely. Moreover he who is under the hand of the pastor should fear to be bound unjustly and should not contradict the judgment of his pastor by temerity: lest, even if he was bound unjustly, he should become guilty of pride from the temerity." [13]

13. C. 11, q. 3, dict. post c. 77, "§1. Iustam sententiam [Gregory] vocat, quando crimen subest, super quod fertur: iniustam, quando illud non subest, que tamen timenda vel servanda est, quia ex alio iam dudum dampnandus erat. Unde, cum premisisset Gregorius: 'Utrum iuste an iniuste obliget pastor, pastoris tamen sententia timenda est gregi,' subsecutus adiecit: 'Ne is, qui subest, et cum iniuste forsitan ligatur, ipsam obligationis suae sententiam ex alia culpa mereatur.' Pastor ergo vel absoluere indiscrete timeat, vel ligare. Is autem, qui sub manu pastoris est ligari timeat vel iniuste nec pastoris sui iudicium temere reprehendat: ne, etsi iniuste ligatus est, ex ipsa tumidae reprehensionis superbia culpa, que non erat, fiat." In C. 2, q. 7, Gratian expounded the doctrine that subjects can accuse their ecclesiastical superiors of abuse of power. Thus, he argues that subjects burdened by an unjust sentence can find redress according to canon law. Until the courts have overturned the bishop's sentence, however, the subjects

120

The same idea is confirmed in a later dictum:

Hence, even if, as was said, he should not be held bound before God, he ought to obey the sentence, lest he should be bound from pride when he was first held absolved from purity of conscience.[14]

This dictum ends Gratian's explanation of the attitude of the council fathers of the early Church toward disobedience. In effect, he has argued that since the nature of injustice is a matter of legal technicality, judgment of injustice ought to be carried out by trained judges. Yet, in discussing the last case, the Magister appears to expound a doctrine that makes the whole treatment of technical injustice superfluous. He wants Christians to follow the decree of the council fathers, even when the sentence in question is unjust in fact as well as in law. This doctrine is close to what Saint Bernard said about perfect obedience. For the sake of humility and for fear of its opposite, the Magister enjoins men to obey where there does not seem to be any need to obey. But though the doctrine of the two authors is the same, their reasons for the exposition of the doctrine are different. It can be seen how this is true by following the Magister's argument in the quaestio to its conclusion. There is one case in which Gratian does advise, or even demand, that men disobey their superiors.

He justifies disobedience to an unjust sentence of excommunication when the condemned man has been sentenced for refusing to perform an evil action on the command of his superior. The doctrine is summed up in the dictum post c. 101:

When, therefore, subjects are excommunicated because they are not able to be forced to [do] evil, then the sentence ought not to be obeyed because just as Gelasius said, "No one is weighed down by an iniquitous sentence before God or in His Church." [15]

---

must obey it. Gregory's statement applies to situations in which no court has acted to strike down the sentence.

14. C. 11, q. 3, dict. post c. 90, "Hec etsi, ut dictum est, non teneatur ligatus apud Deum, sententiae tamen parere debet, ne ex superbia ligetur qui prius ex puritate conscientiae absolutus tenebatur."

15. C. 11, q. 3, dict. post c. 101, "Cum ergo subditi excommunicantur, quia ad malum cogi non possunt, tunc sententia non est obediendum, quia iuxta illud Gelasii, 'Nec apud Deum, nec apud ecclesiam eius, quemquam gravat iniqua sententia.' " Gratian demonstrates that he agrees with Saint Bernard on the mat-

121

It is therefore only when the problem of obedience to a sentence involves that of obedience to a command that Gratian expounds a theory of obedience identical with Saint Bernard's. It is at this point that the community, represented by its prelate, violates its basic purpose by endangering the salvation of one of its members. The Magister agreed with Bernard, but it is clear that he was concerned with the ecclesiological implications of the obligation to obey while Bernard concentrated on the relationship between obedience and the state of the individual's soul. Gratian's theory is therefore more complex than Bernard's and demonstrates that the Magister had an appreciation for the important place held by the theory of obedience in the political theory of the ecclesiastical community.

The idea that underlies Gratian's doctrine of obedience is that the justice or injustice of a sentence is a secondary consideration in deciding whether or not to obey it. Much more important than considerations of justice are considerations of the stability and welfare of the ecclesiastical community. This idea is embodied in the Magister's theory that unjust sentences—*ex causa, ex ordine,* or *ex animo*—ought to be obeyed. In most cases, the Magister sustains the obligation of obedience because the condemned individual deserved the penalty anyway. The sentence, though technically unjust, has a just effect because it protects the community against an undesirable member. Also, Gratian makes it clear in several dicta that he wants to preserve the judicial structure and authority of the community. To permit individuals to act on their own authority would be to endorse the disintegration of the Church by depriving the regularly constituted authority of its power to judge. Even in the passages dealing with the ways in which sentences may be technically unjust, Gratian gives the impression that subjects ought to bear with the faults of those who hold power in order to preserve the power that they hold. He makes the same point more directly elsewhere in the *Causae,* when he says that sentences

---

ter of obedience to commands which contradict divine law in C. 11, q. 3, c. 99 (rubric), "Per obedientiam bonum deserere, numquam malum facere licet." This passage is also from Saint Gregory the Great. *Moralia in Job,* XXXV, c. 12. See C. 11, q. 3, dict. post c. 90, "§1 . . . quando subditi non possunt cogi ad malum, scientes obedientiam non esse servandam prelatis in rebus illicitis."

ought to be obeyed until overturned by a higher court, and when he condemns self-help by the subjects of the Church.[16]

The Magister also shows his concern for the stability of the Church community where he permits a Christian to withdraw his obedience. When a superior commands a subject to perform an evil act, the subject ought not to obey because he endangers his chance for sanctity and attainment of the kingdom of heaven. This idea shows that the highest concern of the Magister, as of Saint Bernard, is to ensure that no ecclesiological doctrine comes between the Christian and his ultimate purpose of achieving beatitude. In this doctrine, Gratian's scale of values becomes evident. The highest importance is attached to the ability of every individual in the Church to attain his goal as a Christian. But the primary vehicle for achieving this goal is the Church, and Gratian's next highest concern is to preserve that community. Only when the Church ceases to be the vehicle of individual sanctification does he counsel that Christians withdraw their obedience to the ecclesiastical authority. By that act of disobedience, the community ceases to exist, for it is obedience born of faith in its divine purpose and character which holds the Church together.

The recognition of the Magister's system of values makes understandable the import of his doctrine where the sentence of excommunication is not deserved at all. He argued that such sentences ought to be humbly obeyed lest the disobedient commit the sin of pride. It is the sin of pride, not the virtue of humility, which is at the center of Gratian's attention in this doctrine, and he is not, as Saint Bernard was, expounding a theory of perfect obedience. Rather, the importance that he attributes to the stability of the community makes him view almost any act contrary to the command of the governors as prideful. The

16. C. 22, q. 3, dict., "Cum ergo, ut ratione et exemplo monstratum est, episcopus reus periurii non esset, consueta obedientia ab archidiacono sibi denegari non debuit, cum etiamsi criminosum illum esse constaret, ante diffinitivam tamen sententiam, ut supra monstratum est, nulli suorum clericorum ab eo liceret discedere. Constat ergo illicitum esse quod archidiaconus iuramento firmavit [He swore that he would not obey his superior.]." C. 16, q. 6, dict. ante c. 1, "Quod autem quisquis sua auctoritate que sibi deberi putat usurpat, nec per iudicem resposcit, cadit a causa." C. 11, q. 3, dict. post c. 40 (n. 9 above). C. 11, q. 3, dict. post c. 64 (n. 10 above). C. 3, q. 1, dict. post c. 6.

Magister has come back to the doctrine expounded at the beginning of the quaestio—that sentences of pastors ought to be obeyed by their flock whether they are just or unjust—but now the import of that doctrine becomes clear. As long as the actions of ecclesiastical governors do not force members of the community to perform evil actions and thus to commit crimes that will condemn them to eternal punishment, then subjects ought to obey their superiors. Gratian agrees with Saint Bernard that commands contrary to divine law ought to be disobeyed. He would probably agree with Bernard that commands merely repetitious of divine law are unnecessary. But what Gratian shows is that the third class of commands—those which are morally indifferent— is larger and raises more complex problems than Bernard had thought. Gratian demonstrates that there is a distinction between divine justice and divine law. The ecclesiastical governor can violate the principles of the first without losing his authority, but he cannot transgress against the second. By focusing on the relationship between actions of human authority and justice, he emphasizes the scope and independence of human power. This is a one-sided view of his theory of governmental power. In his discussion of the sacrament of penitence, he showed that human authority was part of divine governance of the Universe. Approaching the problem of human authority from this point of view, he emphasized the connection between that authority and God.

The sacrament of penitence.

The subject of penitence received extensive treatment in the theological writings of the twelfth century. This was a period of transition in the theology of penitence, and, in fact, not until the middle of the century did writers begin to consider penitence a sacrament. Anciaux says that Peter Lombard is the first writer in whose work penitence definitely takes a place in the catalog of sacraments. But Peter recognized two penitences: an interior penitence, which is a virtue of the mind, and an exterior penitence, which is a sacrament.[17] It is obvious how difficult

17. P. Anciaux, *La Théologie du sacrement de pénitence au XIIe siècle* (Louvain, 1949), pp. 145, *passim.* Kuttner, "Zur Frage der theologischen Vorlagen Gratians," *ZRG,* Kan. Abt., 23 (1934), 246. In fact, Anciaux points out that peni-

it would be to clarify the meaning and conditions of successful penitence beginning from this double definition. During the twelfth
century, much of the discussion about the act of penitence centered on
the question of which penitence brought the remission of sins: interior
contrition or performance of the sacrament through confession and
the reception of a penitential penalty. Writers found biblical and
patristic passages to support both sides of the dispute. Gratian examined the arguments in Causa 33, quaestio 3, what is now the
Tractatus de penitentia in Friedberg's edition. The issue raised a very
difficult ecclesiological problem for the Magister.

The view that contrition alone would suffice for the remission of sins
was based on passages from the Book of Psalms and the Gospel of
Luke. Psalm 50 contains the verse, "A sacrifice to God is an afflicted
spirit: a contrite and humbled heart, O God, thou wilt not despise." [18]
And Psalm 31 reads, "I have acknowledged my sin to thee, and my injustice I have not concealed. I said I will confess against myself my
injustice to the Lord: and thou hast forgiven the wickedness of my
sin." The *Glossa Ordinaria* to this passage explained that God forgave
the sin in his great mercy on the promise of the sinner alone; for he
heard the contrition of the individual in his heart before it was confessed by his mouth.[19]

The passage from Luke held an even more important place in the
argument against the necessity of confession and penitential satisfaction than did the passages from the Psalms. Luke had reported that
Peter, after he had denied the Lord three times, had wept over his

---

tence had already been considered a sacrament in the school of Laon. Gratian,
too, indicates that he thought penitence was a sacrament. C. 1, q. 1, dict. post c.
42. See chap. vii, n. 14 for passages dealing with this matter.

18. C. 33, q. 3, Dist. 1 *de Pen.,* dict. ante c. 1, "Sunt enim qui dicunt, quemlibet criminis veniam sine confessione ecclesiae et sacerdotali iudicio posse promoveri." C. 33, q. 3, Dist. 1 *de Pen.,* c. 3, "Sacrificium Deo spiritus contribulatus; cor
contritum et humiliatum, Deus, non despicies" (Ps. 50:19).

19. C. 33, q. 3, Dist. 1 *de Pen.,* c. 4, "Dixi, confitebor adversum me iniusticiam
meam Domino, et tu remisisti inpietatem peccati mei." (Ps. 31:5). C. 33, q. 3,
Dist. 1 *de Pen.,* c. 5, "Magna pietas Dei, ut ad solam promissionem peccata dimi-
serit. §1. Nondum pronunciat ore, et tamen Deus iam audit in corde, quia ipsum
dicere quasi quoddam pronunciare est. Votum enim pro opere reputatur." Gratian attributes this passage to Saint Augustine.

betrayal and had been forgiven. About this chapter, Saint Ambrose said, "Peter was sad and cried because he had erred as a man. I do not find that he spoke; I know that he cried. I read of his tears, I do not read of satisfaction." This text supported by the similar explanation of Saint John Chrysostom, was the central pillar in the argument of those who said that contrition alone sufficed for the remission of sins.[20] The argument on this side of the question rests on the idea that God is the sole actor in the remission of sin.

The argument on the other side of the question is based on the idea that God acts through his sacerdotal agents in the remission of sin. This argument, too, is supported by texts from the Bible and patristic exegesis. In fact, the first capitulum in the long series that Gratian brings forth in favor of the necessity of confession and satisfaction is from Saint Ambrose's *Liber de Paradiso*. Ambrose says, "No one is able to be justified from sin unless he will have confessed beforehand." [21] And reading through the capitula supporting this view of the matter, it is clear that Ambrose holds the most important place in the patristic exegesis cited. The argument is based on passages from Isaiah, the first letter of John, and Ecclesiastes,[22] and Gratian sums it up in the dictum post c. 60.

20. Luke 22, *passim*. C. 33, q. 3, Dist. 1 *de Pen.*, c. 1, "Petrus doluit et flevit, quia erravit, ut homo. Non invenio quid dixerit; scio, quod fleverit. Lacrimas eius lego, satisfactionem non lego." C. 33, q. 3, Dist. 1 *de Pen.*, c. 2, "Lacrimae lavant delictum, quod voce pudor est confiteri." The argument continues in what is now dict. post c. 30 and dict. post c. 32. (Capitula 6–30 are paleae. See chap. i, p. 14). Gratian refers in these dicta to the passage from Ezechiel 33:12, "In quacumque hora peccator fuerit conversus, et ingemuerit, vita vivet, et non morietur." The Magister concludes the argument in dict. post c. 34, "Conversio autem dicitur quasi cordis undique versio. Si autem cor nostrum undique ad Deum a malo vertitur, mox conversionis suae fructum meretur, ut Deus ab ira ad misericordiam conversus peccati prestet indulgentiam, cuius primo preparabat vindictam. Unde datur intelligi, quod etiam ore tacente veniam consequi possumus." There follow several other biblical examples, such as the story of the cleansing of the lepers and the raising of Lazarus, which support this view further.

21. C. 33, q. 3, Dist. 1 *de Pen.*, c. 38, "Non potest quisquam iustificari a peccato, nisi fuerit peccatum ante confessus." Saint Ambrose, *Liber de Paradiso*, c. 14. Capitula 38, 39, 46–48, 50–56 are from Ambrose.

22. Isa. 43:26, "Dic tu iniquitates tuas, ut iustificeris." (C. 33, q. 3, Dist. 1 *de Pen.*, dict. post c. 37.) 1 John 5:16, "Est peccatum ad mortem: quis orabit pro eo?" (C. 33, q. 3, Dist. 1 *de Pen.*, dict. post c. 58). Eccles. 12:13, "Quis medebitur

From these [cc. 37–60] it appears that without confession of the mouth and satisfaction of work sin is not remitted. For if our iniquities are necessary, as we say, so that afterward we will be justified; if no one is able to be justified from sin unless he will have confessed sin; if confession opens paradise, [and] acquires forgiveness; if that confession alone is useful which is done with penitence . . . ; if he who promises pardon to the one doing penitence secretly before God and not before the Church frustrates the Gospel and the keys given to the Church, also promises to the delinquent what God denies; if no one is able to be granted pardon unless in some way, even if less than he ought, he pays the penalty of sin; if the power of binding and loosing was given to priests alone by God; if no one receives pardon unless he tries to seek it by supplications to the Church: it is concluded that no one abolishes the guilt of sin before confession of the mouth and satisfaction of work.[23]

He concludes the argument for the necessity of confession and satisfaction in the *dictum post* c. 87 in which he reinterprets the doctrine of the first part of the quaestio. The passages from Luke and the Psalms refer only to those who are like Saint Peter and mortify themselves for their sins. They can also refer to the way men receive pardon for secret sins for which only secret confession and satisfaction are necessary.[24] Clearly,

---

incantatori vulnerato a serpente?" (C. 33, q. 3, Dist. 1 de Pen., dict. post c. 58). Also, 1 Kings 2:25, "Si sacerdos peccaverit, quis orabit pro eo?" (C. 33, q. 3, Dist. 1 de Pen., c. 59). Many other texts come into consideration in the capitula.

23. C. 33, q. 3, Dist. 1 de Pen, dict. post 60, "Ex his itaque apparet, quod sine confessione oris et satisfactione operis peccatum non remittitur. Nam si iniquitates nostras necesse est, ut dicamus, ut postea iustificemur; si nemo potest iustificari a peccato, nisi antea fuerit confessus peccatum; si confessio paradysum aperit, veniam acquirit; si illa solum confessio utilis est, que fit cum penitencia . . . ; si ille, que promittit veniam occulte apud Deum non apud ecclesiam penitenciam agenti, frustrat evangelium et claves datas ecclesiae, promittit etiam quod Deus negat delinquenti; si nemo potest consequi veniam nisi quantulamcumque, etsi minorem quam debeat, peccati, soluerit penam; si solis sacerdotibus ligandi solvendique potestas a Deo tradita est; si nullus veniam accipit, nisi ecclesiae supplicationibus ipsam inpetrare contendat: concluditur ergo, quod nullus ante confessionem oris et satisfactionem operis peccati abolet culpam." There follow many biblical examples supporting this view.

24. C. 33, q. 3, Dist. 1 de Pen., dict. post c. 87, "premissae auctoritates, quibus videbatur probari, sola contritione cordis veniam prestari, aliter interpretandae sunt, quam ab eis exponantur. . . . Non ergo necessaria sibi erat certa satisfactio peccati, cuius totum vitae tempus obedientiae inpendebatur sui conditoris. . . . Non ergo illa auctoritate Leonis Papae satisfactio penitenciae negatur esse necessaria cuilibet delinquenti, sed ei tantum, qui B. Petrum imitatus huic seculo

many secret sins ought to be confessed to the priest, but Gratian means those that are secret or have already been confessed once to the priest may be forgiven by God through contrition alone.

Thus, Gratian appears to solve the issue of the quaestio in favor of the necessity of confession, but in the next dictum, he shows that in his mind, he has not decided the issue definitively. He leaves the decision concerning whether contrition suffices to the reader's discretion:

> We have proposed [shown] briefly by what authorities and reasoning each sentence of [each opinion concerning] confession and satisfaction is supported. To which of these one ought to adhere is reserved for the judgment of the reader. Each has wise and religious men for supporters.[25]

This passage has of course raised many questions in the minds of scholars. Why did the Magister leave the issue to the judgment of the reader after he had apparently decided the matter? Scholars have tried to reconcile the discrepancy between the dictum and the rest of the quaestio for over sixty years. Vacandard argued that Gratian left the question open because he favored the argument of the earlier capitula denying the necessity of confession. The Magister could not disregard the strong arguments that were contained in capitula 37 to 87, so he

---

penitus abrenunciat, et cunctorum viciorum fomitem in se funditus mortificat . . . [the texts] non ita intelligendum est, ut sine confessione oris peccata dicantur dimitti, sed sine publica satisfactione. Secreta namque peccata secreta confessione et occulta satisfactione purgantur, nec est necesse, ut que semel sacerdoti confessi fuerimus denuo confiteamur, sed lingua cordis, non carnis apud iudicem verum ea iugiter confiteri debemus."

25. C. 33, q. 3, Dist. 1 de Pen., dict. post 89, "Quibus auctoritatibus, vel quibus rationum firmamentis utraque sentencia confessionis et satisfactionis nitatur, in medium breviter proposuimus. Cui autem harum potius adherendum sit lectoris iudicio reservatur. Utraque enim fautores habet sapientes et religiosos viros." This passage presents another example of Gratian's use of loose and problematic language. The dispute in the quaestio juxtaposes the argument that contrition of the heart satisfies God for the remission of sins and the argument that only through confession can that satisfaction be gained, Here, Gratian is clearly referring to the dispute, but he uses the words *confessio* and *satisfactio* to designate the two sides. In the word *satisfactio* is contained the whole idea that God may be satisfied through contrition alone. Thus, though the language of the dictum is anything but clear, the traditional interpretation, which I have accepted, is correct; Gratian refers here to the dispute he appeared to solve in favor of the necessity of confession in dict. post c. 87. I owe this reading of the passage to a suggestion from Professor Brian Tierney.

left the question undecided. Vacandard therefore concluded that Gratian was not in agreement with most of the writers of his time who supported the necessity of confession, and he suggested that Gratian incorporated the long series of texts supporting this idea in the quaestio because he was concerned to set down all the views of his time.[26]

The French scholars Hugueny and Debil challenged Vacandard's interpretation. They pointed out that it is unclear what issue Gratian left undecided at the end of the quaestio, and they argued that the Magister was indecisive only about whether remission of sins followed or preceded confession to the priest. There was no question that confession was necessary. According to these scholars, therefore, the issue about which Gratian was undecided was only a theological question that did not directly interest him. Both concluded that the Magister favored the view that demanded confession and penitential satisfaction.

26. E. Vacandard, "Confession du Ie au XIIIe siècle," *DTC*, 3 (1911), 838–894. J. Turmel, *Histoire de la Théologie positive* (Paris, 1904), p. 455 n. 4. Andrée Teetaert, *La Confession aux laiques* (Paris, 1926), pp. 198–207. Anciaux, *op. cit.*, pp. 108–111, agrees with Vacandard's interpretation. The theologians solved the problem raised by penitence by showing that sin binds the sinner in two ways and must therefore be remitted in two ways. See, for example, *Duplex est peccati vinculum* (Clm 17100 6^{r-v}), ed. Ludwig Hödl, *Die Geschichte der scholastischen Literatur und der Theologie der Schlüsselgewalt* (Münster, 1960), pp. 48–49, "Duplex est peccati vinculum. . . . Sunt ergo interiores obdurationis, exteriores perpetuae damnationis. . . . Nota prudenter divini operis administrationem: praecedente opere Dei apte ministerium hominis subsequitur: vinculum obdurationis dissolvere opus Dei est, debitum damnationis praevenire correctione hominis est ministerium. . . . Solvitur a Domino a culpa solvitur a poena, cum opere ministrorum corporalis poenitentiae remedio animae languenti subvenitur." See *Vae vobis pharisaeis,* ed. Hödl, *op. cit.,* p. 51, "in scripturis sanctis inveniatur: sacerdotes peccata remittunt, sic intelligendum est, quod per eorum ministerium remittit Deus. Determinanda sunt eodem modo verba Domini 'Quaecumque remiseritis remissa sunt, 'id est quaecumque peccata Deus remiserit nobis per ministerium cooperantibus, non imputabit nec puniet ea in aeternum." These *sententiae* stem from the school of Saint Victor. See also *Summa Sententiarum,* VI, 11, PL 176, col. 147. Hugh of Saint Victor, *de Sac.,* II:14, 8. Peter Abelard recognized the necessity of three conditions for the remission of sins: contrition, confession, and satisfaction. He valued the first most highly, however. Contrition was true penitence. Peter Abelard, *Ethica,* cc. 17, 19. See, the Laon *sententia, Auctoritate sanctorum patrum,* ed. Hödl, *op. cit.,* p. 22, "ita baptizati pro suis criminibus a corpore ecclesiae separati non sunt reconcilianda nisi digne poenitentes."

129

Hugueny added that Gratian was nonetheless embarrassed by the lack of any definitive solution of the knotty theological problem.[27]

The argument of Hugueny and Debil is basically correct, but it does not get to the hub of Gratian's doctrine in the quaestio. Neither scholar answers the question why Gratian supported the necessity of confession when he could not decide whether remission of sins followed or preceded that confession. On the surface at least, these two questions are closely connected, and the views of these writers do not explain why the Magister considered them separate.

The answer to this question is to be found in the reasoning behind Gratian's support of the necessity for confession. The issue raised by the dispute over penitence concerned the power of the hierarchy on earth. The Magister was interested in the problems of defining the power and the position of ecclesiastical authority. This was exhibited in his discussion of the theory of obedience, and it is now seen in his reasoning on the need for maintaining the Christian's obligation to confess his sins. In the *dictum post* c. 60, which was quoted above, he says that those who do not do penitence before the Church frustrate the power of the keys given to the Church by God. In the final dictum of the argument, he makes the same point more succinctly:

How . . . is it to be believed that the right of binding and loosing was given to priests alone by the Lord, if anyone, by his own decision, binds himself by sinning or gives himself the sentence of excommunication [and] by secret penitence, after satisfaction, reconciles himself to God and His altar without the judgment of the priest.[28]

27. Étienne Hugueny, "Gratien et la confession," *Revue des sciences philosophiques et théologiques*, 6 (1912), 81–88. A. Debil, "La première distinction du 'de paenitentia' de Gratian," *RHE*, 15 (1914), 251–273, 442–455. E. H. Fischer, "Bussgewalt, Pfarrzwang und Beichtvater-Wahl nach dem Dekret Gratians," *SG*, 4 (1956–1957), 185–230.

28. C. 33, q. 3, Dist. 1 *de Pen* dict. post c. 87, "§11. Quomodo . . . ius ligandi et solvendi solis sacerdotibus a Domino creditur esse permissum, si quisque suo arbitrio se ipsum peccando ligat, vel secreta penitencia, . . . in se ipsum sentenciam profert excommunicationis, atque post satisfactionem absque sacerdotali iudicio se ipsum Deo vel altario eius reconciliat?" Gratian's contemporaries also connected the power of the keys with remission of sins. From the school of Anselm of Laon, *Liber VII partium*, V:2, ed. Hödl, *op. cit.*, p. 16. The Victorine *sententia Vae vobis pharisaeis*, ed. Hödl, *op. cit.*, p. 50, "Videtur praeterea aliam clavem [clavis potestatis] id est potestam [*sic*] ligandi atque solvendi." Reading

In these dicta, the Magister again shows himself to be primarily concerned about the stability of the community and, in this case, about the power of its governing authority. If no confession was necessary for the remission of sins, then the power of the hierarchy would have no value and the Church could not be seen as necessary for the salvation of men. Gratian saw that to support the view first expounded in the quaestio would be to deny the most basic premises of Christian ecclesiology. There was no doubt in his mind that the obligation of confessing one's sins had to be preserved.

Hugueny and Debil were correct in arguing that Gratian left undecided the theological question of the necessity for confession. The argument for the sufficiency of contrition was too strong to be simply discarded. But leaving this question open did not change the Magister's certainty about the ecclesiological necessity for confession. He made a distinction between these two levels in the discussion, though he recognized there was a connection between them.

The problem can be seen clearly by comparing Gratian's doctrine with the ideas of Peter Lombard, who based his discussion of confession and contrition on the Decretum.[29] The Master of the Sentences expounded the argument for confession much more clearly than the great Bolognese canonist. Confession is necessary, Peter said, "because, even if one should be absolved before God, he is not nevertheless held to be absolved in the face of the Church [*in facie Ecclesiae*] unless through the judgment of the priest." [30] Confession and reception of a

---

through the texts cited by Hödl gives one a sense of the commonness of this view.

29. It is clear from comparison of the texts of Peter's *Sententiae* and the Decretum that the Master of the Sentences used Gratian's work. Paul Fournier, "Deux controverses sur l'origine du Décret de Gratien," *Revue d'histoire et de litterature religieuse*, 3 (1898), 97–116. Vacandard, *op. cit.*, p. 882. Anciaux, *op. cit.*, pp. 110, 228–229. Joseph de Ghellinck, *Le mouvement théologique*, pp. 203–213, 456–460.

30. Peter Lombard, *Sententiae*, IV, *Dist.* 18, c. 6, "quia, etsi aliquis apud Deum sit solutus, non tamen in facie Ecclesiae solutus habetur nisi per sacerdotis iudicium." *Summa Sent.*, VI:11, PL 176, col. 148, "Duobus enim peccator ligatus est: caecitate mentis, videlicet et pro ea debito futurae damnationis; peccato enim et poena peccati tenetur. Per veram cordis contritionem solvitur a caecitate mentis; qui enim mortuus fuerat jam vivit, et quia vivit interius illuminatus est; sed tamen adhuc debito est donec satisfaciat Ecclesiae."

penitential punishment are necessary for the existence of the Church, notwithstanding the relationship between confession and the interior cleansing wrought by God.

Peter conceded the force of the argument against the necessity for confession and based the obligation to confess on ecclesiological grounds. He therefore made a radical distinction between the earthly and heavenly spheres of the Church and satisfied both sides of the dispute. Gratian based his argument on the same distinction, but he refrained from arguing that the two parts of the Ecclesia required different conditions for absolution. He did not fail to see that his argument tended to that conclusion, but he saw that the solution Peter Lombard adopted two decades later would violate the assumptions of Christian ecclesiology. By distinguishing so sharply between heaven and earth, one would only arrive at the conclusion that ecclesiastical authority does not participate in the work of salvation. The whole value of the *potestas clavium* consisted in its being the vehicle for such participation. Thus, Gratian left the basic theological issue to the reader's discretion.

Contradictory ideas determined the character of Gratian's ecclesiology. He definitely made the distinction between the two spheres of the Church, and it helped him to clarify many constitutional issues and to propose solutions satisfactory for the conditions of an earthly community. His theories of membership and the obligation of obedience as well as the need for confession are examples of how the distinction could aid him. But he could not stress the idea of distinction so strongly that it would destroy the bond between the two spheres of the Church and between earthly and divine powers. This bond was the essence of the power of the keys and was a basic part of the Christian's idea of how and why the Church was founded. It had to remain intact, therefore, no matter what sort of trouble it caused for the development of ecclesiological doctrines. In subsequent chapters, the difficulties caused by this article of faith will be met several times, but the next chapter concentrates on a concern limited to the earthly Church—the relationship between ecclesiastical authority and human law.

VI. Human Authority and Its Own Law: The Theory of Legislative Power

The relationship between human authority and the law of the community depends on the theory of legislative power, and Gratian expounded a theory of legislative power according to which the governors of the Church held virtually absolute sovereignty over the laws. The famous Roman law maxim, "Princeps legibus solutus est" (The prince is loosed from the laws) could be applied to the pope. But just as the Roman lawyers did not take the phrase literally when discussing the relationship between the emperor and the laws of his community,[1]

1. Brian Tierney, " 'The Prince Is Not Bound by the Laws.' Accursius and the Origins of the Modern State," *Comparative Studies in Society and History,* 5 (1962–1963), 378–400. There have been two major problems in the scholarship concerning the medieval theory of legislative power. First, there has been acceptance of the view that medieval legal theory did not recognize any right of the ruler to make law. Law was found in the ancient customs of the community —which were assumed to be immemorial; it was never created out of whole cloth. Second, it was generally accepted that the Roman law tradition was absolutist, or, in modern terms, Austinian. The maxim, "Princeps legibus solutus est," was one of the most important pieces of evidence in this interpretation.

The best known proponents of the view that the medieval rulers did not have the right to make law were: Fritz Kern, *Kingship and Law* (Oxford, 1939); Charles H. McIlwain, *The High Court of Parliament* (New Haven, 1910); Idem, *Constitutionalism. Ancient and Modern* (Ithaca, 1940); Idem, *The Growth of Political Thought in the West* (New York, 1932). The argument that medieval legal theory did not recognize the right of the ruler to legislate led to a revision of the interpretation of the early history of the English Parliament. McIlwain (*High Court*) argued that Parliaments in the thirteenth and fourteenth centuries were only judicial assemblies and did not pass laws. His view was based on some observations that Maitland had made relative to the Parliament of 1305. Maitland

so Gratian restricted the import of his ecclesiastical legislative theory. On the one hand, he followed the ancient patristic tradition that balanced the exercise of *potestas* with the considerations of *caritas*. As the Magister said in Dist. 45, "In prelates there ought not to be found the leniency of mercy without the rectitude of severity or the zeal of rectitude without mercy." [2] On the other hand, the Magister limited the legislative power of the ecclesiastical ruler by arguing that he was to obey the laws except when he engaged in the specific act of law-making. The lawmaking power placed the governor in a sovereign position relative to the law, but legislating was only one of the functions performed by him.

Gratian set forth the distinction between the governor as judge and as legislator in the *Tractatus de legibus,* but as was the case with the theories of obedience and penitence, the Magister did not treat the

---

noted that most of the business done at the session was accomplished after the commons was sent home and that it was of a judicial nature. Frederick W. Maitland, "Introduction to *Memoranda de Parliamento, 1305,*" *Selected Historical Essays of F. W. Maitland,* ed. Helen M. Cam (Cambridge, 1957), pp. 52–96. George O. Sayles, *The Mediaeval Foundations of England* (Cambridge, 1950). Sayles and H. G. Richardson, *The Mediaeval Governance of England* (London, 1963).

It is now generally accepted that medieval rulers did legislate and were permitted to do so by the constitutional theories of their times. Sten Gagner, *Studien zur Ideengeschichte der Gesetzgebung* (Upsala, 1960). T. F. T. Plucknett, *The Legislation of Edward I* (Cambridge, 1949). J. W. Gough, *Fundamental Law in English Constitutional History* (Oxford, 1953). Gavin Langmuir, " 'Judei Nostri' and the Beginning of Capetian Legislation," *Traditio,* 16 (1960), 203–239. Tierney, *op. cit.,* pp. 378–382.

The interpretation of the Roman law tradition as absolutist was put forth by A. Esmein, "La maxime Princeps legibus solutus est dans l'ancien droit public français," *Essays in Legal History,* ed. P. Vinogradoff (Oxford, 1913), pp. 201–214. A. J. and R. W. Carlyle, *A History of Mediaeval Political Theory in the West,* II:75. McIlwain, *Growth* p. 383. Tierney, *op. cit.,* p. 380, *passim.* As Tierney points out, McIlwain, "reconsidering the whole question at a time when events in contemporary Germany had produced a general scepticism about theories of innate Teutonic virtue . . . strongly emphasized the contribution of Roman law to the growth of Western constitutionalism." McIlwain, *Constitutionalism,* pp. 43–68.

2. Dist. 45, dict. post c. 13, "Ex his omnibus apparet, quod nec lenitas mansuetudinis sine rectitudine severitatis, nec zelus rectitudinis sine mansuetudine in prelatis debet inveniri." Ludwig Buisson, *Potestas und Caritas* (Cologne-Graz, 1958), pp. 17–73.

theory of legislative power only in the *de legibus*. In Causa 25, he expounded the same ideas as he did earlier, but his perspective changed. In the *de legibus,* he was primarily interested in the law, while in Causa 25, he focused attention on the power of the hierarchy. This shift of interest results in a shift of emphasis which alters the relationship between the governor and the law by giving a different view of the balance between power over law and the necessity of obeying it. Each of these sections of the Decretum will be treated in turn.

The theory of legislative power is interesting not only because it is part of Gratian's constitutional law but also because it is one of the most striking doctrines set forth in the Decretum. The Magister's method in expounding it is peculiar and it possesses a special historical significance. In the third section of this chapter, this significance will be explained.

The Tractatus de legibus

In the *de legibus,* Gratian was primarily concerned with the law and its characteristics, and he considered the problem of lawmaking in order to show how that power affected the authority and stability of the law. By setting the authoritativeness of law against the power of the ecclesiastical hierarchy to change and make law, the Magister exposed with great clarity the central difficulty in the theory of legislative power. It is the paradox that law possesses an authority that makes it superior to the governor, while it is subject to the power of the governor who can abrogate it or change it.[3] The problem is stated early in the *Tractatus* and then examined in more detail in its second to last *Distinctio.*

In Dist. 4, Gratian examined the qualities that laws ought to possess. They ought to be constituted in accordance with justice, practicality, and convenience, because once made, law becomes the standard of judgment. The law is created by the governor, but it becomes a

---

3. Thus, Gratian introduced a tension into his governmental theory. It is the tension between the ruler's sovereign power to make law and the idea that he has to be bound by the laws. It is a tension, as Tierney has said, found in the constitutions of all nonabsolutist political societies. Tierney, *op. cit.,* p. 382.

principle according to which he rules once it is established: "in the constitution [of laws] these things [justice, practicality, and convenience] ought to be considered because when the laws will have been instituted, one will not be free to judge concerning them, but it is necessary to judge according to them." [4] In this passage, it is clear that the ecclesiastical governor possesses legislative power, but it is also clear that this power is limited specifically to the act of legislating. The governor is not simply superior to the law; so that whatever he does is law.

The discussion in Dist. 4 raises a difficulty for the theory of the relationship between the governor and the law by setting his legislative power against his other functions. Gratian recognizes that the different functions of the hierarchy imply different conclusions concerning the hierarchy's power over the law. Furthermore, he cannot separate the discussions of ecclesiastical power as legislator and as judge since all functions of government are exercised by the same offices. In the dictum of Dist. 4, the Magister exposes the distinction between the judge and lawmaker and explains, rather tersely, the position of each relative to the law. Later in the Decretum, he recognizes that in effect the judge who interprets the law makes law and that therefore only he who has the power to make law can act as judge.[5] This statement not only is an explicit recognition of what had been implied in Dist. 4—that judge and legislator are the same person—but also complicates the doctrine contained in the earlier passage. The judge, it is now recognized, must have power over the law in order to be justified, as was said earlier, to be under law. Deciding cases requires the governor to judge concerning and according to the law at the same time. Which aspect of the judge's position is more important, his power over the

4. Dist. 4, dict. post c. 1, "Preterea in ipsa constitutione legum maxime qualitas constituendarum est observanda, ut contineant in se honestatem, iustitiam, possibilitatem, convenientiam et cetera." Dist. 4, dict. post c. 2, "Ideo autem in ipsa constitutione ista consideranda sunt, quia cum leges institutae fuerunt, non erit liberum iudicare de ipsis, sed oportet iudicare secundum ipsas." Gagner, *op. cit., passim.* Gagner considers the Decretum at several points in his work. He is primarily interested in the ideas expressed in these early *Distinctiones* and in the capitula. Like other scholars who have treated the Decretum, Gagner studies the work as the source of later doctrines.

5. C. 25, q. 1, dict. post c. 16, n. 21 below.

law or the necessity that he respect the law? This problem will be further examined in the section on Causa 25.

The problem raised by the passage of Dist. 4 is not the only one raised in the *de legibus* concerning legislative power. There is also the question, related of course to the first problem, of how the governor, acting as a legislator, is bound by the laws of preceding holders of his office. This question is brought to the fore in Dist. 19, which follows a discussion in which Gratian has shown that, with some unimportant reservations, all legislative power in the Church is held by the pope. Even the legal authority of the so-called "canons of the Apostles" and of the canons promulgated by the eight councils of the ancient Church derives from the approval of them by Pope Hadrian I.[6] Furthermore, the pope is the only one who has the authority to summon councils and only those councils that he summons are capable of establishing law for the ecclesiastical community.[7] In contrast, episcopal councils have no power to make general law, though they have the right to correct delinquents and to make provision for local circumstances.[8]

6. Dist. 16, dict. ante c. 1, "Apostolorum canones, qui per Clementem Romanum Pontificem, sicut quidam asserunt, dicuntur esse translati, sunt quinquagenta. Hos non recipiendos, sed inter apocrifa deputatos, Ysidorus scribit dicens." But see Dist. 16, dict. post c. 4, "Item cum Adrianus Papa sextam sinodum recipiat cum omnibus canonibus suis, cum etiam sancta octo universalia concilia professione Romani Pontificis sint roborata, in septima autem sinodo, sive in sexto concilio, apostolorum canones sint recepti et approbati: patet, quod non sunt inter apocrifa deputandi." Dist. 16, c. 8 (rubric), "Auctoritate Romani Pontificis sancta octo concilia roborantur."

7. Dist. 17, dict. ante c. 1, "Auctoritas vero congregandorum conciliorum penes apostolicam sedem est." This doctrine is supported by the example of the council called by Emperor Theodoric to judge the accusations brought against Pope Simachus. Dist. 17, dict. post c. 6, "Hinc etiam cum auctoritas Teodorici regis ex diversis provinciis ad urbem Romam sacerdotes convenire precepisset, ut sanctum concilium iudicaret de his, que venerabili Papae Simacho, presuli apostolicae sedis, ab adversariis ipsius dicebantur impingi, Liguriae Emiliae episcopi, seu Venetiarum suggesserunt, ipsum, qui dicebatur impetitus, debere sinodum convocare: scientes, quia eius sedi primum Petri apostoli meritum, deinde secuta iussione Domini conciliorum venerandorum auctoritas singularem in ecclesiis tradidit potestatem, nec antedictae sedis antistitem minorum subiacuisse iudicio."

8. Dist. 18, dict. ante c. 1, "Episcoporum igitur concilia, ut ex premissis apparet, sunt invalida ad diffiniendum et constituendum, non autem ad corrigendum. Sunt enim necessaria episcoporum concilia ad exortationem et correctionem, que etsi

The pope need not act in council to make valid and authoritative law. In fact, he does not even have to act officially or formally in order to lay down new precepts. In Dist. 19, Gratian argued that decretal letters possess the force of law even if they are not incorporated into the corpus of canon law.[9] The word of the pope needs no corroboration by councils nor any formal statement and procedure to make it a part of the law. This great power gives rise to problems, however, because the pope, without the aid of others, may establish laws that are unjust, impractical, or inconvenient. The Magister therefore added that decretals ought to be obeyed, "in which nothing is found contrary to the decrees of the preceding Fathers or to the evangelical precepts." He has in mind the case of Pope Anastasius II, who acted against the law of the Church and the decrees of God, and who was repudiated by the Church and God for his action.[10]

Anastasius had decreed that those priests ordained by Acatius after he was convicted of heresy and excommunicated should retain their orders and be able to exercise their offices. This decree contradicted the earlier decretal of Pope Gelasius who had commanded that these priests be deprived of their positions in the Church. Gratian explains:

Because therefore he [Anastasius] gave these orders illicitly and not canonically, but against the decrees of God and of his predecessors and successors (as prove Felix and Gelasius, who had excommunicated Acatius before Anastasius, and Hormisdas who was the third pope after him and who damned Acatius afterward), he was repudiated by the Roman Church and it is read that he was struck down by God.[11]

---

non habet vim constituendi, habent tamen auctoritatem imponendi et indicendi, quod alias statutem est et generaliter seu specialiter observari preceptum."

9. Dist. 19, dict. ante c. 1, "De epistolis vero decretalibus queritur, an vim auctoritatis obtineant, cum in corpore canonum non inveniantur." Dist. 19, c. 1 (rubric), "Decretales epistolae vim auctoritatis habent."

10. Dist. 19, dict. post c. 7, "Hoc autem intelligendum est de illis sanctionibus vel decretalibus epistolis, in quibus nec precedentium Patrum decretis, nec evangelicis preceptis aliquid contrarium invenitur. Anastasius enim secundus favore Anastasii imperatoris, quos Acatius post sententiam in se prolatam sacerdotes vel Levitas ordinaverat, acceptis offitiis rite fungi debere decrevit."

11. Dist. 19, dict. post c. 8, "Quia ergo illicite et non canonice, sed contra decreta Dei, predecessorum et successorum suorum hec rescripta dedit (ut probat Felix et Gelasius, qui Acatium ante Anastasium excommunicaverunt, et Hormisda, qui ab ipso Anastasio tertius eundem Acatium postea dampnavit), ideo ab

This passage leaves us in doubt about the relationship between the legislator and the decrees of others who have held or will hold his office. Clearly, it was illicit and uncanonical for Anastasius to contradict the decrees of God, but was it the same for him to contradict the commands of his predecessors and successors? I can suggest an answer to this question by analyzing the language of the dictum.

Two actions were taken against the errant pope. One was his immediate downfall caused by the withdrawal of obedience from him by his clergy. This was interpreted as being the action of God against him.[12] The other was his repudiation by the Church through the action of Hormisdas, and the general disapproval of his decree. But both the divine and the human actions were taken because Anastasius had handed down an illicit and uncanonical decree that was against the decree of God. The relationship of the unfortunate pope's decree to the decrees of his predecessors was not so important. Gratian indicated that the legality of Anastasius's decree was not affected by its opposition to the decrees of other popes. His reference to the actions of Anastasius's successors as well as his predecessors affirms this interpretation. He pointed out that the Church governors, both before and after Anastasius, had judged the matter correctly—that is to say, in accordance with divine law. He did not want to argue that because Anastasius contradicted the earlier popes he acted criminally, but that his action stood out as the more heinous because of the example of his predecessors. If the Magister had sought to make the point that a decree that contra-

---

ecclesia Romana repudiatur, et a Deo percussus fuisse legitur." This dictum and the capitulum following it were borrowed by Gratian, word for word, from Alger of Liège, *Liber de misericordia et iustitia,* III:59.

12. Dist. 19, c. 9, "Anastasius II, natione Romanus, fuit temporibus Teoderici regis. Eodem tempore multi clerici se a communione ipsius abegerunt, eo quod communicasset sine concilio episcoporum vel presbiterorum et clericorum cunctae ecclesiae catholicae diacono Tessalonicensi, nomine Fotino, qui communicaverat Acatio; et quia occulte voluit revocare Acatium, et non potuit, nutu divino percussus est." The idea that Anastasius acted without the counsel of his clergy and fellow bishops and that failure to do so was part of his crime has the potential of being an important notion in the theory of papal legislative action. One might conclude that the pope cannot act without the aid and counsel of his subordinates in the Church. Gratian did not pick up this idea, however, as is shown by the doctrine developed in the *Distinctio.*

dicts earlier ecclesiastical law should be considered illicit and un-canonical, it is hard to imagine why he referred to Hormisdas's action as well as the actions of Felix and Gelasius. Notwithstanding the mention of the decrees of the preceding Fathers in the dictum quoted above, Gratian does not appear to have been interested in the conflict between Anastasius's action and that of Gelasius and Felix, when he discussed the case. He did not mean to use the example of Anastasius to show that the scope of the pope's power to legislate contracted through the ages as more and more law was made. He wanted rather to confirm the doctrine expounded earlier in the *de legibus* that no human law may contradict divine law.[13] The decrees of the Fathers are to be received as examples of good legislation, not as law that limits the later use of legislative authority in the Church.

Even though the pope normally ought to respect the law of his predecessors and Anastasius's action was understood to be evil because he replaced good law with bad law, Gratian did not hesitate to admit that sometimes the ancient law needed to be revised or replaced. In a dictum of Dist. 63, he expressed this recognition very clearly.

—this great authority ought to be held [to be] in the Church: that if among the several things which were done by our predecessors and an-cestors there are some which were able to be [done] without guilt, and afterward turned into error and superstition, then without hesitation and with great authority, they ought to be destroyed by those who come later.[14]

Thus, Anastasius's successor, Hormisdas, was able to repeal his decree with impunity because it was evil and did not deserve obedience.

13. Dist. 9, dict. post c. 11.

14. Dist. 63, dict. post c. 28, "Ac per hoc magna auctoritas ista habenda est in ecclesia, ut, si nonnulli ex predecessoribus et maioribus nostris fecerunt aliqua, que illo tempore potuerunt esse sine culpa, et postea vertuntur in errorem et superstitionem, sine tarditate aliqua et cum magna auctoritate a posteris des-truantur."

Saint Bernard divided laws into three types, *stabile, inviolabile,* and *incom-mutable.* Stable laws were those that the authority of the Church established and therefore had a right to change. Such laws are neither *naturaliter* nor per se good. Inviolable laws are those made by divine power, and these may not be changed at all unless by God Himself. The Ten Commandments are examples of these laws. Incommutable laws are those that God himself cannot change or grant dispensations from. The virtues such as humility, mercy, and love are examples of such precepts. Bernard, *de praecepto et dispensatione,* II:4–5; III:6–8.

The theory of legislative power which emerges from the *Tractatus de legibus* emphasizes the limitations on that power. In Dist. 4 and 19, Gratian opposes the power to make and change the law to the authority of existing law and of divine law. But Gratian did not approach legislative theory directly in the *Distinctiones,* and he therefore did not define the power to make law very clearly. The Magister's concentration on the hierarchy and the character of the laws made him treat lawmaking power as if it was a specific, relatively rare use of power. At the center is the normal authoritativeness of the law, and the obedience due to it. In Causa 25, he took up the pope's lawmaking power *ex professo* and completed his doctrine by discussing the power of the pope to change the law, and the reasons why he ought to obey the law.

Causa 25

Causa 25 involves a conflict of papal privileges granted to a baptismal church and to a monastery in its locale. To the church, the Roman see conceded all the tithes paid by its parish, and to the monastery, it gave exemption from paying tithes. Two questions are raised by the dispute between the church and the monastery. The first one concerns only the privilege granted to the baptismal church. Gratian asked: Can the pope grant all the tithes of a parish to the church when the decrees of the Fathers say that the tax should be divided into four portions assigned to the bishop, the building fund, the poor, and the church in question? [15] This question involved the Magister in the issue that he

15. C. 25, dict. principium, "Sancta Romana ecclesia quandam baptismalem ecclesiam suis munivit privilegiis, decimationes suae diocesis ex integro sibi attribuens. Item quoddam monasterium similiter munivit privilegiis propriis, decernens, ut ex propriis prediis nulli decimas persolveret. Accidit itaque, ut intra diocesim premunitae baptismalis ecclesiae prefatum monasterium alia emptione, alia donatione predia sibi inveniret. Oritur itaque contentio inter monachos et clericos de decimis. Nunc primum queritur, an clerici baptismalis ecclesiae auctoritate privilegii decimas suae diocesis ex integro sibi valeant vendicare?" C. 25, q. 1, dict. ante c. 1, "Quod vero auctoritate illius privilegii decimas sibi ex integro clerici vendicare non valeant, hinc probatur, quia decimae iuxta decreta sanctorum Patrum quadripertito dividuntur, quarum una pars episcopis, secunda clericis, tercia fabricis restaurandis, quarta vero pauperibus est assignata."

141

seemed to treat in Dist. 19—the relationship between papal legislative power and decrees of preceding popes. The issue was raised because he considered granting of privileges to be an exercise of legislative instead of executive power. The privilege is seen as a private law, according to the etymology of its name.[16]

The second question refers more directly to the case. Gratian seeks to determine whether a later privilege abrogates an earlier one.[17] Since the granting of privileges is seen as a legislative act, the second question really concerns the same issue as the first, and Gratian's discussion in the second quaestio simply corroborates the discussion in the first.

The opening dictum of the first quaestio states the problem for the whole Causa. It seems that, "no one more than the pope ought to obey the decrees of the holy canons." [18] All sixteen of the capitula of the first quaestio support the view that the pope must obey the decrees of his predecessors and Gratian sums up the doctrine of these canons in the dictum post c. 16.

If, therefore, it is necessary that the first see observe before all others the statutes of the councils, if it is necessary that that [see] guard the state of the Church with diligence [*inpigro affectu*]; if it is fitting that those things decreed by the Roman Pontiffs be observed by all [and] if those who do not obey the sacred canons ought not to minister at the altars: it is obvious that privileges ought not to be granted by the pope against the statutes of the holy canons according to which the state of the churches is either confounded or perturbed.[19]

16. Dist. 3, dict. post c. 2, "§1. Sunt autem quedam privatae leges, tam ecclesiasticae quam seculares, que privilegia appellantur." C. 25, q. 1, dict. post c. 16, "§1. Licet itaque sibi [pope] contra generalia decreta specialia privilegia indulgere, et speciali benefico concedere quod generali prohibetur decreto." Paragraphs 2 to 4 of this dictum treat privileges as laws and as emanations of the lawmaking power.

17. C. 25, dict. principium, "Secundo, an subsequenti privilegio monachorum derogetur antiquioribus privilegiis baptismalium ecclesiarum?"

18. C. 25, q. 1, dict. ante c. 1, "Decreta vero sanctorum canonum neminem magis quam Apostolicum servare oportet."

19. C. 25, q. 1, dict. post c. 16, "Si ergo primam sedem statuta conciliorum pre omnibus servare oportet, si pro statu ecclesiarum necesse est illam inpigro vigilare affectu; si ea que a Romanis Pontificibus decreta sunt, ab omnibus servari conveniti si illi, qui nesciunt sacris canonibus obedire, altaribus ministrare non debent: patet, quod contra statuta sanctorum canonum, quibus status ecclesiarum vel confundantur vel perturbantur, privilegia ab Apostolice concedi non debent."

This is the doctrine against which the Magister argues in the remainder of the dictum.

He states the opposing argument, supporting papal legislative power, simply. "The sacrosanct Roman Church imparts justice [*ius*] and authority to the sacred canons, but is not bound by them."[20] He then supports this argument by making an analogy between Christ as Legislator and the pope. Christ obeyed the old law by permitting himself to be circumcised and presented in the temple. He was also the first to observe the new law of sacraments which he established. The value of Christ's obedience was to confirm the authority of the law. The ecclesiastical legislator should obey his law for the same reason; through his obedience, he will confirm and sanctify the law that he makes. But sometimes authority shows that it is lord of the law by instituting new and altering old ones. This activity is analogous to the institution of the new sacraments by Christ. Taking into account authority's duty to obey the law and its power to change it, Gratian summed up the theory of authority's position relative to law in a succinct sentence. "In the previous capitula the necessity of obeying is imposed on others: for the highest Pontiffs there is shown to be the authority of observing [*auctoritas observandi*], so that they demonstrate to others that those [laws] handed down by themselves ought not to be despised."[21]

20. C. 25, q. 1, dict. post c. 16, "Sacrosancta Romana ecclesia ius et auctoritatem sacris canonibus impertit, sed non eis alligatur."

21. C. 25, q. 1, dict. post c. 16, "sicut Christus, qui legem dedit, ipsam legem carnaliter inplevit, octava die circumcisus, quadragesimo die cum hostiis in templo presentatus, ut in se ipso eam sanctificaret, postea vero, ut se dominum legis ostenderet, contra litteram legis leprosum tangendo mundavit, Apostolos quoque contra litteram sabbati per sata pretergredientes, spicas vellentes et confricantes manibus suis, probabili exemplo David, circumcisionis et templi excusavit. . . . Sic et conditis reverentiam exhibent, et eis se humiliando ipsos custodiunt, ut aliis observandos exhibeant. Nonnumquam vero seu iubendo, seu diffiniendo, seu decernendo, seu aliter agendo, se decretorum dominos et conditores esse ostendunt. In premissis ergo capitulis aliis inponitur necessitas obsequendi: summis vero Pontificibus ostenditur inesse auctoritas observandi, ut a se tradita observando aliis non contempnenda demonstrent, exemplo Christi, qui sacramenta, que ecclesiae servanda mandavit, primum in se ipso suscepit, ut ea in se ipso sanctificaret. Oportet ergo primam sedem, ut diximus, observare ea, que mandavit decernendo, non necessitate obsequendi, sed auctoritate inpertiendi." Note the similarity be-

The phrase *auctoritas observandi* emphasizes the voluntary nature of authority's obedience to law, and this emphasis shows the difference between the Magister's treatment of the power to make law in this part of the Decretum and the way in which he treated it earlier in the *Tractatus de legibus*. There, the authority of the law held the center of the reader's attention. Here, the power of the pope as the ecclesiastical legislator is most important. The reconciliation of these two aspects of the relationship between the governing power and its law is a delicate matter because Gratian wants to emphasize the authoritative character of the law without injuring the power of the pope to alter it. In Causa 25 the idea of the stability of law is to some extent lost through the use of the phrase *auctoritas observandi,* even though it is clear that Gratian did not mean, by that phrase, to free the ecclesiastical power from the provisions of the law under normal circumstances. In this Causa as in the early part of the *Tractatus de legibus,* Gratian puts forth the view that observance of the law by the hierarchy confirms the law and makes it effective. In Dist. 4, he had gone so far as to say that law that was not obeyed ceased to be law,[22] and this rule includes the obedience rendered by the ruler when he is not acting officially in his capacity as legislator. Yet, the power of the ecclesiastical hierarchy relative to its law is enhanced by the discussion in Causa 25. Authority's respect for laws of the community rests on the good will of the authority.

---

tween Gratian's and Saint Bernard's use of the example of Christ's circumcision. Bernard, *in circum. Dom.,* 1, n. 1–2 (see chap. iii, n. 3).

22. Dist. 4, dict. post c. 3, "Leges instituuntur, cum promulgantur, firmantur, cum moribus utentium approbantur. Sicut enim moribus utentium in contrarium nonnullae leges hodie abrogatae sunt, ita moribus utentium ipsae leges confirmantur." The case of the decrees of the Council of Nicea is an example of how laws are abrogated by disuse. A Pseudo-Isidorian letter attributed to Anastasius of Alexandria, written to Pope Marco (Dist. 16, c. 12), reported that seventy canons were issued by the council. Of these, only twenty were known in Gratian's time and the canonist asks how this can be. Dist. 16, dict. post c. 12, "Quomodo ergo viginti tantum capitula in Nicena sinodo statuta dicuntur, cum septuagenta capitula . . . in ea statuta monstrentur? His ita respondetur: Capitula Nicenae sinodi quedam in desuetudinem abierunt: viginti tantum in Romana ecclesia habentur."

The shift in the perspective of the Magister from the *de legibus* to Causa 25 also affects, as was said before, his view of the judging activity of the hierarchy. In the earlier part of the Decretum, Gratian emphasized the distinction between lawmaking and judging. In the first activity, the power judged concerning the law, while in the second, it judged according to the law. In Causa 25 the Magister recognized that the authority to judge is analogous to the authority to make law. He says, "Those alone are able to interpret the canons who have the right to make them." [23] The different views given by the two sections of the Decretum indicate the difficulty that one has in distinguishing the functions of Church power when the same persons and offices perform all governmental tasks. The statement of the *de legibus* does not necessitate that lawmaker and judge be the same persons, though it implies that this is the case. The passage from Causa 25 states clearly that in Gratian's mind, the governmental theory he expounded required that the same persons perform both functions. Placing all legislative power in the hands of the pope, the Magister reasons, necessitates placing, at least ultimately, all judicial power in his hands also.

The doctrine of the first quaestio of Causa 25 seems to make the governing power virtually free of any restraint in changing and making law. Yet, both in this quaestio and in the second, Gratian shows that he recognized one limitation of legislative power; it is a limitation of power that derives from the prelate's *caritas*. The authority in the Church ought to preserve the laws that serve the cause of good government and moral life in the community. The analogy between Christ and the human ecclesiastical legislator through which the Magister developed his theory of legislation embodies this idea. Like Christ, the pope as legislator and judge stands above the community and in some sense outside of it. But the virtually unfettered legislative power of the pope ought to be used in accordance with justice, as Christ uses

23. C. 25, q. 1, dict. post c. 16, "Sacri siquidem canones ita aliquid constituunt, ut suae interpretationis auctoritatem sanctae Romanae ecclesiae reservent. Ipsi namque soli canones valent interpretari, qui ius condendi eos habent." The same idea is suggested in this dictum several sentences earlier when Gratian says that the popes show themselves to be the lord of the law by defining or discerning as well as by making law. See n. 19 above.

his power.[24] This view was expressed in the *de legibus* when Gratian said that laws ought to be just, practical, and convenient, and when he considered the case of Pope Anastasius. The comparison between Christ and pope in Causa 25 makes the same point more forcefully. But the Magister also makes the requirement explicit by urging the pope to act *considerata tamen rationis equitate* when he grants a privilege against the general provisions of the law. He repeats this phrase in his discussion of the replacement or restriction of one privilege by another in the second quaestio.[25] Having already studied the Magister's theory of obedience, this statement about the pope can be viewed

24. This comparison between Christ and the pope, and its import for the theory of legislative as well as other types of power, may have been connected with the use of the term *vicarius Christi* to describe the supreme pontiff. The term became increasingly important from the mid-twelfth century on. See n. 27 below. Buisson, *op. cit.,* pp. 52–54, 58–59.

25. C. 25, q. 1, dict. post c. 16, "§4. Valet ergo, ut ex premissis colligitur, sancta Romana ecclesia quoslibet suis privilegiis munire, et extra generalia decreta quedam speciali beneficio indulgere, considerata tamen rationis equitate, ut que mater iusticiae est in nullo ab ea dissentire inveniatur, ut privilegia videlicet, que ob religionis, vel necessitatis, vel exhibiti obsequii gratiam conceduntur, neminem relevando ita divitem faciant." C. 25, q. 2, dict. post c. 21, "Si ergo privilegia monasteriorum vel quarumlibet ecclesiarum auctoritate Leonis, Gregorii, Gelasii et nonnullorum aliorum Pontificum sanctae Romanae ecclesiae inviolata servantur . . . si Pontifex non habet liberam licentiam discedendi a documentis, quibus iura ecclesiae firmantur: patet, quod posteriora privilegia antiquioribus derogare non possunt, nec eorum auctoritate eis aliqua obicietur exceptio . . . §1. His ita respondetur: Sancta Romana ecclesia sua auctoritate congregata valet disiungere, et disiuncta congregare; rationis tamen equitate considerata." Note also C. 22, q. 4, dict. post c. 23, "§2. Cum . . . omne preceptum Domini iustum sit, patet ei iustitiam deesse, quod eius precepto contrarium invenitur." Note the similarity of Gratian's statement in §1 of C. 25, q. 2, dict. post c. 21 with Saint Bernard's view in *De Consid.,* III:4, 14, "Subtrahuntur abbates episcopis, episcopi archiepiscopis, archiepiscopi patriarchis sive primatibus. Bonane species haec? Mirum si excusari queat vel opus. Sic factitando probatis vos habere plenitudinem potestatis, sed justitiae forte non ita. Facitis hoc, quia potestis: sed utrum et debeatis, quaestio est." See also, *Ep.* 131, "Plenitudo siquidem potestatis super universas orbis Ecclesias, singulari praerogativa apostolicae Sedi donata est. Qui igitur huic potestati resistit, Dei ordinationi resistit. Potest, si utile judicaverit, novos ordinare episcopatus, ubi hactenus non fuerunt. Potest eos qui sunt, alios deprimere, alios sublimare, prout ratio sibi dictaverit, ita ut de episcopis creare archiepiscopos liceat, et e converso, si necesse visum fuerit."

in the proper light. The pope ought to exercise his power to legislate and judge in accordance with the precepts of God, but if he fails to do so, the subjects have to obey his laws or judgment anyway—with the one exception that they should not perform an evil action.

The Magister's theory of legislative power exhibits the complexity of the relationship between the ecclesiastical governor and his community. The pope as legislator or judge was above the community and could act according to his own will and conscience. The pope as executive was presumably part of the community charged with the task of administering its business in accordance with the laws. The position of the pope with respect to the community therefore changed according to the tasks of government he performed. In addition to the problem created by the variety of governmental functions performed by the pope, Gratian's failure to treat the executive power *ex professo* introduced another difficulty into the problem of determining the relationship between the highest pontiff and the Church community. The doctrine developed in Causa 25 leaves its reader with the impression that the pope is to be considered superior to the community, that he is loosed from the laws.

One of the chief problems of medieval constitutional theory is brought to our attention by this conclusion. In order to assess the possibility of the community exercising control over its governing authority, the relationship between community and authority had to be determined. Furthermore, authority had to be seen as being within the community for there to be a possibility of constitutional government. According to Gratian's theory of papal legislative and judicial power, the possibility of constitutional control was very slight indeed. His doctrine pointed to only one possible solution to bad government in the Church: The community had to ensure that good men were promoted to the see of Saint Peter. It was only in the late twelfth century, when it had become clear that good men were hard to find and that good men did not always remain good, that there began to develop a new mode of controlling the governors. Constitutional lawyers took the first steps toward expounding a theory of government which reserved some authority for the community, enabling it to exercise power against its governors. A part of the foundation for the new constitutionalism will be exposed when the theory of how legitimate authority is established in the Ecclesia is studied.

But it is important to recognize that the problems of constitutional control which emerge from the theory of legislative power involve only the pope. Lower members of the ecclesiastical hierarchy were responsible to those above them and could be accused of misgovernment by their subjects.[26] The pope, in whom all power in the Church ultimately rests, was beyond the reach of his subjects both clerical and lay. This distinction between the pope and his clerical inferiors was based on the hierarchical theory that Gratian and his contemporaries used to describe the relationship between the ranks of the priesthood. This subject demands a separate treatment, later.

The historical importance of the theory of legislative power.

The concern for the moral quality of the holders of power in the Church, which was the consequence of the theory of ecclesiastical authority, linked Gratian with the party of Haimeric in the Curia. The argument of the first quaestio of Causa 25 provides more evidence of this link and also deepens understanding of the movement's ideology.

Gratian constructed the argument of the quaestio in a way different from his usual method in the Decretum. He often supported his views with only a handful of texts from the ancient law, but here he brought forth no canons to support his argument.[27] This characteristic of the discussion in the quaestio is difficult to explain. Why does Gratian reject the unanimous canonical tradition so completely in order to build his theory of legislative power?

26. C. 2, q. 7. Also, this idea is contained in the doctrine that members of the Church ought to obey the sentences of their superiors until a higher court reverses their decisions. See chap. v, n. 16.

27. There are other examples of Gratian setting forth his argument without citing any canons in support of his views; in some cases he cites no canons at all. See, for example, C. 29, q. 1; C. 11, q. 2 (where the Magister's answer to the question rests on C. 11, q. 1, c. 42); C. 13, q. 1 (where the Magister's treatment of the single canon he cites is similar to his treatment of those cited in C. 25, q. 1); C. 17, q. 3; C. 22, q. 3. In these last two examples, the question had been answered, implicitly, in the previous quaestio.

Clearly, the Magister sought to bolster the power of the papacy and to ensure that legal theory would support its active role in the Church. With this much being clear, it seems reasonable to suggest that the Magister's treatment of the problem of lawmaking was one of the earliest expositions of the theory of papal legislative power. It goes considerably beyond the concern of the earlier canonical collections for the primacy of the pope in the Church, and its inclusion in the Decretum shows the shift of interest and political outlook from the Gregorian movement to the new reform movement of Gratian's time.

The collectors of canons associated with the Gregorian papacy always gave much space to ancient texts that supported the primacy of the papal see, but these collectors were interested more in establishing their ideas about the structure of the hierarchy than in exploring the substantive powers of papal authority. This is not to say that the Gregorians of the eleventh century did not expound a theory of legislative power—Gregory himself did so in his letters[28]—but Gratian's doctrine of papal legislative power is considerably more developed than earlier expositions. His discussion represents the next step in the development of the theory of papal primacy, and it also represents an important shift in the interest of the lawyers from the structure of the hierarchy to the nature and use of its power. Two aspects of Gratian's discussion in Causa 25 make this interpretation of its historical importance very convincing.

In the first place, the comparison between the papal governor and Christ is striking evidence of the Magister's concern for the way in which papal power will be exercised. The comparison seems especially apt when one remembers that Saint Bernard was one of the first and certainly the most important of the writers to call the pope the *vicarius Christi*.[29] The vicar of Christ must be like Christ in his gov-

28. G. B. Ladner, "Two Gregorian Letters," *Studi Gregoriani*, 5 (1956), 221–242.

29. Bernard, *De Consid.*, IV:7, 23, "De cetero oportere te [the pope] esse considera formam justitiae . . . sacerdotem Altissimi, vicarium Christi, christum Domini." Bernard, *De Consid.*, II:8, 15, "Quis es? Sacerdos magnus, summus Pontifex. Tu princeps episcoporum, tu haeres Apostolorum, tu primatu Abel, gubernatu Noe, patriarchatu Abraham, ordine Melchisedech, dignitate Aaron, auctoritate Moyses, judicatu Samuel, potestate Petrus, unctione Christus." See

ernance of the Church. In the second place, the theory of legislative power is one of the rare doctrines in the Decretum which is based directly on the work of the Roman lawyers. Gratian did not cite any texts from the codes of Justinian or Theodosius in the Causa, as he did not do so in other parts of the Decretum, but he took the idea of the *ius condendi legem*, the right of making law, from the commentaries on Justinian's great collection.[30] Earlier canonical collections and treatises did not provide an adequate conceptual basis for a theory of legislative power, and the Magister therefore went to a source that he generally avoided. This change in attitude in conjunction with the failure to find any canons to support his doctrine expose the novelty of Gratian's interest in the subject as well as of his ideas themselves. The new movement for reform of the Church required a strong

also Bernard, *De Consid.,* II:1, 4. *Epp.* 59; 251. Kilga counted the titles which Bernard gave to the pope and arrived at the number thirty-four. K. Kilga, *Der Kirchenbegriff des hl. Bernard von Clairvaux,* Sonderdruck: *Cistercienser-Chronik* (1947–1948), pp. 80–81, 92–93. Jacqueline notes a change in Bernard's use of the term *vicarius Christi.* Before 1147, Bernard used the title, he says, to designate abbots and bishops as well as the pope. *Ep.* 59. *De mor. et offic. episc.,* 9, 36. After 1147, when Eugenius was pope and the second crusade was being arranged, Bernard dropped the title *vicarius Petri* for the second pope and reserved that of *vicarius Christi* to him. *Ep.* 251. *De Consid.,* II:8, 15; IV:7, 23. Bernard Jacqueline, *Papauté et épiscopat selon s. Bernard* (Saint-Lô, 1963), pp. 131–132. Yves Congar, "L'ecclésiologie de s. Bernard," *Saint Bernard Théologien,* pp. 159–160.

Other writers of Bernard's period used the title *vicarius Christi* to designate the pope, but they did not use it so frequently, and their use of it does not seem to have had such an effect on later writers. Anselm of Havelberg, *Dialogi,* 3, 10. See Johannes Beumer, "Ein Religionsgesprach aus dem 12. Jahrhundert," *Zeitschrift für katholische Theologie,* 73 [1951], 465–469). Arnulf of Lisieux, *Invectiva,* 4. Peter the Venerable calls the pope *vicarius Dei.* See *Ep.* 11, ed. Constable. Gerhoh of Reichersberg calls the pope *vicarius Christi* without using the exact term. See *de invest. Antichristi,* 19–20. But Gerhoh usually called the pope *vicarius Petri.* See *de aed. Dei,* 69. *Ep. ad Inn., MGH,* Libelli de lite III:203. *de ord. don. Spiritus Sancti, MGH,* Libelli de lite III:274.

The idea that the pope is *vicarius Christi* emphasizes that the pope is above the community of the Church in the same way that Christ is.

30. Pierre Legendre, *La pénétration du droit romain dans le droit canonique classique de Gratien à Innocent IV (1140–1254)* (Paris, 1964), pp. 99–100. Yet, the idea of *ius condendi legem* is contained in C. 25, q. 1, c. 6 (see n. 33 below) which comes from the work of Placidus of Nonantula (see nn. 31, 33 below).

statement in support of the pope's power to change old laws and make new ones.

But there is another historical dimension to the Magister's theory of legislation which must be mentioned. The crisis of 1111 was primarily a crisis of papal authority, and in the writings that it engendered, one of the problems dealt with is the pope's power to make laws. Pascal's concession of the right of investiture to Henry V in April, 1111, was viewed as a legislative act that, like the act of Anastasius II much earlier, contradicted rules enunciated by his predecessors. Placidus of Nonantula, writing probably toward the end of 1111, argued that Pascal ought to repudiate the concession, since it was against the canons and decrees of the holy fathers.[31] In the council of March, 1112, when the concession was retracted, Pascal read a statement that affirmed his intention to uphold the decrees of his predecessors, especially Gregory VII and Urban II.[32] The thrust of

31. Placidus, *de honore ecclesiae, MGH,* Libelli de lite II, c. 117, "Emendandum est igitur quod contra canones et decreta sanctorum patrum eis concessum fuisse." *Ibid.,* c. 118, "Non igitur sanctus papa hoc [the agreement of April, 1111] observare debet, sed magis studiosissime emendare, imitans beatissimi patris sui Petri apostoli fidem . . . " *Ibid.,* c. 127. Chapter 70 in Placidus's work contains perhaps the most striking statement on papal legislative power. See n. 33 below.

32. Mansi, vol. 21, col. 50–51, "Amplector omnem divinam scripturam, scilicet veteris et novi testamenti, legem scriptam a Moyse et a sanctis prophetis: amplector quatuor evangelia, septem canonicas epistolas, et epistolas gloriosi doctoris beati Pauli apostoli, sanctos canones apostolorum, quatuor universalia concilia, sicut quatuor evangelia, Nicaenum, Constantinopolitanum Ephesinum, et Chalcedonense, decreta sanctorum patrum Romanorum pontificum, et praecipue decreta domini mei papae Gregorii, et beatae memoriae Urbani. Quae ipsi laudaverunt, laudo: quae ipsi tenuerunt, teneo; quae confirmaverunt, confirmo; quae damnaverunt, damno; quae repulerunt, repello; quae interdixerunt, interdico; quae prohibuerunt, prohibeo in omnibus, et per omnia, et in his semper perseverabo."

Thus, those who controlled Pascal at the time of the council and who forced him to make this declaration harked back to Gregory VII. Pascal calls Gregory *domini mei* in his statement. Furthermore, this humiliation of the pope was carried out by a group led by Girard of Angoulême, later a leading member of Anaclet's party. Gratian, however, proved himself sympathetic to Pascal by citing his ill-fated agreement of February, 1111, the so-called Agreement of Sutri, in a dictum that will be discussed later (C. 23, q. 8, dict. post c. 20, see chap. ix). The Magister's rejection of Roman law is another sign that he was sympathetic to the notion that the ecclesiastical and secular spheres ought to be radically separated—

151

this declaration and of the argument of Placidus was to limit the papal right to legislate.

Gratian knew Placidus's work well and probably also had read the documents of the Lenten council of 1112. His discussion of lawmaking power appears in many places as a direct answer to the limitations of that power suggested in the heat of the 1111 crisis. In fact, some of his statements asserting the pope's broad authority to make law come directly from Placidus's work, and one of the capitula in Causa 25 is also taken from Placidus, though it is ascribed to Urban II.[33] The Magister's theory of legislation, then, can be related directly to political events of the early twelfth century. In respect to both its general conclusions and its particular arguments, the theory conveyed Gratian's reaction to political issues raised a decade or so before he began compiling his work. Causa 25 is a monument to Gratian's sensitivity to the contemporary political scene.

It is also clear that the Magister's contemporaries were aware of his views and that they were quick to react to them. His theory of legislative power was echoed in the writings of Saint Bernard and others in the reform party, but it also had a direct and specific effect on the practices of the Roman chancery. In 1143–1144, when the reform

---

one of the basic notions of the February, 1111, agreement. Hence, the crisis of 1111 to 1112 cemented in Gratian's mind the connection between his political enemies of a later time and Gregory VII and may explain his rejection of Gregory's letters in his discussion of the episcopal election (Dist. 63). The problem of the participation of the secular rulers in the election involved the question of papal legislative power. This can be seen in Dist. 63, dict. post c. 28, n. 14 above. For a complete discussion of the episcopal election and Gratian's argument in Dist. 63, see chap. viii.

33. Much of Dist. 63, dict. post c. 28 (n. 14 above) is taken verbatim from Placidus, *op. cit.*, c. 69 though it is interesting to note that in Placidus's work, the sentences used so effectively by Gratian are not directly concerned with papal legislative authority. The implication contained in Placidus's text was clear, however. C. 25, q. 1, c. 6 comes from Placidus, *op. cit.*, c. 70, "Sunt autem quidam dicentes Romano Pontifici semper bene licuisse novas condere leges. Quod et nos non solum non negamus, sed etiam valde affirmamus. Sed sciendum summopere est, quia inde novas leges condere potest, unde sancti patres et praecipue sic apostoli et eos sequentes sancti patres sententialiter aliquid diffinierunt, ibi est usque ad animam et sanguinem confirmare debet." Dist. 19, dict. post c. 7. Kuttner, "Urban II and Gratian," *Traditio* (Institute of Medieval Canon Law Bulletin for 1968), 24 (1968), 504–505.

party had won complete control of papal government, the chancery began to include the phrase *salva sedis apostolicae auctoritate* in its privileges. This practice derived from Gratian's discussion in Causa 25, quaestio 1. All privileges and laws of the pope, according to Gratian, contained explicitly, or implicitly, this phrase or one like it as a recognition of papal legislative power.[34] It was only during the pontificate of Celestine II, however, that the papal chancery began to make this reservation explicit in its grants. It cannot of course be certain whether the chancery borrowed the phrase and its suggested usage from the Decretum or both the chancery and Gratian obtained the idea from a common source.[35] But it is clear that the idea was new and must have stemmed from a source close to the papacy, and to Gratian, during the period of Haimeric's ascendancy at Rome. Whatever the exact circumstances of its use in the Decretum and the chancery, its appearance in both places makes the connection between the Magister and the new curial powers entirely probable.

By attributing all legislative and ultimately all judicial power to the pope, Gratian exposed another facet of his governmental theory. It was a hierarchical theory that provided a feeble basis for arguing that the episcopate, in addition to the pope, held real governmental authority. All exercise of authority in the Church was concentrated in the pope. But the pope was one of the bishops, and his order of priesthood did not differ from theirs. What then was the foundation on which his greater power was based? In the next chapter, Gratian's ideas about the division of authority in the Church are examined.

34. C. 25, q. 1, dict. post c. 16, "Sacri siquidem canones ita aliquid constituunt, ut suae interpretationis auctoritatem sanctae Romanae ecclesiae reservent. . . . Unde in nonnullis capitulis conciliorum, cum aliquid observandum decernitur statim subinfertur: 'Nisi auctoritas Romanae ecclesiae inperaverit aliter,' vel: 'salvo tamen in omnibus iure sanctae Romanae ecclesiae,' vel: 'salva tamen in omnibus apostolica auctoritate.' "

35. Friedrich Thaner, "Über Entstehung und Bedeutung der Formel: Salva sedis apostolicae auctoritate in den päpstlichen Privilegien," *Sitzungsberichte der Wiener Akademie der Wissenschaft,* Phil.-Hist. Cl., 72 (1872), 809–851. Johannes B. Sägmüller, "Die Entstehung und Bedeutung der Formel 'salva Sedis apostolicae auctoritate' in den päpstlichen Privilegien," *Theologische Quartalschrift,* 89 (1907), 93–117.

VII. Sacerdotal Power and the Hierarchy of the Church

According to the hierarchical principle of Church government, all power tends to concentrate in the hands of the hierarchy's highest member. But this tendency goes against many of the basic ideas that medieval writers expressed about the power held by inferiors of the Roman pontiff. Bishops and presbyters possessed the indelible character of the priesthood which they, like the pope who was often called *summus sacerdos,* received directly from God. One must be willing to deny this basic tenet of ecclesiology if he is to contend that the pope's supreme position curtailed or diminished the authority of his co-priests. Also, the pope is not to be too much separated from the episcopacy. He is a bishop himself. Thus, what can be said about his relationship with all other priests can be stated even more strongly about his relationship with his fellow bishops. His power is not different in essentials from theirs. Yet, there is a considerable difference between the power of the pope and other members of his order. It is this difference, and that between bishops and presbyters, which is discussed here.

The problem raised by the examination of grade differences in the ecclesiastical hierarchy concerns the nature of sacerdotal power.[1] All

1. In this context, sacerdotal power denotes only the powers received by the priest and not his *officium.* There will be a discussion of the priest's power in the Church, his *potestas* and *officium,* in this chapter and again in the next chapter where establishment of legitimate ecclesiastical authority will be considered. See the recent book by Robert L. Benson, *The Bishop-Elect: A Study in Medieval Ecclesiastical Office* (Princeton, N.J., 1968), pp. 45–55. See also, M. van de Kerckhove, "La notion de juridiction chez les Décrétistes et les premiers Décrétalistes

154

members of the hierarchy have this power; do they have it in varying degrees or is there some other, nonsacerdotal, authority at the base of the distinction between them? The preceding chapter detailed the difference in the power of the members of the hierarchy to make laws and judge cases. This chapter investigates the relationship between such powers, generally thought of today as governmental powers, and sacerdotal power; it is not difficult to understand the complexity of this problem. Priests perform sacramental as well as governmental functions in the earthly Church community, and many of the sacraments themselves served both as spiritual and juridical actions. Are the hierarchy's governmental powers simply derivative of its sacramental authority? Modern theory of sacerdotal power answers no to this question, and suggests that the priest holds two distinct types of authority. Before turning to the doctrine of the early and mid-twelfth century, the problem of sacerdotal power as it is illuminated by modern doctrine should be described.

The problem of sacerdotal power.

Traditionally, the power of the priesthood has been divided into two parts, the power of order and the power of jurisdiction. One purpose in studying Gratian's thought on this division is to determine whether the tradition goes as far back as the Decretum or whether it stems from a period after the completion of the work. On this point, scholarly opinion has been divided. Sohm argued that the idea of jurisdictional power was introduced into the conception of ecclesiastical authority after Gratian completed the Decretum.[2] The introduction of this idea was an important part of the transition between the sacramental phase of canon law and its modern, we might say jurisdictional, phase. According to Sohm's view therefore, Gratian did not recognize the distinction between the powers of order and jurisdiction.

(1140–1250)," *Études franciscaines,* 49 (1937), 420–421, 425–426, 440–443. Donald E. Heintschel, *The Mediaeval Concept of an Ecclesiastical Office* (Washington, D.C., 1956).

2. Rudolph Sohm, *Das altkatholische Kirchenrecht und das Dekret Gratians,* Festschrift der Leipziger Juristenfakultät für Adolf Wach (Munich-Leipzig, 1918), pp. 536–674.

155

Ladislav Orsy has disagreed with Sohm's interpretation of Gratian's theory. Orsy argues that the Magister did recognize the two elements of priestly power and concludes that while Gratian thought all *sacerdotes* held the same sacramental power, he thought the power to govern varied among the ranks of the hierarchy and accounted for the differences between them.[3] The distinction between the two parts of the sacerdotal power is to be found, says Orsy, in Gratian's conception of the sacerdotium—what it is to be a priest. A passage from Saint Isidore's *Etymologies* defined the *sacerdos* as one who performs sacrifices. Gratian incorporated this passage, and its simple definition of the priest, at the very beginning of the *Tractatus ordinandorum,* at Dist. 21, c. 1. But Orsy believes that in his dicta, the Magister broadened Isidore's idea of the *sacerdos* to include the power to govern as well as to perform sacraments. When the Magister took up the problem of the monk-priests, he was forced to note that some priests had the power to sacrifice, but not to govern. His doctrine on this matter implies, says Orsy, that he recognized two separable elements in the priesthood.[4] This interpretation imposes ideas on Gratian which he did not express, but it also exposes the importance of the doctrine of sacerdotal power for distinguishing between the *ordines* of ecclesiastical hierarchy. A closer look should be taken at the way in which the two parts of that power are analyzed today.[5]

According to modern canonical theory, powers of order and jurisdiction differ in purpose, mode of transmission, and nature. Power of order has for its object sanctification of men through performance of the sacraments. Power of jurisdiction gives prelates authority to gov-

3. Ladislav Orsy, "Bishops, Presbyters, and Priesthood in Gratian's Decretum," *Gregorianum,* 44 (1963), 788–826.

4. *Ibid.,* pp. 802–809. Dist. 21, c. 1, "sacerdos a sacrificando dictus est: consecrat enim et sacrificat." On the problem of monk-priests, see C. 16, q. 1. The doctrine expounded by the Magister in this Causa will be discussed in this chapter.

5. R. Naz, "Ordre en droit occidental," *DDC,* 6:1148–1150. R. J. Banks, "Jurisdiction (Canon Law)," *New Catholic Encyclopedia,* 8:61–62. S. E. Donlon, "Power of Jurisdiction," *New Catholic Encyclopedia,* 8:62–63. The terminology of this basic distinction in the sacerdotal powers did not arise, according to Van de Kerckhove, until the thirteenth century. Van de Kerckhove, *La notion de juridiction dans la doctrine des Décrétistes et des premiers Décrétalistes de Gratien (1140) à Bernard de Bottone (1250)* (Assisi, 1937), p. 35.

ern their flocks. Power of order is received through ordination, while power of jurisdiction is granted by ecclesiastical authority. The bishop grants power to govern when he commits a parish to the priest. Finally, power of order is immutable and stable since it comes directly from God, while power of jurisdiction can, once granted, be taken away, extended, or contracted at the pleasure of higher authority. Orsy does not assume that Gratian analyzed the differences between the two powers exactly as modern canon lawyers do, but he argues that the Magister made a distinction between the two elements of priestly authority similar to the one made today. He argues, in effect, that Gratian saw the differences among the parts of sacerdotal power in the same way as his successors in canon law schools, even if his conceptions were not so well expressed or conceived as theirs.

The question whether Gratian recognized any division in the kinds of power held by priests is a very difficult one. The Magister did not devote any one section of the Decretum to a systematic study of the theory of sacerdotal power, and in those dicta that do touch upon the problem, he expressed himself cryptically. The problem of sacerdotal power was bound up with the theology of the keys, and Gratian's comments on this subject can be understood significantly better by comparing them with the speculations of contemporary theological schools than by considering them *in vacuo*. Looking at the views of the three most important schools—those of Laon, Saint Victor, and Peter Abelard—will fill in the lacunae in Gratian's treatment of sacerdotal power and make it easier to judge the merits of Sohm's and Orsy's interpretations of it.

In the early Church, the keys had represented the whole power of the priest;[6] in Gratian's time, this simple equation was being studied and analyzed. The early scholastic theologians found the patristic tradition concerning the keys to be confused and self-contradictory, and they set about to remedy the situation. Peter Abelard's attempts in this direction were met by the charge of unorthodoxy,[7] but others remained

6. Charles Lefebvre, "Pouvoirs de l'Église," *DDC,* 7:73–74.
7. Peter Abelard set forth the patristic tradition on the relationship between the power of the keys and the remission of sins in: *Sic et Non,* c. 151, "Quod sine confessione non dimittantur peccata, et contra." He took up the subject of

157

close enough to the older tradition to escape such charges. In particular, two aspects of the early scholastic theology of the keys are of interest: first, the views of these writers concerning the number of keys received by the priest and the types of power represented by them; second, their thought about the source of the keys.

the keys again in his *Ethica, c. 26,* "Utrum generaliter ad omnes pertineat praelatos solvere et ligare?" There Peter points out, "Cum enim multi sint episcopi nec religionem, nec discretionem habentes, quamvis episcopalem habeant potestatem; quomodo eis aeque ut apostolis convenire dicemus: 'Quorum remiseritis peccata, remittentur eis, et quorum retinueritis, retenta sunt?'" After citing passages from Saint Jerome and Origen, he concludes, "Ex his, ni fallor, verbis Hieronymi apostolis dictum est de ligandis vel solvendis peccatorum vinculis, magis de personis eorum, quam generaliter de omnibus episcopis accipiendum esse. . . . Patenter itaque Origenes ostendit, sicut et manifesta ratio habet, quod in his quae diximus, Petro concessum est, nequaquam omnibus episcopis a Domino collatum esse; sed his solis, qui Petrum non ex sublimitate cathedrae, sed meritorum imitantur dignitate." These views stemmed from problems raised by the theology of the key of knowledge. These problems will be treated in the next section.

Peter's views were attacked in capitulum 12 of the list of errors charged against him at the Council of Sens in 1140. PL 182, col. 1053-1054. Hödl has pointed out that while the charge of c. 12 obviously refers to the views set forth by Peter in c. 26 of the *Ethica,* the quotations in the charge do not correspond to the text of the work edited in PL 178, col. 633-678. There was a second redaction of the work, however, contained in Oxford, Balliol College, Cod. 296 from which C. Ottaviano has edited the most important fragments. Hödl thinks that the twelfth capitulum of the list of errors refers to this text of the *Ethica.* Peter retracted his views in the *confessio fidei* that he offered at Sens. Hödl quotes Cousin's edition of the confession. "Potestatem ligandi atque solvendi successoribus apostolorum omnibus aeque ut ipsis apostolis concessam esse profiteor et tam dignis quam indignis episcopis, quamdiu eos ecclesia susceperit." This doctrine is that set forth by Gratian. Dist. 23, dict. post c. 6; C. 1, q. 1, dict. post c. 95; C. 15, q. 8, c. 5. See chap. iii, n. 36. Ludwig Hödl, *Die Geschichte der scholastischen Literatur und der Theologie der Schlüsselgewalt* (Münster, 1960), pp. 78-86. On the two redactions of the *Ethica,* see Artur M. Landgraf, *Einführung in die Geschichte der theologischen Literatur der Frühscholastik* (Regensburg, 1948), p. 64. For the fragments of the second redaction, see C. Ottaviano, "Frammenti Abelardiani," *Rivista di Cultura,* 12 (1931), 442-443. Hödl quotes some passages from this article. Hödl, *op. cit.,* pp. 84-85. On the synod of Sens in 1140, see Arno Borst, "Abälard und Bernhard," *Historische Zeitschrift,* 186 (1958), 497-526. Jean Rivière, "Les 'capitula' d'Abélard condamnés au concile de Sens," *Recherches de Théologie ancienne et médiévale,* 5 (1933), 5-22.

*Sacerdotal power according to the schools
of Laon, Saint Victor, and Peter Abelard.*

In the school of Anselm of Laon, writers followed the traditional division of the keys into two parts, the key of knowledge and the key of power. This view of key power stemmed from the works of the Venerable Bede who had argued that the power of the keys consisted in the knowledge of who should be excluded from and who received in the Church and the power to act on that knowledge.[8] A Laon *sententia, Auctoritate sanctorum patrum,* repeated Bede's exposition.

By the authority of the holy fathers, the keys of the Church are knowledge and power, (knowledge) is that by which it is discerned who ought to be admitted to the Church and who excluded. . . . That is called power by which pastors of the Church receive the elect, [and] cast out the reprobate.[9]

But writers of this school made an addition to the traditional teaching. They said that the *clavis scientiae* was analogous to *discretio,*[10] and this equation of knowledge and discretion raised certain difficulties for the theory of sacerdotal power. How could it be said that the key of discretion was possessed by priests who were conspicuously lacking in just that virtue? How was the discretion possessed by non-priests different from that possessed by those who had been consecrated?

8. Bede, *Hom.* 16, PL 94, col. 222, "Claves regni caelorum ipsam discernendi scientiam potentiamque nominat qua dignos recipere in regnum, indignos secludere debet a regno." Hödl, *op. cit.* Hödl provides an extensive review of the literature dealing with this problem in the writings of the early scholastic period.

9. *Auctoritate sanctorum patrum,* ed. Hödl, *op. cit.,* pp. 20–21, "Auctoritate sanctorum patrum testante ecclesiae sunt claves scientia et potestas, (scientia) scilicet qua discernitur qui sunt in ecclesia intromittendi vel excludendi. . . . Potestas autem dicitur qua pastores ecclesiae possunt electos suscipere, reprobatos abicere."

10. See the *Sententia* of the school of Laon contained in Clm 22272, ed. Hödl, *op. cit.,* p. 11, "Claves illae sunt scientia et potentia. Scientia autem est discretio illa, qua discernunt, quos debent in templum recipere, quos ut leprosos abicere." See also the *Summa Sententiarum* of the Victorine school sometimes attributed to Hugh of Saint Victor. Here the problem raised by the equation of *scientia* and *discretio* is recognized and discussed. *Summa Sent.,* VI:14, PL 176, col. 152, "Sed non videtur, quod vel soli vel omnes sacerdotes habeant eas [the keys], quia multi ante ordinationem habent discretionem, qui sint ligandi, qui etiam solvendi, plures post consecrationem carent illa discretione." This passage will be referred to again.

A writer of Peter Abelard's school analyzed these issues with admirable skill and loyalty to logic, and he came to the conclusion that the *auctoritas,* presumably the passage from Bede, lied when it said there were two keys. It is clear, said the writer, that no key of discretion is given to priests who have no powers of discretion and that, therefore, there is only one key. This one key was called two in the Gospel, he continues, because it represents a double office—that of opening and closing the gates of heaven.[11] The opinion expressed by this writer was not the common one in the middle of the twelfth century—to put it mildly. In fact, Abelard's disciple was being rather bold to exercise his skill in dialectics on a point about which the patristic texts held an *opinio communis.* There are two keys.

Writers of the school of Saint Victor approached the problem of discretion from another point of view. They sought to distinguish between the discretion of normal persons and that attributed to priests through the *clavis scientiae.* Recognizing that discretion is discretion, these writers made their distinction by arguing that the priest received an office of discerning even if he did not actually receive discretion when he was consecrated.[12] Gratian considered this problem of dis-

---

11. See the *sententia* contained in Clm 13088, fol. 156ʳ (and in Clm 12519, fol. 120ʳ⁻ᵛ), edited by Hödl, *op. cit.,* p. 94, "Quaeritur, cum certum sit duas claves Petro datas esse a Deo scilicet discretionem et potestatem, si omnes eius successores dicuntur habere duas claves. Quod non datur omnibus discretio, probatur hoc modo: alicui indiscreto accedenti ad sacerdotium non datur discretio, nam sic indiscretus recedit sicuti indiscretus accessit. Igitur tali non datur discretio. Item discretio accedenti non datur, quia prius habuit eam: si autem nec discreto nec indiscreto datur, igitur nulli in consecratione datur discretio; igitur mentitur auctoritas dicens omni sacerdoti duas claves dari in consecratione . . . quamvis auctoritas dicat omni sacerdoti duas claves in consecratione, non tamen datur ei magis quam una clavis, scilicet potestas. Sed placuit scripturae hanc unam clavem appellare duas claves propter duplex officium ligandi et solvendi. Et quia hoc duplex officium datur per simile, nam una eadem clave clauditur ianua et aperitur." Note that the question set forth at the beginning of the passage is the same as that set forth by Peter Abelard himself in *Ethica,* c. 26. Concern about the keys in Abelard's school was restricted to the problems discussed in the *Ethica* and the *sententia* quoted here. The Magister and his disciples did not consider the problem of the source of the keys.

12. *Summa Sent.,* VI, 14, PL 176, col. 152, n. 20 below. See the *sententia* quoted in the next note.

cretion in Dist. 20. When his views are discussed, it will be useful to quote the passage from the Victorine writing that treats this subject.

The key of discretion provided the priest with much more than the office of discerning according to the writers associated with the school of Saint Victor. The author of the Victorine *sententia, Vae vobis pharisaeis,* says that it includes all the sacramental power held by the *sacerdos.*

The Lord gave this key, that is the office of discretion to his disciples when He "sent them in pairs" to preach "in every place where He would come." Then indeed they received the faculty of preaching, of instructing, of correcting, of baptizing, of curing the infirm, of chasing demons; also at the last supper they received the power [of offering] the body and blood of the Lord.[13]

All these powers are included in the key of knowledge. The same author continues by explaining that the key of power is the power of binding and loosing. This power permits the priest to excommunicate and absolve.[14]

The author of *Vae vobis pharisaeis* does not seem to have associated the power of binding and loosing with the sacramental power included in the *clavis scientiae,* though he does see this power as that connected with the remission of sins. As noted in a previous chapter, the giving of penance was not generally viewed as a sacrament until the middle of the twelfth century.[15] This *sententia,* therefore, has at least the sug-

13. *Vae vobis pharisaeis,* ed. Hödl, *op. cit.,* p. 50, "Hanc clavem id est officium discretionis dedit Dominus discipulis suis, quando 'misit eos binos' ad praedicandum 'in omnem locum quo erat ipse venturus' [Luke 10:1]. Tunc enim acceperunt facultatem praedicandi, instruendi, corrigendi, baptizandi, infirmos curandi, daemonia effugandi; in Coena etiam potestatem acceperunt [conficiendi] corpus et sanguinem Domini." Medieval writers did not look upon preaching in the same way as we do. The preacher sanctified his listeners according to medieval theory, and, therefore, he performed a sacerdotal duty and exercised a sacerdotal power when he spoke. Erich Kleineidam, "Bernhard von Clairvaux über die Predigt," *Sacramentum Ordinis,* Geschichtliche und systematische Beiträge, ed. E. Puzik and O. Kuss (Breslau, 1942), pp. 169–199.

14. *Vae vobis pharisaeis,* ed. Hödl, *op. cit.,* p. 50, "Videtur praeterea aliam clavem id est potestam [sic] ligandi atque solvendi. . . . Potestas ligandi et solvendi est facultas malos excommunicandi et absolvendi."

15. P. Anciaux (*La Théologie du sacrement de pénitence au XIIe siècle*

gestion of a distinction between two parts of sacerdotal power. The author does not explicitly make the distinction, but readers of his work are led to ask what the difference is between the powers included in the two keys. The uncertainty on this point is decreased when one considers the views of the schoolmen about the source from which the priest receives the keys.

Writers of the school of Laon considered this problem, and the prevailing view in the school was that a man who was consecrated a priest without receiving the *cura pastoralis* did not receive the power of the keys.[16] Implied in this view is a separation between the power of the keys and the sacramental power of the priest. In his ordination,

[Louvain, 1949], p. 145) points out that the school of Laon already had enrolled penitence in the catalog of sacraments. He cites the *sententia* no. 369, Odon Lottin, ed., "Nouveaux fragments théologiques de l'école d'Anselme de Laon," *Recherches de Théologie ancienne et médiévale,* 13 (1946), 172, "Sunt enim quedam sacramenta que nisi per ministros assumpserit homo non potest salvari, ut baptismus, penitentia, confessio et communicatio corporis et sanguinis Christi, si spatium habuerit." This passage implies the distinction between sacraments of dignity and of necessity made by Gratian and others in the middle of the century. Gratian, too, included penitence in the list of sacraments. C. 1, q. 1, dict. post c. 42, "Non est enim de hoc sacramento [ordination] ut de ceteris; cetera enim vel ad culpas abluendas dantur, ut baptismus et penitentia." J. Spitzig, *Sacramental Penance in the Twelfth and Thirteenth Centuries* (Washington D.C., 1947). P. Schmoll, *Die Busslehre der Frühscholastik* (Munich, 1909). K. Müller, "Der Umschwung in der Lehre von der Busse während des 12. Jahrhunderts," *Theologische Abhandlungen Carl von Weizäcker gewidmet* (Freiburg i. Br., 1892), pp. 287–320. Landgraf, "Grundlagen für ein Verständnis der Busslehre der Früh- und Hochscholastik," *Zeitschrift für katholishe Theologie,* 51 (1927), 161–194.

16. *Auctoritate sanctorum patrum,* ed. Hödl, *op. cit.,* p. 21, "Neque putandum, quod ubi sacerdotes consecrentur, claves et pastoralem curam accipiant omnes. Sacerdotes enim sunt qui populis non praesunt, qui scilicet divina peragunt tantum sacramenta nulla sibi congregatione populi commissa. . . . Hac itaque differentia clericorum et monachorum ecclesiam Dei pascere et regere, ligare et solvere monachis non constat, qui tamen per episcopos pastores ecclesiae constitui possunt." The view that the power of the keys are received through the sacrament of orders was not, however, absent from the writings of the school of Laon. It is implied in the following passage from a Laon *sententia* in Clm 22272, ed. Hödl, *op. cit.,* pp. 11–12, "Et scientia [the key of knowledge] datur illis, qui idonei promoventur ad ministerium illud, etsi idiotae sint et simplices, quia, cum in illa consecratione sua, si digni sunt, accipiant et sacramenta et res sacramentorum, per Spiritum etiam accipiunt illam discretionem." This passage also hints at the problem raised by the key of knowledge. See nn. 10 and 11 above.

the priest receives power to perform sacraments, but he receives the power of the keys only when the bishop commits a parish to him. It would seem that this writer equated key power with power to govern in the Church and that he therefore distinguished, in a vague way, between the powers of order and jurisdiction.

The writers of the school at Saint Victor did not expound a set theory about the way in which the power of the keys was transmitted to the priest. Instead, they recognized two possible explanations of this transference and left the question undecided. The author of *Vae vobis pharisaeis* expressed the ambivalent attitude of the school well. Like Gratian, the Victorine writer raised the problem when he considered the status of monk-priests.

It is asked whether monks who are ordained into the priesthood or clerics who do not have parishes receive the keys. About this it is said that they do not actually receive the power of using the keys, but that the ordination makes them worthy to do so; so that they are able to use the keys if a flock is committed to them. Or it is possible to say that when a *cura animarum* is given, they receive the keys.[17]

The author of this passage included all the powers of the priesthood in the keys. The key of discretion included the power of performing the sacraments, while the key of power was connected with the remission of sins. The Victorine theology of the keys precludes separation between sacramental powers of the priest and his governmental power that was implied by the *sententia* connected with the school of Laon. And separation between the two types of power is precluded by the view of the Victorine author notwithstanding that the second opinion that he expresses about the source of the keys is identical with that held by the writer of Laon. All that is implied by the two opinions about the transmission of the keys found in the Victorine text is that there are two ways of viewing the sacrament of orders. According to the first opinion, the priest receives the keys in the ordination and only

17. *Vae vobis pharisaeis,* ed. Hödl, *op. cit.,* pp. 50–51, "Sed quaeritur de monachis qui in presbyteros ordinantur vel de clericis qui parochias non habent, utrum has claves recipiunt. Ad quod dicitur, quod potestatem utendi his clavibus actualiter non recipiunt, sed ipsa ordinatio ad hoc idoneos effect, ut possint hii uti clavibus si grex eis commissus fuerit. Vel potest dici, quod cum datur cura animarum has claves recipiunt."

the right to exercise the powers associated with the keys when the bishop commits a *cura* to him. According to the second opinion, the priest is only made capable of receiving the power of the keys in his ordination, but he actually receives that power in the *licentia episcopi*.

Comparison of the views of Laon and Saint Victor on the source of the keys shows that in Gratian's time theologians were developing their theology of the keys in such a way as to preclude the distinction between powers of order and jurisdiction. The two keys did not represent these two types of power, and the source from which the priest received the power of the keys did not affect the character of that power. As was seen, the theologians of Saint Victor defined the content of key power more precisely than did their predecessors in the school of Laon, and Gratian's treatment of the power of the keys reflects that of the school of Saint Victor. But Gratian's theory of the keys is bound up, in most of the passages concerning the subject, with his description of the ecclesiastical hierarchy, and, in addition, he was not so careful or explicit in his discussion of key power as the author of *Vae vobis pharisaeis* had been. The character of his discussion and his concentration on the hierarchical structure of Church government raised problems concerning the definition of sacerdotal power which the decretists took up in their commentaries. The division of sacerdotal power into two types of authority was based on the Decretum, but was postulated for the first time by those who commented on the work.

Sacerdotal power according to Gratian.

Gratian's theory of sacerdotal power exhibits the same duality that characterizes his basic ecclesiological conceptions. When he considered the nature of the Church, the Magister made a conceptual distinction between its spiritual and temporal aspects. His theory of Church membership is founded on this distinction, and, thus, a man could receive the sacrament of baptism and become a member only of the earthly community of the Church. Likewise, the priest could act so that his action affected the juridical condition of a Church member but not the member's spiritual condition. This was seen to be true when Gratian's theory of obedience was studied. An unjust sentence, he said, is effective insofar as the earthly ecclesiastical community is concerned, but it has no force before God. Is the distinction between the temporal and spiritual aspects of sacerdotal power the same as the distinction between the power of order and the power of jurisdiction? It is not.

The spiritual power of the priest is separated from his temporal power only when he acts unjustly. When the priest acts in accordance with divine law, his action possesses both spiritual and temporal effect. Gratian's ecclesiological theory does not permit him to postulate the existence of a type of priestly power that does not have this duality. He cannot, therefore, divide the sacerdotal power into the power to govern and the power to perform sacraments; performing sacraments is governing within the ecclesiastical community. In contrast with the interpretation of the Magister's thought set forth by Orsy, the conclusion reached here is that while there are elements of Gratian's doctrine which might lead others to make a distinction between two separable parts of sacerdotal power, he did not make the distinction himself.

Gratian was interested in the same aspects of the keys as his contemporaries in the theological schools. He treated three problems connected with the power. First, he took up the question of what the keys represented and divided them into two—discretion and power. Equating the key of knowledge with discretion, however, led him to consider the related question of how learned and wise individuals who were not priests could be said to lack the key of knowledge. Second, he connected the keys with remission of sins, but also appears to have connected them with other sacramental powers. Third, he considered the source of sacerdotal power when he examined the difference between monk-priests and secular priests.

The issue of Dist. 20 concerns the relationship between judgments or opinions of the pope and the views of learned and holy individuals who do not possess his power. It is a problem that follows from the discussion of the previous *Distinctio* where Gratian had argued that decretal letters of the popes ought to be considered legally binding, even when they are not formally incorporated into canon law. The discussion continues:

Now it is asked concerning the expositors of the sacred scriptures whether their opinions are superior or inferior to those [of the popes]? For some

165

say, with much reason, that the words of these [expositors] seem to be of greater authority. Many of the authors are proved to possess more of the grace of the Holy Spirit as well as being more knowledgeable than others [and] with greater reason [their opinion] ought to be followed. Whence the sayings of Augustine, Jerome, and other authors, it seems, ought to be preferred to the opinions of those constituted in the highest priesthood.[18]

Gratian answers this argument by making a distinction between those who do not possess the power of the keys and those who do have this power. The expositors do not hold the keys while the popes do. And there are two keys according to the Magister, the key of knowledge and the key of power, and both are necessary for the judgment of cases. Thus, he answers the contention of the above passage:

But to impose an end on cases is one thing and to expose [the meaning of] the sacred scriptures is another. For deciding cases not only is knowledge necessary, but also power. Thus, when Christ said to Peter: "Whatsoever you shall bind on earth, it shall be bound also in heaven, etc." he first gave to him the keys of the kingdom of heaven: in the one giving him knowledge for discerning between lepers, in the other giving him power for ejecting anyone from the Church, or receiving him back.[19]

Gratian continues in the passage to make clear that one key will not

18. Dist. 20, dict. ante c. 1, "Decretales itaque epistolae canonibus conciliorum pari iure exequantur. Nunc autem queritur de expositoribus sacrae scripturae, an exequentur, an subiciantur eis? Quo enim quisque magis ratione nititur, eo maioris auctoritatis eius verba esse videntur. Plurimi autem tractatorum, sicut pleniori gratia Spiritus sancti, ita ampliori scientia aliis precellentes, rationi magis adhesisse probantur. Unde nonnullorum Pontificum constitutis Augustini, Ieronimi atque aliorum tractatorum dicta eis videntur esse preferenda."

19. Dist. 20, dict. ante c. 1, "§1. Sed aliud est causis terminum imponere aliud scripturas sacras diligenter exponere. Negotiis diffiniendis non solum est necessaria scientia, sed etiam potestas. Unde Christus dicturus Petro: 'Quodcumque ligaveris super terram, erit ligatum et in celis, etc.' prius dedit sibi claves regni celorum: in altera dans ei scientiam discernendi inter lepram et lepram, in altera dans sibi potestatem eiciendi aliquos ab ecclesia, vel recipiendi. Cum ergo quelibet negotia finem accipiant vel in absolutione innocentium, vel in condempnatione delinquentium, absolutio vero vel condempnatio non scientiam tantum, sed etiam potestatem presidentium desiderant: aparet, quod divinarum scripturarum tractatores, etsi scientia Pontificibus premineant, tamen, quia dignitatis eorum apicem non sunt adepti, in sacrarum scripturarum expositionibus eis preponuntur, in causis vero diffiniendis secundum post eos locum merentur."

166

suffice, but that both are inexorably connected in the performance of priestly duties.

The Magister's solution leaves several points unclear, however. Although he implies that there is a difference between the key of knowledge and the knowledge of Augustine and Jerome, he does not make the distinction clear. In fact, he is saying that the key of discretion is not simply the knowledge of how to distinguish the good from the bad in the Church but also the power or office to do so. This idea was brought out in a text from the contemporary Victorine *Summa Sententiarum* which has been attributed to Hugh of Saint Victor himself:

It does not seem that either priests alone or all priests have these [the keys], because many have discretion before the ordination . . . [and] many lack that discretion after consecration. And so not all priests have those two [keys]. . . . [But] although someone should have that discretion before the consecration, he does not nevertheless have the key because he does not have to do this [make a distinction between who ought to be bound and who absolved] nor is he able to close or open [the gates of the Church and heaven]. . . . Again, the indiscrete priest, even if he lacks that discretion, nonetheless has the office of discerning . . .[20]

Gratian's argument is founded on the distinction made in this passage.

20. *Summa Sent.*, VI, 14, PL 176, col. 152, "Sed non videtur, quod vel soli vel omnes sacerdotes habeant eas (claves), quia multi ante ordinationem habent discretionem . . . (et) plures post consecrationem carent illa discretione. Et ita non omnes sacerdotes illas duas (claves) habent. . . . (Sed) Licet enim aliquis ante consecrationem habeat illam discretionem, non tamen in eo clavis est, quia non habet ex officio hoc facere nec potest claudere vel aperire. . . . Iterum indiscretus sacerdos, etsi careat illa discretione, tamen habet officium sic discernendi." The authorship of the *Summa* (PL 176, col. 41–174) has been disputed since 1887. In that year, Denifle raised serious objections to the accepted view that it was the work of Hugh of Saint Victor. H. Denifle, *Archiv für Literatur und Kirche des Mittelalters*, 3 (1887), 634–640. P. Portalie, in his article about Peter Abelard in the *DTC*, 1 (1909), 53–54, supported the view of Denifle. Other scholars held to the position that Hugh wrote the *Summa*. Since the late nineteenth century, nearly every scholar working on the theology of the twelfth century has had something to say about the authorship of the work. The question remains unsolved, however. Ott has shown that the *terminus ante quem* for the composition of the work was 1141. Ludwig Ott, "Vivianus von Prémontré der früheste Zeuge für die Benutzung der Summa Sententiarum," *Scholastik*, 14 (1939), 81–90. Hödl reviews the scholarly debate over the authorship of the *Summa*. Hödl, *op. cit.*, pp. 57–58. See also, Landgraf, *Einführung in die Geschichte der theologischen Literatur der Frühscholastik*, pp. 75–79.

He says that the pope has the key of discretion, while he recognizes that his powers of discretion are not necessarily as great as those of the learned expositors. But the discussion in Dist. 20 raises problems not raised in the text from the Victorine *sententia*. The distinction that Gratian makes in his dictum is not simply that between priests and non-priests. It is between the pope and learned theologians, and some of these men—like Augustine whom the Magister mentions—were bishops. Thus, the dictum can be understood as referring to the distinction between the pope and other bishops, and when it is understood in this way, it suggests that there is a difference in sacerdotal power, the power of the keys, between the pope and his fellow bishops. Furthermore, it is the power to decide cases, a specifically juridical power, which is the basis for the distinction between the pope and the expositors in the dictum. Thus, in the first passage in which he treats the power of the keys, Gratian recognizes that they represent the power to govern in the Church. Nonetheless, a close reading of the passage shows that the Magister did not mean to distinguish between the power to govern and the sacramental power held by the priest.

The power to decide cases is an extension of the power to excommunicate and reconcile, and elsewhere in the Decretum, Gratian makes it clear that this latter power is sacramental in nature. In a dictum of Causa 24, he grouped the power of excommunicating and reconciling with the power to perform the Eucharist, and in Causa 33, he connected the power of binding and loosing with the sacramental remission of sins.[21] The power of the keys was thus at once sacramental and juridical.

21. Benson (*op. cit.,* pp. 48–49) points out the juridical character of the power of the keys discussed in Dist. 20. He interprets the keys mentioned in the dictum as "the 'knowledge' needed for the judgment of those crimes which are tried in an ecclesiastical court . . . [and the] 'power,' including the power to excommunicate or to reconcile, as well as the power to decide certain criminal cases" (Benson, *op. cit.,* p. 48). But the power to decide cases is the same as the power of binding and loosing. By receiving the keys, both of them, Peter received the power to bind and loose. Gratian demonstrated that he associates both keys with the power of binding and loosing when he connects that power with the remission of sins. C. 24, q. 1, dict. post c. 39, n. 28 below. C. 33, q. 3, Dist. 1 *de Pen.,* dict. post cc. 60, 87, nn. 22 and 23 below. Peter Huizing, "The Earliest Development of *excommunicatio latae sententiae* by Gratian," *SG,* 3 (1955), 285.

Another aspect of the discussion in Dist. 20 ought to be mentioned. The doctrine developed there is analogous to Gratian's theory of obedience in that it deals with the comparison between the imperfections of the earthly community and the ideal implied by its spiritual nature. In his discussion of obedience, the Magister was concerned with unjust sentences, and his separation of the earthly from the spiritual effect of the sentence of the bishop depended on the injustice of the sentence. In Dist. 20, the problem of whether to follow the opinion of the pope or the expositors of the scriptures is based on the assumption that the pope is not so learned or wise as the Fathers. No problem is raised by the comparison between Gregory I and Augustine or Jerome. Thus, in the discussion of obedience, it is the injustice of the prelate which creates the problem and leads Gratian to distinguish between the temporal and spiritual aspect of priestly authority. In the discussion of making decisions, it is the prelate's lack of wisdom.

The Magister followed the common opinion about the number of the keys. What did he have to say further about the powers represented by the keys? He connected the keys with the sacrament of penitence in Causa 33 where he took up the dispute over the necessity of confession for remission of sins. But in making the connection, he was less precise than his contemporaries. They thought that the key of power, the power of binding and loosing, was the basis of the essential place that the priest held in the remission of sins. Gratian did not distinguish between the two keys in making the connection between them and penitence. In his first reference to the connection, he writes of the keys, with no further definition of what he means by them.[22] In his second reference, he concentrates on the power of binding and loosing.[23] Is this power the *clavis potestatis* or is it identical with the

22. C. 33, q. 3, Dist. 1 *de Pen.,* dict. post c. 60, "ille, qui promittit veniam occulte apud Deum non apud ecclesiam penitenciam agenti, frustrat evangelium et claves datas ecclesiae."

23. C. 33, q. 3, Dist. 1 *de Pen.,* dict. post c. 87, "§11. Quomodo . . . ius ligandi et solvendi solis sacerdotibus a Domino creditur esse permissum, si quisque suo arbitrio se ipsum peccando ligat, vel secreta penitencia . . . in se ipsum sentenciam profert excommunicationis, atque post satisfactionem absque sacerdotali iudicio se ipsum Deo vel altario eius reconciliat?" But see also *ibid.,* §10, where Gratian does not distinguish between the two keys in referring to their connection with penitence. "frustrat claves ecclesiae qui sine arbitrio sacerdotis penitenciam agit."

169

power represented by both keys? The Magister implies that the keys, together, represent the power of binding and loosing.

These two sections of the Decretum, Dist. 20 and Causa 33, were the only ones in which Gratian gave an explicit indication of what powers he thought were represented by the image of the keys. It signifies the power to judge cases, give sentences, and remit sins. But there is another dictum that can be interpreted as referring to the power of the keys, and if this interpretation is correct, the passage adds a great deal to understanding Gratian's idea of the keys. The Causa in which the dictum is found concerns the difference between monk-priests and other priests, and the Magister is particularly interested in the question whether monk-priests should be permitted to celebrate the offices for the people. It is a dictum in the first quaestio of Causa 16.

Monks, though they receive (just as other priests) the power of preaching, baptizing, giving penitence, remitting sins, enjoying ecclesiastical benefices in the dedication of their priesthood, so that they do those things which are proven by the constitutions of the holy fathers to be [part] of the sacerdotal office; nevertheless they do not have the execution of the power, unless they will have been elected by the people and ordained by the bishop with the consent of the abbot.[24]

This passage refers to the problem of the transmission of power to the priest as well as to content of that power, and it exposes the intimate connection between the two issues. With respect to the content of the sacerdotal power, it appears from the dictum that the sacramental powers, associated with the key of discretion by the author of *Vae vobis pharisaeis,* were also considered to be part of the key power by Gratian. Since the Magister thought the remission of sins and giving of penitence were part of the power of the keys, by inference he seems to have included the ability to preach and to baptize in that power. This interpretation of the dictum is confirmed when we con-

24. C. 16, q. 1, dict. post c. 19, "Monachi autem, et si in dedicatione sui presbiteratus (sicut et ceteri sacerdotes) predicandi, baptizandi, penitenciam dandi, peccata remittendi, beneficiis ecclesiasticis perfruendi rite potestatem accipiant, ut amplius et perfectius agant ea, que sacerdotalis offitii esse sanctorum Patrum constitutionibus conprobantur: tamen executionem suae potestatis non habent, nisi a populo fuerint electi, et ab episcopo cum consensu abbatis ordinati."

sider what the Magister has to say about the transmission of the sacerdotal power to the priest.

Gratian disagreed with the opinion, expressed by the *sententia* from the school of Laon, that sacerdotal power represented by the keys is received in the *licentia episcopi*. He argues instead that the priest receives his powers in the sacrament of orders and that the bishop only gives him the right to use his power when he commits a parish to his care. This was the first of two views set forth by the Victorine author of *Vae vobis pharisaeis*. By expounding a view similar to the one expounded in the *sententia* from Saint Victor, Gratian implied that he also agreed with the author of that work about the content of key power. The bishop does not transmit any substantive power to the priest when he grants a *cura animarum* to him. The *sacerdos* has already received his power in his consecration. And his power is the power of the keys. Gratian is within the tradition of the new scholastic theology of his times. He did not deviate from the tradition when he considered the source of sacerdotal power; there is no reason to suppose that he deviated from it by not equating sacerdotal power with the keys.[25]

25. The dict. post c. 19 in C. 16, q. 1 raises two other difficulties concerning the establishment of legitimate authority in the Church. The last sentences of the passage quoted in the text of the chapter seems to attribute the source of the priest's *executio potestatis* to election by the people as well as license of the bishop. This implication stems from Gratian's careless use of language. Although election is necessary before the grant of the *executio*, it is actually analogous to the consent of the monk's abbot. The bishop grants the use of sacerdotal power to the monk-priest through the sacrament of orders, but he cannot do so unless the people will have asked that the monk be made their pastor and unless the monk's abbot will have agreed to permit him to take up his charge. The exact relationship between the election through which the monk is chosen as the prospective pastor and the ordination through which he is invested with his authority to act in that capacity is very difficult to determine. This problem will be taken up in detail in the next chapter.

Another problem that is raised by the dictum and will be considered in the next chapter is the apparent distinction between the consecration and the ordination of the priest. In the context of the dictum, the term *ordinare* clearly means to receive the *cura animarum* from the bishop rather than to receive the sacrament of orders. It is the condition of the monk-priest who has not received the cura which causes Gratian to make the distinction between consecration and

Gration did not, as Orsy thinks, make a distinction between the priest's power to govern and his power to offer sacrifices. He saw the sacerdotal power, like his contemporaries, as a whole and integral power represented by the image of the keys. There is no dictum in the Decretum where the Magister distinguished between the types of power held by the priest according to their purposes, character, or modes of transmission. The distinction that the Magister did make was between the *potestas* and the *executio potestatis*. He clarified the doctrine set forth in Causa 16 in another Causa where he considered the power held by an excommunicated priest.

---

ordination and leads to the question: What is the relationship between these two acts? Gerard Fransen, "La tradition des canonistes au moyen-âge," *Études sur le sacrement de l'ordre* (Paris, 1957), pp. 259, *passim*. Benson, *op. cit.,* pp. 23–45.

The distinction drawn between consecration and ordination in the Decretum and in the decretist commentaries was not perfect, however. The monk who received the sacrament of orders but not a *cura animarum* was prohibited from exercising his power in the Church, but he could still perform the sacraments and offices for those within the walls of his monastery. C. 16, q. 1, dict. post c. 12, "Auctoritas illa Nicenae sinodi [c. 1] prohibet monachos de monasteriis exire, et per capellas sepulturas mortuorum celebrare, confluere videlicet more clericorum ad cuiuslibet exequias celebrandas. Ceterum si apud monasterium aliquis semetipsum tumulari voluerit, non est prohibendus." C. 16, q. 1, dict. post c. 16. The decretist Rufinus expanded on this idea. Rufinus, *Summa decretorum,* ed. H. Singer (Paderborn, 1902) p. 353, "Cenobite ergo ipsi sunt, ex quibus si alicui cum licentia abbatis vel prioris sui et auctoritate episcopi ecclesiis parochialibus deputentur, libere poterunt et officia populis celebrare et penitentiam dare, baptizare, predicare decimasque a populo exigere et cetera sacerdotalia officia exercere. . . . Aliis autem cenobitis hec officia non est licitum exercere, possunt tamen fratribus suis vel ad eorum conversationem venientibus vel positis in extremo necessitatis articulo predicare, penitentiam dare, baptizare eosque sepelire."

Benson, (*op. cit.,* pp. 50–51) points out that the distinction between the *potestas* and the *executio potestatis* adopted by Gratian is similar to one that had a long history in the theology of the ecclesiastical office. Augustine had distinguished between the power or *sacramentum* and the use of the power, the *usus sacramenti* or *officium*. The decretists, notably Rufinus, went far beyond the Magister in their analysis of this distinction. Yet, the doctrine, set forth by Gratian and Rufinus, that monk-priests have the right to use their sacerdotal power within the monastery seems to weaken the distinction. At least some sort of *executio potestatis* is granted in the sacrament of orders when it is given to monks. What is needed is an explicit recognition by the canonists that when they speak of the *officium,* they mean the right to use the power of the priesthood in the Church at large.

Although no excommunicated priest can exercise the power of binding and loosing, he can, says Gratian, perform the sacrament of baptism. This doctrine has already been studied in chapter iii. But in Causa 24, the distinction drawn between baptism and the other sacraments causes a special problem. The Magister notes that since the power of binding and loosing and the power to baptize are granted to the priest in the same act, it would seem that both should either be lost or retained by him after he is excommunicated.[26] The Magister attempts to clarify the doctrine concerning what the priest loses when he is excommunicated by again making the distinction between the *potestas* and its *executio*. He argues:

The power of office is one thing and the execution another. Sometimes the power of office is received without its execution as by monks in their sacerdotal unction and sometimes it is retained without its execution just as by suspended [priests], to whom the administration is interdicted, [but] the power not denied.[27]

26. C. 24, q. 1, dict. post c. 4, "Ligandi namque vel solvendi potestas veris, non falsis sacerdotibus a Domino tradita est. . . . Cum ergo dimittere peccata vel tenere, excommunicare vel reconciliare opus sit Spiritus sancti et virtus Christi: apparet, quod hii, qui extra ecclesiam sunt, nec ligare, nec solvere possunt . . . liquido constat, eum qui ab integritate catholicae fidei recedit, maledicendi vel benedicendi potestatem minime habere. . . . Hec autem, que de hereticis, atque scismaticis vel excommunicatis dicta sunt, videlicet, quod ligandi vel solvendi potestatem non habeant, multorum auctoritatibus probantur." C. 24, q. 1, dict. post c. 37, "His auctoritatibus perspicue monstratur, quod, ex quo aliquis contra fidem ceperit aliqua docere, nec deicere aliquem valet nec dampnare. §1. Obicitur tamen illud Augustini: 'Recedentes a fide nec baptisma, nec baptizandi potestatem ammittunt.' Cum ergo sacerdotalem unctionem utraque potestas, baptizandi videlicet et excommunicandi, sequatur, a fide recedentes aut utraque retinebut, aut utraque carebunt."

27. C. 24, q. 1, dict. post c. 37, "Sed aliud est potestas offitii, aliud executio. Plerumque offitii potestas vel accipitur, veluti a monachis in sacerdotali unctione, vel accepta sine sui executione retinetur, veluti a suspensis, quibus amministratio interdicitur, potestas non aufertur." C. 1, q. 1, dict. post c. 97. The Magister distinguished the *ius territorii* which derives from property rights from the power to govern in the Church, and in the dictum in which he does this, he appears to make a distinction between the power of governing and the power of performing the sacraments. He does not follow out the distinction, however. C. 16, q. 2, dict. post c. 7, "Tales [abbots], etsi ius territorii habeant, tamen potestatem gubernandi populum, et spiritualia ministrandi non habent. Quod etiam de episcopo intelligendum est." This passage refers to the rights held by the founders of

173

This doctrine clarifies the immutable character of the powers of priesthood received in the sacrament of orders, even if it does not solve the difficulty created by the special position of the baptizing power.[28] What is clear from the dictum is that Gratian considered the powers

churches. The rubric of the next capitulum shows what Gratian means by the last sentence of his dictum. C. 16, q. 2, c. 8 (rubric), "Episcopus, qui in alterius diocesi ecclesiam edificat, eius consecrationem sibi vendicare non audeat." The Magister thus wants to underscore the doctrine that only the bishop of a diocese has power over the churches. Furthermore, the phrase *potestas gubernandi populum* is very vague. Gratian uses it in one other place, C. 8, q. 1, dict. post c. 17 where he calls it *gubernatio populi*. But in that passage, the phrase means specifically the power of civil government. The dictum is closely connected with the passages that precede and follow it and in both the topic is the leadership of the Hebrew people. I do not think that the phrase should be understood to mean the power of jurisdiction, but the more vague notion of leadership of the people. On the *ius territorii*, see Ulrich Stutz, "Gratian und die Eigenkirchen," *ZRG*, Kan. Abt., 1 (1911), 1–32; 2 (1912), 342–343.

Orsy ("Bishops, Presbyters, and Priesthood," pp. 816–817) argues that the famous electoral decree of 1059 (Dist. 23, c. 1) distinguishes between the pope's power of order and his power of jurisdiction. This doctrine is implied, says Orsy, by the rule that the newly elected pope has the right to exercise the power to govern the Roman church even before he is consecrated. But the Magister does not take this rule into account in developing his own theory of sacerdotal power. Also, the rule is set down by the framers of the electoral decree in order to protect the Church in a case of necessity—when, for some reason, the pope cannot be consecrated shortly after his election. Dist. 23, c. 1, "§6. Plane, postquam electio fuerit facta, si bellica tempestas vel qualiscumque hominum conatus malignitatis studio restiterit, ut is, qui electus est, in apostolica sede iuxta consuetudinem inthronizari non valeat, electum, tamen, sicut vere Papa auctoritatem obtineat regendi Romanam ecclesiam et disponendi omnes facultates illius; quod beatum Gregorium ante consecrationem suam fecisse cognovimus." Benson (*op. cit.,* p. 42) notes that the provision is included in the decree in order to meet emergencies. He also notes that the writers of the decree were correct when they pointed to the example of Gregory. He exercised his powers as pope for seven months before he could be consecrated.

28. C. 24, q. 1, dict. post c. 39, "Baptisma namque sive ab heretico, sive etiam a laico ministratum fuerit, dummodo in unitate catholicae fidei accipiatur, non carebit effectu. Alia vero sacramenta, ut sacri corporis et sanguinis Domini, excommunicationis vel reconciliationis, si ab heretico vel catholico non sacerdote ministrentur, vel nullum, vel letalem habebunt effectum." This dictum demonstrates that the distinction between baptism and the other sacraments is based on its character and importance. It also demonstrates again that Gratian considered the power of the keys to be sacramental power. The fundamental work on the exercise of sacerdotal authority by excommunicated priests is L. Saltet's *Les réordinations: Étude sur le sacrement de l'ordre* (Paris, 1907). Anton Michel

of the priest to be granted by God and not subject to the power of the ecclesiastical hierarchy. The functions performed by the governors of the Church were, for Gratian, both earthly and spiritual, and this duality is characteristic of all sacerdotal power. There can be no distinction between those powers that are spiritual and those that are only juridical. Thus, Gratian did not recognize the existence of two separable elements in sacerdotal power which differ in purpose, character, or mode of transmission.

This conclusion about the Magister's theory of sacerdotal power is confirmed by the way in which he distinguished between the episcopate and the presbyterate. Orsy argued that while some passages in the Decretum supported the idea that the difference between these two grades depended on a difference in sacerdotal power as well as jurisdiction, the favored opinion in the work was that the difference between them was only jurisdictional. He supported this interpretation by showing that Gratian used the term *sacerdos* to refer to all grades of the hierarchy and by arguing that the *sacerdotium* of all these *sacerdotes* was the same.[29]

Orsy's interpretation cannot be accepted. Certainly, Gratian recognized that the jurisdiction of a bishop was significantly greater than that of a presbyter, but he thought the essential difference between the two grades consisted in the difference in their sacramental power. Bishops perform sacraments that presbyters are not permitted to perform. The bishop alone can perform the sacrament of confirmation, the consecration of churches and shrines, the blessing of the holy chrism. Also, the bishop excommunicates the delinquent from and reconciles the penitent to the Church.[30] While the bishop and presbyter

---

follows Saltet in "Ordre," *DTC*, XI:1275–1298. See A. Schleber, *Die Reordinationen in der "altkatholischen" Kirche* (Bonn, 1936). This last work is part of the literature concerning Rudolf Sohm's interpretations.

29. Orsy, "Bishops, Presbyters, and Priesthood," p. 808. The term *sacerdos* could refer to bishops in the Decretum as it does at Dist. 86, dict. post c. 5. Orsy also points to Dist. 17, dict. post c. 6 in this connection, but the word *sacerdotes* is not so obviously limited to bishops in that dictum. Gratian used the term to describe presbyters in opposition to bishops at Dist. 28, dict. post 13. C. 26, q. 6, dict. ante c. 1. Orsy, "Bishops, Presbyters, and Priesthood," p. 804.

30. Blessing the chrism, Dist. 25, c. 1; Dist. 95, cc. 2–3; Dist. 95, dict. post c. 3; C. 26, q. 6, c. 2. Consecrating churches Dist. 1, *de consec.*, c. 2. Although the

share the power to perform baptism and the Eucharist, give penitence, preach, and enjoy ecclesiastical benefices, the difference between the two grades is clearly connected with their sacramental power as well as the extent of the area in which they exercise that power.

Orsy has tried to explain away some of the differences in sacramental power by arguing that when there was necessity, the presbyter could perform some duties normally permitted only to bishops.[31] But necessity has no law, and measures taken to meet extreme need do not make general law. Medieval canonists recognized this principle as clearly as modern lawyers do. Also, Orsy tries to interpret some of the sacramental duties of the bishop as part of his power to govern. By doing this, he can preserve the view that the Magister made a distinction between the power of jurisdiction and the power of order. Thus, Orsy explains the bishop's superiority in conferring orders as part of his power of government.[32] This interpretation overlooks the sacramental character of the juridical act through which one receives sacred office. Gratian made a distinction between the sacrament of orders and the sacraments of baptism, the Eucharist, and penitence when he distinguished between sacraments of dignity and necessity. But the ordination was not less of a sacrament because of this distinction. When, therefore, Gratian distinguished between *maiores* and *minores*

---

de consecratione does not belong to the original Decretum, it is a contemporary work that contains the generally accepted doctrine on these technical matters. Confirming, Dist. 4 *de consec.,* cc. 88, 119, 120; Dist. 5 *de consec.,* cc. 1, 3, 5. On the performance of the sacraments of confirmation and ordination, see Franz Gillmann, *Zur Lehre der Scholastik vom Spender der Firmung und des Weihesakraments* (Paderborn, 1920), pp. 15–17. Excommunication, C. 26, q. 6, dict. post c. 11; C. 26, q. 6, dict. post c. 13. On all these powers, Orsy, "Bishops, Presbyters, and Priesthood," *passim.*

31. Thus, the power of giving the Holy Spirit through anointment with the holy chrism is reserved to the bishop unless he is absent and there is a case of emergency. Dist. 95, c. 1 (rubric). Orsy, "Bishops, Presbyters, and Priesthood," pp. 820–821.

32. Orsy, "Bishops, Presbyters, and Priesthood," p. 824, "the fact that the Bishop has the power and right to confer major orders *may* [*sic*] be a sign of the Bishop's superiority in the Priesthood itself. However, as by the episcopal consecration the power to govern is conferred as well, it cannot be ruled out as theologically impossible that the power and right to ordain is part of the power to rule. But, obviously, no fact would corroborate such a hypothesis."

sacerdotes in Dist. 21, he meant to say that the bishop, the *maior sacerdos,* is a priest who holds a greater measure of the power granted to the priesthood than that held by the presbyter. The episcopate is an *ordo.*[33]

It is clear from the dictum of Causa 24 cited above that Gratian did recognize two elements in sacerdotal authority, whether episcopal or presbyterial. The *executio potestatis* is, for the Magister, an essential part of the priest's authority even though it is not a substantive power, analogous to the power of baptizing for example. Furthermore, the *executio* derives from the *licentia episcopi* while the *potestas* itself comes from God through the sacrament of orders. The two elements of sacerdotal power therefore derive from different sources. There is in this doctrine at least a part of the distinction between the powers of order and jurisdiction which is made in modern canon law.[34] And

33. Robert P. Stenger supports this interpretation of Gratian's thought. Stenger concludes that though Gratian did not give a clear answer to the question of whether the episcopate constituted a separate *ordo* from the presbyterate, the canonists, especially after Huguccio, did hold a definite opinion on the subject. According to Huguccio, the bishop was distinguished from the presbyter by name, administration, office, and the power over the sacraments, and these special powers constituted a proper *ordo.* This opinion became common among the later canonists of the medieval period. My study leads to the conclusion that Gratian did consider the episcopate a separate *ordo.* Stenger, "The Episcopacy as an *ordo* According to the Medieval Canonists," *Mediaeval Studies,* 29 (1967), 66–112.

34. Michael J. Wilks has argued that the distinction between *potestas* and *executio* which Gratian draws in his discussion of excommunicated priests and bishops (C. 1, q. 1 and C. 24, q. 1) is not analogous to the distinction later drawn between *ordo* and *jurisdictio.* Benson repeats this view, but adds that when the Magister draws the same distinction between *potestas* and *executio* in his discussion of monk-priests (C. 16, q. 1), he does imply the later distinction between *ordo* and *jurisdictio.* The basis for Benson's interpretation is Gratian's relatively clear equation of *executio* and *officium* or *jurisdictio* in C. 16, q. 1, dict. post c. 19. The monk-priest receives the executio when he is given a parish by the bishop. Actually, the Magister seems to have held the same idea in Causae 1 and 24, but there he did not explicitly say that loss of the executio was the same as loss of the cure of souls—the right to exercise sacerdotal authority within the excommunicated priest's jurisdictio. Interpreting the executio referred to in these dicta as something general and unconnected with a jurisdiction leads to the conclusion that having the executio meant, for Gratian, that the priest could exercise his powers in the universal Church rather than in a specific church. But the executio was limited to the jurisdiction granted to a priest or bishop. No member of the hierarchy could leave his church nor could he exercise his power outside his own

this is not the only indication in the Decretum that Gratian recognized the existence of an element of sacerdotal authority which was in some way distinct from the power of the keys. The difference in jurisdiction was a basis for ranking the members of the episcopate, even if it did not play a significant role in marking the difference between bishop and presbyter.

The ordo episcopalis and the position of the Pope.

While Gratian explicitly recognized that the difference between the ranks of the episcopate was founded on differences in jurisdiction, he set forth this theory in only one passage. In considering the problem of whether a metropolitan has the right to judge in the matter of a cleric belonging to the diocese of one of his suffragans, the Magister argues that the primate has this right, but that he must exercise it with the consent and counsel of his bishops. In the course of the argument, the Magister cites the famous distinction between those who hold a position in the Church in partem sollicitudinis and those who hold one in plenitudinem potestatis. Pope Leo I had been the first one to draw this distinction, and he was referring to the difference between the bishops' authority over their dioceses and the pope's authority over the universal Church.

Gratian uses the distinction in referring to the difference between the metropolitan and his bishops. The metropolitan has care over the whole province while the bishop is responsible only for the affairs of a single diocese.[35] Thus, the metropolitan is permitted to meddle in the

---

parish or diocese. As Gratian says, paraphrasing Leo I, the bishops are called in partem sollicitudinis in the administration of the Church. C. 9, q. 3, dict. ante c. 1 and other passages cited in n. 35 below. Wilks, "Papa est nomen iurisdictionis," Journal of Theological Studies, 8 (1957), 74–75. Benson, op. cit., p. 52.

35. Leo made the distinction in reference to the difference between the pope, who holds a plenitude of power in the Church, and the bishop, whose jurisdiction is limited to a small part of the Church. Leo I, Ep., 14 n. 1. See C. 9, q. 3, dict. ante c. 1, "Sicut totius episcopatus ecclesiae in potestate sunt episcopi, sic et ecclesiae totius archiepiscopatus ad diocesim pertinent archiepiscopi. Vocantur enim episcopi a metropolitano in partem sollicitudinis, non in plenitudinem potestatis." The doctrine of this dictum is confirmed by dicta that prohibit bishops from ordaining the clerics of another's diocese. C. 9, q. 2, dict. ante c. 1, "autem

affairs of an individual diocese if he considers the affair important to his whole jurisdiction.

The Magister leaves no doubt that he thought this doctrine described the difference between the pope and the bishops as well as between the metropolitan and his suffragans. But in the same dictum in which he extends the doctrine to the relationship between the *Pontifex Romanus* and the *episcopi,* he also shows that the distinction between these two ranks cannot be fully accounted for by the difference in jurisdiction. While the metropolitan must seek the counsel and consent of his suffragans when he acts, "the Roman church is able, on its own authority, to judge concerning all; concerning that [church] however, it is permitted to no one to judge." [36] It is clear from this passage, that Gratian recognized a qualitative difference between pope and bishops and the difference is founded on the hierarchical theory of Church government. In fact, it is with respect to the pope's judicial supremacy and immunity that the Magister usually treats the pope's place in the constitution of the Church. Only twice in the Decretum did the Magister take up the constitutional position of the pope without reference to a specific power of the papal office. More about these passages later; they raise more problems than they solve.

In studying the lawmaking power in the Church, it was noted that the pope held a power that gave him a preeminent position in the hierarchy. The concentration of legislative authority in the papacy leads to the view that the pope held a place not just at the top of a scale of offices, but apart from the other members of that scale. At least with respect to legislative power, there does not seem to be a link between the pope and those below him. They do not share in his power except when he summons them to council in order to aid him. Then

---

episcopus vel quilibet superiorum clericos alterius sine propriis litteris ordinare non debeat." C. 9, q. 2, dict. post c. 9. See also Saint Bernard, *De Consid.* II:8, 16. Orsy, "Irregular Ordinations in Gratian's Decretum," *Heythrop Journal,* 4 (1963), 163–173. Paul Remy Oliger, *Les évêques reguliers* (Paris, 1958).

36. C. 9, q. 3, dict. post c. 9, "Sola enim Romana ecclesia sua auctoritate valet de omnibus iudicare; de ea vero nulli iudicare permittitur." In contrast, the metropolitan must seek the counsel of his suffragan when he meddles in the affairs of his diocese. C. 9, q. 3, c. 8 (rubric), "In suffraganei parrochia nichil absque eius consilio metropolitanus agat."

they participate in the making of law without it being possible to say that they share the power of establishing law.

But this view of the pope's position in the Church—as, in effect, the sole holder of authority—contradicted the normal way in which Gratian and his contemporaries looked upon the hierarchical structure of Church government. Saint Bernard, for example, told his protégé Eugene III that he would err if, because he was the highest power in the Church, he should also consider himself to be the only power. All lesser authorities were also ordained by God and, "he that resisteth the power, resisteth the ordinance of God." [37] Gratian said the same thing in the opening dictum of the *Tractatus ordinandorum:* Christ instituted the greater and lesser priests in the Church.[38] This idea—that the pope

37. Saint Bernard, *De Consid.,* III:4, 17, "Tunc denique tibi licitum censeas, suis ecclesias mutilare membris, confundere ordinem, perturbare terminos, quos posuerunt patres tui? Si iustitiae est ius cuique servare suum, auferre cuiquam sua iusto quomodo poterit convenire? Erras si, ut summam, ita et solam institutam a Deo vestram apostolicam potestatem existimas. Si hoc sentis, dissentis ab eo qui ait: 'Non est potestas nisi a Deo.' Proinde quod sequitur: 'Qui potestati resistit, Dei ordinationi resistit,' esti principaliter pro te facit, non tamen singulariter." Klemens Kilga, *Der Kirchenbegriff des hl. Bernard von Clairvaux,* Sonderdruck: *Cistercienser-Chronik* (1947), pp. 48, 53–54. Yves Congar, "L'ecclésiologie de s. Bernard," *Saint Bernard Théologien,* pp. 151–152. Jerzy von Kozlowski, *Kirche, Staat und Kirchenstaat im hl. Bernhard von Clairvaux* (Poznan, 1916), p. 9. Gerhoh of Reichersberg, *de invest. Antichristi,* 12. Idem, *Ep. ad Inn., MGH,* Libelli de lite III:204.

38. Dist. 21, dict. ante c. 1, "maiorum et minorum sacerdotum discretio in novo testamento ab ipso Christo sumpsit exordium, qui XII. apostolos tanquam maiores sacerdotes, et LXXII. discipulos quasi minores sacerdotes instituit." Orsy has argued that Gratian did not mean to say here that the distinction between bishops and presbyters stemmed from Christ himself. Instead, he suggests that the Magister thought *maiores et minores sacerdotes* were created by the early Church community following the model set forth by Christ, who had distinguished between apostles and disciples. Orsy interprets the phrase *sumpsit exordium* to refer to the example set by Christ. Orsy, "Bishops, Presbyters, and Priesthood," pp. 810–811. This interpretation cannot be accepted. The Magister says that Christ instituted the lesser and greater priests by way of making a comparison between this basic division—stemming from Christ—and the distinctions between other ranks of the hierarchy which were introduced by the members of the early Church. See chap. iii, pp. 72–73. As Stickler points out, Gratian expressed his belief in the divine institution of the hierarchy especially when he mentioned the primacy of Peter and his successors. Alfons M. Stickler, "Magistri

180

was only the highest of the powers in the hierarchy and that the authority of the lesser ranks could not be denied without contradicting divine law—was the foundation of Gratian's theory of judicial power in the Church. In the hierarchy of ecclesiastical judges, the pope stands as the highest judge, the final court of appeals, but not as the only judge from whom all others receive their authority by delegation.

The Magister's treatment of the judicial aspect of papal authority raises many problems, however. The doctrine of papal judicial supremacy that emerges from his dicta places the pope in a position considerably stronger than would be expected of a chief justice. The strength of this position can be appreciated by looking again at the connection that Gratian made between the power to make law and the right to interpret it. The authority to interpret law belongs solely to the one who has the power to make law.[39] But Gratian did not want to prove that all judicial power is actually concentrated in the hands of the pope. Elsewhere in the Decretum, he argued only that the court of the pope was the highest court of appeal to which every Christian has the right to take his case if he thinks he has been unjustly treated by a lower court.[40] This doctrine implies that the pope holds the position of the supreme judge, not of the only judge.

The conflict between the view of the pope as the sole interpreter of the law because he alone has legislative power and the view of him as supreme judge in a hierarchy of judges established by Christ is an important one. In it is contained the basic contradiction in the theory of the Church's governmental structure. If ecclesiastical government is strictly hierarchical, then ultimately all governmental power is con-

---

Gratiani sentencia de potestate ecclesiae in statum," *Apollinaris*, 21 (1948), 49. Dist. 36, dict. post c. 2, §9.

39. C. 25, q. 1, dict. post c. 16, "Ipsi namque soli canones valent interpretari, qui ius condendi eos habent."

40. C. 2, q. 6, dict. ante c. 1, "Causa vero viciata remedio appellationis sublevari poterit." C. 2, q. 6, dict. post c. 10, "patet, quod accusato (sive gravetur, sive non) appellationis vox non est deneganda." According to C. 6, q. 4, a disagreement among the judges hearing a case leads to an appeal to a higher court. Even if the judgment is unanimous, however, the defendant can appeal to a higher court. C. 9, q. 3, dict. post c. 9, n. 34 above.

181

centrated in the highest member of the hierarchy. The power of the lesser authorities is insignificant when compared with the power of the pope. But the theory of the foundation of the hierarchy does not permit Gratian or his contemporaries to enunciate a theory of government according to which only papal power counts. The authority of the bishops and lesser priests must be preserved.

The tension between the hierarchical theory of Church government and the idea that the constitution of the Church is divinely ordained can be seen when the connection that writers of Gratian's time made between the judicial supremacy of the pope and his judicial immunity is studied. Saint Bernard set forth the connection simply, paraphrasing 1 Corinthians 2:15, "The spiritual man is he who judges all things, so that he himself is judged by no one." [41] Gratian made the connection in the context of his discussion of the structure of the hierarchy at the beginning of the *Tractatus ordinandorum:* "the greater ought not to be judged by the lesser." [42] This doctrine embodies the rigid hierarchical ordering of Church government, and it also sets the pope above the rest of the hierarchy. Only the pope is truly immune from judgment according to the theory, and, in fact, judicial immunity is almost always mentioned in connection with the pope. He judges all and is judged by no one. The hierarchical theory therefore sets the pope above and outside the remainder of the hierarchy. As Gratian says, "the election of the highest priests [the popes] ought to be done by the Cardinals and religious clergy; the ejection of these however is reserved to the divine judgment." [43]

41. Saint Bernard, *De Consid.,* III:4, 15, "Spiritualis homo ille qui omnia diiudicat, ut ipse a nemini iudicetur."

42. Dist. 22, dict. ante c. 1, "Quia ergo maior a minori iudicari non debet videndum est, que inter ceteras ecclesias primum locum, que secundum, vel tertium obtineat."

43. Dist. 79, dict. post c. 10, "Sicut supra monstratum est, electio summorum sacerdotum a Cardinalibus et religiosis clericis debet fieri: erectio vero eorum divino iudicio est reservata." Dist. 17, dict. post c. 6, "scientes [the prelates summoned by Emperor Theodoric to judge Pope Simachus], quia eius sedi primum Petri apostoli meritum, deinde secuta iussione Domini conciliorum venerandorum auctoritas singularem in ecclesiis tradidit potestatem, nec antedictae sedis antistitem minorum subiacuisse iudicio. . . . Episcopi vero in sinodo residentes

Gratian seems, therefore, to support the idea that all power in the Church is held by the pope and that the pope is set apart from the earthly community over which he presides. He is the head of the earthly Church in the same way that Christ is the head of the mystical Church; neither can he be considered a part of the body in the sense that the body possesses any power or rights independent of him. But there is a very important reservation to this theory, which in fact contradicts it. At Dist. 40, c. 6, Gratian included a passage from the writings of Humbert of Silva-Candida which contained the doctrine that the pope's judicial immunity was preserved unless he deviated from the faith.[44] This text became the basis of an elaborate decretist commentary that sought to determine the special cases in which the pope could be judged and by whom he could be judged. These glosses played an important role in the development of conciliar theory during the thirteenth and fourteenth centuries.[45] The incorporation of Humbert's text into the Decretum would not be so important in this study, however, if the Magister had not expounded the same doctrine in a dictum later in the work.

In discussing the liability of prelates to accusations of their subjects, Gratian set down an argument that supported the prelates' contention

---

congregata auctoritate eiusdem Simachi [the pope had consented to call the council for the purpose of clearing his name] dixerunt: 'Simachus Papa sedis apostolicae presul ab huiusmodi oppositionibus impetitus quantum ad homines respicit, sit immunis et liber, cuius causam totam Dei iudicio reservamus.' " C. 9, q. 3, dict. post c. 9, n. 34 above. See C. 3, q. 1, dict. post c. 6. Moynihan argued that the connection between judicial supremacy and immunity was based on a misconceived notion of these two qualities. He pointed out that today the two aspects of a governor's character are recognized to be completely separate. For medieval writers, however, the connection was perfectly logical because it stemmed from the hierarchical principle of government. One's capacity to judge another was based on one's superiority to him in rank. The principle of immunity was based on the same scale. J. M. Moynihan, *Papal Immunity and Liability in the Writings of the Medieval Canonists* (Rome, 1961).

44. Dist. 40, c. 6, "Huius [the pope] culpas istic redarguere presumit mortalium nullus, quia cunctos ipse iudicaturus a nemine est iudicandus, nisi deprehendatur a fide devius."

45. Brian Tierney, *The Foundations of the Conciliar Theory* (Cambridge, 1955), pp. 57–67, *passim*.

that they did not have to receive those accusations. Gratian did not reject this argument when he worked out a compromise doctrine on the issue.

Again, Paul reproached Peter who was prince of the apostles. From which we understand that subjects are able to reproach their prelates if they will have been reprehensible. But this is easily refuted [say the prelates] if it is shown why he [Peter] should have been reproached. Peter forced the people to judaize [follow the practice of the Jews] and to recede from the truth of the Gospel when he made the flock like the Jews and secretly withdrew from [eating] the foods of the gentiles. This is equal to leaving the faith and to leading others away from the faith by example and word. By this example therefore it is not proven that prelates ought to be accused by subjects unless they deviate from the faith or force others to leave the faith.[46]

The Magister did not pursue the argument in this passage because he was not interested in the judicial immunity of the pope in that place. Yet, he did set down a theory identical to the one in Dist. 40, c. 6, and this theory, once taken up by the decretists, was like Pandora's box. It gave rise to a host of difficult questions. Who was to decide when the pope had deviated from the faith? Who was to judge him? Was heresy the only crime for which the pope could be judged or would actions that endangered the state of the Church justify ecclesiastical measures against him? Of these questions, those concerning the judges of the pope were the most important. Was it the hierarchy or the whole Church that would take action against an errant holder of the papal see? After a long dispute in the schools, canonical theory finally recognized that the right of judging lay with the whole Church represented

46. C. 2, q. 7, dict. post c. 39, "Item Paulus Petrum reprehendit, qui princeps apostolorum erat. Unde datur intelligi, quod subditi possunt reprehendere prelatos suos, si reprehensibiles fuerint. Sed hoc facile refellitur, si, unde sit reprehensis, advertitur. Petrus cogebat gentes iudaizare, et a veritate evangelii recedere, cum Iudeis gregem faciens, et a cibis gentilium latenter se subtrahens. Par autem est in se a fide exorbitare et alios exemplo vel verbo a fide deicere. Hoc ergo exemplo non probantur prelate accusandi a subditis, nisi a fide forte exorbitaverint, vel alios exorbitare coegerint." The argument in this passage may represent an opinion common among Gratian's contemporaries. The canonist's failure to comment on this particular part of the prelates' position is another example of how he often passed over issues that would become of central importance for the theory of Church government soon after he wrote.

in a general council.[47] Gratian added little to the discussion of this issue. He did not consider the relationship between the pope and the Church as a whole, but only between the pope and the hierarchy. In the passages in which he considered this problem, he set forth an interesting conception of this relationship. The ideas expressed there complete his teaching on the ecclesiastical hierarchy.

In Dist. 21, the Magister reviews the founding of the ecclesiastical hierarchy by Christ. Peter was one of the twelve whom Christ instituted as *maiores sacerdotes,* but he was chosen as *summus sacerdos* when the Lord gave him the keys of the kingdom of heaven *pre omnibus et pro omnibus.* He was thus the representative of the whole hierarchy at the same time that he was its highest member. Here, however, Gratian emphasized Peter's reception of the keys *pre omnibus* by adding that he was raised above his fellow apostles in order to monitor their faith.[48] It is the special quality of the pope's faith as successor of Peter which the Magister points out here, indicating that he saw the pope as mediator between the community and God.

A passage in Causa 24 contains the same double phrase to describe Peter's position as recipient of the keys. But in this dictum, Gratian shifts the emphasis to Peter's reception of the power *pro omnibus.* The pope is the symbol of unity of the ecclesiastical community. The passage concerns the power of heretical bishops, especially their right to exercise the power of the keys. The bishop who separates himself from unity with the pope, says the Magister, loses his right to exercise this power.[49] This doctrine implies that the Church is a corporate body

47. Tierney, *op. cit., passim.*

48. Dist. 21, dict. ante c. 1, "Simpliciter vero maiorum et minorum sacerdotum discretio in novo testamento ab ipso Christo sumpsit exordium, qui XII. apostolos tanquam maiores sacerdotes, et LXXII. discipulos quasi minores sacerdotes instituit. Petrum vero quasi in summum sacerdotem elegit, dum ei pre omnibus et pro omnibus claves regni celorum tribuit, et a se petra Petri sibi nomen imposuit, atque pro eius fide se specialiter rogasse, testatus est, et ut ceteros confirmaret subiunxit."

49. C. 24, q. 1, dict. post c. 4, "Unde, cum Dominus omnibus discipulis parem ligandi atque solvendi potestatem daret, Petro pro omnibus et pre omnibus claves regni celorum se daturum promisit. . . . Quicumque ergo ab unitate ecclesiae (que per Petrum intelligitur) fuerit alienus, execrare non potest, consecrare non valet; excommunicationis vel reconciliationis potestatem non habet." See the

185

headed by the pope, and according to medieval legal theory, the head of the corporation represents the body in himself. But it remains unclear from the passage whether the power of the keys resides in the pope or in the Church that he represents. Does the bishop receive his power from the pope as a delegation or does he hold it because he is a member of the hierarchy in which the power resides?

This question arises not only from the ambiguity of Gratian's dictum in Causa 24 but also from the central petrine text of Matthew 16:18 on which papal primacy rests. The text from Matthew is inadequate as a basis for constitutional theory. As Tierney has pointed out, the passage "You are Peter . . ." was ambiguous because it referred both to Peter and the Church. Peter received the power of binding and loosing, and Christ promised that the Church would not succumb to the powers of Hell. Did Peter receive the power for himself or for the Church? [50] Gratian's treatment of this question was unsatisfactory. He simply and cryptically said that Peter received the keys *pre omnibus et pro omnibus*. But if he received them before all—so that he held supreme power in the Church—in what sense could he have received them for all? And of course this question can be reversed. If Peter received the keys simply as the representative of the Church, how could his primatial power be justified? Thus, as was said previously, Gratian's treatment of the relationship between the pope and his inferiors raises more questions than it solves. In conjunction with the importance of the subject itself, this ambiguity in the Magister's statements was one of the most significant catalysts for the development of canonical political theory after 1140.

---

earlier part of this dictum cited in n. 26 above. Note that Gratian has reversed the two prepositions here.

50. Tierney, *op. cit.,* pp. 23–46. Van de Kerckhove, "La notion de juridiction," pp. 440–443. Anciaux, *op. cit.,* p. 547.

VIII. The Source of Legitimate
Authority in the Church

Political theorists have always been profoundly interested in questions concerning the legitimacy of power, and establishing legitimacy has always presented a complex problem. There are two levels on which one can talk about the legitimacy of rulers in a community. The first is general: Where does the power to rule come from? The answer to this question is a commonplace, an assumption, of the political theory of the community. In the case of the Christian Church, it is a commonplace of ecclesiology that the ecclesiastical hierarchy received its governmental authority when Christ granted the power of the keys to Peter and his fellow apostles. The successors of the apostles, the bishops, rule with the power first granted by Christ. But the establishment of the apostles by Christ has to be distinguished from the establishment of their successors, and this distinction leads to the second level on which the theory of legitimacy must be considered. The community must justify the exercise of authority by those who follow the first rulers, and this justification consists in delineating the rules of succession to power. On this level of the discussion, the theorist concentrates his attention on the choice of the individual who will hold power rather than on the source of the power itself.

While the two levels of the problem of legitimacy are neatly distinguished in the political theory of almost every society, they cannot be separated in the theory of the Christian Church community. The dual nature of both the ecclesiastical community and the power of its sacerdotal rulers makes it impossible to separate the divine source of

187

legitimate authority from the human transmission of that authority. Men cannot pass on divine power to other men; in every act of creating a ruler of the Church, God must participate. Thus, establishment of legitimate authority in the Church leads again to a consideration of the central problem of ecclesiastical political theory, and a discussion of Gratian's ideas will corroborate what has been said again and again in earlier chapters. The Magister recognizes that the ecclesiastical community, as a juridical community analogous to other communities, needs a constitutional doctrine that is reasonably clear-cut and takes into account the imperfections of human society. He also recognizes that it is difficult to explain how God participates in the governance of an imperfect community. In developing the theory of legitimacy, this problem produces some of the most confusing dicta in the Decretum.

Gratian's doctrine of election has been studied by several scholars. The most important early work was a pamphlet by J. B. Sägmüller, *Die Bischofswahl bei Gratian*.[1] Recently, R. L. Benson has reconsidered the Magister's treatment of the subject in the context of a study of the status of the bishop-elect.[2] Both these scholars, and others who have discussed the establishment of episcopal power more briefly, concentrate on the process of election, confirmation, and consecration of the bishop in order to explicate the Magister's constitutional doctrine. It is not my purpose here to repeat the findings of these writers, and indeed, it is not necessary to repeat them, especially now that Benson has brought scholarship on the question up to date. I want to concentrate attention on the general problem of legitimacy—on the questions, how is power transmitted to the priest and by whom is a man chosen to receive the power?—and in the final section of the chapter, on the historical significance of Gratian's discussion of election.

Benson has divided the acts performed in the establishment of legitimate authority in the Church into several classes. There are, he

1. Johannes B. Sägmüller, *Die Bischofswahl bei Gratian* (Cologne, 1908).
2. Robert L. Benson, *The Bishop-Elect: A Study in Medieval Ecclesiastical Office* (Princeton, N.J., 1968). Anscar Parsons, *Canonical Election: An Historical Synopsis and Commentary* (Washington, D.C., 1939), pp. 47–51. Marcel Pacaut, *Louis VII et les elections épiscopales dans le royaume de France* (Paris, 1957), pp. 37–41.

188

says, prerequisite acts such as introducing a man into lower orders before he is permitted to be made a priest or ultimately a bishop. There are designative acts through which an individual is chosen to receive power. Then there are consentaneous acts through which approval of the choice is expressed and constitutive acts through which the power is transmitted to the *electus*. Finally, the declarative acts only promulgate the results of the other actions.[3] Of these actions, the choice of the individual and the transmission of authority to him were most important to medieval writers as well as to us.[4] In these actions, represented by the election of and consent to a man and by ordination or consecration, the cooperation of God and man in the establishment of authority works.

The election: Choice of God or the community?

The issue raised by the theory of election can be stated simply, but for medieval writers, it was not a simple problem. If God chooses the bishop, then the electorate can only be seen as an instrument of His will. If the human electors choose the man to fill the episcopal chair, then God's role in the process is put into question. Orthodox writers could never deny that God participates in the choice of a new bishop for He is the true ruler of the Church. Yet, at the same time, these writers had to face the problem of succession to power as a problem of the here and now. They could not sit by and watch evil or incompetent men obtain ecclesiastical power, if they could do something to prevent such occurrences. The tension between faith in God's governance and confidence in the human community's ability to establish good men in the seats of power was greatest in the works of the canonists. It was for them in particular to bring the divine and human constitutions of the Church into harmonious coexistence.

3. Benson, *op. cit.*, p. 4. Benson points out that prerequisite acts are distinct from prerequisite conditions such as celibacy, age, and other characteristics required of those who will be raised to the priesthood. *Ibid.*, p. 4 n. 2.

4. *Ibid.*, p. 24. Note, as does Benson, Dist. 40, c. 8, "electio et consecratio . . . faciunt episcopum." Dist. 62, dict. ante c. 1, "videndum est, a quibus sunt eligendi et consecrandi." This dictum reflects the statement of Leo I. Dist. 62, c. 1.

Gratian took up the issue of the election in Causa 8 where he discussed the case of a bishop who had named his own successor in his will. The Magister denies that the bishop has the right to designate his successor, though it is licit for him to discuss the subject of the next bishop with those who will elect him. But as often happens with doctrines enunciated by Gratian, there existed a precedent that seems to contradict the rule. Just as Saint Peter's atonement without confession caused trouble for the doctrine that confession is necessary for the remission of sins, so Peter's personal choice of Clement as his successor in the Roman see caused trouble for the doctrine of Causa 8. The Magister solved this dialectical problem in the same way that he handled the one involving confession. He singled out the case of Peter as something extraordinary, explainable by Peter's excellence as a man and by his special relationship with God. Since bishops do not usually choose men of the caliber of Clement—and are not themselves the equals of Peter—the Fathers decreed that bishops be chosen by election of the people.[5] This argument answered the constitutional

5. Gratian bases the case in favor of the bishop's right to name his own successor on two papal decretals as well as on the precedent of Saint Peter. It is the example of Peter, however, which attracts his attention in answering the argument. C. 8, q. 1, dict. ante c. 1, "Quod autem episcopo successorem sibi instituere liceat, ex verbis Zachariae Papae [C. 7, q. 1, c. 17] conicitur, quibus Maguntino archiepiscopo permisit adiutorem sibi statuere, qui ei defuncto in plenitudinem succederet potestatis. §1. Item ex verbis Symachi Papae dicentis [Dist. 79, c. 10]: 'Si transitus Papae inopinatus evenerit, ut de sui electione successoris non possit ante decernere' apparet, quod episcopi successores sibi instituere possunt. §2. Item exemplo B. Petri illud idem probatur, qui B. Clementem sibi successorem instituit." Against this doctrine, the Magister set a canon from the Council of Antioch held in A.D. 332. C. 8, q. 1, c. 3, "Episcopo non licere decernimus pro se alterum sibi successorem constituere, licet ad exitum vitae perveniat. Quod si tale aliquid factum fuerit, irritum sit huiusmodi constitutum." Gratian reconciles these doctrines in C. 8, q. 1, dict. post c. 7, "His omnibus auctoritatibus prohibentur episcopi successores sibi instituere. Sed aliud est de sui successoris electione cum fratribus deliberare, et aliud est ex testamento tamquam suae dignitatis heredem sibi querere. Illud fieri permittitur: hoc autem penitus prohibetur. Illud autem B. Petri ab illis valet in argumentum assumi, qui sibi substituunt, qualem sibi successorem B. Petrus quesivit. Verum, quia offitium non vitae, sed sanguini cepit deferri, atque ad episcopatum tales quisque successores sibi querere cepit, qui vel odiosi populis vel a plebe docendi invenirentur, sacris canonibus constitutum est, ne quisquam sibi sui offitii querat successorem, sed populi electione queratur qui eorum utilitati

question of how a man was to be chosen for the episcopate, but Gratian did not stop there. He delved into the theological problem of God's role in the election.

Peter's choice of Clement was extraordinary not only because of the exceptional character of the men involved but also because of the direct action of God. Gratian cites a passage from Origen's commentary on the Book of Numbers which shows that the will of God is made known through an individual only on the rarest of occasions. The case of Moses' choice of Joshua as his successor was a *figura* of the case of Peter and Clement. The text of the passage is important in this discussion.

If one so great as Moses was not permitted to act by his own judgment concerning the election of the prince of the people . . . who among the people . . . or the priests will dare to consider himself worthy to do this unless it [the choice of a successor] will be revealed to him by God? . . . [In the case of Joshua] the governance of the people was given to the one who God chose, namely to the man who had . . . in himself, the spirit of God and in his eyes, the precepts of God.[6]

How does Gratian understand this passage? In the dictum that follows the canon, he paraphrases Origen, "When it is commanded that the governance of the people be given to the one whom God chooses, we understand that sometimes it is given to those whom God does not choose."[7] This dictum shows that the Magister is interested in the role of God in the choice of the new prelate but does not make

---

digne deserviat, qui illorum utilitatem, non sua lucra querat, qui Christo semen velit suscitare, non sibi divitas congregare. Quod qui facere contempserit iure ab ecclesia repudiatur."

6. C. 8, q. 1, c. 16, "Si ergo tantus ille ac talis Moyses non permittit iudicio suo de eligendo populi principe, de constituendo successore, quis erit qui audeat, vel ex plebe . . . vel ex ipsis etiam sacerdotibus quis erit, qui se ydoneum ad hoc iudicet, nisi si cui oranti et petenti a Domino reveletur? . . . Gubernatio populi illi tradatur, quem Deus elegerit, homini scilicet tali, qui habet . . . in semetipso spiritum Dei et precepta Dei in conspectu eius sunt, et qui Moysi valde notus et familiaris sit, id est in quo sit claritas legis et scientia, ut possint eum audire filii Israel." This passage is more complete than the one translated in the text.

7. C. 8, q. 1, dict. post c. 17, "Cum autem gubernatio populi ei tradi iubetur, quem Deus eligit, datur intelligi, quod aliquando quibusdam traditur, quos Deus non elegit."

clear what his idea is of that role. Origen saw the active participation of God in the choice as a rare event. Gratian seems to see it as the norm. But he could be saying that God does not always choose the bishop. Instead men choose their rulers either in accordance with God's will or not. Part of the interpretative problem raised by the dictum appears to stem from the Magister's attempt to reconcile in it the doctrine of the passages between which it stands. While its language reflects the canon that it follows, its idea seems to point to the canon that it precedes. This passage also comes from Origen's writings, though Gratian attributes it to Saint Jerome, and it concerns God's choice of Saul as king of the Hebrews.

Perhaps what we say is audacious, but we say what is written. The prince of the people and the judge of the Church is not always given through the decision of God, but according to our merits. If our acts are evil and we do bad things in the eyes of God, princes are given to us according to our heart. . . . This seems to be said about Saul whom God chose and ordered to be made king. But since he was elected according to the merits of a sinful people and not according to the will of God, He denied that he [Saul] was constituted with His consent and counsel.[8]

Origen has outdone himself in obscuring his meaning; he presents a very curious argument, the terms of which seem to change at least twice in its short course. Leaders are not always given by God's decision, but if our acts are evil, then they are given (by whom if not by God?) according to our merits. God ordered that Saul be made king, but Saul was elected (by God, presumably) according to the merits of a sinful people, and so God denied that he had been made king through divine consent and counsel. What is the great Greek theologian trying to say and what does Gratian understand him to be saying?

8. C. 8, q. 1, c. 18, "Audaciter fortasse aliquid dicimus, tamen quod scriptum est dicimus. Non semper princeps populi et iudex ecclesiae per Dei arbitrium datur, sed prout merita nostra deposcunt. Si mali sunt actus nostri et operamur maligna in conspectu Dei, dantur nobis principes secundum cor nostrum. . . . Et hoc dictum videtur de Saule illo, quem utique ipse Dominus elegerat, et regem fieri iusserat. Sed quoniam non secundum Dei voluntatem, sed secundum peccatoris populi meritum fuerat electus, negat eum cum sua voluntate vel consilio constitutum." Origen continues, saying that the same thing happens in the Church. Of course, there is a canon between c. 16 and the dictum post c. 17, but Gratian does not take note of it.

Origen appears to distinguish two aspects of God's action in choosing Saul as king. God does act as elector of the man who will receive authority, but he does not approve of the man unless he is a ruler who follows the precepts of divine justice. The phrase *arbitrium Dei* seems to mean that God chooses the ruler, while the phrase *voluntas Dei* indicates that He desires rulers to be morally good men. The divine power gave Saul to the Jews because they deserved such an evil ruler, but Saul was repudiated by God because he ruled evilly. Stating the argument of the passage in this way makes one shake his head in quiet bewilderment, but it seems to be the only possible interpretation of the text. What is clear both from Gratian's dictum and his use of the passage is that he considered God to be a principal participant in the choice of new bishops. An attempt should be made to reconcile this view with that set forth earlier in the same quaestio, giving the principal place to the election of the people.

This is very difficult to do. The doctrine that emerges from the passages is that God acts through a human agent. In special cases, he inspires single individuals to act, and these cases were exemplified by the actions of Moses and Saint Peter. Presumably, however, he usually works through the electorate of the people in the diocese. But in order for God's role to be considered effective, he must choose the method through which his will is made known. Man cannot establish the method by which divine power is exercised. When Gratian settles the original issue of the quaestio concerning whether a bishop may choose his successor, he shows clearly that the electoral principle stemmed from conciliar legislation and was based on practical considerations.[9] While God did choose to act through Moses and Saint Peter, the election is part of human constitutional law and is a means through which human will is made known. God's action in the two special cases noted by the Magister and his sources could be interpreted as events demonstrating the prerogatives of divine power, but these cases do not put the canonical norm in question. The establishment of legitimate authority is a purely human affair.

Gratian confirmed this view of the election in his discussion of the role secular powers played in it and through his conception of an

9. C. 8, q. 1, dict. post c. 7, n. 5 above.

193

ecclesiastical office. In Dist. 63, he argued that while secular governors had once been given a special place in the electoral process, their abuse of the position had convinced the Church Fathers to change the law.[10] Throughout the discussion, the Magister assumes that the establishment of authority through election is a matter of human legislation and subject to change by the ecclesiastical powers. The process of election was created in the interests of justice, practicality, and convenience, and the law of election must preserve these characteristics of the act. At the same time, the Magister's idea of an ecclesiastical office emphasized its political nature and its place in the community of Christians. In Causa 8, Gratian said that the prelate ought to serve the utility of the people.[11] In Causa 1, he had argued that the ordination is given with special concern for the moral character of both the performer and the recipient, because it is given for the good of the people rather than for the good of the recipient alone.[12] It is clear that for Gratian the office of bishop or priest should be exercised in the interests of the community, and that the community itself must take care to ensure that the ideal is met. In this doctrine, as in his theory of election, the

10. Dist. 63, dict. post c. 25, "Electiones quoque summorum Pontificum atque aliorum infra presulum quondam inperatoribus representabantur, sicut de electione B. Ambrosii et B. Gregorii legitur. Quibus exemplis et premissis auctoritatibus liquido colligitur, laicos non excludendos esse ab electione. . . ." Dist. 63, dict. post c. 28, "Verum quia inperatores quandoque modum suum ignorantes non in numero consentientium, sed primi distribuentium, immo exterminantium esse voluerunt, frequenter etiam in hereticorum perfidiam prolapsi catholicae matris ecclesiae unitatem inpugnare conati sunt, sanctorum Patrum statuta adversus eos prodierunt, ut semet electioni non insererent." As Sägmüller (*op. cit.,* pp. 17–18) points out, Gratian borrowed much of this dictum from Placidus of Nonantula, *Liber de honore ecclesiae,* c. 69.

11. C. 8, q. 1, dict. post c. 7. See n. 5 above, toward the end.

12. C. 1, q. 1, dict. post c. 43, "notandum est, quod sacramentum sacerdotalis promotionis pre ceteris omnibus magis accurate et digne dandum et accipiendum est, quia nisi ita collatum fuerit, eo desinet esse ratum, quo non fuerit rite perfectum. Cetera enim sacramenta unicuique propter se dantur, et unicuique talia fiunt quali corde vel conscientia accipiuntur. Istud solum non propter se solum, sed propter alios datur, et ideo necesse est, ut vero corde mundaque conscientia, quantum ad se, sumatur, quantum ad alios vero non solum sine omni culpa, sed etiam sine omni infamia, propter fratrum scandalum, ad quorum utilitatem, non solum ut presint, sed etiam ut prosint, sacerdotium datur."

Magister, loses sight of the place of God in the process of raising an individual to power.

The role of God cannot be ignored, however, when the sacrament of orders—the act through which sacerdotal power is transmitted to the priest or bishop—is considered. This second essential part in the establishment of legitimate authority thus presents a more difficult problem than the electoral theory.

The ordination: The priest's reception of power and authority.

Gratian expounded his theory of ordination in the course of solving two constitutional problems concerning the establishment of legitimate authority in the Church. One, discussed in Causa 16, is the issue raised by those who denied that monks could be given the *cura animarum*. The Magister supported the monks and explained how they could be introduced into the parochial government of the Church. The other problem, raised in Causa 1, stemmed from the Magister's examination of the legal status of simoniacal bishops. After establishing that such bishops are outside the Church, he comes to consider the effect of sacramental acts performed by them. The part of this discussion dealing with the sacraments of baptism and the Eucharist has already been studied.[13] The discussion that follows delves into the sacrament of orders. In both Causa 16 and Causa 1, Gratian treated the relationship between God and man in the establishment of authority. He distinguished the role of each by separating the grant of sacerdotal power from the grant of authority to use the power. The first grant took place through the sacrament of orders; the second through the giving of the *licentia episcopi*. The Magister drew the distinction clearly in Causa 16.

As stated in chapter ii, those who opposed giving *curae* to monks argued that the monastic profession and life were incompatible with the exercise of ecclesiastical government. The argument brought forth by the monks and their supporters denied the incompatibility of the

13. See chap. iii.

195

two types of life and emphasized the need of the Church for rulers with the qualifications possessed by monks.[14] This argument shows that the monks of Gratian's time valued the earthly Church community very highly. They were more concerned about the quality and well being of the community than about the peace and quiet of the monastery. This statement of their view is of course exaggerated, but monks of Gratian's time do appear to have held the idea that monastic life was intimately connected with the life of the Church as a whole. They dedicated themselves to the improvement of the priesthood and allied themselves with the party of Haimeric in the Curia. In the Decretum, concern for the quality of priests resulted in emphasis being placed on the role of the Church community itself in the establishment of its authority. There had always been more than one element in the ordination according to Church law. While the prayers of ordination indicated that God was the grantor of power to the priest,[15] the ordination ceremony also involved an effective grant of authority to use that power by the performing bishop. This understanding of the ordination was confirmed by the rule of law that prohibited what were called "absolute" ordinations.[16] An absolute ordination occurred when a bishop consecrated a priest without granting to him a title or parish in which he could exercise his new power. Gratian designated the two parts of the ordination ceremony consecration, or dedication, and ordination, and he showed that in the case of monk-priests, the grant of the bishop's *licentia* could be separated from the performance of the sacrament of orders.[17] This doctrine enhanced the importance of the *licentia*.

14. See in particular, chap. ii, nn. 40–41.

15. Bernard Botte, "L'ordre d'après les prières d'ordination," *Études sur le sacrement de l'ordre* (Paris, 1957), pp. 13–35.

16. Dist. 70, dict. ante c. 1, "nec etiam a proprio [bishop] absolute ordinandus est [a cleric]: absoluta autem ordinatio Calcedoniensi concilio prohibetur." Dist. 70, c. 2 is canon 15 of the Council of Piacenza held in 1095 by Urban II. The prohibition was repeated in the Council of Esztergom (Gran), Hungary (1114), c. 18, Mansi, XXI, col. 103–104, and the Council of London (1125), c. 8, Mansi, XXI, col. 331. Benson, *op. cit.*, pp. 51–53. V. Fuchs, *Der Ordinationstitel von seine Entstehung bis auf Innocenz III* (Boss, 1930).

17. C. 16, q. 1, dict. post c. 19, "Monachi autem, et si in dedicatione sui presbiteratus (sicut et ceteri sacerdotes) predicandi, baptizandi, penitenciam dandi,

The license of the bishop, which Gratian calls the *executio potestatis,* constitutes the effective act in the establishment of monk-priests as rulers in the Church. The monks receive all the powers attributed to priests in their consecration, but they may not exercise their power in the body of the Church until they will have been ordained to a parish by the proper bishop. By implication, other priests also depend on the juridical action of the bishop for their legitimate exercise of authority, and the implication is made explicit by the doctrine that no bishop may ordain a priest of another diocese. The bishop may give the sacrament of orders to a man from another diocese, but he may not grant a *cura* to the new priest, except in his own diocese.[18] The right to govern in the Church depends on the permission of the proper bishop. By separating the reception of power by the priest from the grant of authority to him, Gratian emphasizes the role of the ecclesiastical community in setting up its governing power.

In Causa 1, discussing another problem in the establishment of authority, the Magister sets forth the same doctrine. The simoniacal bishop, once he is excommunicated, loses the right to grant the power to govern in the Church. He can perform a valid, if not licit, sacrament

---

peccata remittendi, beneficiis ecclesiasticiis refruendi rite potestatem accipiant, ut amplius et perfectius agant ea, que sacerdotalis offitii esse sanctorum Patrum constitutionibus conprobantur: tamen executionem suae potestatis non habent, nisi a populo fuerint electi, et ab episcopo cum consensu abbatis ordinati." E. H. Fischer, "Bussgewalt, Pfarrzwang, und Beichtvater-wahl nach dem Dekret Gratians," *SG,* 4 (1956–1957), 187–230.

18. Dist. 70, dict. ante c. 1, "Ab episcopis alterius civitatis clericus ordinari non poterit." Dist. 71, *passim.* C. 9, q. 2, dict. post c. 9, "His auctoritatibus prohibentur quilibet episcopi clericos alterius ordinare. Sed queritur, si contingat eos aliquibus sacros ordines distribuere, an ordinati ab episcopis suis in propriis ordinibus recipi possint?" C. 9, q. 2, c. 10 (rubric), "Clerici ab episcopo alterius parrochiae ordinati a proprio in suis ordinibus recipi possunt." This capitulum comes from Urban II. It should be noted that the use of the term *ordinare* here refers to the sacrament of orders. The terminology had not been standardized in this period. See on ordinations by irregular bishops, Ladislav Orsy, "Irregular Ordinations in Gratian's Decretum," *Heythrop Journal,* 4 (1963), 163–173. Marie-Joseph Gerland, "Le ministre extraordinaire du sacrement de l'ordre," *Revue thomiste,* 36 (1931), 874–885. Artur M. Landgraf, "Zur Lehre von der Konsekrationsgewalt des von der Kirche getrennten Priesters im 12. Jahrhundert," *Scholastik,* 15 (1946), 204–227.

of orders, however.[19] The two aspects of the ordination are again separated in this doctrine, and the nature of each part is made clear. In the sacrament of orders, God grants the priestly powers, and the evil or schismatic bishop cannot hinder the effect of the divine act. But the bishop cannot give the newly consecrated priest a legitimate license to exercise his powers. Only those within the body of the Church are permitted to grant authority to govern the Church. It is apparent that while there is a technical difference in the irregularity discussed by the Magister in the passages that have been considered, the doctrine that he expounds is the same. In every case, the essential action in the establishment of legitimate authority is the action of the episcopal power.

The sacerdotal powers are received directly from God in the sacrament of orders and cannot be changed or taken away by the ecclesiastical hierarchy. As an often-quoted dictum of Causa 24 says, the suspended priest does not lose his *potestas,* but only his *executio potestatis.*[20] Yet from the standpoint of the Church, the suspended priest's or the monk-priest's possession of all their powers makes no difference when the governance of the ecclesiastical community is in question. The establishment of authority in the Church has to be considered an

---

19. C. 1, q. 1, dict. post c. 43, n. 12 above. C. 24, q. 1, dict. post c. 37, "Unde ab hereticis baptizati vel ordinati, cum ad unitatem fidei catholicae redierint, si forte intuitu ecclesiasticae pacis in suis recipiantur ordinibus, non iterabitur sacramentum, quod in forma ecclesiae probabitur ministratum, sed per inpositionem manus prestabitur virtus sacramenti, que extra ecclesiam nulli docetur esse collata." Orsy, "Sacred Ordinations in Gratian's Decretum," *Heythrop Journal,* 3 (1962), 152–162.

20. C. 24, q. 1, dict. post c. 37 "§1. Plerumque offitii potestas vel accipitur, veluti a monachis in sacerdotali unctione, vel accepta sine sui executione retinetur, veluti a suspensis, quibus amministratio interdicitur, potestas non aufertur." Benson, *op. cit.,* p. 51. Benson notes that Rufinus went considerably beyond Gratian on this matter. He distinguished between four things that were given to a priest in a complete ordination—the *potestas aptitudinis,* which is the sacramental power; the *potestas regularitatis,* which is the personal capacity needed to perform sacerdotal duties; the *usus officii,* which is the right to exercise sacerdotal authority; and the *potestas habilitatis,* which is the possession of an office or title in which to exercise the authority. Rufinus, *Summa decretorum,* ed. H. Singer (Paderborn, 1902), pp. 161–162.

act of cooperation between God and man, but in Gratian's discussions of this act, God's role is deemphasized—deemphasized but not diminished. No one can govern the Church without having received the sacrament of orders. Truly, the balance between God and man in the establishment of legitimate authority in the Church is impossible to gauge; both are indispensable because the community is both spiritual and temporal. It is Gratian's concern for the earthly community which makes him emphasize the constitutional aspects of the setting-up of the rulers, but his discussions, recognizing the two separate but integrally connected parts of the process, imply that his emphasis is artificial and misleading.

There is one further comment that can be made about Gratian's theory of ordination. The two elements of the ceremony imply that the priest receives his authority from two separate sources and that he is responsible to two powers. His power descends from God to him and at the same time comes from the Church. In the case of a lesser priest, it can be said that all power descends—from God and the bishop—but in the case of the bishop, or the pope, the issue is more complex. Looking at the establishment of the bishop, it appears that power descends from God and ascends from the Church. The Magister's theory of episcopal elections focuses attention on the relationship between the community and its ruler and has broad constitutional importance. It raises the question of who performs the election, and ultimately, whether the electors retain any rights over their chosen ruler.

The theory of the electorate: Its historical and constitutional importance.

Although the canons designated the performer of the ordination and elaborated on the formulas to be used in the ceremony,[21] they did not define very precisely the electorate that chose a new bishop or the procedure to be followed. By Gratian's time, the electoral principle was very ancient. It had been expounded early in the history of the Church by Pope Celestine I (422–432) and Pope Leo I (450–464). Leo

21. Dist. 64 and 65.

199

wrote to Rusticus, bishop of Narbonne, that no one ought to be considered a bishop unless he has been elected by the clergy, sought out by the people, and consecrated by his conprovincials with the cooperation of the metropolitan.[22] This doctrine was almost completely forgotten in the ensuing centuries during which the secular powers exercised the right to choose men to fill episcopal sees under their domination. By the eleventh century, bishoprics were being treated as private churches by the emperor and other powerful lay rulers of Europe. The reformers of the eleventh century set themselves against this situation and sought to free the episcopacy, as well as the papacy, from the control of the secular powers. Members of the reformed hierarchy could not owe their position to the grant of some secular prince, if they were to carry out the moral regeneration of the Church and to guide the spiritual life of Christians in the way envisaged by the reform party. The ancient theory of election of bishops furnished the reformers with a replacement for the discredited lay investiture as a way of establishing legitimate authority in the Church.[23]

The letter of Pope Leo was perhaps the most important ancient document in the reemergence of the electoral principle during the eleventh century, and Gratian made Leo's doctrine his own.[24] But while this doctrine clearly makes election necessary for the legitimate holding of authority, it does not make clear who performs the election or how it is carried out. The Magister's statements on these problems are simply an elaboration on Leo's idea. In Dist. 63, where he

22. Leo I, *Ep.* 167, "Nulla ratio sinit ut inter episcopos habeantur qui nec a clericis sunt electi, nec a plebibus sunt expetiti, nec a provincialibus episcopis cum metropolitani iudicio consecrati." Dist. 62, c. 1 where wording is very slightly different. Celestine I, *Ep.* 4, n. 5, "Nullus invitis detur episcopus. Cleri, plebis et ordinis consensus ac desiderium requiratur." Dist. 61, c. 13 and Dist. 63, c. 26.

23. Paul Schmid, *Der Begriff der kanonischen Wahl in den Anfängen des Investiturstreits* (Stuttgart, 1926). Schmid only studied the period up to the reign of Gregory VII. Gerd Tellenbach, *Church, State, and Christian Society at the Time of the Investiture Contest,* trans. R. G. Bennet (Oxford, 1940), pp. 111–114, *passim.* Tellenbach sees the movement for canonical election as a manifestation of a revolution in the way of looking at world order.

24. Dist. 62, dict. ante c. 1, "Nunc videndum est, a quibus [bishops] sunt eligendi et consecrandi. Electio clericorum est, consensus plebis." Dist. 62, dict. post c. 2, "Nisi autem canonice electus fuerit, consecrari non debet."

treats the participation of the secular powers in episcopal elections, he says:

In the Church of God, a ruler is rightly established when the people acclaim the one whom the clergy will have elected by common vote.[25]

Sägmüller argued, on the basis of this dictum, that Gratian wanted to diminish the role played by the people in the election of a new bishop. The Magister saw the election as an act of the clergy. The German scholar did not found his interpretation only on Gratian's explicit statements in the dicta but also pointed to the curious omission of canons stemming from the writings of Gregory VII. He noted, further, that the Magister did not avoid the use of Gregory's statements in other parts of his work. Thus, he concluded that Gratian rejected Gregory's dicta on the election because he disagreed with the reform pope's notion of the electorate. Gregory had written vaguely of the election by clergy and people, while Gratian sought to remove the *populus* from effective participation in the choice of a new bishop.[26]

25. Dist. 63, dict. post c. 25, "Tunc enim in ecclesia Dei rite preficietur antistes, cum populus pariter in eum acclamaverit, quem clerus communi voto elegerit." Note the end of Dist. 62, dict. ante c. 1 as well.

26. Sägmüller, *op. cit.,* pp. 17–18, *passim.* Benson, *op. cit.,* pp. 34–35 n. 60. Benson points out there that it is "misleading to assert, as Sägmüller (*op. cit.* [*Bischofswahl,* p.] 19) and Schulte (*Geschichte der Quellen [und Literatur des canonischen Rechts von Gratian bis auf die Gegenwart* (Stuttgart, 1875–1880), vol.] I, 92ff) have done, that Gratian was, in his electoral doctrine and elsewhere, an 'ausgesprochener Gregorianer.'" I agree with Benson's doubts. The Magister cited passages from Gregory VII at Dist. 96, cc. 9, 10; Dist. 8, c. 5; C. 1, q. 3, c. 1; and C. 15, q. 6, c. 3. In each case the issue was either a technical point of law or a question of reform that had become standard since the mid-eleventh century.

Sägmüller overemphasizes the degree to which Gratian wants to remove the people from the electoral process. In a dictum from Causa 8 (C. 8, q. 1, dict. post c. 7), the Magister referred to the election simply as an *electio populi.* The term obviously refers to the whole community of the electorate and indicates that the people, as opposed to the clergy, are part of that electorate. In the context of Dist. 63, Gratian associates the people with the clergy in the election. The position of the people is distinct from that of the lay rulers. In the ancient Church, the Magister says, the *electus* was presented to the civil authority in order to receive its consent to the choice. The disruption and corruption that arose from this practice, however, caused the fathers to remove the royal power from any par-

As Benson has pointed out, the Magister's opposition to the views expressed in a canon cannot explain its omission from the Decretum.[27] In asking questions about the absence of canons from the work, Gratian's dialectical method must be kept in mind; the Magister rejected the doctrine of a great many canons that he incorporated in the Decretum. The omission of Gregory VII's pronouncements on the canonical election should be seen, I think, as yet another clue to Gratian's political sympathies and, more important, to the political significance of the theory of the electorate in the mid-twelfth century.

Sägmüller and Benson focused attention on the respective places held by the clergy and the people in the election of a bishop. It is the place held by the monastic leaders of the diocese, the so-called *religiosi viri*, which should be at the center of this discussion. Under the aegis of the new reform movement headed by Haimeric and symbolized by Saint Bernard, the abbots had begun to insert themselves into the electoral procedure of some dioceses. At the Second Lateran Council,

---

ticipation in the choice of the new bishop. The lay people retained their role though. (Dist. 63, dict. post cc. 25, 27, 28. Michel, *Papstwahl und Königsrecht* [Munich, 1936].)

Gratian says that the people ought to exercise humility in giving its assent to the choice made by the clergy in elections (Dist. 63, dict. post c. 25), but such admonitions did not weaken the effect of the role that the people could play. The case of the papal schism of 1130 shows the possible importance, both political and canonical, of the laity's participation in the election. In one of his letters on this affair, Saint Bernard compared the reception of Anaclet II by the Romans to the general European acceptance of Innocent II's legitimacy. This argument was repeated by other supporters of Innocent, and, as Bloch has pointed out, it was a canonical principle. Anaclet and his supporters also sought to win the adherence of the peoples of the Church. Saint Bernard, *Ep.* 124, n. 2, "Pulsus Urbe, ab orbe suscipitur." Peter the Venerable, *Ep.* 40, ed. Constable, "Hoc considerate, ubi aecclesia esse existimanda sit, quae in omnibus mundi nationibus esse credenda est, in angulo urbis Romae, an in toto orbe." Arnulf of Lisieux, *Invectiva,* 7. Arnulf was trained as a canonist at Bolognia. H. Bloch, "The Schism of Anacletus II and the Glanfeuil Forgeries," *Traditio,* 8 (1952), 167–169.

Gratian himself confirmed the importance of popular acceptance in his discussion concerning a bishop's right to choose his own successor. Bishops were prohibited from choosing their successors because too often they chose men who were hated by the people. (C. 8, q. 1, dict. post c. 7.) Thus, though the Magister definitely does emphasize the role played by the clergy, he does not, as Sagmüller argues, so completely disregard the place of the people.

27. Benson, *op. cit.,* p. 34, n. 60.

202

the victorious party of the reformers promulgated a canon that legalized the participation of the religious men in the election. The new rule required the clergy that was to elect a new bishop to consult with the abbots before they voted. If they failed to do this, the election was to be considered invalid. Gratian included this canon in Dist. 63 where, to the surprise of scholars, he omitted the appropriate texts on the structure of the electorate contained in the writings of Gregory VII. He also gave it very strong support in the dictum that precedes the canon.[28]

The discussion of Dist. 63 should therefore be connected with that of Causa 16. Both these sections of the Decretum are affected by the contemporary dispute over the participation of monks in the governance of the Church, and this dispute involved the ecclesiastical parties of the 1120's and 1130's.[29] The discussion of Dist. 63 is not the only con-

---

28. Conc. Lat. II, c. 28, ed. J. Alberigo *et al., Conciliorum Oecumenicorum Decreta* (Freiburg i. Br., 1962), p. 179. Dist. 63, c. 35, "Obeuntibus sane episcopis, quoniam ultra tres menses vacare ecclesiam sanctorum Patrum prohibent sanctiones, sub anathemate interdicimus, ne canonici de sede episcopali ab electione episcoporum excludant religiosos viros, sed eorum consilio honestam et idoneam personam in episcopum eligant. Quod si exclusis religiosis electio facta fuerit, quod absque eorum consensu et conniventia factum fuerit, irritum habeatur et vacuum." Pope Eugene III interpreted the term *religiosi viri* to mean the monks of the diocese. Eugenie III, *Ep.* 548, PL 180, col. 1566-7. Dist. 63, dict. post c. 34, "Nunc autem sicut electio summi Pontificis non a Cardinalibus tantum, immo etiam ab aliis religiosis clericis auctoritate Nicolai Papae est facienda, ita et episcoporum electio non a canonicis tantum, sed etiam ab aliis religiosis clericis, sicut in generali sinodo Innocentii Papae Romae habita constitutum est."

29. See chap. ii, pp. 42–46. The newly won rights of the monks in the election of bishops were reflected in a transition in the conception of the monastic status within society as a whole. The transition was from the ancient tripartite division of society into *coniugati, continentes,* and *praelati*—deriving chiefly from Gregory the Great (*Moralia in Job,* XXXII, 20, XXV)—to a simple twofold division that saw the clergy, including the monks, opposed to the laity. The change was not complete during Gratian's time nor did all the members of Haimeric's party agree with the new mode. The Magister incorporated a passage supporting the new view in the Decretum, but the source of the text has not been found. C. 12, q. 1, c. 7, "Duo sunt genera Christianorum. Est autem genus unum, quod mancipatum divino offitio, et deditum contemplationi et orationi, ab omni strepitu temporalium cessare convenit, ut sunt clerici, et Deo devoti, videlicet conversi . . . §1. Aliud vero est genus Christianorum, ut sunt laici." Gratian attributes the passage to Saint Jerome. Luigi Prosdocimi, "Chierci e laici nella societa occidentale del secolo XII: A proposito di Decr. Grat. C. 12, q. 1, c. 7: 'Duo

temporary evidence that the process of election and the determination of who should participate caused difficulties for the new reformers. In 1144, Saint Bernard thought it necessary to remind the cathedral chapter of Sens, then engaged in choosing a new archbishop, that they should consult with the monks of the diocese.[30] It is reasonable to suppose that opposition to the intrusion of the monks into the electoral process was widespread in the period of the party disputes and that it continued to exist for sometime afterward.

Gratian's omission of Gregory VII's canons on the election is another sign of the influence of politics on the discussion in Dist. 63. Gregory was one of the chief representatives and *auctoritates* of the political tradition that Gratian opposed, and the pope's views on the electorate were very likely used by those opposed to the participation of the monks in the election.[31] In addition, the corpus of canons did not provide an adequate counterweight to the doctrine set forth by Gregory. The only canons that the Magister might have been able to set against those of Gregory would have been the electoral decree of 1059 and the one promulgated by the Second Lateran Council, and he must have recognized that such a procedure would not convince

---

sunt genera Christianorum'," *Proceedings of the Second International Congress of Medieval Canon Law, Boston College, 1963,* ed. Stephan Kuttner and J. J. Ryan (Rome, 1965), pp. 105–122.

Hugh of Saint Victor also supported the new twofold division. *de Sac.,* II:2, 3. Saint Bernard and Gerhoh of Reichersberg gave strong support to the ancient view. Bernard, *in Nat. Domini,* 1, n. 7. Idem, *de div.,* 35, n. 1. Gerhoh, *de invest. Antichristi,* 10. On the Carolingian background of the tripartite view of the *populus christianus,* see James M. Wallace-Hadrill, "The *via regia* of the Carolingian Age," *Trends in Medieval Political Thought,* ed. B. Smalley (Oxford, 1965), pp. 37–38.

30. Saint Bernard, *Ep.* 202, "Expectandum proinde suffraganeorum concilium episcoporum, expectandus assensus religiosorum qui sunt in episcopatu, atque in commune tractandum commune negotium."

31. As Sägmüller (*op. cit.,* p. 19) pointed out, Gregory recognized only two participants in the election, *clerus et populus.* It is probably the exclusion of any other elements of the community rather than the overemphasis of the role of the people which concerned Gratian. The restrictiveness of Gregory's comments made them effective counterweights to the new electoral theory of Haimeric's group. See the comments in n. 33 below. See also the comments on the connection between Gregory VII and Gratian's political enemies established during the crisis of 1111–1112 in chap. vi, n. 32.

opponents or skeptics of the legal soundness of his doctrine.[32] He therefore went back to the ancient canons of the Church Fathers, chiefly to the views expressed by Leo I and Celestine I, in order to construct his theory of the electorate. These canons permitted him to argue the main point of the *Distinctio*—that secular rulers have no place in the election—without jeopardizing the argument that monks do have a place in it.[33] Gratian omitted Gregory's dicta on the election because they were associated with the views of his political opponents, not because they gave the people too great a role in the election. He would incorporate texts in the Decretum to which he was opposed on doctrinal grounds but not those which represented opposing political views, where his opposition might be construed as stemming only from political sympathy.

There is other evidence that contemporary politics influenced the content and argument of Gratian's discussion of the election. In his letter to the clergy of Sens, Saint Bernard argued that they ought to consult the monastic leaders of the diocese because the election would affect these men, and they ought to give consent therefore to the choice that would be made.[34] The principle on which this argument was based derived from Roman law, but it had been incorporated into canonical jurisprudence by the fifth century. The history of the idea has been studied by Gaines Post and Yves Congar.[35]

32. The electoral decree of 1059, Dist. 23, c. 1, was too vague on this point though Gratian mentions it in the dict. post c. 34 of Dist. 63 (see n. 28 above). Dist. 23, c. 1, "§2 . . . obeunte huius Romanae ecclesiae universalis Pontifice, inprimis cardinales episcopi diligentissima simul consideratione tractantes, mox sibi clericos cardinales adhibeant: sicque reliquus clerus et populus ad consensum novae electionis accedant."

33. Benson (*op. cit.,* p. 24 n. 5) notes that of the forty-eight capitula in Dist. 61–63, twenty stem from the writings of Celestine I, Leo I, and Gregory I. Note that the letter of Leo I Dist. 63, c. 27) mentions the consent of the *conventus ordinis* as well as of the honored men of the diocese. This text could not be effectively cited in opposition to the Magister's doctrine.

34. Saint Bernard, *Ep.* 202, n. 30 above.

35. Gaines Post, "A Romano-Canonical Maxim, Quod Omnes Tangit, in Bracton and in Early Parliaments," *Studies in Medieval Legal Thought* (Princeton, 1964), pp. 163–240. This article originally appeared in *Traditio,* 4 (1946), 197–251. Post has revised and enlarged it for its reprint in his *Studies.* Yves Congar, "Quod omnes tangit, ab omnibus tractari et approbari debet," *RHD,* 36 (1958), 210–259.

205

The principle was contained in the Roman law maxim, "Quod omnes similiter tangit, ab omnibus comprobetur" (what touches all in the same way, ought to be approved by all [*q.o.t.*]) which had been expounded by classical jurists to govern actions concerning *tutela* (a charge or guardianship). If the charge was governed by more than one person or *tutor,* they said, then no action could be taken effecting the charge unless all the *tutores* consented.[36] In Church law, the maxim was applied to episcopal elections by Celestine I and Leo I. Celestine stated briefly that "no bishop ought to be given to those who are unwilling [to receive him]." Leo wrote more precisely that "he who will be placed above all ought to be elected by all." [37] The passage from this pope's letter to Rusticus of Narbonne, cited above, implies the same doctrine, and the idea became current again in the mid-twelfth century, after a long period when it, like the idea of the election itself, lay buried in the ancient papal letters. And after the period of Saint Bernard and Gratian, the *q.o.t.* maxim became even more important. As Post has shown, the canonists of the late twelfth and early thirteenth century used the *q.o.t.* maxim to explain the electoral acts of corporations and communities. In the thirteenth century, the doctrine was used to justify claims by the cathedral chapters to participate in the governance of the dioceses in the Church, and it also played a role in the development of arguments according to which kings could not tax the realm unless all whom the tax would touch approved through their representatives.[38] In view of the importance of the idea contained in *q.o.t.* and derivative maxims, Gratian's treatment of it is very strange.

36. The maxim occurs at C. 5, 59, 5, 2 of the *Corpus Juris Civilis*. Post, *op. cit.,* p. 169. As Post points out, the rule was an extension of the general notion of classical law that all those involved in an affair in law ought to be consulted and summoned.

37. Celestine I, *Ep.* 4, n. 5, "Nullus invitis detur episcopus." This sentence is the first one in Dist. 61, c. 13. On this text, see n. 40 below. Leo I, *Ep.* 10, n. 6, "Qui praefuturus est omnibus, ab omnibus eligatur." See on these and later references to the principle in canon law, Congar, *op. cit., passim.*

38. Post, *op. cit., passim*. Historians have recognized the importance of the principle of *q.o.t.* since the mid-nineteenth century. Stubbs claimed that Edward I was the one who made the principle into a pillar of constitutional government in his writ to the Archbishop of Canterbury of 1295: "Sicut lex justissima . . . hortatur et statuit ut quod omnes tangit ab omnibus approbetur, sic et nimis evidenter ut communibus periculis per remedia provisa communiter obvietur."

The Magister cites the letter of Celestine in which that pope has expressed, briefly, the principle of *q.o.t.*, but the passage occurs in Dist. 61 as part of the proof that clerics belonging to the diocese ought to be preferred over outsiders, when a new bishop is elected. As a result, it is not the statement of the general principle justifying the theory of election which interests Gratian in the canon, but the argument summarized in the rubric of the preceding capitulum, "Men from other dioceses ought not to be put before outstanding men from their own diocese [by electors]." [39] But Celestine's text is cited again in connection with the electoral principle itself, and in that capitulum, the Magister deleted the sentence that contained the *q.o.t.* principle. Leo's more explicit, and more famous, statement of the principle was excluded from the Decretum altogether. Like the passage from Celestine's letter, Gratian cites the Leonine text in connection with his enunciation of the electoral principle and deletes the sentence containing the reference to *q.o.t.* He might have been expected to cite both texts in full. [40]

The passages occur at Dist. 63, cc. 26 and 27. In the preceding dictum, Gratian set forth the doctrine that lay people and lay rulers

---

William Stubbs, *Constitutional History of England*, 4th ed., 2:133–134, 369. Post (*op. cit.*, pp. 166–167) reviews the historiography of *q.o.t.*, and quotes the writ of Edward. Post set out to show that the maxim had had a considerable history in the law of the Church and of England before it was used by King Edward.

39. Dist. 61, c. 12 (rubric), "Extranei emeritis in suis ecclesiis non preponantur." Dist. 61, c. 13 (rubric), "De eodem." Dist. 61, dict. post c. 11, "Item clerici unius ecclesiae non sunt preferendi in electione his, qui bene militant in propria ecclesia."

40. Celestine I, *Ep.* 4, n. 5, "Nullus invitis detur episcopus. Cleri, plebis et ordinis consensus ac desiderium requiratur." Gratian deletes the second sentence of the passage from his citation of it at Dist. 61, c. 13. He quotes only the second sentence, with slight textual variation, at Dist. 63, c. 26. Leo I, *Ep.* 10, n. 4, "Exspectarentur certe vota civium, testimonia populorum; quaereretur honoratorum arbitrium, electio clericorum, quae in sacerdotium solent ordinationibus ab his qui noverunt patrum regulas, custodiri. . . . [n. 6], Per pacem et quietem sacerdotes qui futuri sunt postulentur. Teneatur subscriptio clericorum, honoratorum testimonium, ordinis consensus et plebis. Qui praefuturus est omnibus, ab omnibus eligatur." Then compare Dist. 63, c. 27, "Vota civium, testimonia populorum, honoratorum arbitrium, electio clericorum in ordinationibus sacerdotum constituantur. *Et infra*: Per pacem et quietem sacerdotes, qui futuri sunt, postulentur, teneatur subscriptio clericorum, honoratorum testimonium, ordinis conventus et plebis."

ought not to be excluded from the electoral process.[41] In the dictum that follows c. 27, he explains why, in the ancient Church, the *electus* was presented to the civil authority in order to receive its consent to the choice. The role of the emperor or king was based, according to the Magister, on two principles. First, the civil ruler was considered to be the guardian of the Church against the danger posed by heretics and schismatics. Having military power, the king or emperor could keep such men from invading ecclesiastical sees. Second, the secular ruler would become the son of the man who filled the episcopal or papal chair, and those who were to be placed under the guidance of another man ought to consent to the one who would fill that position.[42] The second reason thus approximated the general principle supporting the electoral theory that Celestine and Leo, in the passages quoted immediately before this dictum, had so clearly enunciated and that Gratian had deleted from these canons. All is not plainly visible in the Magister's treatment of the electoral theory.

Gratian certainly knew the principle set forth by Celestine and Leo and current in the electoral theory of his time, but he must also have known the origin of the idea. For Saint Bernard, the principle embodied by *q.o.t.* probably appeared to be an orthodox canonical rule. He could therefore cite it without qualms in his letter to the canons

41. Dist. 63, dict. post c. 25, "Quibus exemplis et premissis auctoritatibus liquido colligitur, laicos non exludendos esse ab electione, neque principes esse reiciendos ab ordinatione ecclesiarum. Sed quod populus iubetur electioni interesse, non precipitur advocari ad electionem faciendam, sed ad consensum electioni adhibendum. Sacerdotum . . . est electio, et fidelis populi est humiliter consentire. Desiderium ergo plebis requiritur an clericorum electioni concordet. Tunc enim in ecclesia Dei rite preficietur antistes, cum populus pariter in eum acclamaverit, quem clerus communi voto elegerit." In stating the same doctrine, Celestine and Leo had also stated the principle of *q.o.t.* Gratian here carefully avoids stating that principle and in the next capitula, he prevents Celestine and Leo from stating it as well.

42. Dist. 63, dict. post c. 27, "Principibus vero atque inperatoribus electiones Romanorum Pontificum atque aliorum episcoporum referendas usus et constitutio tradidit pro scismaticorum atque hereticorum dissensionibus, quibus nonnumquam ecclesia Dei concussa periclitabatur, contra quos legibus fidelissimorum inperatorum frequenter ecclesia munita legitur. Representabatur ergo electio catholicorum principibus, ut eorum auctoritate roborata nullus hereticorum vel scismaticorum auderet contraire, et ut ipsi principes tamquam devotissimi filii in eum consentirent quem sibi in patrem eligi viderent."

of Sens. For Gratian, the most learned canonist of his day and a man well read in the Roman law commentaries as well, the principle was part of the Roman law tradition that he and his political allies wanted to remove from canonical jurisprudence. His omission of the crucial sentence from the letters of Celestine and Leo cited at cc. 26 and 27 was, it seems, connected with his general attitude toward Roman law. How then can his reference to the principle of *q.o.t.* in the subsequent dictum be explained?

There are two possible answers to this question. The first is rather simple and straightforward; the second is a bit involved, but attractive nonetheless. On the one hand, it is possible that Gratian did not see the similarity between the sentences deleted from Celestine's and Leo's canons and the idea that the participation of the secular powers in the election was based, at least in part, on the need for consent of subjects to newly established rulers. This answer to the question supposes that the Magister was fairly dense and also implies that he was unaware of the famous principle enunciated by Leo and Celestine. Both these suppositions appear unjustified. On the other hand, then, it is possible that Gratian, associating the principle with Roman law, also associated it with the participation of secular powers in elections. The reasons for this participation given in the dictum post c. 27 did not prevent the Fathers from depriving the civil rulers of their role when it became clear that such rulers interfered with and disrupted elections instead of aiding in carrying them out. In the dictum post c. 28, the Magister confirms this new constitutional theory and supports the right of the ecclesiastical legislators to make it part of the law of the Church.[43] The implication is that *q.o.t.* is a bit of secular law that canonical jurisprudence can do without.[44]

Gratian had already made the point in the *Distinctio* that the Roman law maxim was not necessary for supporting the doctrine of election of bishops. The *auctoritates* made it clear that the election was the proper way to establish episcopal authority. Getting rid of the principle was analogous to, indeed part of, getting rid of the participation of the

43. See n. 10 above.

44. The right of ecclesiastical authority to accept or reject secular law, as regards the Church, is set forth in Dist. 10.

princes in the election. What Gratian seems to be indicating by his argument in the *Distinctio* is that he accepts the doctrine of the Gregorian reformers of the previous century, but goes beyond them as well. The process of freeing the Church from secular control includes not only prohibiting lay interference in ecclesiastical affairs, but also cleansing Church law of troublesome secular ideas and doctrines. The problem raised by the *q.o.t.* is its inclusiveness. It justifies the participation of the secular rulers, as well as other elements of the community, in episcopal and papal elections, a point that the Magister plainly recognizes. It must, therefore, be expunged from ecclesiastical law; a task that he subtly undertakes. And like other principles of the Roman law which Gratian carefully avoided in the Decretum, the *q.o.t.* idea was reintroduced into canonical jurisprudence by his successors. The party disputes of the 1120's and 1130's were defunct by the time they took up the theory of canonical election.[45]

45. In fact, the doctrine of the reform party itself provided the basis for the later reintroduction of *q.o.t.* into the law of the Church. During the late eleventh and twelfth centuries, the canons of the cathedral, organized into a chapter, won the exclusive right to act as the clerical participants in the election. This victory for the chapter was implied in the canon of the Second Lateran Council (c. 28= Dist. 63, c. 35) studied above. Conc. Lat. II, c. 28, "ne canonici de sede episcopali ab electione excludant religiosos viros." It was formally recognized by Innocent III in the Fourth Lateran Council of 1215. Conc. Lat. IV, c. 24, "in collatione adhibita eligatur, in quem omnes vel maior vel sanior pars capituli consentit." The chapter also began to participate actively in the administration of affairs in the diocese. One result of this activity was that disputes between bishops and their chapters abounded in the twelfth and thirteenth centuries. Another result was that the lawyers began to develop doctrines to describe and justify the corporate activities of the chapter and the relationship between it and the bishop. They used the *q.o.t.* principle as one of the bases of this legal doctrine. Post, *op cit., passim.* For a brief history of the cathedral chapters, see John Gilchrist, "Cathedral Chapter," *New Catholic Encyclopedia,* 3:249–251. Kathleen Edwards, *The English Secular Cathedrals* (Manchester, 1949), pp. 1–22.

In the thirteenth century, the cardinals began to apply the new legal doctrines to their own juridical status and to their relationship with the pope. They called themselves *pars corporis papae* indicating that they thought they ought to participate in papal government. Joseph Lecler, "Pars corporis papae. . . . Le Sacré Collège dans l'ecclésiologie médiévale," *Mélanges Henri de Lubac,* 2 (Paris, 1964), 183–198. Brian Tierney, *Foundations of the Conciliar Theory* (Cambridge, 1955), pp. 68–84.

IX. The Division of Governmental Responsibilities Between Regnum and Sacerdotium: The Ecclesiastical Community and Other Communities

The struggle to free the Church from the control and interference of the secular powers became the preoccupation of the Gregorian reformers during the Investiture Contest. Papal writers began to assert that the Ecclesia was an independent juridical community, and after the end of the Contest, the new reformers elaborated on the theory of its constitutional structure. But the new emphasis on the juridical *communitas ecclesiae* exacerbated the problems of coexistence for the two powers. The governmental authority of the Church revived ancient claims of leadership in certain areas of law and social life and pushed into new areas. The division of governmental responsibilities between regnum and sacerdotium within *Christianitas,* which had been a relatively unimportant matter in the early Middle Ages, became a central fact of political life after 1122. A great need arose for legal theory to regulate the sharing of power.

There are two aspects of the juridical relationship between regnum and sacerdotium. First, there is the problem of juridical independence and of the authority of each relative to the other. Such questions about the relationship were the underlying issues of the Investiture Contest, and they have attracted a great amount of attention from scholars. Second, there is the more prosaic problem of how the two powers are to get on with the day to day business of governing. Gratian did not consider the first aspect of the regnum-sacerdotium relationship, but he had significant things to say about the second. A study of the Magister's ideas about the division of governmental responsibilities between the two powers will complete this explication of his ecclesiology. Determining Gratian's conception of the relationship between the powers clarifies his view of the scope and character of ecclesiastical authority.

Focusing attention on the division of governmental responsibilities between regnum and sacerdotium also gives a good perspective of scholarly disputes over the juridical position of the two powers vis-à-vis each other. The dispute has been long-lived and often acrimonious, and no one on either side has been in any way convinced by the arguments of his opponents.

Walter Ullmann argues, on one side, that medieval political thinkers considered the Church to be an all-embracing community in which there was a single governing authority, the ecclesiastical hierarchy.[1] Ullmann considers the idea of the *societas christiana,* identical to *Christianitas,* to be the basis of medieval theory on the relationship between regnum and sacerdotium. This society was oriented toward the goals specifically associated with the Ecclesia, the moral education of men and the salvation of souls. The rulers best suited for guiding men toward these goals were the priests who were therefore given the principal role of governing in the universal community. According to Ullmann, medieval Church writers, including Gratian, recognized the force of this reasoning and argued consistently for the superiority of priestly power in all matters of temporal as well as spiritual life. Yet, according to Ullmann, the ecclesiastical theory of order in the universal community of Christians was opposed by another. The supporters of the emperor during and after the Investiture Contest expounded the view that the secular authority was the supreme governor of the community. Their argument was strengthened by the actual predominance of imperial power in the period before the advent of the reform papacy and the apparent acquiescence of Church leaders to this arrangement before the rise of the reform party. Ullmann argues that while history

1. Walter Ullmann, *The Growth of Papal Government in the Middle Ages,* 2d ed. (London, 1962), *passim.* Idem, *Medieval Papalism* (London, 1949), *passim.*

212

was on the side of the imperial writers, ecclesiastical writers had ancient texts on which to base their claim that the sacerdotium was the superior power. The reform movement, according to him, was aimed at the realization of the ancient ecclesiastical view of world order.

Alfons Stickler and Friedrich Kempf have argued, on the other side, that Church writers always recognized the existence of two independent and essentially equal powers.[2] While Ullmann views medieval political thought as monistic, they consider it dualistic. Stickler, who has studied Gratian's ideas on regnum-sacerdotium relations, argues that the Magister and his contemporaries recognized the independence of civil authority. For them, secular power pursues its own goals and is juridically equal to ecclesiastical power. Examples of one governmental authority intruding on the sphere of the other do not, according to Stickler, lead medieval thinkers to claim that one of the two is juridically superior. For Stickler, *Christianitas* is not identical to the *societas christiana,* and medieval writers do not put forth a theory of government for such a society. *Christianitas* was, in his view, a vague term referring only to the cultural-religious body of Christians, not to the juridical community of Christians.[3]

2. As noted, the dispute between Kempf and Stickler on the one side and Ullmann on the other has been vehement. Its flavor can be seen in the preface to the second edition of Ullmann's *Growth of Papal Government* (see n. 1) and from Kempf's articles, Friedrich Kempf, "Die päpstliche Gewalt in der mittelalterlichen Welt," *Miscellanea Historica Pontificalis,* 21 (1959), 153–166. *Idem,* "Das Problem der Christianitas im 12. und 13. Jahrhundert," *Historisches Jahrbuch,* 79 (1961), 104–123. See Alfons M. Stickler, "Concerning the Political Theories of the Medieval Canonists," *Traditio,* 7 (1949–1951), 450–463. Three other articles by Stickler are especially important for this study on Gratian. Stickler, "De ecclesiae potestate coactiva materiali apud Magistrum Gratianum," *Salesianum,* 4 (1942), 2–23, 96–119. *Idem,* "Magistri Gratiani sentencia de potestate ecclesiae in statum," *Apollinaris,* 21 (1948), 36–111. *Idem,* "I 'gladius' negli atti dei concili e dei RR. Pontefici sino a Graziano e Bernardo di Clairvaux," *Salesianum,* 13 (1951), 414–445.

3. The equation of *Ecclesia and Christianitas* is, of course, the basis of Ullmann's interpretation of medieval theory of regnum-sacerdotium relations. But as Ladner has shown, twelfth-century writers did not equate these two notions. Gratian and Bernard assumed the existence of parallel systems of secular and ecclesiastical government, and this assumption precludes the absolute equation of *Ecclesia* and *Christianitas.* Gerhard Ladner, "The Concepts of Ecclesia and Christianitas and Their Relation to the Idea of Papal 'Plenitudo Potestatis' from Gregory VII to

213

The view of Ullmann has been termed hierocratic, while that of Stickler and Kempf has been called dualistic. Both views emphasize the extreme positions on the relations of regnum and sacerdotium, and they possess the advantage of extreme positions. They permit scholars to give a simple interpretation of medieval theory about the two powers. But as Tierney has pointed out, no medieval writer committed himself to such extreme theories as hierocracy and dualism.[4] The use of these terms in modern scholarship, while perhaps useful when scholars began to study medieval theories of regnum and sacerdotium, are now tending to misrepresent the views of medieval thinkers. All writers of the twelfth century agreed that both powers were necessary because there were governmental functions that only one of the two was competent to perform. The priesthood could not pass sentences requiring the shedding of blood and could not be involved in carrying out any penalty that entailed mutilation or death. The secular powers could not judge cases concerning marriage law or the status of oaths. The juridical relationship between the two powers, the structure of government within *Christianitas,* was very complex, and to obtain an understanding of it, the scholar must carefully analyze the division of governmental responsibilities between them. This chapter will give substance to Tierney's criticism of scholars' interpretation of medieval ideas on regnum and sacerdotium.

In the first section, a study is made of Gratian's idea of the division of legislative and judicial authority between the powers. This serves as an introduction to the second section where the complex theory of the exercise of coercive power in the interests of the Church will be taken up. The coercive activity was the most important area of cooperation between regnum and sacerdotium, and Gratian discussed it extensively. He examines not only the right of the Church power to use force, but also the use of force by political powers in general.

Boniface VIII," *Sacerdozio e Regno da Gregorio VII a Bonifacio VIII* (Rome, 1954), pp. 49–77. Kempf, "Das Problem der Christianitas im 12. und 13. Jahrhundert."

4. Brian Tierney, "The Continuity of Papal Political Theory in the Thirteenth Century. Some Methodological Considerations," *Mediaeval Studies,* 27 (1965), 227–245.

The division of legislative and judicial powers.

Gratian's treatment of human law in the *Tractatus de legibus* shows that he recognized a distinction between secular and ecclesiastical powers and their spheres of jurisdiction. He divided human law into two parallel systems, secular and ecclesiastical, and these corpora of laws represent the independent legislative and judicial power of the Church and the secular communities.[5] But the division of human law itself does not imply any relationship between the two parts of the law or the authorities from which they emanate. In fact, Gratian did not take up this problem, even when he discussed conflicts of laws. His only interest in discussing the relationship between the laws of the Church and of secular princes is to examine the use of secular law in the ecclesiastical community per se. In ecclesiastical courts, he says, the constitutions of princes yield to ecclesiastical statutes. When Church law does not cover a case, however, the ecclesiastical judge can use secular law, and when there is no conflict of law, secular law, filling a lacuna in Church law, deserves full obedience.[6]

Conflicts of law would not be frequent according to Gratian's conception of the division of authority. The two powers did not duplicate each other's efforts in all phases of legislation. Rather, the whole legislative and judicial authority to which Christians were subject was

5. Dist. 2, dict. ante c. 1, "Constat autem ius Quiritum ex legibus et plebisscitis et senatusconsultis et constitutionibus principum et edictis sive prudentum responsis." Dist. 3, dict. ante c. 1, "Omnes he species secularium legum partes sunt. Sed quia constitutio alia est civilis, alia ecclesiastica: civilis vero forense vel civile ius appellatur, quo nomine ecclesiastica constitutio appelletur videamus. §1. Ecclesiastica constitutio nomine canonis censetur." Dist. 3, dict. post c. 2, "Porro canonum alii sunt decreta Pontificum, alii statuta conciliorum. Conciliorum vero alia sunt universalia, alia provincialia."

6. Dist. 10, dict. ante c. 1, "Constitutiones vero principum ecclesiasticis constitutionibus non preminent, sed obsecuntur." Dist. 10, dict. post c. 6, "Ecce quod constitutiones principum ecclesiasticis legibus postponendae sunt. Ubi autem evangelicis atque canonicis decretis non obviaverint, omni reverentia dignae habeantur." These dicta are not to be taken as having a general bearing; they only mean that secular laws are put after ecclesiastical laws within the Church. Dist. 10, c. 7 (rubric), "Leges imperatorum in adiutorium ecclesiae licet assumi." Charles Munier, "Droit canonique et droit romain d'après Gratien et les Décrétistes," *Études Le Bras,* II:946. See chap. ii, p. 54.

divided between secular and ecclesiastical authorities. The laws of marriage, probate of wills, economic morality, contracts, and dowry were under the authority of the Church while property institutions arose from secular law and were under the authority of secular power. The legitimizing of children was a power shared by the two authorities. Since legitimacy was legal status connected with the exercise of a right, such as the right to become a priest or the right to inherit land, each authority legitimized children for those rights that were part of its sphere. A child could be legitimate in secular law, so that he could receive the inheritance of his father, at the same time that he was illegitimate before the Church and could not be raised to sacred office. The canons therefore made clear that there were areas of legislation assigned to regnum and sacerdotium, but that each authority possessed legislative and judicial powers that affected the operation or stability of the other authority. The division of authority was not so neat as it seems at first.

In the social and political structure of feudal society, the law of oaths, professions, and promises played an important role. This law was under the authority of the ecclesiastical rulers. In the Decretum, there is a passage from a letter of Fulbert, bishop of Chartres (written in 1020 to William of Aquitaine), which enumerates the content of the oath of fealty between vassal and lord.[7] The power of the Church to judge concerning such oaths is defended in another context. When Gratian considered the validity of oaths made under the threat of violence, he set forth the doctrine that the pope could invalidate such oaths. This power of the pope to dissolve oaths attracted his attention, and he delved into it further, referring to the deposition of Childeric III. Pope Zacharias had dissolved the oath of fidelity that the Franks had taken to the deposed king.[8] The passage describing this action came from Gregory VII's famous letter to Hermann of Metz in which the deposition of Childeric was used as an example of papal power over evil or useless kings. According to Gregory, there were three steps in

7. C. 22, q. 5, dict. post c. 17, "De forma vero fidelitatis, et quid quisque debeat domino, vel e converso, sic invenitur in epistola Filiberti Episcopi." C. 22, q. 5, c. 18, "Qui domino suo fidelitatem iurat, ista sex in memoria semper habere debet: incolume, tutum, honestum, utile, facile, possibile."

8. C. 15, q. 6, dict. post c. 2, "A fidelitatis etiam iuramento Romanus Pontifex nonnullos absoluit, cum aliquos a suis dignitatibus deponit."

the deposition—depriving Childeric of his power, appointing his successor, and absolving the Franks from their oaths.[9] Gratian was only interested in the third step, but the connection between the powers to dissolve oaths and to depose led to the theory that ecclesiastical power held a juridical superiority over secular power. While the Magister did not consider the relationship between these two powers, some of the decretists based discussions of this problem on the capitulum from Gregory's letter.[10]

The Church, in turn, was not free from intrusion by secular power into its life and institutions. Before the Investiture Contest, civil authority had a place in the election of bishops and the pope. The secular lord was supposed to prevent heretics and schismatics from obtaining offices in the Church.[11] In Gratian's time, the direct participation of secular power in the establishment of legitimate ecclesiastical authority was no longer permitted, but all men recognized that cooperation and consent of the kings and emperor were important. The members of Haimeric's party made this recognition more readily than their opponents in the party of Pierleoni because they were more conciliatory toward the secular powers than the last representatives of the Gregorian epoch. Saint Bernard called on the kings of Europe to affirm their al-

9. C. 15, q. 6, c. 3, "Alius item Romanus Pontifex, Zacharias scilicet regem Francorum non pro suis iniquitatibus, quam pro eo, quod tantae potestati erat inutilis, a regno deposuit, et Pipinum, Karoli inperatoris patrem, in eius loco substituit, omnesque Francigenas a iuramento fidelitatis absoluit. Quod etiam ex frequenti auctoritate agit sancta ecclesia, cum milites absoluit a vinculo iuramenti, quod factum est his episcopis, qui apostolica auctoritate a pontificali gradu deponuntur." Gratian seems to be most interested in the part of the capitulum following "omnesque Francigenas . . ." James Muldoon, "The Medieval Origins of the State: The Contribution of the Canonists From Gratian to Hostiensis," (Ph.D. dist., Cornell University, 1965), pp. 146–148. Note that the Magister cited this letter of Gregory at Dist. 96, cc. 9, 10. He took the text from Ivo of Chartres' *Panormia*, V:107–108, but in citing it in Dist. 96, he deleted the part dealing with the deposition of Childeric. He was only interested in the part of the letter concerning the intrusion of secular powers into ecclesiastical affairs. See chap. ii, n. 55.

10. See, for example, Rufinus, *Summa decretorum*, ed. H. Singer (Paderborn, 1902), p. 350. Muldoon (*op. cit.*, pp. 146–148) discusses this passage and other commentary by the later canonists. Most recently, see Edward M. Peters, *The Shadow King* (New Haven, 1970).

11. Dist. 63, dict. post cc. 27, 28. See chap. viii, nn. 10 and 42.

legiance to Innocent II during the schism of 1130, and he wrote letters
to monarchs and urban communes urging them to take military action
against the supporters of Anaclet II. He often sought royal confirmation
of episcopal elections as well.[12] Gratian showed that he agreed with
Bernard's attitude when he said that since there was no one who could
judge a pope, when the papacy was occupied by a heretic or schismatic,
armed force had to be used to oust him.[13] The Magister did not elaborate on this argument, but he may have been thinking of the occupa-
tion of the Holy See by Anaclet II when he wrote it. In any case, it is
clear that Gratian and his contemporaries considered the two powers to
be closely associated in the exercise of their authority.

The secular governor also controlled the use of property by members
of the Church and by the Church itself, and he was the legitimate
judge for deciding cases involving property rights. Gratian treated this
issue in the context of a case involving clerics and approached it by
asking who had the right to judge cases involving clerics.[14] Most of
the *auctoritates* cited denied that the secular ruler could judge the case;
Gratian reviewed the argument for the other side in a dictum. The

12. Saint Bernard, *Epp.* 128, 129, 130, 131, 138, 139, 255. On episcopal elections,
Epp. 170, 449.

13. C. 3, q. 1, dict. post c. 6, "Patet ergo, quod expoliati prius sunt presentialiter
restituendi, antequam ad causam sint vocandi. Sed obicitur, ubi non fuit legitima
institucio, ibi non potest esse restitucio. Non enim probatur destitutus qui prius
non fuit institutus, ac per hoc nec restaurationem postulare potest. Illi ergo,
quorum electio viciosa est, vel qui a clero non sunt electi, vel a populo expetiti,
vel qui per symoniam inrepserunt, non sunt habendi inter episcopos, et ideo, si a
sedibus, quas tenere videbantur, expulsi fuerint, non possunt restitutionem petere
ante, quam vocentur ad causam. Unde supra in tractatu ordinandorum 'Si quis
pecunia vel gratia humana, seu populari vel militari tumultu, etc.' [Dist. 79, c.
9] Sed hoc in eo tantum casu intelligitur, quo apostolica sedes per violentiam oc-
cupatur, quo casu iudex non invenitur, cuius offitio ille apostaticus possit excludi.
In aliis autem locum non habet, cum violenta possessio, nisi per iudicis sententiam,
violento detentori detrahi non possit."

14. C. 11, q. 1. Causa 11 concerns a suit brought by one cleric against another
involving rights over farms. C. 11, dict. principium, "Clericus adversus clericum
questionem de prediis agitavit, quem ad civilem iudicem producere voluit reus
non nisi ante iudicem ecclesiasticum stare volebat; actor vero potentia civilis
iudicis illum a possessione sua deiecit. Quo audito episcopus eum ab offitio sus-
pendit; ille contempta episcopi sui sententiam offitium suum administravit. Hoc
conperto episcopus sine spe restitutionis in eum sententiam dedit. Hic primum
queritur, utrum clericus ante civilem iudicem sit producendus?"

priest or cleric, said the Magister, is under the bishop *ex officio* and under the emperor *ex possessionibus,* since he receives his right to hold property from the emperor. From this argument, it follows that in civil cases clerics ought to seek judgment before civil judges. Just as the ecclesiastical judge is the administrator of ecclesiastical law, so the civil judge is the administrator of civil statutes. Gratian repeats the idea he expressed in his consideration of papal legislative power: Only he who has power to make law has power to interpret law. The bishop should not, therefore, hear cases involving an infringement of secular law.[15]

Gratian admits that this reasoning is sound, but he rejects the conclusion that clerics may be taken before civil judges. It makes no difference what issues the case involves. Clerics are exempt from the jurisdiction of secular judges because of the *privilegium fori,* which

15. The first twenty-six capitula of quaestio 1 support the view that no cleric may be brought before a secular court. Gratian reviews the issue in C. 11, q. 1, dict. post c. 26, "Cum ergo his omnibus auctoritatibus clerici ante civilem iudicem denegentur producendi, cum (nisi prius depositi, vel nudati fuerint) curiae non sunt representandi, patet, quod ad secularia iudicia clerici non sunt pertrahendi. §1. His ita respondetur: Clerici ex offitio sunt subpositi episcopo, ex possessionibus prediorum inperatori sunt obnoxii. Ab episcopo unctionem, decimationes et primitias accipiunt; ab inperatore vero prediorum possessiones nanciscuntur. Unde Augustinus ait super Iohannem: 'Quo iure villas defendis? divino, an humano etc.?' [Dist. 8, c. 1] Require in principio, ubi differentia designatur inter ius naturae et ius constitutionis. Quia ergo ut predia possideantur inperiali lege factum est, patet, quod clerici ex prediorum possessionibus inperatori sunt obnoxii." C. 11, q. 1, dict. post c. 30, "Ex his omnibus datur intelligi, quod in civili causa clericus ante civilem iudicem est conveniendus. Sicut enim ecclesiasticarum legum ecclesiasticus iudex est administrator, ita et civilium non nisi civilis debet esse executor. Sicut enim ille solus habet ius interpretandi canones, qui habet potestatem condendi eos, ita ille solus legum civilium debet esse interpres, qui eis ius et auctoritatem inpertit. In criminali vero causa non nisi ante episcopum clericus examinandus est. Et hoc est illud, quod legibus et canonibus supra diffinitum est, ut in criminali videlicet causa ante civilem iudicem nullus clericus producatur, nisi forte cum consensu episcopi sui; veluti, quando incorrigibiles inveniuntur, tunc detracto eis offitio curiae tradendi sunt." C. 11, q. 1, dict. post c. 31, "Quia ergo iste non in criminali, sed in civili causa clericum ante civilem iudicem produxit, non est iudicandus transgressor canonum, nec est dicendus pertraxisse reum ad iudicem non suum, quia de civili causa non nisi civilis iudex cognoscere debet." The argument that only he who has the right to make the law has the right to interpret it is expounded in: C. 25, q. 1, dict. post c. 16, "Ipsi namque soli canones valent interpretari, qui ius condendi eos habent."

219

was granted by the emperor as well as promulgated in ecclesiastical law. Having set forth this argument, the Magister cites passages from the Theodosian Code and the Capitularies of Charlemagne, which add weight to the canons already brought forth in the discussion.[16] It is of interest that the Magister uses secular law to strengthen the legal basis for his doctrine. This is not a case in which the canons have nothing to say but in which they do not speak authoritatively enough. The recipient of a privilege can hardly claim it in the absence of the grantor's consent.

As its name makes explicit, the *privilegium fori* is a privilege. This characteristic of the rule should be noted because in the discussion that concludes the quaestio, Gratian treats it as general law, and he does not hesitate to draw some general conclusions concerning the jurisdiction of episcopal judges from his discussion. According to the Magister, the bishop's exclusive right to hear cases involving clerics does not derive from imperial privilege but from the very nature of the prelate's jurisdiction as it is defined in the New Testament. The biblical text is from Paul's second letter to Timothy, "No man, being a soldier of god, entangleth himself with secular businesses." (2 Tim. 2:4). As Clement had said, "God does not wish you [the bishop] to be a man of secular affairs." But a distinction must be made, says Gratian, between secular business and the business of secular men. Since clerics may be engaged in secular business, as in the administration of Church property, it is clear that bishops may judge concerning secular business if it is the business of a cleric.[17] Episcopal jurisdiction is defined in terms

16. C. 11, q. 1, dict. post c. 31, "§1. Econtra ea, que in actoris [he who sought judgment from a secular court] defensione dicta sunt, verisimilia quidem videntur, sed pondere carent. Sacris enim canonibus et forensibus legibus tam in civili quam in criminali causa clericus ad civilem iudicem pertrahendus negatur." C. 11, q. 1, cc. 35–37. These capitula stem from secular law.

17. C. 11, q. 1, dict. post c. 47, "Ex his omnibus datur intelligi, quod clericus ad publica iudicia nec in civili, nec in criminali causa est producendus, nisi forte civilem causam episcopus decidere noluerit, vel in criminali sui honoris cingulo eum nudavert. §1. Illud autem quod in epistola Clementis dictum est: 'Non cognitorem secularium negotiorum te vult Deus esse,' [C. 11, q. 1, c. 29] ex episcopali unctione intelligendum est. Non enim in episcopum ungitur, ut cognitor secularium negotiorum resideat, sed ut procurator animarum et distributor spiritualium existat. Prohibetur ergo secularibus negotiis occupari, non ad tempus sequester fieri. Vel secularia iudicia non de rebus secularibus sed sec-

DIVISION OF GOVERNMENTAL RESPONSIBILITIES

of persons instead of types of affairs, and this definition stems from Saint Paul, not from Theodosius or Charlemagne.

It is clear, therefore, that for Gratian, the *privilegium fori* is not a privilege at all, but a recognition, in law, of the right order of things. The name of the rule is but a vestige of a time when kings and emperors did not recognize the true division of jurisdiction between themselves and the episcopate of the Church. In fact, however, the argument that Gratian expounded earlier in the quaestio—that the cleric was subject to his bishop *ex officio* and to the emperor *ex possessionibus*—is very strong and has in its support the authority of Saint Augustine.[18] The Magister's rejection of this argument and his later explanation of episcopal jurisdiction reflect a change in the view of the Ecclesia after the Investiture Contest. The struggle to remove secular powers from participation in the governance and affairs of the Church had a positive side in the development of constitutional law to replace the discredited practices of earlier centuries.[19] The revival of the electoral theory of establishing legitimate authority in the Church was only one aspect of this development. The idea of ecclesiastical jurisdiction which emerges from Causa 11, quaestio 1 brings to the fore the general notion behind the particular constitutional developments. Breaking away from the secular powers, the Ecclesia became, in the eyes of Church writers, a juridical community possessing its own jurisdiction, its own constitution, and its own complement of juridical powers exercised by its rulers. There remained types of legislation and

---

ularium virorum intelligenda sunt. Iudicia de rebus secularibus secularia appellantur iuxta illud Apostoli: 'Secularia igitur iudicia si habueritis contemptibiles qui sunt in ecclesia constituite.' [1 Cor. 6:4] Iudicia vero secularium secularia appellantur in epistola Clementis, quod ex subsequentibus datur intelligi, cum dicitur: 'Hec opera, que tibi minus congruere diximus, exhibeant sibi invicem vacantes laici.' Prohibentur ergo Clerici a cognitione negotiorum secularium virorum, non secularium causarum. Negotia quippe clericorum, sive criminalia sive civilia fuerint, non nisi apud ecclesiasticum iudicem ventilanda sunt."

18. Dist. 8, c. 1

19. On the revolutionary change in the view of the Church during the Investiture Contest, see Gerd Tellenbach, *Church, State and Christian Society at the Time of the Investiture Contest,* trans. R. F. Bennet (Oxford, 1940). See also Stickler, 'Il 'gladius' negli atti." In this article, Stickler traces the history of the sword image in the late eleventh century.

judgments which the Church did not claim, but these diminished both in number and in importance from the mid-eleventh century on.[20] The discussion of Causa 11, quaestio 1 makes this clear.

According to the doctrine set forth by the Magister, the *privilegium fori* affects the property rights of clerics, while the rights of laymen are adjudicated in civil courts. Yet, in the same dicta in which he states this argument, he demonstrates that the Church possesses some authority over the property rights of its lay subjects. The ecclesiastical community makes claims on the land and produce of its subjects in the form of tithes and first fruits, even though Church law recognized that land was held according to imperial statutes. Ecclesiastical taxes were not considered to be a special grant of imperial or royal power as was the *privilegium fori*. Gratian argued that the pastor's right to receive tithes was granted to him when the bishop gave him a *licentia* to exercise a *cura animarum*.[21] According to this doctrine, the bishop's jurisdiction applies to temporal things, and his power must be described in terms of cases as well as persons.

The Church is an independent community and its episcopal rulers

20. The famous decretal of Innocent III, *Per Venerabilem,* is a monument in the history of this development and extension of ecclesiastical jurisdiction. There the pope claimed to be supreme judge in all cases, secular as well as ecclesiastical. The statement was based on a little used text from Deut. [17:8–12]. In other decretal letters, Innocent made claims that were not so broad as that in *Per Venerabilem,* but made the same point. Tierney, " 'Tria Quippe Distinguit Iudicia . . .' A Note on Innocent III's Decretal Per Venerabilem," *Speculum,* 37 (1962), 48–59.

21. C. 11, q. 1, dict. post c. 26, n. 15 above. Causae 12 and 13 involve cases in which tithes are in dispute. Causa 25 involves a dispute over tithes as well, but the issues concern the legislative power of the pope rather than the rules concerning the division or collection of tithes. Giles Constable, *Monastic Tithes* (Cambridge, 1964), pp. 125–126.

The traditional explanation of the division of jurisdiction between the two powers is based on the distinction between *temporalia* and *spiritualia*. See, for example, Stickler, "Magistri Gratiani sentencia de potestate ecclesiae in statum." This view does not receive any support in the Decretum. It has already been shown that the bishop possesses power over temporal business as well as over lay persons. The distinction between the business of secular men and that of clerics which the Magister made shows no clear-cut division of temporal and spiritual things.

hold an independent juridical authority in Gratian's eyes. The idea of the Church which emerges from his discussion in Causa 11 is that it should be considered as an entity complete in itself separate from secular communities. Just as the rules for establishing legitimate ecclesiastical authority and receiving secular law into the corpus of canon law are governed by Church law, so Church law has in its jurisdiction the economic foundations of the community. There is no need to look to secular law or power to support the ecclesiastical community or to help it live its own life. This idea, so basic to the development of constitutional theory for the Church, is most dramatically set forth in the legal doctrine governing the Church's use of force. Up to the mid-eleventh century, this area of governmental activity was the one most susceptible to cooperation between the two powers. In the twelfth century, cooperation between the powers still was the rule when force was used in the interests of the Church, but the way of looking at the act of cooperation had changed radically.

The use of force by the Church.

Church writers claimed that the ecclesiastical power had the right to use force in carrying out its governmental tasks, but they recognized that members of the ecclesiastical hierarchy had only a limited exercise of the right. Only lay persons could actually use force when it led to the shedding of blood, and the Church had to rely on them when it sought to take drastic action against its members or against external enemies. In most cases, it was the secular power that was called upon to exercise the sword in the interests of the Church, and this led to a very complicated theory of the relationship between the two powers. Gratian devoted a whole Causa to the use of force by and for the ecclesiastical community.

In medieval writings, the image of the sword was often used to signify the exercise of governmental power. There were two swords, one for spiritual and one for material power, and scholars have generally interpreted them as conveying the distinction between the authority of ecclesiastical and secular rulers. This interpretation has been challenged by Stickler who thinks that up to the time of Gratian and Saint Bernard, the image of the swords represented coercive power.[22] The power of spiritual coercion was associated with the ecclesiastical governor, but according to Stickler's argument, the power of material coercion could be exercised in either the ecclesiastical or the secular sphere. His account of the history of the sword imagery and its meaning in the mid-twelfth century is persuasive; a review of his argument serves as a good basis for study of Gratian's views about coercive power.

There are several passages in the New Testament in which the image of the sword is used, and Stickler argues that even in those texts, the sword signified primarily the power to coerce. A passage from Saint Paul's letter to the Romans was most important: "For he [the civil governor] is God's minister to thee, for good. But if thou do that which is evil fear: for he beareth not the sword in vain. For he is God's minister: an avenger to execute wrath upon him that doth evil." (Rom. 13:4).[23] In this text, the Apostle asserts that the secular authority legitimately exercises coercive power for attaining its ends. The passage became the justification of the use of force in the Middle Ages. The image of the spiritual sword, attributed to the Church, was con-

---

22. Stickler, "Il 'gladius' negli atti," *passim*. Stickler has studied the use of the sword imagery in several other articles as well. *Idem*, "De potestate gladii materialis ecclesiae secundum 'Quaestiones Bambergenses ineditas,'" *Salesianum*, 6 (1944), 113–140. *Idem*, "Der Schwerterbegriff bei Huguccio," *Ephemerides Juris Canonici*, 3 (1947), 1–44. *Idem*, "Il 'gladius' nel Registro di Gregorio VII," *Studi Gregoriani*, 3 (1948), 89–103. Stickler's views on Bernard of Clairvaux have been reviewed and supported by Kennan in a recent article, Elizabeth Kennan, "The 'De Consideratione' of St. Bernard and the Papacy in the Mid-Twelfth Century: A Review of Scholarship," *Traditio*, 23 (1967), 73–115. For the older view of the use of the image of the swords in medieval writings, see J. Lecler, "L'argument des deux glaives dans les controverses politiques du moyen-âge," *Recherches de Science religieuse*, 21 (1931), 299–339. See chap. ii, n. 57. Ullmann accepts the older view of the swords as representing the two powers. See the works cited in n. 1 above.

23. The most important biblical text for the history of the sword image is Luke 22:38, "Lord, behold here are two swords. And he said to them, It is enough." This verse established the number of swords, and became the chief basis for medieval exegesis on them. Strictly speaking however, the passage from Luke does not itself use the sword as an image for governmental authority. Stickler therefore leaves it aside.

tained in a text from Ephesians (6:17): "And take unto you the helmet of salvation, and the sword of the Spirit (which is the word of God)." The same idea was put forth in the letter to the Hebrews and in the Apocalypse.[24]

The Church itself never repudiated the use of force for its interests, according to Stickler. He argues that references to the swords in early Christian literature cannot be understood except as references to coercive power.[25] The primary meaning of the sword image was as a symbol for the use of force in the material sense—incarceration, whipping, or even death. The connection between the sword and spiritual penalties such as excommunication and anathema was made less frequently and gained currency more slowly. Once the connection was established, however, no one denied that Church power could coerce with spiritual penalties and could do so through its own agency. The use of material force was more complicated. While the Church did not hesitate to claim that material force could be used in its interests, it repeatedly prohibited clerics from exercising some kinds of coercive power with their own hands. The early councils enacted these prohibitions and called on the secular power to cooperate with the ecclesiastical governors in carrying out the governmental tasks of the Church.[26]

The doctrine that force could be used to solve problems of Church government, while only secular powers could perform many of the necessary actions, causes some confusion about who actually possesses the right to use force. If the ecclesiastical governors could request that the secular rulers take up the sword in favor of the Church, then it appears that the ecclesiastical governors themselves have the *ius coactivae potestatis* if not the *executio iuris*. Until the period of the Carolingians, however, the power of coercion in the hands of the Church was restricted to spiritual penalties, and no conclusions were drawn from the doctrine that the Church could request secular cooperation in protecting itself or punishing recalcitrant criminals. The civil power was thought to have the *ius coercitionis* and an ill-defined duty to

24. Heb. 4:12 and Apoc. 2:16.
25. Stickler, "Il 'gladius' negli atti," pp. 422–429.
26. *Ibid.*, pp. 422–424.

use it in the interests of the Ecclesia when it was asked to do so. Such an idea may have been part of the significance of the *patronatus* title that the papacy gave to Pepin and Charlemagne.

Stickler finds the first hints of the claim that the Church holds an independent power of material coercion in writings of the Carolingian era. The claim was made at times when secular authority was slow to carry out its duty to protect the Church or aid in its work. It was also made in passages that referred to cases or situations in which the Church exercised temporal authority as well as the pastorate, as it did in the papal states. Stickler cites passages from the letters of several eighth- and ninth-century popes to support his argument. A sentence from John VIII (872–882) is perhaps the clearest of these statements: "We pursue external enemies not only with the visible but also with the invisible sword." [27] Up to the time of the Investiture Contest, Stickler concludes, the image of the sword was first and foremost a symbol of the power of material coercion and only gradually became used, on the basis of the text from Ephesians, as a symbol for the power of spiritual coercion.

Stickler thinks that one aspect of the dispute between the pope and emperor in the late eleventh and early twelfth century was a struggle for the independent use of coercive power by the Church. During this period, he finds that Church writers claimed both swords for the Church, thereby making the ecclesiastical body a more complete and autonomous juridical entity. The claim was not supported by all the leading reformers, but it gained currency as the dispute between pope and emperor progressed. The most striking practical result of the idea was the proclamation of the Crusade by Pope Urban II at Clermont in 1095,[28] but taking responsibility for the crusading movement was not the only evidence that the ecclesiastical hierarchy was making claim to an independent power of material coercion. During the pe-

---

27. *Ibid.*, p. 427. JL 3307, "Velut exteros inimicos non solum visibili sed etiam invisibili gladio pariter persequamur." Stephen II (752–757), *MGH*, Epistolae, III:498. (Stickler calls this pope Stephen III.) Leo IV (847–855), JL 2611. Stephen VI (885–891), JL 3414. The terminology of the swords was unstable in this period. They were variously called visible-invisible, spiritual-material, and corporal-sword of anathema. Stickler, "Il 'gladius' negli atti," pp. 429–430.

28. Stickler, "Il 'gladius' negli atti," pp. 430–435.

riod when Gratian and Saint Bernard were writing their works, the papacy was taking the initiative in a myriad of petty daily actions involving the use of force. In the letters of popes Innocent II and Eugene III there are many examples of the pope ordering local civil powers to act forcefully where a monastery was being despoiled or molested, or ecclesiastical dignitaries had been ill treated.[29] Also, the extensive activity of Eugene III and Saint Bernard in the launching of the Second Crusade shows that in the fifty years since Urban II, the conception of the power of the ecclesiastical rulers with respect to the use of force for ecclesiastical ends had grown considerably. In fact, when the Second Crusade failed and plans for a third were being made, the prospective crusaders wanted Bernard to lead them.[30]

Notwithstanding new powers of the Ecclesia in the realm of coercive action, ecclesiastical law did not alter its stance on the exercise of such power by clerics. No cleric was to carry out the policies of the Church with his own hands, if shedding blood was necessary. Clerical judges were not even permitted to condemn a man to mutilation or death.[31] The new claims did result, however, in a refinement of the theory of how churchmen could bring about forceful measures on behalf of the Church. The ecclesiastical governor could deputize any layman for the task and no longer had to rely wholly on the goodwill of the civil powers.[32] This doctrine was a logical extension of the theory that churchmen possessed the right to use force on their own authority but could not exercise the right.

Stickler shows that Gratian and Saint Bernard followed the tradition of the eleventh-century reformers in connecting the sword image to the coercive power of the Church.[33] His argument is convincing. Both writers use the image of the two swords when considering actions of the Church alone. In the case of Bernard, the references seem to be to the action of Eugene III in leading a force against the citizens of

29. Innocent II, JL 7617, 8067, 8123, 8172, 8203. Eugene III, JL 8764, 8765, 8985, 8986, 8987, 9103.

30. Bernard, *Ep.* 256. E. Vacandard, *Vie de s. Bernard* (Paris, 1895), 2:431.

31. Conc. Toledo XI (A.D. 675), c. 6, "His a quibus domini sacramenta tractanda sunt, iudicium sanguinis agitare non licet." (C. 23, q. 8, c. 30).

32. Stickler, "Il 'gladius' negli atti," p. 437.

33. *Ibid.,* pp. 440–445.

Rome in order to reestablish himself in the city.[34] Bernard attributes the *ius coactivae potestatis* to Church authority, but he denies the *executio iuris* to it. The material sword is used, "at the nod of the priest and at the order of the emperor." [35] For Bernard, the exercise of force for the purpose of ecclesiastical authority involved an act of cooperation between the two powers. This is brought out in a letter to King Conrad III concerning the same Roman affair. The king is portrayed as equal to the pope in power and governmental authority, and he is called upon to recognize the unity of purpose between himself and the pope. That unity originated in Christ himself who was king and priest.[36]

Gratian examined the problem of the use of force more extensively than Bernard. In some passages, he too emphasized that exercise of coercive power for the Church was a cooperative act between the two powers, but most of the time the cooperative nature of the act is deemphasized, while the activity and power of the Church is brought to the fore. The discussion is located in Causa 23, which concerns a group of

34. E. Jordan, "Dante et S. Bernard," *Bulletin du Jubilé* (Paris 1921), 4:311.

35. Saint Bernard, *De Consid.*, IV:3, 7, "Dracones, inquis, me mones pascere, et scorpiones, non oves. Propter hoc, inquam, magis aggredere eos, sed verbo, non ferro. Quid denuo usurpare gladium tentes, quem semel jussus es reponere in vaginam? Quem tamen qui tuum negat, non satis mihi videtur attendere verbum Domini dicentis sic: 'Converte gladium tuum in vaginam' Tuus ergo et ipse, tuo forsitan nutu, etsi non tua manu, evaginandus. Alioquin, si nullo modo ad te pertineret et is, dicentibus Apostolis: 'Ecce gladii duo hic,' non respondisset Dominus: 'Satis est,' sed: 'nimis est.' [Luke 22:38] Uterque ergo Ecclesiae, et spiritualis scilicet gladius, et materialis, sed is quidem pro Ecclesia, ille vero et ab Ecclesia exserendus: ille sacerdotes, is militis manu, sed sane ad nutum sacerdotis et iussum imperatoris."

36. Bernard, *Ep.* 244, n. 1, "Nec dulcius, nec amicabilius, sed nec arctius omnino regnum sacerdotiumque conjungi seu complanatori in invicem potuerunt, quam ut in persona Domini ambo haec pariter convenirent; utpote qui factus est nobis ex utraque tribu secundum carnem summus et Sacerdos, et Rex. Non solum autem, sed et commiscuit ea nihilominus ac confoederavit in suo corpore, quod est populus christianus. . . . Non veniat mea anima inconsilium eorum qui dicunt, vel imperio pacem et libertatem Ecclesiarum, vel Ecclesiis prosperitatem et exaltationem imperii nocituram. Non enim utriusque institutor Deus in destructionem ea connexuit, sed in aedificationem. . . . Quamobrem accingere gladio tuo super femur tuum, potentissime, et restituat sibi Caesar quae Caesaris sunt, quae sunt Dei Deo. Utrumque interesse Caesaris constat, et propriam tueri coronam, et Ecclesiam defensare." See chap. ii, pp. 58–59.

bishops who hold jurisdiction from the emperor. The pope commands them to take measures against heretics in their midst, and they use armed force to compel the heretics to return to the faith. The questions raised concern the legitimacy of the use of force for social and political purposes and the capacity of churchmen to exercise the right to use force. The terms of the argument bring the use of force in general into question first and then take up the problem of the shedding of blood by ecclesiastical rulers. Gratian does not separate these two issues, however. For him, the right to use force implies the right to kill or mutilate. The first time he discusses this problem, he is not specifically interested in the rights of churchmen, but in the general question of whether any person has the right to shed blood.[37] The argument progresses through Gratian's successive answers to objections raised against the use of force. At the end of the Causa, his doctrine and his reasoning about the justification of coercive action by the Church and by secular powers are fairly evident.

The first objection to the use of force by Christians comes from its apparent opposition to the virtue of *caritas*. Fighting seems to be sinful for Christians, and many passages from the New Testament appear to condemn the use of the sword. The most prominent among these

37. C. 23, dict. principium, "Quidam episcopi cum plebe sibi conmissa in heresim lapsi sunt; circumadiacentes catholicos minis et cruciatibus ad heresim conpellere ceperunt, quo conperto Apostolicus catholicis episcopis circumadiacentium regionum, qui ab inperatore civilem iurisdictionem acceperant, inperavit, ut catholicos ab hereticis defenderent, et quibus modis possent eos ad fidei veritatem redire conpellerent. Episcopi, hec mandata Apostolica accipientes, convocatis militibus aperte et per insidias contra hereticos pugnare ceperunt. Tandem nonnullis eorum neci traditis, aliis rebus suis vel ecclesiasticis expoliatis, aliis carcere te ergastulo reclusis, ad unitatem catholicae fidei coacti redierunt." Stickler, who believes that the questions of the Causa concern the different forms of coercive action, has studied C. 23 very fully. He set out to prove that Gratian recognized the right of the Church to use force in pursuing its ends, and he succeeded admirably in achieving his purpose. He did not follow the argument of the Causa in building his case, but organized the relevant texts around the points he wished to cover. I am not attempting the proof that Stickler has already furnished, but wish to examine the relations between the two powers in the exercise of force by the Church. I will follow Gratian's argument more closely than Stickler did, but I am indebted to him for the readings of several texts. Stickler, "De ecclesiae potestate coactiva materiali apud Magistrum Gratianum," *Salesianum*, 4 (1942), 2–23, 96–119.

229

texts was the famous verse from Matthew: "Put up again thy sword into its place: for all that take the sword shall perish with the sword." [38] Gratian answers the argument based on this passage by saying that the precepts of patience and caritas do not hinder the use of force because they refer to the attitudes of men, not to their actions. Our approach to others ought to be infused by the spirit of caritas, he says, and caritas itself may lead us to use force.[39] The idea that the Magister seems to be conveying is that sometimes we must use force to protect a man against himself.

The second objection is related to the first by also being based the dictates of the Christian spirit. We should not use force to meet the threat of force because Christ advised his disciples, "And when they shall persecute you in this city, flee into another." [40] Christ's kingdom is not of this world. Christians, turning their thoughts toward heaven, ought not to value anything enough to use force to protect it. Gratian

38. C. 23, q. 1, dict. ante c. 1, "Quod militare alienum videatur ab evangelica disciplina, hinc videtur posse probari, quia omnis milicia vel ob iniuriam propulsandam, vel propter vindictam inferendam est instituta, iniuria autem vel a propria persona, vel a socio repellitur, quod utrumque evangelica prohibetur. . . . §1. Item, cum Petro gladio defendenti magistrum, Christus dixerit: 'Converte gladium tuum in vaginam; an putas, quia non possum rogare patrem meum, et exhibebit michi plus quam duodecim milia legiones angelorum?'" Other biblical texts supporting this argument are Matt. 5:39; Rom. 12:19; Matt. 26:52 (that quoted in the text of the chapter); Matt. 7:1; Matt. 13:30; Rom. 14:4. C. 23, q. 1, dict. ante c. 1, *passim.*

39. C. 23, q. 1, dict. post c. 1, "His ita respondetur: Precepta patienciae non tam ostentatione corporis quam preparatione cordis sunt retinenda." C. 23, q. 1, dict. post c. 7, "Ex his omnibus colligitur, quod militare non est peccatum, et quod precepta patienciae in preparatione cordis, non ostentatione corporis servanda sunt." Dist. 45, dict. post c. 13, "nec lenitas mansuetudinis sine rectitudine severitatis, nec zelus rectitudinis sine mansuetudine in prelatis debet inveniri."

40. C. 23, q. 3, dict. ante c. 1, "Quod vero iniuria sociorum armis propulsanda non sit, exemplis et auctoritatibus probatur. . . . Cum ergo ille, qui ab iniuria armis arcetur, non minus scandalizetur quam ille, a quo ablata coram iudice reposcuntur, patet, quod ad propulsandam iniuriam non sunt petenda armorum auxilia. Quod autem petendum non est, illud iure prestari non debet. §2. Sed multa rite prestantur, que tamen iure non petuntur. Bonus enim non rite iniuriae vindictam peteret quia malum pro malo redderet quam tamen iudex recte infligeret, nec nisi bonum pro malo redderet." The biblical text cited in the chapter is Matt. 10:23.

answers that this objection, too, refers to the attitudes of men and not to their actions. He argues that the divine orientation of Christians is compatible with use of force. The Church plays an essential role in guiding men toward their spiritual goal; it must be protected and its character preserved so that it can go on with its work. Thus, Saint Paul sought soldiers from the Roman praetor of Judea in order to protect himself against some Jews who had sworn not to eat until they had killed him (Acts 23). Also, the Church uses force not only to protect itself but also to carry out its work. The Magister continues his argument by saying that evil will is thwarted and good will is given effect through the judicious use of coercive power.[41]

Gratian's answer to the second objection justifies the use of force within the ecclesiastical community. The social good associated with the correct use of coercion is compatible with the divine goals of the community. But the emphasis in these passages is on the repelling of threatened violence. The next objection to the use of force directs attention to the revenge of evil already done. The argument against taking revenge rests on the idea that evil persons ought to be tolerated by the Church. If evildoers should be punished, they ought to be given only spiritual penalties.[42] Like the earlier objections, this one is based

41. C. 23, q. 3, dict. post c. 1, "§1. Aliud est enim iniuriam propellere, ut sibi liceat voluptuose vivere, aliud, ut aliorum utilitati libere possit vacare. Sicque aliud est suffragium ab homine tamquam a ministro iusticiae postulare, ut mala voluntas adversantium eius ministerio careat effectu, et bonorum voluntas eius suffragio sortiatur effectum; aliud spem suam a Deo in hominem transferre, ut adversa, que inferuntur a Deo ad vitae correctionem, humano pellantur auxilio nulla precedente correctione. . . . Petere ergo vel prestare in tribulatione subsidium, ut voluptuose quis in crimine vivat, dampnabile est. Petere autem vel prestare solacium, ut malis facultas delinquendi adimatur, ut ecclesia pacem adipiscatur, ut aliquis multorum utilitati servetur, utile est et honestum; dissimilare vero est gravissimum. Hinc de Paulo legitur, quod, cum quidam Iudeorum iurassent, se non comesturos panem, nisi eum interficerent, petiit milites a pretore, quorum presidio illesus scruaretur ab iniuria Iudeorum, non suae voluptati, sed omnium utilitati victurus. . . . Hinc etiam ecclesia auxilium ab inperatore ad sui defensionem petere monetur." C. 23, q. 3, dict. post c. 10.

42. C. 23, q. 4, dict. ante c. 1, "Quod autem vindicta inferenda non sit, multis modis probatur. Mali enim tollerandi sunt, non abiciendi; in crepatione feriendi, non corporaliter expellendi." C. 23, q. 4, dict. post c. 12, "Ecce, quod mali tol-

on the requirements of the Christian spirit, but it also involves the purpose of the ecclesiastical community. If the purpose of the Church is to lead all men toward salvation, then evil persons, who are most in need of guidance and correction, ought not to be expelled or put under a heavy burden of physical punishment.

The emphasis of this third objection shows that Gratian is concerned with coercion of all types, spiritual as well as material. At this point in his discussion, the Magister wants to justify the use of force in general as a legitimate means for carrying out the governance of the community. It is also clear from his argument that the Church community is at the center of his attention. He answers the objection by explaining its implications. What his opponents are arguing, he says, is that punishment of wrongdoers ought to be reserved to God, that in other words, the Church has no governmental jurisdiction over its members. But the texts that his opponents use to prove their point do not, says Gratian, imply that all punishment ought to be reserved to God. While some evil persons should be corrected by admonitions only, judgment and punishment of others is reserved to God only in cases where the delinquents are not within the jurisdiction of the Church or when their crimes cannot be proven in court. Saint Paul implicitly recognized the Church's jurisdiction over its members when he told the Corinthians, "For what have I to do to judge them that are without? . . . For them that are without, God will judge." (1 Cor. 5:12–13). In addition, argues the Magister, the position of his opponents can be construed as referring to cases when corporal punishment of wrongdoers is impossible, when, for example, the multitude is in

---

lerandi sunt, nec corporali, sed spirituali vindicta sunt puniendi. Unde, cum discipuli non recepti a Samaritanis ignem celitus super eos deducere voluerunt, dicentes magistro: 'Vis dicimus descendat ignis de celo, et consumat eos?' audierunt: 'Nescitis, cuius spiritus estis?' [Luke 9:54] Item: 'Omnis qui gladium acceperit, gladio peribit.'" C. 23, q. 4, dict. post c. 15, "Unde Christus ait in evangelio: 'Audistis quia dictum est in lege . . .' 'Oculum pro oculo, dentem pro dente.' Ego autem hanc vicissitudinem tollens et ad mansuetudinem et karitatis perfectionem vos invitans, dico vobis: 'Nolite resistere malo, sed diligite inimicos vestros. . . .' [Matt. 5:38] In lege enim veteris testamenti corporalis pena statuta est: in lege vero evangelii omni peccanti per penitenciam venia pro mittitur. Unde illa a terrore incepit. . . . Hec vero a lenitate mansuetudinis et misericordiae."

sin and penalties cannot be doled out without disturbing the peace of the Church. In such cases, evil persons ought to be tolerated.[43]

The Magister continues this discussion by considering the conditions under which force ought to be used to revenge an evil already done. He repeats the usual admonition that the judge should act from a zeal for justice, not from a love of punishing,[44] but he also makes an interesting distinction between evils done to oneself and those done to others. Christ said in Matthew, "Blessed are ye when they shall revile you, and persecute you, and speak all that is evil against you, untruly, for my sake: Be glad and rejoice for your reward is very great in heaven." (Matt. 5:11–12). In discussing this text and others from the New Testament, Gratian says that sins against God or a neighbor ought to be punished by us, but those committed against ourselves ought to be patiently tolerated.[45] In the ensuing passages, he broadens

43. C. 23, q. 4, dict. post c. 15, "Ex his omnibus [the capitula cited by his opponents] colligitur, quod malorum vindicta Deo reservanda est, nec sunt corporaliter puniendi, sed crebra ammonitione, et karitatis beneficio ad correctionem invitandi." C. 23, q. 4, dict. post c. 16, "His ita respondetur: Sunt quedam, que salubri tantum ammonitione sunt corripienda, non corporalibus flagellis sunt animadvertenda; sed eorum vindicta divino examini tantum est reservanda, quando in delinquentes disciplinam videlicet exercere non possumus, vel quia non sunt nostri iuris, vel quia illorum crimina, etsi nobis nota sunt, tamen manifestis indiciis probari non possunt. §1. De his qui non sunt nostri iuris, ait Apostolus in epistola prima ad Chorinthios: 'Quid enim michi attinet de his, qui foris sunt, iudicare? de his enim Dominus iudicabit.'" C. 23, q. 4, dict. post c. 17, "§1. Item, quando multitudo est in scelere nec salva pace ecclesiae mala puniri possunt, tolleranda sunt pocius, quam violata pace ecclesiae punienda." C. 23, q. 4, dict. post c. 25, "Ecce, quod crimina sunt punienda, quando salva pace ecclesiae feriri possunt; in quo tamen discretio adhibenda est. Aliquando enim delinquentium multitudo diu per patienciam est expectanda. . . ." On the Church's jurisdiction over only open crimes, see Kuttner, "Ecclesia de occultis non indicat," *Acta Congressus Iuridici Internationalis*, 3 (Rome, 1934), 225–246.

44. C. 23, q. 4, dict. post c. 26, "[in asking Christ to bring the fire of heaven upon the Samaritans, Luke 9:54] Apostoli non zelo iusticiae, sed amaritudinis odio ob iniuriam suae expulsionis vindicandam Samaritanos igne voluerunt consumere." C. 23, q. 4, dict. post c. 32. Dist. 45, dict. post c. 13, n. 39 above.

45. C. 23, q. 4, dict. post c. 26, "Dominus autem volens eos iniuriam propriae personae cum patiencia et gaudio tollerare. . . . Hinc etiam Petrus, qui, cum aliis audierat: 'Beati eritis, cum maledixerint vobis homines, et dixerint omne malum adversum vos; gaudete in illa die, et exultate, quoniam merces vestra copiosa est in celis.'" C. 23, q. 4, dict. post c. 27, "Hinc, idem [Gregory I] in omeliis, osten-

this argument to include crimes against the Church. An objection is raised on the basis of an action of Pope Silverius (536–537) against the *patricius* of Rome. It is alleged that the pope acted in order to avenge an injury done to himself. Gratian argues, however, that injury to the pope constituted injury to the Church and that avenging the crime was therefore justified.[46]

The argument that crimes against the Church ought to be punished amounts to an assertion that force is rightfully used in the interests of the social body. The same idea is conveyed by the argument that it is justifiable to punish the few in order to induce the many to behave correctly.[47] Having arrived at this point, Gratian takes up the problem of who can use the sword for these actions. Again, it is an objection to the use of force which launches the discussion.

Basing their argument on the biblical text, "For all that take the sword shall perish with the sword," the Magister's imaginary opponents argue that no one ought to use force. This is really a repetition of the old argument against the use of coercive power in general, but Gratian treats it differently than he did before. He has already shown

---

dens, quod peccata, que in Deum vel in proximum conmittuntur, a nobis punienda sunt, ea vero, quibus in nos delinquitur, patientier tolleranda."

46. The case of Silverius is described in C. 23, q. 4, c. 30. Silverius was exiled by the *patricius* of Rome and instead of going into exile, he convened a council of bishops and anathematized the *patricius*. Gratian's opponents argue that this case is a precedent showing that crimes against oneself could be revenged. Gratian answers C. 23, q. 4, dict. post c. 30, "Sed et his non suam, sed ecclesiae iniuriam ultus est."

47. C. 23, q. 4, dict. post c. 25, "aliquando in paucis est punienda, ut eorum exemplo ceteri terreantur, et ad penitenciam provocentur. Hinc, cum discipuli celesti igne Samaritanos vellent consumere, prohibiti sunt, et Samaritani ad penitenciam sunt expectati, ut Christo predicante converterentur ad fidem." C. 23, q. 4, dict. post c. 30, "Quid autem peccatum populi in paucis puniendum sit, Moyse exemplo docuit, qui peccatum ydolatriae in paucos cultores vituli vindicavit, morte paucorum expians peccata multorum, in presens terrens, posterum disciplinam sanctiens."

Justifying the use of force in the interests of the social body and especially of a social body such as the Church, is a striking indication of the discrepancy between the two aspects of the Church community. While it is easy to see why Gratian and others considered the use of force by the ecclesiastical authority to be justified and even necessary, it is nonetheless strange to see such a doctrine in the constitution of the most perfect human community.

234

that force can and ought to be used for the purposes of the community, and he takes the objection now raised as a reference to the question of who shall exercise the power. His argument is based on ideas that he expounded in other parts of the Decretum. Just as only legitimate governmental authority has the right to exercise the power of the keys, so legitimate authority alone has the right to exercise the power of the sword.[48] A passage from the works of Saint Jerome seemed to oppose this doctrine, but the Magister explains that when Jerome says that the Church cannot persecute anyone, he means only that the Church cannot persecute anyone unjustly. It is reasonable, he argues, to persecute heretics just as Christ persecuted those whom he expelled from the temple.[49]

This argument is acceptable, but it fails to take up an important distinction in the theory of coercive power. While no one denied that force in the form of excommunication, anathema, or even incarceration could be used by the Church, all recognized that shedding blood was forbidden to priests. The next stage of Gratian's argument concerns the exercise of this extreme kind of coercive action. The Magister's opponents ask the question in its more general sense, however, inquiring whether there is justification for acts of mutilation or killing by any judge. Gratian takes up this problem in the fifth quaestio and because of the general nature of the question, his discussion produces some confusion. Whereas the discussion up to this point very apparently concerned the use of force within the Church community, the Magister now transfers at least some of his attention to the actions of secular judges and their agents. The relationship between the Church and the use of force by which blood is shed is very complex, as is pointed out below, when the argument of the eighth quaestio is taken

48. C. 23, q. 4, dict. post c. 35, "Item illud evangelii, quod obiciebatur: 'Qui gladio usus fuerit gladio cadet,' Augustinus exponit in lib. 2. contra Manichoes [c. 70] ita discens." C. 23, q. 4, c. 36, "Ille gladium accipit, qui, nulla superiori ac legitima potestate vel iubente, vel concedente, in sanguinem alicuius armatur."

49. C. 23, q. 4, dict. post c. 36, "Porro illud Ieronimi [c. 13], quo ecclesia negatur aliquem persequi, non ita intelligendum est, ut generaliter ecclesia nullum persequatur, sed quod nullum iniuste persequatur. Non enim omnis persecutio culpabilis est, sed rationabiliter hereticos persequimur, sicut et Christus corporaliter persecutus est eos, quos de templo expulit."

up. The argument in the fifth quaestio adds a further element of confusion to this problem because it does not make a clear distinction between the governors of the Church and of the secular communities.

The opposition to the exercise of the power of life and death over men is based on the commandment, "Thou shalt not kill" as well as on the Gospel text, "For all that take the sword shall perish with the sword." [50] Gratian answers this argument:

If holy men and public powers [who are] waging wars are not transgressors of that mandate: "Thou shalt not kill," although they kill some criminals worthy of death; if a knight obeying his power [ruler] is not guilty of homicide when he kills any criminal by his [the ruler's] command; if it is not shedding blood to punish murderers and poisoners, but the ministry of the laws; if [the cause of] the peace of the Church consoles the long line of the lost; if those who kill excommunicates who rise against the catholic mother [the Church] are not judged to be murderers: it is obvious that it is permitted not only to whip the evil, but also to kill them.[51]

The point is simply that the exercise of coercive power, even if it leads to mutilation and killing, is permitted as long as it is done as a function of the legitimate exercise of governmental authority by men who are legitimate holders of that authority. But the text of this dictum

---

50. C. 23, q. 4, dict. post c. 54, "Sed cum vindicta aliquando inferatur dampnis rerum, aliquando flagellis, aliquando etiam morte: queritur, an sit peccatum iudici vel ministro reos morti tradere?" C. 23, p. 5, dict. ante c. 1, "Quod autem nulli liceat aliquem occidere, illo precepto probatur, quo Dominus in lege homicidium prohibuit, dicens: 'Non occides.' Item in evangelio: 'Omnis, qui gladium acceperit, gladio peribit.'" C. 23, q. 5, dict. post c. 7, "Hinc apparet, quod mali flagellis sunt cohercendi, non membrorum truncatione vel temporali morte plectendi."

51. C. 23, q. 5, dict. post c. 48, "Si ergo viri sancti et publicae potestates bella gerentes non fuerunt transgressores illius mandati: 'Non occides,' quamvis quosque flagitiosos digna morte perimerent; si miles suae potestati obediens non est reus homicidii, si eius inperio quemlibet flagitiosum interfecerit; si homicidas, et venenarios punire non est effusio sanquinis, sed legum ministerium; si pax ecclesiae mesticiam consolatur perditorum; si illi, qui zelo catholicae matris accensi excommunicatos interficiunt, homicidae non iudicantur: patet, quod malos non solum flagellari, sed etiam interfici licet." C. 23, q. 5, dict. post c. 7, "§2. Prohibetur ergo illo precepto quisque sua auctoritate in necem alicuius armari, non legis inperio malos perimit, nec illius precepti transgressor, nec a celesti patria alienus habetur."

236

raises some difficult problems for the understanding of Gratian's ecclesiological doctrine. The Magister seems to introduce a very fine distinction into the conception of shedding blood and seems to justify the use of force by churchmen even if it leads to bloodshed.

The dictum quoted above can be put into its proper context by reviewing the argument about the power to shed blood in some earlier passages of the quaestio. Gratian distinguishes, at one point, between the roles of regal and sacerdotal power. A capitulum from a letter of Saint Jerome informs us that royal power was instituted to control the evil and protect the good.[52] The rubric of another nearby capitulum deriving from Isidore's works says, "What priests are not able to do by teaching; the power [*potestas*] compels by the terror of discipline."[53] The "power" in this sentence is royal authority; Gratian makes this clear in two subsequent dicta.[54] In one of these, he says:

Further, just as we are forced to show faith and reverence to the princes and powers, so there is a necessity incumbent upon the administrators of the secular dignities to protect the churches. If they refuse to do this, they ought to be expelled from communion.[55]

In this and preceding passages, the Magister expresses the ancient view that the material sword is in the hands of secular princes, and they have a duty to use it in the interests of the Church. Here at least, Gratian does not recognize any right to use material force in the Church itself.

The language of the dictum quoted earlier seems to contradict this view. The reference, in the first sentence of the dictum, to the holy

52. C. 23, q. 5, c. 18, "Non frustra sunt instituta potestas regis, ius cognitoris, ungulae carnificis, arma militis, disciplina dominantis, severitas etiam boni patris; habeant ista omnia modos suos, causas, rationes, utilitates. Hec cum timentur, et mali cohercentur, et boni quieti inter malos vivunt."

53. C. 23, q. 5, c. 20 (rubric), "Quod sacerdotes efficere docendo non valent; disciplinae terrore potestas extorqueat."

54. C. 23, q. 5, dict. post c. 23, "Ipsis autem principibus et potestatibus fidem et reverentiam servari oportet, quam qui non exhibuerit apud Deum premia invenire non poterit."

55. C. 23, q. 5, dict. post c. 25, "Preterea, sicut principibus et potestatibus fidem et reverentiam exhibere cogimur, ita secularium dignitatum amministratoribus defendendarum ecclesiarum necessitas incumbit. Quod si facere contempserint, a communione sunt repellendi."

men and public powers suggests that churchmen also could kill criminals without transgressing the commandment, "Thou shalt not kill." The words *viri sancti* are not a very clear reference to prelates and even can be interpreted as meaning that men who kill in the name of governmental authority remain holy men in spite of the sixth commandment. Yet, *viri sancti* seems to be opposed to *publicae potestates* in the Magister's mind.[56] He is apparently justifying the use of force in its extreme form by two independent groups of men. Since *publicae potestates* clearly refers to secular authorities, *viri sancti* would seem to refer to rulers of the Church. This interpretation is supported by Gratian's treatment of the phrase *effusio sanguinis* later in the dictum. "To punish murderers and poisoners is not the shedding of blood, but the ministry of the laws." This sentence implies that if priests, acting as legitimate governors, were to kill or mutilate vicious criminals, they would not be committing the crime of shedding blood which was condemned by the ancient canons of the Church.

Does Gratian mean to expound the doctrine that priests can spill blood as long as they act in the name of legitimate authority? If he is seriously putting forth this doctrine, then he is contradicting the view he supported only a few pages earlier in the quaestio. He gives no indication that he is trying to refute that view, and though the theory that priests can use force in its extreme form is present in the troublesome dictum, it is there only for those who might want to find it. Gratian did not mean to say that priests could kill or otherwise shed the blood of other men. He does not use the phrase *viri sancti* to mean members of the ecclesiastical hierarchy. He is only summing up what he has said earlier in the quaestio, and he is being perfectly conventional about the relationship between priests and the spilling of blood.

56. He says "viri sancti et publicae potestatibus." See n. 51 above. Professor Gerald Caspary has suggested to me that *viri sancti* might refer to the patriarchs of the Old Testament. He tells me that the term was commonly used to refer to these figures. I have not been able to find any use of the term in the capitula of the quaestio, but Gratian certainly could have been using it as Professor Caspary suggests. This understanding of the term would solve the problem it raises in the context of the dictum since the patriarchs were not prohibited from shedding blood.

238

While Gratian granted that priests could impose material punishments, he argued that they were not permitted to use physical force involving the shedding of blood. His doctrine on this matter is contained in quaestio 8 of the Causa.

The argument in the eighth quaestio concerns the power of churchmen to shed blood. Though this is not perfectly clear from the language of the Magister, it is clear from the progress of the argument in the Causa. Before he comes to the problem of quaestio 8, Gratian has approved of the exercise of force in another form by the ecclesiastical rulers. They can, he says, confiscate the lands of heretics.[57] In the discussion of quaestio 8, coercive power means specifically the power to shed blood.

Gratian's argument again develops through his answers to objections raised against the right of the Church to use force. The Magister's opponents ask whether the Church possesses the right to use force, if bishops and other clerics are not permitted to exercise coercive power themselves. The sword of the Church, they argue, is the spiritual sword, which is the word of God. Only legitimate secular power possesses the material sword as Saint Paul wrote to the Romans, "For he beareth not the sword in vain."[58] This argument corresponds to

57. C. 23, q. 7, dict. ante c. 1, "Nunc autem queritur, an heretici suis et ecclesiae rebus sint expoliandi? et qui possident hereticis ablata an dicantur possidere aliena." C. 23, q. 7, dict. post c. 4, "His igitur auctoritatibus liquido monstratur, quod ea, que ab hereticis male possidentur, a catholicis iuste auferuntur, nec ideo aliena possidere dicuntur." Although the argument in these passages seems to be directed at confiscation by Christians and not specifically by bishops, it should be remembered that the case on which this question is based indicates that the bishops were the confiscators. Gratian must have had this fact in mind when he wrote the dicta of the quaestio.

58. C. 23, q. 8, dict. ante c. 1, "De episcopis vero vel quibuslibet clericis, quod nec sua auctoritate, nec auctoritate Romani Pontificis arma arripere valeant, facile probatur. Cum enim Petrus, qui primus apostolorum a Domino fuerat electus, materialem exerceret gladium, ut magistrum a Iudeorum iniuria defensaret, audivit: 'Converte gladium tuum in vaginam, omnis enim, qui acceperit gladium, gladio peribit,' ac si aperte ei diceretur: hactenus tibi tuisque predecessoribus inimicos Dei corporali gladio licuit persequi; deinceps in exemplum patienciae gladium tuum, id est tibi hactenus concessum, in vaginam converte et spiritualem tantum gladium, qui est verbum Dei, in mactatione veteris vitae

239

Stickler's view of the ancient theory of the two swords. The swords represent coercive power, and each of the authorities holds one of them. Gratian argues first that priests can urge (*hortari*) others to take up arms against oppressors and the enemies of God.[59] He shows what he means by "urge" in a dictum referring to an action of Pope Gregory I:

In the register it is read that the Blessed Gregory ordered the citizens of Tuscany to take up arms against the Lombards, and that he decreed stipends for the knights. From this example and the cited authorities, it is therefore clear that priests, even if they ought not to seize arms with their own hands, can either persuade those to whom such offices are committed or order anyone [other than the legitimate ruler] by their own authority to seize them.[60]

The doctrine is recapitulated in a later dictum.[61]

---

exerce. Omnis enim preter illum, vel auctoritatem eius, qui legitima potestate utitur, qui, ut Apostolos ait, non sine causa gladium portat, cui etiam omnis anima subdita esse debet, omnis, inquam, qui preter huius auctoritatem gladium acceperit gladio peribit." C. 33, q. 2, dict. post c. 5.

59. C. 23, q. 8, dict. post c. 6, "His ita respondetur: Sacerdotes propria manu arma arripere non debent; sed alios ad arripiendum, ad oppressorum defensionem, atque ad inimicorum Dei oppugnationem eis licet hortari."

60. C. 23, q. 8, dict. post c. 18, "In registro enim legitur, quod B. Gregorius civibus Tusciae, ut contra Longobardos arma pararent, mandavit, et militantibus stipendia decrevit. Hoc igitur exemplo et premissis auctoritatibus claret, quod sacerdotes, etsi propria manu arma arripere non debeant, tamen vel his, quibus huiusmodi offitia conmissa sunt, persuadere, vel quibuslibet, ut ea arripiant, sua auctoritate valeant inperare."

61. C. 23, q. 8, dict. post c. 28, "Licet ergo prelatis ecclesiae exemplo B. Gregorii ab inperatoribus vel quibuslibet ducibus defensionem fidelibus postulare. Licet etiam cum B. Leone quoslibet ad sui defensionem contra adversarios sanctae fidei viriliter adhortari, atque ad vim infidelium procul arcendam quosque citare." I have discussed these dicta with Professor Caspary, who has been working on the history of the sword imagery. In studying the passages, he was sensitive to the change in the verbs Gratian used. In the dictum post c. 18, Gregory *mandavit* that the Italians arm themselves against the Lombards. In drawing a rule from Gregory's example, the Magister said that priests could order (*inperare*) laymen to take up arms in defense of the Church. In the dictum post c. 28, Gregory is said to have asked (*postulare*) the emperors and dukes to come to his aid and Leo urged (*adhortari*) others to do the same. Caspary thinks that the change of verbs from the first dictum to the second indicates a retreat on Gratian's part from the extreme position he enunciated in the dictum post

240

The meaning of Gratian's language is clear. The Church does have the right to use armed force for its own purposes, but the members of the hierarchy themselves cannot participate in the action. Here again is the distinction between *potestas* and *executio potestatis,* now put into terms of a *ius* and *executio iuris.* The Church authority can exercise its power through the agency of laymen. In addition to expecting aid from those to whom a material sword was granted for their own governing activities, Gratian permits the ecclesiastical hierarchy to order others to take up arms. The existence of two material swords is implied in this recognition. The secular material sword is committed to the civil authority and should be used in the interests of the Church when the ecclesiastical rulers ask for aid. But the Church possesses a material sword of its own which it can use through the agency of ordinary laymen. This doctrine is important for understanding a difficult dictum that follows the one cited above.

Gratian's opponents are imaginative as well as imaginary, and they bring forth yet another objection to the use of force by prelates: Bishops ought not to implicate themselves in secular business. The relevant biblical passage comes from 2 Timothy 2:4: "No man, being a soldier to God, entangleth himself with secular businesses." [62] Gratian an-

---

c. 18. Gratian's final position on the Church's possession of the sword is thus relatively conservative.

Caspary's interpretation has merit and adds something to my own reading of the argument. I have concentrated on the reference, in both dicta, to the example of Gregory and think that by coming back to the earlier example, Gratian is implying that he has not retreated from the earlier doctrine. If I am right, then the change in verbs would be due to a looseness in the Magister's usage rather than to a doctrinal retreat. Nonetheless, I am confused by the dictum post c. 28 because it seems to go both ways, and I think there is support for both Caspary's and my interpretations. As will be seen, however, I too conclude that Gratian was setting forth a more conservative position than is contained in these dicta. The basis of my conclusion is different from the basis of Caspary's.

62. C. 23, q. 8, c. 19, "Reprehensibile valde esse constat quod subintulisti, dicendo, maiorem partem omnium episcoporum die noctuque, cum aliis fidelibus tuis contra piratas maritimos invigilare, ob idque episcopi inpediantur venire, cum militum Christi sit Christo servire, milites vero seculi serviant seculo, sicut scriptum est: 'Nemo militans Deo inplicat se negociis secularibus.' Quod si seculi milites miliciae student, quid ad episcopos et milites Christi, nisi ut vacent orationibus?" This passage is from a letter of Pope Nicholas I, JL 2788.

swers in effect that this text refers only to some bishops, basing his argument on a distinction between those bishops who hold regalia and those who renounce it. The bishops involved in the action against the heretics in the case under discussion held jurisdiction from the emperor. Bishops who accept imperial lands or offices are bound to pay the tribute due to the secular lord and to perform the duties required by their titles. Bishops who renounce the regalia and are content to live on tithes and other legitimate ecclesiastical revenues should not have anything to do with the secular community.[63] Those prelates who hold regalia may go to the camp of the emperor if the pope consents, but they may not render any aid personally except through daily prayers.[64]

Gratian's answer to the objection of his opponents is based on his understanding of the term "secular business." In the first section of

---

63. C. 23, q. 8, dict. post c. 20, "Sed notandum est, quosdam episcopos Levitica tantum portione esse contentos, qui, sicut in Dei sorte tantum numerantur, sic ipsum Deum solummodo in hereditatem accipiunt, dicentes: 'Dominus pars hereditatis meae est' [Ps. 15:5]. His nichil commune est cum principibus seculi, quia temporalia penitus abiciunt, ne eorum occasione legibus inperatorum obnoxii teneantur. Talibus nulla occasio relinquitur occupationis secularis miliciae, quia cum de decimis et primiciis vivunt tamquam summi regis filii in omni regno a terrenis exactionibus liberi sunt ita ut dicere valeant: 'Venit princeps mundi huius, et in nobis non habet quicquam' [John 14:30]. Porro alii sunt, qui non contenti decimis et primiciis, predia, villas, et castella, et civitates possident, ex quibus Cesari debent tributa, nisi inperiali benignitate inmunitatem promerverint ab huiusmodi. Quibus a Domino dicitur: 'Reddite que sunt Cesaris Cesari; et que sunt Dei Deo' [Matt. 22:21]. Quibus idem Apostolus: 'Reddite omnibus debita, cui tributum, tributum; cui vectigal, vectigal' [Rom. 13:2]." Hubrecht has concluded, on the basis of this dictum, that Gratian did not attribute the material sword to the Church. He argues that the Magister permits only those bishops who hold regalia to use the material sword. They receive the material sword from the emperor or king. This interpretation cannot be accepted. Hubrecht isolates the dictum from the rest of the Causa. G. Hubrecht, "La 'juste guerre' dans le Décret de Gratien," *SG*, 3 (1954), 161–177.

64. C. 23, q. 8, dict. post c. 25, "De his vero, que a quiluslibet emerit vel vivorum donationibus acceperit, principibus consueta debet obsequia, ut et annua eis persolvat tributa, et convocato exercitu cum eis proficiscatur ad castra. Quod tamen hoc ipsum non sine consensu Romani Pontificis fieri debet." C. 23, q. 8, dict. post c. 27, "Quam proficiscentes ad comitatum possunt intelligi non secuti inperatorem, ut armis sibi auxilientur, sed ipsum cum exercitu suo cottidianis orationibus Deo commendent."

this chapter, it was shown that the Magister made a distinction between the secular business of clerics and the secular business of secular men.[65] Here in Causa 23, he takes the phrase *negotia secularia* in 2 Timothy to mean the business of secular men. His distinction between the two types of bishops permitted him to point out that the biblical text referred only to those who had separated themselves from the worldly power by refusing to accept regalia.

Furthermore, the argument that he is making concerns the relationship between ecclesiastical governors and the secular material sword. It does not concern the Church's own material sword. Presumably, bishops who live on tithes can still command laymen to take up arms in the name of the Church, even if they cannot participate in actions undertaken by the emperor or kings. Gratian's response therefore avoids the issue raised by the objection. Starting from the premise that the passage from 2 Timothy refers only to the business of secular men, the Magister does not have to consider any actions other than the rather special ones in which bishops are called upon to act in the interests of the emperor. In these dicta, Gratian preserved his essential argument that bishops and the pope could call on civil authorities to aid the Church with arms or could command ordinary laymen to act in behalf of the Church.

Gratian's statement here, nevertheless, is a bit peculiar. He is trying to reconcile the actions of popes Leo II and Gregory II, who went out against the Saracens raiding the Italian coast and urged the people to take up arms, with the prescription of the Pauline letter concerning the involvement of priests in secular business. He could have accomplished this reconciliation, as he did in C. 11, q. 1, dictum post c. 47, without making the distinction between bishops who accept the regalia and those who renounce them. In fact, it is difficult to see the relevance of the distinction for the argument that Gratian is constructing.

In Gratian's period, the idea that bishops ought to renounce their regalia had been brought forth in the so-called Agreement of Sutri of 1111. It had met with a rather lively opposition from the bishops and had been given up. There appears to be a connection between the Agreement of Sutri and this *dictum Gratiani,* and the Magister very

65. See n. 17 above.

clearly favors the idea that bishops ought to be separated from their regalia. This idea, though not stated explicitly, was common among the supporters of Haimeric. In the writings of Bernard of Clairvaux and Gerhoh of Reichersberg, one constantly encounters pleas that bishops and the pope disengage themselves from worldly occupations and devote themselves to the spiritual life. In the great uproar that followed the announcement of the Sutri treaty, the basic idea of this treaty was lost and attention was shifted to other issues arising from Pascal II's imprisonment and its result. This dictum of Gratian and the oft-repeated pleas of others among the new reform party would seem to show that the treaty's basic message was not lost upon the Magister's generation, who were in their twenties when the agreement was made. It was a model of ecclesiastical life, an ideal model, which Gratian's generation strove for, but which, as the Magister's dictum shows, they did not expect to achieve.

To return to the Magister's doctrine concerning the use of force, it would seem that the doctrine he consistently expounded in the eighth quaestio contradicts the rule, also consistently set forth, that priests are entirely prohibited from spilling blood; this prohibition extended also to passing judgments involving the spilling of blood.[66] How can passing a judgment of blood be distinguished from commanding laymen to take up arms or urging civil rulers to use the power committed to them? It can only be concluded that while the prelate cannot tell laymen to kill a criminal or enemy, they can urge them to take appropriate action. To modern lawyers, this distinction is at best very weak, but it does not seem to have troubled Gratian and his contemporaries.

There is an interesting observation that can be made about Gratian's treatment of the image of the material sword and the power it signified. The Magister never discards the distinction between the legitimate secular authorities and the ordinary laymen in the exercise of the material sword. In his work, the older theory, according to which the secular material sword was to be used in the interests of the Church, coexisted with the newer theory that the Church itself possessed a material sword. Stickler has suggested that according to

66. C. 23, q. 8, c. 30, n. 31 above.

Gratian, priests urge or persuade civil authority to use its own sword power in the interests of the Church and order or command laymen when it is a matter of the ecclesiastical material sword.[67] This interpretation seems correct. From the dicta of quaestio 8, the reader gets the impression that the ecclesiastical material sword was to be used only when the secular power refused to act promptly on a request from a bishop or the pope. The same interpretation may be applied to the passages from the work of Saint Bernard. In his letter to Conrad III, Bernard stressed the ancient idea of cooperation between emperor and pope. In the famous passage from the *De Consideratione,* he recognized that the Church itself possessed the material as well as the spiritual sword.[68] The coexistence of these ideas in Bernard's and Gratian's works shows that the claim the theologians of the eleventh-century reform movement made, according to Stickler, had not taken very deep root in the tradition of ecclesiastical political and ecclesiological thought. The claim that the Church possessed its own material sword and did not need the help of the emperor or kings for carrying out its tasks was made, perhaps strongly, by writers of the eleventh-century reform movement, but it remained secondary in the writings associated with chancellor Haimeric's party in the twelfth century. Stickler's argument is misleading on this point; Bernard and Gratian followed not only the tradition of the reformers but also the more ancient tradition.

It is tempting to see the views of Gratian and Bernard on the Church's material sword and the cooperation between the two powers as a manifestation of their shared political outlook. If Stickler's interpretation of the attitude of the eleventh-century reformers is correct, then these authors would seem to have significantly weakened the Church's claim to the material sword by giving more emphasis to the older ideas of cooperation between the two powers. Since Gratian and Bernard looked upon imperial and royal power with more amity than their political opponents in the party of Pierleoni, they might be expected to favor theories of cooperation between regnum and sacer-

67. Stickler, "Magistri Gratiani sentencia de potestate ecclesiae in statum," p. 101.

68. Bernard, *Ep.* 244, n. 1, n. 36 above. Idem. *De Consid.,* IV:3, 7, n. 35 above.

dotium. At the same time, they may have been attracted by doctrines that deemphasize the coercive activities of the Church, since they sought to make the ecclesiastical community less worldly than it had been under Gregorian leadership. They would not have discarded the new ideas altogether, of course, because these ideas were part of the view of the Church which the new reformers accepted from the old reformers. The most important ecclesiological result of the eleventh-century reform movement was the creation of a free and independent Church; the new reformers of the twelfth century seized on this creation and sought to transform it according to their image of the ideal Christian community. Yet, to ascribe the theory of the Church's use of force expounded by Bernard and Gratian to their political attitudes is purely speculative. It is not known and cannot be discovered what the members of Pierleoni's party thought about the Church's material sword. This speculation, like others, retains some value however. They are the salt of the historian, and they stimulate asking new questions of the sources.

X. Conclusions

The Decretum in the twelfth century.

Until the circulation of the Decretum Gratiani, Church law consisted of a great mass of documents. It was the sum total of all the decretal letters and conciliar decrees, plus snippets from the writings of exegetes, theologians, and historians whose statements touched on some aspect of the Church's legal system. Magister Gratian brought order to the mass of material, deriving a set of legal rules on a large number of the questions traditionally covered by the canons. Historians have appreciated Gratian's effect on the body of Church law; they call him the father of canonical jurisprudence. They have also passed judgment on his methodological originality, and of late, they have studied a considerable number of his doctrines. But with rare exceptions, students of Gratian's work have asked historical questions that deepen only our knowledge of its place in the history of law. While it has been recognized that the Magister did not treat many important areas of canon law,[1] it has not been asked why he left out some topics or

1. As Lefebvre points out, Gratian's work was deficient on the matters of rescripts, delegation of authority, judicial procedure, the effect of sentences when appeal is made, benefices, criminal procedure (especially as regards accusations), and marriage. The members of the schools remedied some of these lacunae by the addition of paleae to the Decretum itself. Much of this material came from Roman law. After about 1170, however, the canonists began making new, supplementary collections of decretal letters that went beyond the Magister's discussions on many issues and covered the areas he had skipped. Charles Lefebvre, *L'âge classique* (Paris, 1965), pp. 140–141. On the paleae and beginning of the new collections of decretals, see the section of the same book written by Jacqueline Rambaud [-Buhot], and see chap. i above.

why he included others. When the Decretum is read as a whole, with no specific purpose in mind except to discover what Gratian was writing about, the unity of the work and its cohesiveness is striking. The recognition of a central theme leads to the question: What was Gratian trying to do?

Gratian presented the ancient ecclesiastical law to his contemporaries in a manageable form. In doing this he founded a new science of canon law parallel to the system of Roman law, and there is no doubt that part of the Magister's purpose was to establish this new science. But that was not his whole purpose. His thought, apparent in the structure as well as the content of his work, was not shaped by scholastic purposes but by the situation within the Church during the period when he wrote. This study has shown that Gratian's reform of the Church's legal system was connected with the party of Haimeric and Saint Bernard.

The reform movement of the eleventh century had focused attention on the earthly Church. Early in the movement's history, leaders of the reform were concerned with the structure and moral condition of the Church. After the Investiture Contest started, the emphasis shifted to the Church's place in the world order. The new reformers of the twelfth century wanted to return the attention of the hierarchy to the constitutional and moral state of the Church. In the Decretum, Gratian expressed the views and concerns of the reformers. He organized the law of the Church according to subject, treating the legal and moral condition of candidates for the clergy. He set forth the constitutional law of an autonomous community whose essential purpose is spiritual. Gratian's work thus exhibits the same interests and comes to the same conclusions as the works of Saint Bernard, Gerhoh of Reichersberg, and others of the reform movement. Gratian does not, of course, emphasize the mystical aspects of Bernard's or others' ecclesiology, but his is the best and fullest exposition of its mundane, constitutional aspects.

This interpretation of the Decretum forces historians to take a new look at the party dispute in the Church of the mid-twelfth century. The schism of 1130 was the event that signaled the beginning of the last stage of a struggle for power which had begun earlier. It is now possible to see that struggle as something more than a faction fight within the Roman Curia which, when it resulted in the schism, attracted the attention of the general European Church. The party dispute of the 1120's and 1130's should be seen as a great controversy over the needs of a Church freed from the interference of secular power and interests. By linking Gratian, Bernard, and other writers of the period with the fight for power in the Curia, it has been shown that there were principles and policies at issue in the struggle. Chancellor Haimeric's faction was actually a movement of great importance in the history of the period. It succeeded not only in changing the leadership of the Church but also in changing the view of the Church—its needs and its place in the world.

The effects of the movement were manifold. The works of its major writers, Gratian and Bernard, became basic source books of political thought in the High Middle Ages. At the same time, the movement established the monastic orders and canons regular in the constitutional fabric of the Ecclesia. Monks were now associated with the clergy in the governance of the Church. They participated in the election of bishops, and they were considered to be part of the clergy when writers set forth the division of the ecclesiastical body. The new orders of monks and canons played an essential role in the reform movement of the twelfth century, and the new view of their status within the Church reflected their importance.

The connection between the monks and the papacy in the twelfth century was very similar to what had existed at the beginning of the eleventh-century reform. But unlike the connection between Cluny and reform in the 1040's and 1050's, the alliance between pope and monks in the mid-twelfth century was a lasting one. By the end of the Investiture Contest, the monks and canons had entered the life of the Church as parish priests, and they controlled churches that had once been owned by secular lords. The monasteries were now not only the source of manpower for the hierarchy—as they had been since the beginning of the eleventh-century reform movement—but also active participants in the governance of the Church. The new reform movement and the period immediately following its victory coincided with the establishment of canons regular in the cathedral churches of Europe. The development of cathedral chapters had far-reaching effects on the constitution of the medieval church.

Historians have chronicled the later years of the Investiture Contest, focusing their attention on the playing out of the great issues and political struggles that arose in the eleventh century. Now it is clear that the period has to be looked at from another point of view. It is probable that by seeking the origins of the new reform movement of the 1120's and 1130's a new dimension will be added to understanding the early years of the twelfth century. What were the antecedents of the new movement that, as Klewitz's brilliant insight showed, brought an end to the great reform papacy of the previous century? Which of the events of the early decades of the century spurred the new party's development? Historians have seen these years and events as the last stages of something old; they must now look at them as the first stages of something new. The pontificates of Pascal II, Gelasius II, and Calixtus II demand the attention of the historian again.

The place of the Decretum in medieval political theory.

Some very general remarks on the place of the Decretum in the history of political theory in the Middle Ages are called for in conclusion to this study. The Decretum presents the new reformers' theory of the ecclesiastical community; it is therefore an important document. Before the twelfth century, Christian political theory focused on the secular political community. It was only after the Church won its independence from secular power that ecclesiastical writers began to view it as a political community in its own right. The political theory of the Church which such writers—and Gratian was one of the most important among them—expounded was based on earlier works dealing with secular kingdoms.

The writers of the Carolingian period had concerned themselves with the nature of kingship.[2] For them, the king was the vicar of God,

2. James M. Wallace-Hadrill, "The *via regia* of the Carolingian Age," *Trends in Medieval Political Thought,* ed. B. Smalley (Oxford, 1965), pp. 22–41. This article, given as a lecture, is an excellent survey of the interests and main ideas of the Carolingian political thinkers.

and the hierarchy of authority atop which he sat corresponded to the hierarchy of heaven over which God presided. This conception led Carolingian political thinkers to take up many of the problems later found to be important by Gratian when he considered the nature of ecclesiastical authority. Thus, they treated the relationship between king and divine law, and then went on to consider his power over human law. Hincmar, the great archbishop of Reims, cited the passage from Augustine's *de vera religione* which said that rulers could no longer judge concerning the laws once those laws had been made. Gratian cited this passage and repeated its message in a dictum in the *Tractatus de legibus*.[3]

In many aspects of his theory of authority, then, Gratian followed older medieval views, simply using them to describe ecclesiastical instead of secular authority. But the Church, and especially the Church of the twelfth century, presented problems for the political thinker which earlier writers, treating the secular community, had not faced. In particular, the membership of the Church was not natural or tribal, but artificial. It was therefore more subject to scrutiny by lawyers than membership of those communities into which one was simply born. Moreover, the heretical sects of the twelfth century made the definition of membership in the ecclesiastical community a subject of great importance by attacking the traditional understanding of it. Orthodox writers, trying to meet heretical arguments about the sacrament of baptism, brought to the fore their notions of how one became and remained a member of the Church. While these writers, Gratian included, did not discuss the ecclesiological aspects of baptism *ex professo*, they did introduce this important problem, in essence the problem of citizenship, into political discourse. It remains for scholars to follow out the later history of their discussions.

Another area in which Gratian surpassed earlier medieval political thinkers was in his treatment of political obedience. This problem was not raised by any theory of social contract which would make acceptance of the duty of obedience a voluntary affair, but by the rela-

---

3. Hincmar, *De ordine palatii*, c. 8. See the discussion of this passage by Wallace-Hadrill (*op. cit.*, pp. 35-36). In the Decretum, the Augustinian passage occurs at Dist. 4, c. 3, but see also Dist. 4, dict. post c. 2.

tionship between the governor of the Church and God. Carolingian writers had set forth a theory of the secular community which emphasized that the king was only a minister of the true ruler. The king ruled over a *populus christianus* that was the people of God. But these writers did not derive any theory of resistance from their doctrine on this matter. Gratian did take up this issue because the Church was both a more perfect and, for the Christian, a more important community than the secular community. Since the ecclesiastical governor participates in the divine governance of the universe, his authoritative actions must be judged carefully. The effect that the political authority in the Church could have on the spiritual life of Christians made it imperative for them to determine the limits of that authority and to propose a method of dealing with the evil exercise of authority. Thus, in this matter too, transferring the attention of the political theorist from the secular community to the Church led to a broadening of the scope of political discussion and to a more detailed study of the nature of the polity than had been undertaken earlier in the Middle Ages.

Enlarging the view of the political thinker, bringing more problems into his consideration, and making him examine them more carefully, was not the most important result of the transference of his attention to the Church in the twelfth century. The Christian's conception of the political community of the Church was fundamentally different from his idea of the secular kingdom. The king was a God-given ruler and his kingdom was a model of the heavenly kingdom, but he did not rule a perfect community in the Christian sense. The kingdom could become a parody of the heavenly community or a degenerate model; the Church would always remain good. The gates of Hell would not prevail against the Church; all too often, they prevailed against the secular communities. More important, the Church is a spiritual as well as worldly community. It remains perfect by virtue of its essential spirituality, even though it can never be perfect in its earthly manifestation. The duality of the Church created great difficulties for Gratian's political thought, but it also made his doctrine true Christian political theory in a way that the political theory of the secular community could never be true. His political theory of the Church is a description of the perfect community existing imperfectly; it is

Plato's *Republic* and *Laws* in one. And it is, therefore, a failure from the standpoint of the political theorist. Ultimately, the political theory of the perfect-imperfect community remains a mystery; it is part of the mystery that for the Christian is the essential characteristic of the Church.

Appendix I

The Date of the Decretum

The arguments on the date the Decretum appeared have been constructed without reference to the career of its author. So little is known about Gratian's life and career, that scholars have relied on internal evidence and the relationship of the Decretum to contemporary works and events. The traditional date established for the work was 1150–1151. This period was chosen by the Roman Correctors and was accepted by most nineteenth-century scholars. It was based on a tradition preserved by the medieval canonists. (For a review of the scholarly opinion on the date of the Decretum from the Middle Ages until 1898, see Paul Fournier, "Deux controverses sur les origines du Décret de Gratien," *Revue d'histoire et de litterature religieuse,* 3 [1898], 253–255.) In 1872, however, the German legal historian Thaner published an argument that the Decretum was completed shortly after 1139. The inclusion of decrees from the Second Lateran Council made that date the *terminus a quo,* while a change of practice within the papal chancery seemed to establish a *terminus ad quem* in 1143–1144. In those years, during the pontificate of Celestine II, papal privileges began to contain a clause that reserved the power of the pope to alter or abrogate them. The introduction of this clause, "salva sedis apostolicae auctoritate," stemmed, according to Thaner, from the theory of legislative power Gratian had developed. In Causa 25, the Magister argued that every papal decree contained an explicit or implicit recognition of papal legislative power. On the basis of the use of the Decretum by the scribes of the papal chancery, Thaner dated the work about 1140. (Friedrich Thaner, "Über Entstehung und Bedeutung der Formel: Salva sedies apostolicae auctoritate in den päpstlichen Privilegien," *Sitzungsberichte der Wiener Akademie der Wissenschaft,* Phil.-Hist.

Cl., 72 [1872], 809–851. Thaner's date was not universally accepted, but in 1898 it received strong support from Paul Fournier. Against Thaner, see for example, J. B. Sägmüller, "Die Entstehung und Bedeutung der Formel 'salva Sedis apostolicae auctoritate' in den päpstlichen Privilegien," *Theologische Quartalschrift,* 89 [1907], 93–117. Fournier, *op. cit.,* pp. 97–116, 253–280.)

Fournier argued from the use of the Decretum in literary works as well as from the dates of the earliest commentaries and internal evidence. The earliest use of Gratian's work was by Anselm of Havelberg and Peter Lombard. Fournier dated the *de ordine canonicorum* of Anselm in 1149–1150, and though Peter Lombard's *Sententiae* could be dated any time from 1150 to 1158, he preferred 1150–1152. Thus, he argued, by about 1150 Gratian's work was known in Germany and Paris, and sufficient time must be reckoned between its date of composition and its circulation north of the Alps. Friedberg, in the introduction to his edition of the Decretum, indicates the sources from which the Magister took his canons. The last one on his list is Peter Lombard's *Sententiae,* which were written considerably after the Decretum. Fournier's date for the *Sententiae* is no longer accepted. Van den Eynde has argued persuasively that the work should be dated about 1158. (D. Van den Eynde, "Précisions chronologiques sur quelques ouvrages théologiques du XIIe siècle," *Antonianum,* 26 [1951], 223–246.)

The dates of the first commentaries also help in the dating of the Decretum, according to Fournier. The *Summa* of Rolandus, who became Alexander III, was written about 1148 and the work of Paucapalea, Gratian's first known pupil, must be dated in the early or mid-1140's. These dates suggest that Gratian completed the Decretum about 1140. This date is confirmed by evidence from the Decretum itself. Fournier showed that three bishops mentioned by the Magister held their sees in 1140.

The bishops are Henry, bishop of Bologna, 1130–1145; Adeline, bishop of Reggio, 1130–1140; and Gautier, archbishop of Ravenna, 1119–1145. (See C. 2, q. 6, dict. post c. 31.) The names are used in model forms of appeal and Fournier thought that Gratian would have used the names of living bishops. The best date, he thought, was 1140 when all three bishops held their sees and after the *terminus a quo* set by the presence of decrees from the Second Lateran Council (1139) in the work. In the same dictum, a date is given in one of the model appeals. This is, in Friedberg's edition, April 30, 1105, a Wednesday. The year appears as 1105, 1128, and 1161 in the manuscripts, and Fournier pointed out that according to local calendars, April 30 did not fall on Wednesday in any of these years. It did fall on that day in 1130 and 1141. Although Fournier favored 1130 as the original date, he thought that neither date would injure his case for the date of the Decretum. (Fournier, *op. cit.,* pp. 264–266.) There are two conclusions that can be derived from Fournier's reasoning. First, Gratian may have written C. 2, q. 6 about 1130 and therefore used that date in his model. Later, there would have been no reason to change the date. Second, Gratian may have completed this section, and the Decretum, around April 30, 1141. Of course, the Magister may have chosen the day at random, leaving twentieth-century scholars to argue over a meaningless point.

The evidence brought forth by Fournier is very convincing, and his argument has been generally accepted. Only Vetulani, working on a newly found abridgment of the Decretum, and trying to solve the Roman law problem at the same time, has rejected the date 1140 and suggested a much earlier date. The abridgment was found in a manuscript from Danzig Vetulani discovered before the Second World War. He thinks it predates Paucapalea's *Summa,* and he argues that Paucapalea relied on the abridgment's introduction and on some of its glosses. The author of the summary also said that the Decretum was well known when he began to write. Vetulani thinks that the epitome was made about 1140, and he points out that some time would have been necessary for Gratian's work to achieve the notoriety attributed to it then. With respect to the Roman law problem, Vetulani says that Gratian's careful avoidance of that law is extremely difficult to understand if it is supposed that the Decretum was completed in 1140. By that period, Bologna was already a center of active Roman law studies, and it is unlikely that a well-trained and brilliant lawyer like Gratian would not have been infected with the general interest in Justinian's great compilation. In fact, studies on Decretum manuscripts show that within a very short time the members of the early canonical schools supplied the missing Roman law texts to the Decretum demonstrating the impact of Roman law studies in the 1140's.

According to Vetulani, the solution of the problems raised by the Danzig manuscript and the absence of Roman law from the Decretum lies in moving the date of Gratian's activities back to the first decades of the twelfth century. Gratian, he argues, was a member of Pascal II's party in the period of Sutri and thus he believed in the radical separation of the Church from secular affairs. This attitude would naturally extend also to secular law. Furthermore, Vetulani thinks it likely that Gratian worked away from the center of legal studies and that he was actually living in Rome when he made his collection. There, he would have been in closer touch with Pascal and his supporters and would not have been influenced by the trend in legal scholarship at the schools in Bologna. The date Vetulani supports is between 1105 and 1120 when the party of Pascal was still in existence and its ideas still alive. (A. Vetulani, "Le Décret de Gratien et les premiers Décrétistes à la lumière d'une source nouvelle," *SG*, 7 [1959], 273–353. This article was originally published in Polish in 1955.) Vetulani argues that the best manuscripts of the Decretum contain the date April 30, 1105 in C. 2, q. 6, dict. post c. 31; see above. Thus, the manuscript evidence supports his argument, he says. Vetulani's arguments have been rejected by nearly all scholars working on Gratian. Fransen has attacked his dating of the Danzig manuscript, which is one of the bases of his position. (G. Fransen, "Le date du Décret de Gratien," *RHE*, 51 [1956], 521–531. Vetulani answered Fransen in the French translation of his study published in *SG op. cit.*, p. 299 n. 16a. See also H. F. Schmid, review of Vetulani's study in *ZRG*, Kan. Abt., 43 [1957], 365–375. Fransen and R. Gansiniec debate the importance of the Danzig manuscript in "Le premier abrégé du Décret de Gratien," *RHE*, 52 [1957], 865–870. G. Le Bras has commented on Vetulani's thesis in *RHD*, 4th ser., 33 [1955], 622.) Madame Rambaud has said that the manuscript evidence does not support his case. In the first place, the earliest manuscripts of the Decretum come from the middle of the century; and in the second place, the decrees of the Second Lateran

Council do not appear to be paleae as Vetulani's view makes necessary. (J. Rambaud, *L'Âge Classique* [Paris, 1965], pp. 57–58.) Fournier's date still appears to be the best one offered. But Vetulani's arguments are stimulating and point up the need to look at the Decretum in the context of its historical background.

Appendix II

Saint Bernard and the Law

The dispute over Saint Bernard's attitude to the law and the judicial activities of the Church is important for our understanding of the Bernard's ideas about the nature of the ecclesiastical hierarchy. The dispute has involved many scholars, and a great amount of the discussion has centered on *De Consideratione,* I:4, 5.

Walter Ullmann (*The Growth of Papal Government in the Middle Ages* [London, 1954], pp. 426–436) argues that Bernard is pro-Gregorian and pro-legalistic. In fact, Ullmann sees Bernard's writings as the final statement of the hierocratic theory of world order. After the middle of the twelfth century, all hierocratic political thinkers repeated Bernard's ideas and even his words. (On the later use of Bernard's work, see also Jean Rivière, *Le problème de l'Église et de l'État au temps de Philippe le Bel* [Louvain, 1926]. Rivière points out that Bernard's works were used by both parties to the dispute.) Jacqueline has supported the view that Bernard was interested in and even knowledgeable about the law. (Bernard Jacqueline, "Saint Bernard et le droit romain," *RHD,* 4th ser., 29 [1952], 223–228. *Idem,* "Catalogue des manuscrits juridiques de la bibliothèque de Clairvaux," *24e Congrès de l'Association bourguignonne des sociétés savants* [Dijon, 1955], pp. 157–175. Idem, *Papauté et épiscopat selon saint Bernard de Clairvaux* [Saint-Lô, 1963]. *Idem,* "Yves de Chartres et saint Bernard," *Études Le Bras,* I:179–184. See also B. H. D. Hermesdorf, "Bernardus van Clairvaux als jurist," *Annalen voor Rechtsgeleerdheid en Staatswetenschappen,* 13 [1953], 345–363.)

The view that Bernard was antilegalistic is held by White. (H. V. White, "The Gregorian Ideal and St. Bernard of Clairvaux," *Journal of the History of Ideas,* 21 [1960], 321–348. *Idem,* "The Conflict of

Papal Leadership Ideals from Gregory VII to Bernard of Clairvaux,"
[Ph.D. diss. University of Michigan, 1956].) A. Fliche argued that
Bernard was antilegalistic, but pro-Gregorian. The conflict between the
views of Fliche and Ullmann on these points demonstrates that the
definition of Gregorianism holds an essential place in the dispute over
Bernard's views. Fliche has argued that the Gregorian papacy was
essentially interested in reform and that Gregorianism is a reform
ideology rather than a movement toward centralization and constitutional development of the Church. Ullmann and White hold the
view that the most important aspect of the Gregorian movement was
its constitutional reform and its views of world order. (A. Fliche, *La
reforme gregorienne, Histoire de l'Église,* 8 [Paris, 1950], 179–198.
Idem, "Bernard et la société civile de son temps," *Bernard de Clairvaux,*
355–378. *Idem,* "L'influence de Gregoire VII et des idées gregoriennes
sur la pensée de s. Bernard," *Saint Bernard et son temps,* 1:137–150.
See also A. Fliche, R. Foreville, and P. Rousset, *Du premier concile du
Latran à l'avenement d'Innocent III, Histoire de l'Église,* vol. 9, pt. 1
[Paris, 1944].) Recently, E. Kennan has reviewed the scholarship on the
dispute in the context of an article dealing with interpretations of
Bernard's *De Consideratione.* Kennan supports those who argue that
Bernard had an interest in the law. (E. Kennan, "The 'De Conside-
ratione' of St. Bernard and the Papacy in the Mid-Twelfth Century:
A Review of Scholarship," *Traditio,* 23 [1967], 73–115.)

Jacqueline ("Saint Bernard et le droit romain") has offered the most
concrete evidence of Bernard's supposed knowledge of the law, in
this case the Roman law. He points to a passage in the *De gradibus
humilitatis,* IV:14, "Et legibus humanis statutum et in causis, tam
ecclesiasticis quam saecularibus servatum scio, speciales amicos causantium non debere admitti ad judicium: ne vel fallant vel fallantur
amore suorum." This text was borrowed verbatim by the compiler
of the *Collection in Ten Parts* and by the author of the first collection
of Châlons, both canonical collections. (On these collections, see
P. Fournier and G. Le Bras, *Histoire des collections canoniques,* 2
[Paris, 1932], 296–306, 308–311.) Jacqueline believes that Bernard was
citing a Roman law text from the commentary *Summa Codicis* which
has been attributed variously to Irnerius and Rogerius. A copy of this

relatively rare work was in the library of Clairvaux during the twelfth century. Actually, the textual basis for Jacqueline's argument that Bernard was citing the *Summa* is not strong. I must agree with Jacqueline that Bernard tended to quote texts from memory and that he often made slight errors, but in this case the argument for literary relationship between the texts is based only on the appearance of certain words in each of them. In fact, the content of the two passages is not the same. If Bernard is recalling the passage from the Roman law commentary, he has had a significant lapse of memory.

There are other reasons why Jacqueline's argument cannot be accepted. The chronology of the works in question is a bit confusing. Some, as was said, think that the *Summa Codicis* was written by Irnerius who died after 1125. Most appear to place the work in the period around 1150. (E. H. Fitting, *Summa Codicis des Irnerius* [Berlin, 1894]. H. Kantorowicz, *Studies in the Glossators of the Roman Law* [Cambridge, 1938], pp. 145–171. Kantorowicz sees it as the work of Rogerius done between 1140 and 1159. See also E. Besta, *Storia del diritto italiano,* 2 [Milan, 1923], 798–799. Besta thinks the work was written around 1150, but he does not think it can be firmly attributed to any known civilists.) Jacqueline's argument presumes that Fitting is correct on this matter, and the presumption is certainly not a strong foundation upon which to rest his interpretation. But his argument also assumes that the work was in the library at Clairvaux very early in the abbey's history and very early in the history of Bernard's literary activity. The *De gradibus humilitatis* was probably the first treatise written by the abbot and can be dated between 1120 and 1125. (J. Leclercq, introduction to *De gradibus humilitatis, Opera,* 3:3–4. D. Van den Eynde, "Les débuts literaires de Saint Bernard," *Analecta sacris ordinis Cisterciensis,* 19 [1963], 189–198.) It must be accepted that Bernard used the summa shortly after it was written (if indeed it was written so early as Fitting and Jacqueline argue), that he used it in Clairvaux shortly after the monastery was founded, and that he used it in his first literary work, a work written before Bernard became entangled in the affairs of the world. The evidence for all this is not convincing. Jacqueline's argument seems improbable at best.

Jacqueline may have started to develop his argument after reading the passage from the *De gradibus humilitatis,* IV:14. The passage strikes the reader as being unusual in the context of the treatise, and Jacqueline's instinct on this matter is probably correct. But it would be more reasonable to suppose that Bernard borrowed this legalistic passage from some canonical work. Jacqueline himself notes that there were several works of canon law in the library at Clairvaux during Bernard's abbacy (*op. cit.,* p. 224 n. 1). These collections included Alger of Liège's *Liber de misericordia et justitia,* Gerland of Besancon's *Candela,* Ivo of Chartres' *Panormia,* and the Pseudo-Isidorian Decretals. There was a copy of Gratian's Decretum at Clairvaux from 1166 when Alan of Auxerre, a disciple of Bernard, donated one to the monastery. In addition, a study of the language of the passage may point to canonical rather than Roman origin. Bernard notes that the rule he is citing is common to ecclesiastical as well as secular cases, and this reference to both types of human law reminds one of canonical works. The canonists often referred to the two codes giving the impression that they wanted to indicate the equality of the two types of jurisprudence. Gratian, for example, says in the *Tractatus de legibus* (Dist. 3, dict. ante c. 1), "constitutio alia est civilis, alia ecclesiastica." Dist. 3, dict. post c. 3, "Officium vero secularium, sive ecclesiasticarum legum est."

At the same time, it is known that Roman law played an important part in the development of canonical jurisprudence during the twelfth century. Even Gratian, who scrupulously avoided using texts from Justinian and other Roman law compilations, borrowed some of his most important legal conceptions from the commentaries of the Roman lawyers (e.g., the idea of *ius condendi,* C. 25, q. 1, dict. post c. 16; see chap. vi). The Magister's treatment of Roman law was not caused by ignorance of it. It is possible, therefore, that Bernard borrowed the passage in question from a canonist who had in turn borrowed it from Roman law.

Bernard himself provides an example of how this process could work. In his *Epistola* 202 to the clergy of Sens, he cites the ancient rule that all those who were affected by an episcopal election ought to participate in that election. In its origins, this rule came from a Roman legal maxim governing the treatment of a *tutela,* but it had been accepted into canonical jurisprudence as early as Pope Celestine I, at the beginning of the fifth century. Bernard certainly thought that he was informing the clergy of Sens on an ancient canon law principle. Gratian seems to have recognized the Roman origins of the maxim and his treatment of it, discussed in chapter viii, is in accordance with his approach to nearly all Roman law.

Bernard, as Jacqueline has noted (*op. cit.,* p. 224 n. 1), wrote a treatise that was legalistic in name if not in content. This work was the *De praecepto et dispensatione,* treating a topic common to the canon lawyers. In addition, Bernard quoted from the canons of the Council of Reims (1148) in his *De Consideratione* (III:5, 20). A list of these canons was in the library of the monastery. On the basis of this evidence, there seems no justification for claiming that Bernard was antilegalistic. But historians should be careful to distinguish the limits of his interest in the law. The evidence of interest in and knowledge of Roman law which Jacqueline presents appears to be too weak to support the assertions that Jacqueline wants to make. It would seem that the famous text of *De Consideratione,* I:4, 5, is a true indication of Bernard's attitude toward civil law.

Herbert Bloch has pointed out evidence that indicates the party of Haimeric as a whole was influenced by the canonists. Arnulf of Lisieux, who wrote one of the most vitriolic and most widely read tracts against Anaclet, had studied law, probably at Bologna. Peter the Venerable mentioned the notion of *sanior pars* in a letter to Aegidius of Tusculum, a former monk of Cluny and one of the cardinal bishops who sided with Anaclet. *Ep.,* 40 (ca. 1133), ed. Giles Constable, 2:135, "canonica decreta hoc habeant, ut maiori et saniori parti in omni negotio caedendum sit." In the same letter, Peter refers to a distinction, derived from the canon law tradition, between the *urbs* and *orbis.* *Ep.,* 40 (ca. 1133), ed. Constable, 2:135, "ubi aecclesia esse existimanda sit, quae in omnibus mundi nationibus esse credenda est, in angulo urbis Romae, an in toto orbe." Saint Bernard made the same distinction in a famous phrase from *Ep.* 124 (1131) in which he described Innocent as, "Pulsus urbe, ab orbe suscipitur." Gratian incorporated a canon in the Decretum which contained the same opposition of *urbs* and *orbis.* (Dist. 93, c. 24. H. Bloch, "The Schism of Anacletus II and the Glanfeuil Forgeries of Peter the Deacon," *Traditio,* 8 [1952], 169. Bloch received this information from Professor S. Kuttner. It should be noted that Bloch's reference, in n. 36 on p. 169, to Dist. 73, c. 24 is a misprint.)

Yet, in spite of the evidence cited in the preceding paragraphs, it should not be asserted too readily that Bernard was deeply interested in the canon law either. He may have read some canonical works as a result of his general interest in the Church and its problems, but when he debated with the famous canonist Peter of Pisa at the court of Roger of Sicily in 1137, he is reported to have conspicuously avoided arguing the legal niceties of the double election of 1130. Instead, he concentrated on the character of the two popes arguing that Innocent II deserved to be pope and was more suited to be pope, than Anaclet II. He won the debate on these grounds. (See *vita Bernardi,* II:7. Falco of Beneventum, *Chronicon,* ed. Muratori, *Rerum Italicarum SS,* 5:125.) Bernard's inspiration in the fight for recognition of the legitimacy of Innocent did not come from reading works dealing with canon law. He was inspired by his commitment to the monastic vocation and by his belief that this vocation would save the Church. He was infused with a spirit that entered the mainstream of canon law jurisprudence in the *Distinctiones* of Gratian's Decretum. By making the law of the Church sensitive to the reformers' ideals, Gratian changed the image of canon law and made it a vital part of the new Church of the mid-twelfth century. Bernard certainly knew some law and used legal conceptions on occasion, but it is more important to understand another aspect of the intellectual history of his time. In the hands of Gratian, the law came to Bernard.

Bibliography

Many articles cited below appear in collections (e.g., *Proceedings of the Second International Congress of Medieval Canon Law*). In order to save space and avoid repetition, I have noted only the title and page numbers when citing such articles. The complete bibliographical information for these collections is presented under the title of each. In addition, where I cite many single works of a medieval writer which appear in a collection of their works, I have presented the complete bibliographical information in the first citation only. I have used the standard abbreviation (PL) where I cite J.-P. Migne's *Patrologiae cursus complectens,* series latina.

Algerus Leodiensis. *Liber de misericordia et justitia.* PL 180, col. 857–968.

Amelineau, E. "St. Bernard et le schisme d'Anaclet II," *Revue des questions historiques,* 30 (1881), 47–112.

Anciaux, P. *La Théologie du sacrement de pénitence au XIIe siècle.* Louvain: E. Nauwelaerts, 1949 (Universitas Catholica Lovaniensis. Dissertationes ad gradum magistri in Facultate Theologica vel in Facultate Iuris Canonici consequendum conscriptae, ser. 2, vol. 41).

Arnold, Franz. "Die Rechtslehre des Magisters Gratians," *Studia Gratiana,* 1 (1953), 453–482.

Arnulfus Lexoviensis episc. *Invectiva in Girardum Engolismensem Episcopum (De schismate).* Ed. Julius Dieterich. *Monumenta Germaniae Historica,* Libelli de lite III, 81–108 (PL 201, col. 173–194).

Arquillière, H.-X. "Sur la formation de la 'theocratie' pontificale," *Mélanges d'Histoire du moyen-âge offerts à F. Lot.* Paris, 1925. Pp. 1–24.

Bainvel, J. "L'idée de l'Église au moyen-âge. S. Anselme et S. Bernard," *La Science Catholique,* 13 (1899), 193–24.

Banks, R. J. "Jurisdiction (Canon Law)." In *New Catholic Encyclopedia.* 8:61–62.

Barion, Hans. *Rudolph Sohm und die Grundlegung des Kirchenrechts.* Recht und Staat in Geschichte und Gegenwart. Vol. 81. Tübingen: J. C. Mohr, 1931.

———. "Der Rechtsbegriff Rudolph Sohms," *Deutsche Rechtswissenschaft,* 7 (1942), 47–51.

Barraclough, Geoffrey. *The Origins of Modern Germany*. Oxford: B. Blackwell, 1946.

Bennington, J. Clement. *The Recipient of Confirmation*. Canon Law Studies 267. Washington, D.C.: Catholic University of America Press, 1952.

Benson, Robert L. "The Obligations of Bishops with 'Regalia': Canonistic Views from Gratian to the Early Thirteenth Century," *Proceedings of the Second International Congress of Medieval Canon Law*. Pp. 123–137.

——. *The Bishop-Elect: A Study in Medieval Ecclesiastical Office*. Princeton, N.J.: Princeton University Press, 1968.

Bergamo, Mario da. "Osservazioni sulle fonte per la duplice elezione papale del 1130," *Aevum*, 39 (1965), 45–65.

Berlière, Ursmer. "Le cardinal Matthieu d'Albano," *Revue Benedictine*, 18 (1901), 280–303.

——. "L'exercice du ministère paroissial par les moines du XIIe au XVIIIe siècle," *Revue Benedictine*, 39 (1927), 340–364.

——. "L'exercice du ministère paroissial par les moines dans le haut moyen-âge," *Revue Benedictine*, 39 (1927), 227–250.

Bernardus Claravallensis. *Ad clericos de conversione*. Ed. J. Leclercq and H. Rochais. *Sancti Bernardi Opera*. Rome: Editiones Cistercienses, 1957 to present. 4:61–116.

——. *De Consideratione*. Ed. J. Leclercq and H. Rochias. *Opera*. 3:381–493.

——. *De festivitatibus sancti Stephani, sancti Joannis et sanctorum innocentium* (de tempore 4). Ed. J. Leclercq and H. Rochais. *Opera*. 4:270–273.

——. *Epistolae*. PL 182, col. 67–722.

——. *In adventu Domini* (de tempore 1). Ed. J. Leclercq and H. Rochais. *Opera*. 4:161–196.

——. *In Nativitate Domini* (de tempore 3). Ed. J. Leclercq and H. Rochais. *Opera*. 4:244–270.

——. *In Quadragesima* (de tempore 10). Ed. J. Leclercq and H. Rochais. *Opera*. 4:353–380.

——. *In Septuagesima* (de tempore 9). Ed. J. Leclercq and H. Rochais. *Opera*. 4:344–352.

——. *In vigilia nativitatis Domini* (de tempore 2). Ed. J. Leclercq and H. Rochais. *Opera*. 4:197–244.

——. *Liber ad milites templi de laude novae militiae*. Ed. J. Leclercq and H. Rochais. *Opera*. 3:207–239.

——. *Liber de praecepto et dispensatione*. Ed. J. Leclercq, H. Rochais, and C. H. Talbot. *Opera*. 3:243–294.

——. *Sermo in conversione Sancti Pauli* (de Sanctis 1). Ed. J. Lerclercq and H. Rochais. *Opera*. 4:327–334.

——. *Sermo in octava Epiphaniae* (de tempore 7). Ed. J. Leclercq and H. Rochais. *Opera*. 4:310–313.

———. *Sermones super cantica canticorum.* Ed. J. Leclercq, H. Rochais, and C. H. Talbot. *Opera.* Vols. 1–2.

———. *Tractatus de baptismo aliisque quaestionibus.* PL 182, col. 1031–1046.

———. *Vita S. Malachi.* Ed. J. Leclercq and H. Rochais. *Opera.* 3:297–378.

———. *Bernard de Clairvaux.* Commission d'histoire de l'Ordre de Citeaux. Publications. Vol. 3. Paris: Editions Alsatia, 1953.

———. *Saint Bernard et son temps.* Congrès de 1927 de l'Association bourguignonne des Sociétés savantes. 2 vols. Dijon, 1928.

———. *Saint Bernard: homme d'Église. Temoignages.* Vols. 38–39. 1953.

———. *San Bernardo.* Pubblicazione Commemorativa nell 'VIII centenario della sua morte. Milan: Società Editrice "Vita e Pensiero," 1954 (Milan: Università Cattolica del Sacro Cuore. Publicazioni. N.S. 46).

———. *Saint Bernard Théologien. Analecta sacris ordinis Cisterciensis.* Vol. 9. 1953.

———. "Bernardus Bibliographie," *Citeaux in de Nederlanden,* 6 (1955), 31–75.

———. *Bernhard von Clairvaux, Mönch und Mystiker.* Ed. J. Lortz. Wiesbaden: Veröffentlichungen des Instituts für Europäische Geschichte-Mainz, 1955.

Bernheim, E. *Das Wormser Konkordat und seine Vorurkunden hinsichtlich Entstehung, Formulierung, Rechtsgültigkeit.* Breslau: M & H Marcus, 1906 (Untersuchungen zur deutschen Staats- und Rechtsgeschichte. Vol. 81).

Beumer, Johannes. "Ekklesiologische Probleme der Frühscholastik," *Scholastik,* 27 (1952), 183–209.

———. "Zur Ekklesiologie der Frühscholastik," *Scholastik,* 26 (1951), 364–389.

———. "Ein Religionsgespräch aus dem 12. Jahrhundert," *Zeitschrift für katholische Theologie,* 73 (1951), 465–469.

Bliemetzrieder, Franz. *Anselms von Laon systematische Sentenzen.* Münster: Aschendorf, 1919 (Beiträge zur Geschichte der Philosophie des Mittelalters. Texte und Untersuchungen. 81:2–3).

———. "Gratian und die Schule Anselms von Laon," *Archiv für katholisches Kirchenrecht,* 112 (1932), 37–63.

Bloch, Herbert. "The Schism of Anacletus II and the Glanfeuil Forgeries of Peter the Deacon," *Traditio,* 8 (1952), 159–264.

Borst, Arno. "Neue Funde und Forschungen zur Geschichte der Katharer," *Historische Zeitschrift,* 174 (1952), 17–30.

———. "Abälard und Bernhard," *Historische Zeitschrift,* 186 (1958), 497–526.

———. *Die Katharer.* Stuttgart: Hiersemann Verlag, 1953 (*Monumenta Germaniae Historica.* Schriften 12).

Botte, Bernard. "L'ordre d'àpres les prières d'ordination," *Études sur le sacrement de l'ordre,* Lex Orandi 22. Paris, 1957. Pp. 13–35.

——— et al. *Le Concile et les Conciles.* Paris: Editions du Cerf, Editions de Chevetogne, 1960.

Boulet-Sautel, Marguerite. "Les 'paleae' empruntées au Droit Romain dans quelques manuscrits du Décret de Gratien conservés en France," *Studia Gratiana,* 1 (1953), 149–158.

Brixius, J. M. *Die Mitglieder des Kardinalkollegiums von 1130–1181.* Berlin: R. Trenkel, 1912.

Browe, Peter. "Die Kinderkommunion im Mittelalter," *Scholastik,* 5 (1930), 1–40.

———. *Die Pflichtkommunion im Mittelalter.* Regensburg: Regensburgische Verlagsbuchhandlung, 1940.

Brys, Johannes. *De dispensatione in iure canonico praesertim apud decretistas et decretalistas usque ad medium saeculum decimum quartum.* Bruges: C. Beyaert, 1925 (Universitas Catholica Lovaniensis. Dissertationes ad gradum magistri in Facultate Theologica consequendum conscriptae. Ser. 12. Vol. 14).

Buisson, Ludwig. *Potestas und Caritas.* Die päpstlichen Gewalt im Spätmittelalter. Cologne-Graz: Böhlau, 1958 (Forschungen zur kirchlichen Rechtsgeschichte und zum Kirchenrecht. Vol. 2).

———. "Die Entstehung des Kirchenrechts," *Zeitschrift der Savigny-Stiftung für Rechtsgeschichte,* Kan. Abt., 52 (1966), 1–175.

Calcaterra, C. *Alma Mater Studiorum.* L'Università di Bologna nella storia della cultura e della civiltà. Bologna: N. Zanichelli, 1948.

Capelle, Catherine. *Le voeu d'obéissance, des origines au XIIe siècle; étude juridique.* Paris: R. Pichon et R. Durand-Auzias, 1959 (Bibliothèque d'histoire du droit et droit romain 2).

Carlyle, A. J., and R. W. Carlyle. *A History of Mediaeval Political Theory in the West.* 6 vols. London: W. Blackwood and Sons, 1903–1936.

Caron, Pier Gr. "I poteri del metropolita secondo Graziano," *Studia Gratiana,* 2 (1954), 251–278.

———. "Appunti sui concetti de 'auctoritas' e di 'potestas' nel decreto di Graziano e nella dottrina decretistica della seconda meta del secolo XII," *Il diritto ecclesiastico,* 67 (1958), 393–438.

Châtillon, Jean. "Une ecclésiologie médiévale: l'idée de l'Église dans la théologie de l'école de St. Victor au XIIe siècle," *Irenikon,* 22 (1949), 115–138, 395–411.

Chenu, M.-D. *La Théologie au douzième siècle.* Paris: J. Vrin, 1957 (Études de Philosophie médiévale 45).

Chibnall, Marjorie. "Monks and Pastoral Work: A Problem in Anglo-Norman History," *Journal of Ecclesiastical History,* 18 (1967), 165–172.

Citterio, B. "La riforma del Clero nella trilogia di S. Bernardo," *La scuola Cattolica,* 82 (1954), 111–132.

Classen, Peter. *Gerhoch von Reichersberg: eine Biographie.* Wiesbaden: F. Steiner, 1960.

Claude, H. "Autour du schisme d'Anaclet: Saint Bernard et Girard d'Angoulême," *Mélanges Saint Bernard.* Dijon, 1954. Pp. 80–94.

Composta, Dario. "Il diritto naturale in Graziano," *Studia Gratiana,* 2 (1954), 153–210.

Conciliorum Oecumenicorum Decreta. Ed. J. Alberigo, P. P. Joannou, C. Leonardi, P. Prodi. Freiburg i. Br.: Herder, 1962.

Congar, Yves. "L'ecclésiologie de s. Bernard." *Saint Bernard Théologien.* Pp. 136–190. Trans. in Ger.: "Das Ekklesiologie des hl. Bernhard," *Bernhard von Clairvaux: Mönch und Mystiker.* Ed. J. Lortz. Pp. 76–119.

———. "Quod omnes tangit, ab omnibus tractari et approbari debet," *Revue historique de droit français et étranger,* 36 (1958), 210–259.

Constable, Giles. *Monastic Tithes From Their Origins to the Twelfth Century.* Cambridge: Cambridge University Press, 1964.

Cosme, R. L. "La teoria de las fuentes del derecho eclesiastico en la renascencia juridica de principios des siglo XII," *Rivista espanola de derecho canonico,* 15 (1960), 317–370.

Cox, R. J. *A Study of the Juridic Status of Laymen in the Writings of the Medieval Canonists.* Canon Law Studies 395, Washington, D.C.: Catholic University of America Press, 1959.

Czerwinski, Francis C. "Innocent III and the Jews." Master's thesis, Cornell University, 1965.

Dauvillier, Jean. "La juridiction arbitrale de l'Église dans de Décret de Gratien," *Studia Gratiana,* 4 (1956–1957), 121–129.

David, Marcel. "Parjure et mensonge dans de Décret de Gratien," *Studia Gratiana,* 3 (1954), 117–141.

Debil, A. "La première dist. du 'de paenitentia' de Gratien," *Revue d'histoire ecclesiastique,* 15 (1914), 251–273.

Déchanet, Jean-Marie. "Aux sources de la pensée philosophique de s. Bernard." *Saint Bernard Théologien.* Pp.56–77.

———. "La Christologie de saint Bernard." *Saint Bernard Théologien.* Pp. 78–91.

Delhaye, Philippe. "L' 'ignorantia juris' et la situation morale de l'heretique dans l'Église ancienne et médiévale." *Études Le Bras.* 2:1131–1142.

Depoorter, A. "De argumento duorum gladiorum apud s. Bernardum," *Collationes Brugenses,* 48 (1952), 22–26, 95–99.

Dereine, Charles. "Les origines de Prémontré," *Revue d'histoire ecclesiastique,* 42 (1947), 352–378.

———. "Le problème de la vie commune chez les canonistes d'Anselme de Lucques à Gratien," *Studi Gregoriani,* 3 (1948), 287–298.

———. "L'élaboration du statut canonique des chanoines reguliers specialement sous Urbain II," *Revue d'histoire ecclesiastique,* 46 (1951), 534–565.

Didier, J. Ch. "La question du baptême des enfants chez s. Bernard et ses contemporains." *Saint Bernard Théologien.* Pp. 191–201.

Die Chimaere seines Jahrhunderts. Vier Vorträge über Bernhard von Clairvaux. Ed. J. Spoerl. Würzburg: Werkbund-Verlag, 1953.

Diener, H. "Das Verhältnis Clunys zu den Bischöfen, vor allem in der Zeit seines Abtes Hugo (1049–1109)." *Neue Forschungen über Cluny und die Cluniacenser.* Ed. G. Tellenbach. Freiburg i. Br.: Herder, 1959. Pp. 219–252.

271

Dimier, Anselme. "Saint Bernard et le droit en matière de Transitus," *Revue Mabillon,* 43 (1953), 48–82.

Donlon, S. E. "Power of Jurisdiction." In *New Catholic Encyclopedia.* 8:62–63.

Duchesne, Louis. "Le nom d'Anaclet II au palais de Latran," *Memoires de la Société des Antiquaires de France,* 5th ser., 9 (1888), 197–206.

Edwards, Kathleen. *The English Secular Cathedrals in the Middle Ages.* Manchester: Manchester University Press, 1949.

Ehrle, F. "Die Frangipani und der Untergang des Archivs und der Bibliothek der Päpste am Anfang des 13. Jahrhunderts." *Mélanges offerts à M. Emile Chatelain.* Paris: Champion, 1910.

Ekbertus Schonaugiensis. *Sermones Contra Catharos.* PL 195, col. 11–98.

Elze, R. "Die päpstliche Kapelle im 12. und 13. Jahrhundert," *Zeitschrift der Savigny-Stiftung für Rechtsgeschichte,* Kan. Abt., 36 (1950), 145–204.

Esmein, A. "La maxime Princeps legibus solutus est dans l'ancien droit public français." *Essays in Legal History.* Ed. P. Vinogradoff. Oxford: Oxford University Press, 1913. Pp. 201–214.

Études d'histoire du droit canonique dediées à Gabriel Le Bras. 2 vols. Paris: Sirey, 1965.

Eugenius III papa. *Epistolae et Privilegia. Regesta Pontificum Romanorum.* 2:8714–9735. PL 180, col. 1013–1614.

Evervinus Steinveldensis. *Ep.* 472 *inter Bernardinas Epistolas.* PL 182, col. 676–680.

Farlati, D. *Illyricum Sacrum.* 8 vols. Venice: Apud Sebastianum Coleti, 1751–1819.

Fedele, Pietro. "Le famiglie di Anacleto II e di Gelasio II," *Archivio della Società Romana di storia patria,* 27 (1904), 399–433.

———. "Pierleoni e Frangipani nella Storia medievale di Roma," *Roma,* 15 (1937), 1–12.

———. "Sull'origine dei Frangipane (a proposito di un recente lavoro)," *Archivio della Società Romana di storia patria,* 33 (1910), 493–506.

———. *Tabularium S. Mariae Novae ab. an. 982 ad an. 1200.* Rome: Società Romana di storia patria, 1903. (*Archivio della Società Romana di storia patria,* vols. 23–25, 1901–1903.)

Feine, Hans Erich. *Kirchliche Rechtsgeschichte.* Vol. 1. Weimar: H. Böhlaus, 1950 (only volume to appear).

———. "Gliederung und Aufbau des Decretum Gratiani," *Studia Gratiana,* 1 (1953), 353–370.

Festschrift zum 800-Jahrgedächtnis des Todes Bernhard von Clairvaux. Oesterreichische Beiträge zur Geschichte des Cistercienserordens. Vienna-Munich: Herold, 1953.

Fischer, Eugen H. "Bussgewalt, Pfarrzwang und Beichtvater-Wahl nach dem Dekret Gratians," *Studia Gratiana,* 4 (1956–1957), 185–230.

Fliche, Augustin. "L'influence de Gregoire VII et des idées gregoriennes sur la pensée de saint Bernard." *Saint Bernard et son temps.* 1:137–150.

———. "Bernard et la société civile de son temps." *Bernard de Clairvaux.* Pp. 355–378.

Fliche, Augustin, Raymonde Foreville, and R. Rousset. *Du premier Concile du Latran à l'avenement d' Innocent III. Histoire de l'Église.* Vol. 9 (in 2 parts). Paris: Bloud & Gay, 1944 and 1953.

Foreville, Raymonde. *Latran I, II, III et Latran IV.* Histoire des conciles oecumeniques. Vol. 6. Paris: Editions de l'Orante, 1965.

Foreville, Raymonde, and Jean Leclercq. "Un débat sur le sacerdoce des moines au XIIe siècle." *Anaclecta Monastica.* 4th ser. Rome, 1957. Pp. 8–118 (*Studia Anselmia.* Vol. 41).

Föster, Erich. "Sohm widerlegt?" *Zeitschrift für Kirchengeschichte,* 48 (1929), 307–343.

———. "Rudolph Sohms Kritik des Kirchenrechts zur 100. Wiederkehr seines Geburtstages 29 Oktober 1841 untersucht," *Teyler's Godgeleerd genootschap bekroente Preisschrift* (1942).

Fournier, Paul. "Une collection canonique italienne du commencement du XIIe siècle," *Annales de l'Enseignement superieur de Grenoble,* 6 (1894), 343–438.

———. "Deux controverses sur les origines du Décret de Gratien," *Revue d'histoire et de litterature religieuse,* 3 (1898), 97–116, 253–280.

———. "Un tournant de l'histoire du droit (1060–1140)," *Revue historique de droit français et étranger,* 40–41 (1917), 129–180.

Fournier, Paul, and Gabriel Le Bras. *Histoire des collections canoniques en Occident depuis les Fausses décrétales jusqu'au Décret de Gratien.* 2 vols. Paris: Recueil Sirey, 1931–1932.

Fransen, Girard. "La date du Décret de Gratien," *Revue d'histoire ecclesiastique,* 51 (1956), 521–531.

———. "Manuscrits canoniques conservés en Espagne," *Revue d'histoire ecclesiastique,* 51 (1956), 935–941.

———. "La tradition des canonistes au moyen-âge." *Études sur le sacrement de l'ordre.* Paris: Editions du Cerf, 1957 (Lex Orandi 22).

Freçon, P. "Calixte II et la querelle des Investitures," *Bulletin de la Société des Amis de Vienne 1967,* 63 (1968), 43–54.

Friedberg, Emil. "Erörterungen über die Entstehungszeit des Decretum Gratiani," *Zeitschrift für Kirchenrecht,* 17 (1882), 397–408.

Fuchs, V. *Der Ordinationstitel von seine Entstehung bis auf Innozenz III.* Eine Untersuchung zur kirchlichen Rechtsgeschichte mit besonderes Berücksicht der Anschauungen Rudolph Sohms. Bonn: L. Röhrscheid, 1930.

Gagner, S. *Studien zur Ideengeschichte der Gesetzgebung.* Upsala: Almquist & Wiksells. Boktryckeri Ab, 1960.

Gansiniec, R., and Girard Fransen, "Le premier abrégé du Décret de Gratien," *Revue d'histoire ecclesiastique,* 52 (1957), 865–870.

Ganzer, K. "Das Mehrheitsprinzip bei den kirchlichen Wählen des Mittelalters," *Tübinger theologische Quartalschrift*, 147 (1967), 60–87.

Gaudemet, Jean. "La doctrine des sources du droit dans le Décret de Gratien," *Revue de droit canonique*, 1 (1951), 5–31.

————. "Das römische Recht in Gratians Dekret," *Oesterreichisches Archiv für Kirchenrecht*, 12 (1961), 177–191.

————. "Patristique et Pastorale, La contribution de Gregoire le Grand au 'Miroir de l'Évêque' dans le Décret de Gratien." *Études Le Bras*. 1:129–140.

————. "Equité et droit chez Gratien et les premiers décrétistes." *La Storia del Diritto nel quadro della scienze storiche*. Atti del Primo Congresso Internazionale della Società Italiana di Storia del Diritto. Florence, 1966.

Gaudenzi, A. "L'Età del Decreto di Graziano e l'antichissimo Ms. Cassinese di esso," *Studi e Memorie per la Storia del Universita di Bologna*, 1 (1909), 65–96.

Gebhardt, Bruno. *Handbuch der deutschen Geschichte*. Ed. Herbert Grundmann. Vol. 1. Stuttgart: Union Deutsche Verlagsgesellschaft, 1954.

Gerhohus Reichersbergensis. *De investigatione Antichristi*. Ed. J. Scheibelberger. *Opera inedita*, I (1875) (complete). *Monumenta Germaniae Historica*, Libelli de lite III:304–395 (bk. I). Ed. E. Sackur.

————. *De quarta vigilia noctis*. *Monumenta Germaniae Historica*, Libelli de lite III:503–525 (complete). Ed. E. Sackur.

————. *Epistola ad Innocentium Papam missa quid distet inter clericos seculares et regulares*. PL 194, col. 1375–1426 (complete). *Monumenta Germaniae Historica*, Libelli de lite III, 209–239 (complete). Ed. E. Sackur.

————. *Libellus de eo, quod princeps mundi huius iam indicatus sit (Liber de simoniacis)*. PL 194, col. 1335–1372 (incomplete). *Monumenta Germaniae Historica*, Libelli de lite III:239–272 (complete). Ed. E. Sackur.

————. *Liber de novitatibus huius temporis*. Ed. D. J. Thatcher. *The Decennial Publication of the University of Chicago*, 1 (1906), 186–238 (complete). *Monumenta Germaniae Historica*, Libelli de lite III:288–304 (partial). Ed. E. Sackur.

————. *Opusculum ad Cardinales*. *Monumenta Germaniae Historica*, Libelli de lite III:399–411. Ed. E. Sackur.

————. *Opusculum de aedificio Dei*. PL 194, col. 1187–1336 (complete). *Monumenta Germaniae Historica*, Libelli de lite III:136–202 (most). Ed. E. Sackur.

————. *Tractatus de ecclesiasticiis negotiis (Expositio sexagesimi quarti psalmi)*. PL 194, 9–118 (complete). *Monumenta Germaniae Historica*, Libelli de lite III:439–492 (most). Ed. E. Sackur.

Gerland, Marie-Joseph. "Le ministre extraordinaire du sacrement de l'ordre," *Revue thomiste*, 36 (1931), 874–885.

Ghellinck, Joseph de. "La 'Species quadriformis Sacramentorum' des canonistes du XIIe siècle et Hugues de Saint-Victor," *Revue des Sciences philosophiques et théologiques*, 6 (1912), 527–537.

————. "Un chapitre dans l'histoire de la définition des sacrements an XIIe siècle," *Mélanges Mandonnet*, vol. 2, *Bibliothèque thomiste*, 14 (1930), 79–96.

274

——. *Le mouvement théologique du XIIe siècle.* 2d ed. Bruges: Editions "De Tempel," 1948.

Giet, Stanislas. "Saint Bernard et le troisième degré d'obéissance ou la soumission du jugement," *L'année théologique,* 7 (1946), 192–221.

——. "De trois textes de Gratien sur la propriété," *Studia Gratiana,* 2 (1954), 321–332.

Gilchrist, John. "'Simoniaca haeresis' and the Problem of Order from Leo IX to Gratian," *Proceedings of the Second International Congress of Medieval Canon Law.* Boston College, 1963. Ed. S. Kuttner and J. J. Ryan. Vatican City, 1965. Pp. 209–235.

——. "Cathedral Chapter," In *New Catholic Encyclopedia.* 3:249–251.

Gillmann, Franz. "Paucapalea et paleae bei Huguccio," *Archiv für katholisches Kirchenrecht,* 88 (1908), 466–479.

——. "Die Siebenzahl der Sakramente bei den Glossatoren des Gratianischen Dekrets," *Der Katholik,* 89 (1909), 182–214.

——. *Zur Lehre der Scholastik vom Spender der Firmung und des Weihesakraments.* Paderborn: F. Schöningh, 1920.

——. "Zu Gratians und der Glossatoren inbesondere des Johannes Teutonicus Lehre über die Bedeutung der justa causa für die Wirksamkeit der Excommunikation," *Archiv für katholisches Kirchenrecht,* 104 (1924), 5–40.

——. "Zur scholastischen Auslegung von Mt. 16, 18," *Archiv für katholisches Kirchenrecht,* 104 (1924), 41–53.

——. "Einleitung und System des Gratianischen Dekrets nach den alten Dekretglossatoren bis Johannes Teutonicus," *Archiv für katholisches Kirchenrecht,* 106 (1926), 472–574.

——. *Die 'anni discretionis' im Kanon Omnis utriusque sexus (c. 21, Conc. Lat. IV).* Mainz: Kirchheim, 1929.

——. "Rührt die Distinctioneneinteilung des ersten und dritten Dekretteils von Gratian selbst her?" *Archiv für katholisches Kirchenrecht,* 112 (1932), 504–533.

Gilson, Étienne. *The Mystical Theology of S. Bernard.* Trans. A. H. C. Downes. London: Sheed & Ward, 1940.

——. "La cité de Dieu de s. Bernard." *S. Bernard, homme d'Eglise.* Pp. 101–105.

Gough, J. W. *Fundamental Law in English Constitutional History.* Oxford: Clarendon Press, 1953.

Grabmann, Martin. *Die Geschichte der scholastischen Methode.* 2 vols. Graz: Akademische Druck- und Verlagsanstalt, 1957 (original Freiburg i. Br., 1909–1911).

——. "Das Naturrecht der Scholastik von Gratian bis Thomas von Aquin," *Archiv für Rechts- und Wirtschaftsphilosophie,* 16 (1923), 12–53.

Gratianus. *Concordia discordantium canonum* (Decretum). Ed. E. Friedberg. *Corpus Iuris Canonici.* Vol. 1. Graz: Akademische Druck- und Verlagsanstalt, 1959 (reprint of Leipzig: B. Tauchnitz, 1879 edition).

275

Greenaway, G. W. *Arnold of Brescia.* Cambridge: Cambridge University Press, 1931.

Gressier, J. "Gratien et le ministre de la pénitence." Ph. D. dissertation, Pontificia Universitas Gregoriana, 1955.

Grill, Leopold. "Saint Bernard et la question sociale." *Mélanges Saint Bernard.* Pp. 194–211.

Grundmann, Herbert. *Religiöse Bewegungen im Mittelalter.* Hildesheim: Georg Olms Verlagsbuchhandlung, 1961 (reprint of Historischen Studien 267. Berlin: Verlag Dr. Emil Ebering, 1935 with addition of an appendix: "Neue Beiträge zur Geschichte der religiösen Bewegungen im Mittelalter").

Hackett, J. H. "State of the Church: A Concept of the Medieval Canonists," *The Jurist,* 23 (1963), 259–290.

Haid, Kassian. "Der hl. Bernhard über Kirche und Staat," *Cistercienser Chronik,* 28 (1916), 269–270.

Haller, Johannes. *Das Papsttum: Idee und Wirklichkeit.* 5 vols. Munich: Rowohlt, 1965.

Häring, Nicholas M. "Character, Signum und Signaculum. Die Einführung in die Sakramententheologie des 12. Jahrhunderts," *Scholastik,* 31 (1956), 182–212.

Hauck, Albert. *Der Gedanke der päpstlichen Weltherrschaft bis auf Bonifaz VIII.* Leipzig: A. Edelmann, 1904.

Hauck, W. A. *Rudolph Sohm und Leo Tolstoi,* Rechtsordnung und Gottesreich. Heidelberg: Winter Universität. Verlag, 1950.

Hefele, C. J. von. *Conciliengeschichte. Nach den Quellen bearbeitet.* 11 vols. Freiburg im Breisgau: Herder, 1873–1890. Trans. into French: H. Leclercq, *Histoire des conciles.* 12 vols. Paris: Letouzey, 1907–1912.

Heggelbacher, O. *Die christliche Taufe als Rechtsakt nach dem Zeugnis der fruhen Christenheit.* Freiburg, Switz.: Universitätsverlag, 1953.

Heintschel, Donald E. *The Medieval Concept of an Ecclesiastical Office.* Canon Law Studies 363. Washington, D.C.: Catholic University of America Press, 1956.

Henry, A.-M. "Moines et chanoines," *La vie spirituelle,* 80 (1949), 50–69.

Hermesdorf, B. H. D. "Bernardus van Clairvaux als jurist," *Annalen voor Rechtsgeleerdheid en Staatswetenschappen,* 13 (1953), 345–363 (*Annales de droit et sciences politiques*).

Hessel, A. "Cluny und Mâcon. Ein Beitrag zur Geschichte der päpstlichen Exemptions privilegien," *Zeitschrift für Kirchengeschichte,* 22 (1901), 516–524.

Heyer, Friedrich. "Der Titel der Kanonessammlung Gratians," *Zeitschrift der Savigny-Stiftung für Rechtsgeschichte,* Kan. Abt., 2 (1912), 336–342.

———. "Namen und Titel des Gratianischen Dekretes," *Archiv für katholisches Kirchenrecht,* 94 (1914), 501–517.

Hilling, Nicholas. "Die Bedeutung der jurisdictio voluntaria und involuntaria im römischen Recht und im kanonischen Recht des Mittelalters und der Neuzeit," *Archiv für katholisches Kirchenrecht,* 105 (1925), 449–473.

———. "Über den Gebrauch des Ausdrucks jurisdictio im kanonischen Recht während der ersten Hälfe des Mittelalters," *Archiv für katholisches Kirchenrecht,* 118 (1938), 165–170.

Hödl, Ludwig. *Die Geschichte der scholastischen Literatur und der Theologie der Schlüsselgewalt.* Vol. 1. Münster: Aschendorffsche Verlagsbuchhandlung, 1960 (Beiträge zur Geschichte der Philosophie des Mittelalters. Vol. 38:4).

Hoffman, H. "Die beiden Schwerter im hohen Mittelalter," *Deutsches Archiv für Erforschung des Mittelalters,* 20 (1965), 78–114.

Hofmeister, Philipp. *Bischof und Domkapitel nach altem und neuem Recht.* Wurttemburg: Abtei Neresheim, 1931.

———. "Mönchtum und Seelsorge bis zum 13. Jahrhundert," *Studien und Mitteilungen zur Geschichte des Benediktiner-Ordens und seine Zeige,* 65 (1953–54), 209–273.

———. "Kardinäle aus dem Ordensstände," *Studien und Mitteilungen zur Geschichte des Benediktiner-Ordens und seine Zeige,* 72 (1961), 153–170.

Holböck, F. *Der eucharistische und der mystische Leib Christi in ihren Beziehungen zueinander nach der Lehre der Frühscholastik.* Rome: Verlag "Officium libri catholici," 1941.

Holtzmann, Walter. "Die Benutzung Gratians in der päpstlichen Kanzlei im 12. Jahrhundert." *Beiträge zur Reichs- und Papstgeschichte des hohen Mittelalters.* Bonn, 1957. Pp. 177–196.

Horoy, C. A. *Droit international et droit des gens public d'après le Decretum de Gratien.* Paris: Chevalier-Marescq, 1887.

Hubrecht, G. "La 'juste guerre' dans le Décret de Gratien," *Studia Gratiana,* 3 (1954), 161–177.

Hugelmann, Karl G. *Die deutsche Königswahl im Corpus Iuris Canonici.* Breslau: M. & H. Marcus, 1909 (Untersuchungen zur deutschen Staats- und Rechtesgeschichte. Vol. 98).

Hugo Ambianensis. *Contra haereticos sui temporis (De ecclesia et ejus ministris libri tres).* PL 192, col. 1255–1298.

———. *Dialogorum libri septem.* PL 192, col. 1137–1248.

Hugo de S. Victore. *De arca Noe mystica.* PL 176, col. 681–704.

———. *De duabus civitatibus et duobus populis et regibus.* PL 177, col. 496–497. Miscellanea, I:48.

———. *De oboedientia quibus sit praestanda.* PL 177, col. 581. Miscellanea, I:185.

———. *De sacramentis Christianae fidei.* PL 176, col. 183–618.

———. *De sacramentis legis naturalis et scriptae Dialogus.* PL 176, col. 17–42.

———. *Institutiones in decalogum legis dominicae.* PL 176, col. 9–15.

———. *Quod spiritualis diiudicat omnia.* PL 177, col. 469–477. Miscellanea, I:1.

———. *Sermo de officio et potestate praelatorum.* PL 177, col. 497–499. Miscellanea, I:49.

277

Hugueny, Étienne. "Gratien et la confession," *Revue des Sciences philosophiques et théologiques*, 6 (1912), 81–88.

Huizing, Peter. "The Earliest Development of Excommunication 'latae sententiae' by Gratian and the Earliest Decretists," *Studia Gratiana*, 3 (1955), 277–320.

Hyland, Francis E. *Excommunication, Its Nature, Historical Development and Effects.* Canon Law Studies 49, Washington, D.C.: Catholic University of America Press, 1928.

Innocentius II papa. *Epistolae et Privilegia. Regesta Pontificium Romanorum.* 1:840–911 (PL 179, col. 25–674).

Iung, N. "Confirmation dans l'église occidentale." *Dictionnaire de droit canonique.* 4:99–103.

Jacqueline, Bernard. "Saint Bernard et le droit romain. A propos d'une citation du Tractatus de gradibus humilitatis: Speciales amicos causantium non debere admitti ad judicium," *Revue historique de droit français et étranger*, 30 (1952), 223–228. (See *Bernard de Clairvaux.* Pp. 429–433.)

——. "Bernard et l'expression 'plenitudo potestatis.' " *Bernard de Clairvaux.* Pp. 345–348. (See *Papauté et épiscopat.*)

——. "Bernard et le schisme d'Anaclet II." *Bernard de Clairvaux.* Pp. 349–354. (See *Papauté et épiscopat.*)

——. "A propos de l'exemption monastique." *Bernard de Clairvaux.* Pp. 339–343.

——. "Saint Bernard et la Curie romaine," *Rivista di storia della chiesa in Italia*, 7 (1953), 27–44. (See *Papauté et épiscopat.*)

——. "Le pouvoir pontifical selon saint Bernard, l'argument des deux glaives," *Année canonique*, 2 (1953), 197–201. (See *Collectanea ordinis Cisterciensis reformatae*, 17 (1955), 130–138.)

——. "Le Décret de Gratien à l'abbaye de Clairvaux," *Studia Gratiana*, 3 (1955), 426–432. (See *Collectanea ordinis Cisterciensis reformatae*, 14 (1952), 259–264.)

——. *Papauté et épiscopat selon saint Bernard de Clairvaux.* Saint-Lô: Éditions du Centurion, 1963.

——. "Yves de Chartres et saint Bernard." *Études Le Bras.* 1:179–184.

Jordan, E. "Dante et S. Bernard," *Bulletin de Jubilé*, Paris, 1921. 4:267–330 (Comité francais catholique pour le célébration du 6e centenaire de Dante).

Kane, Thomas A. *The Jurisdiction of the Patriarchs of the Major Sees in Antiquity and in the Middle Ages.* Canon Law Studies 276. Washington, D.C.: Catholic University of America Press, 1949.

Kantorowicz, Ernst. *The King's Two Bodies.* Princeton, N.J.: Princeton University Press, 1957.

——. "Kingship Under the Impact of Scientific Jurisprudence." *Twelfth Century Europe and the Foundations of Modern Society.* Ed. G. Post, M. Clagett, and R. Reynolds. Madison: University of Wisconsin Press, 1961. Pp. 89–111.

Kehr, Paul. "Diploma purpurea di re Roggero II per la casa Pierleoni," *Archivio della R. Società Romana di storia patria,* 24 (1901), 253–259.

———. "Die Belehnungen der süditalienische Normannenfürsten durch die Päpste 1059–1192." *Abhandlungen der preussischen Akademie der Wissenschaften,* Phil.-Hist. Kl. n. 1. Berlin, 1934.

Kempf, Friedrich, "Die päpstliche Gewalt in der mittelalterlichen Welt," *Miscellanea Historica Pontificalis,* 21 (1959), 153–16.

———. "Das Problem der Christianitas im 12. und 13. Jahrhundert," *Historisches Jahrbuch,* 79 (1960), 104–123.

———. "Kanonistik und kuriale Politik im 12. Jahrhundert," *Archivum Historiae Pontificiae,* 1 (1963), 11–52.

Kennan, Elizabeth. "The 'De Consideratione' of St. Bernard and the Papacy in the Mid-Twelfth Century: A Review of Scholarship," *Traditio,* 23 (1967), 73–115.

Kerckhove, M. van de. *La notion de juridiction dans la doctrine des Décrétistes et des premiers Décrétalistes.* Assisi, 1937.

———. "De notione jurisdictionis apud Decretistas et priores Decretalistas (1140–1250)," *Jus Pontificium,* 18 (1938), 10–14.

Kern, Fritz. *Kingship and Law in the Middle Ages.* Trans. S. B. Chrimes. Oxford: B. Blackwell, 1939.

Kilga, Klemens. *Der Kirchenbegriff des hl. Bernard von Clairvaux.* Sonderdruck: Cistercienser Chronik, 1947–1948.

Kirsch, P. A. "Der sacerdos proprius in der abendländischen Kirche vor dem Jahre 1215," *Archiv für katholisches Kirchenrecht,* 84 (1904), 527–537.

Kleineidam, Erich. "Bernhard von Clairvaux über die Predigt." *Sacramentum Ordinis.* Geschichtliche und systematische Beiträge. Ed. E. Puzik and O. Kuss. Breslau: Verlag de Schleswig Bonifatiusvereins-Blattes, 1942. Pp. 169–199.

Klewitz, Hans Walter. "Die Entstehung des Kardinalkollegiums," *Zeitschrift der Savigny-Stiftung für Rechtsgeschichte,* Kan. Abt., 25 (1936), 115–221. (Reprinted in *Reformpapsttum und Kardinalkolleg.* Darmstadt: H. Gentner, 1957.)

———. "Das Ende des Reformpapsttums," *Deutsches Archiv für Geschichte des Mittelalters,* 3 (1939), 371–412. (Reprinted in *Reformpapsttum und Kardinalkolleg.* Darmstadt: H. Gentner, 1957.)

Knotzinger, K. "Das Amt des Bischofs nach Bernhard von Clairvaux. Ein Traditionsbeitrag," *Scholastik,* 38 (1963), 519–535.

Kohlmeyer, Ernst. "Charisma oder Recht? Vom Wesen des ältesten Kirchenrechts," *Zeitschrift der Savigny-Stiftung für Rechtsgeschichte,* Kan. Abt., 38 (1952), 1–26.

Köstler, Rudolf. "Zum Titel des Gratianischen Dekrets," *Zeitschrift der Savigny-Stiftung für Rechtsgeschichte,* Kan. Abt., 32 (1932), 370–373.

———. "Noch einmal: Zum Titel des Gratianischen Dekrets," *Zeitschrift der Savigny-Stiftung für Rechtsgeschichte,* Kan. Abt., 34 (1934), 378–380.

Kozlowski, Jerzy von. *Kirche, Staat und Kirchenstaat im hl. Bernhard von Clairvaux.* Poznan: Winiewicz, 1916.

Kuhlmann, G. "Rudolph Sohm und unsere gegenwärtigen kirchenrechtlichen Situation," *Archiv für Kirchenrecht,* 5 (1941), 155–172.

Kurze, D. *Pfarrerwählen im Mittelalter.* Ein Beitrag zur Geschichte der Gemeinde und des Niederkirchenwesens. Cologne-Graz: Böhlau, 1966 (Forschungen zur kirchlichen Rechtsgeschichte und zum Kirchenrecht, 6).

Kuttner, Stephan. "Zur Frage der theologischen Vorlagen Gratians," *Zeitschrift der Savigny-Stiftung für Rechtsgeschichte,* Kan. Abt., 23 (1934), 268.

——. "Ecclesia de occultis non iudicat." *Acta Congressus Iuridici Internationalis.* Rome, 1934. 3:225–246.

——. *Kanonistische Schuldlehre von Gratian bis auf die Decretalen Gregors IX.* *Studi e Testi.* Vol. 64. Vatican City: Biblioteca apostolica vaticana, 1935.

——. *Repertorium der Kanonistik.* Prodomus corporis glossarium. *Studi e Testi.* Vol. 71. Vatican City: Biblioteca apostolica vaticana, 1937.

——. "Les débuts de l'école canoniste française," *Studia et documenta historiae et iuris,* 4 (1938), 1–14.

——. "The Father of the Science of Canon Law," *The Jurist,* 1 (1941), 2–19.

——. "De Gratiani opere noviter edendo," *Apollinaris,* 21 (1948), 118–128.

——. "New Studies in the Roman Law in Gratian's Decretum," *Seminar,* 11 (1953), 12–50.

——. "Additional Notes on the Roman Law in Gratian," *Seminar,* 12 (1954), 68–74.

——. "Urban II and Gratian," *Traditio,* 24 (1968), 504–505.

Kuttner, Stephan, and E. Rathbone. "Anglo-Norman Canonists of the Twelfth Century," *Traditio,* 7 (1949–1951), 279–358.

Lackner, Bede. "The Priestly Ideal of St. Bernard," *American Ecclesiastical Review,* 140 (1959), 237–244.

Ladner, Gerhard B. "I mosaici e gli affreschi ecclesiastico-politico nell'antico palazzo Lateranense," *Rivista di archeologia Cristiana,* 12 (1935), 265–292.

——. "Aspects of Medieval Thought on Church and State," *Review of Politics,* 9 (1943), 403–422.

——. "The Concepts of Ecclesia and Christianitas and Their Relation to the Idea of Papal 'Plenitudo potestatis' from Gregory VII to Boniface VIII," *Sacerdozio e Regno da Gregorio VII a Bonifacio VIII,* Miscellanea Historiae Pontificiae 18 (1958), 49–77.

——. "Two Gregorian Letters," *Studi Gregoriani,* 5 (1956), 221–242.

Landgraf, Artur M. "Grundlagen für ein Verständnis der Busslehre der Früh- und Hochscholastik," *Zeitschrift für katholische Theologie,* 51 (1927), 161–194.

——. "Kindertaufe und Glaube in der Frühscholastik," *Gregorianum,* 9 (1928), 337–373, 497–543.

——. "Sünde und Trennung von der Kirche in der Frühscholastik," *Scholastik,* 5 (1930), 210–247.

——. "Das sacramentum in voto in der Frühscholastik," *Mélanges Mandonnet,* vol. 2, *Bibliothèque Thomiste,* 14 (1930), 97–144.

——. *Écrits théologiques de l'école d'Abélard.* Textes inedits. Louvain: Spicilegium Sacrum Lovaniensis 14, 1934.

——. "Scattered Remarks on the Development of Dogma and on Papal Infallibility in Early Scholastic Writings," *Theological Studies,* 7 (1946), 577–582.

——. "Zur Lehre von der Konsekrationsgewalt des von der Kirche getrennten Priesters im 12. Jahrhundert," *Scholastik,* 15 (1946), 204–227.

——. "Die Lehre vom geheimnisvollen Leib in den fruhen Paulienkommentaren und in der Frühscholastik," *Divus Thomas,* 24 (1946), 217–248, 393–428; 25 (1947), 365–394; 26 (1948), 160–180, 291–323, 395–434.

——. *Einführung in die Geschichte der theologischen Literatur der Frühscholastik.* Regensburg: Gregorius Verlag, 1948.

——. "Die Lehre der Frühscholastik vom Episcopat als ordo," *Scholastik,* 26 (1951), 496–519.

——. *Dogmengeschichte der Frühscholastik.* 8 vols. Regensburg: F. Pustet, 1952–1956.

Langmuir, Gavin. "'Judei Nostri' and the Beginning of Capetian Legislation," *Traditio,* 16 (1960), 203–239.

Le Bras, Gabriel. *L'Immunité réelle, étude sur la formation de la théorie canonique de la participation de l'Église aux Charges de l'Etat, et sur son application dans la monarchie française au XIIIe siècle.* Rennes: "La Presse de Bretagne," 1920.

——. "Alger de Liège et Gratien," *Revue des Sciences philosophiques et théologiques,* 20 (1931), 5–26.

——. "Les écritures dans le Décret de Gratien," *Zeitschrift der Savigny-Stiftung für Rechtsgeschichte,* Kan. Abt., 27 (1938), 47–80.

——. "Inventaire théologique du Gratien et de la Glose ordinaire." *Mélanges J. de Ghellinck.* Gembloux: J. Duculot, 1951. 2:605–613.

——. "Quelques Problèmes posés par le Décret de Gratien," *Apollinaris,* 21 (1948), 112–117.

——. "Le droit classique de l'Église contre la puissance arbitraire," *Rivista Storia Diritto,* 26–27 (1953–1954), 25–37.

——. Note on Vetulani 1955 (See *Studia Gratiana,* 7 [1959]). *Revue historique de droit français et étranger,* 33 (1955), 622.

Le Bras, Gabriel, Charles Lefebvre, and Jacqueline Rambaud, eds., *L'âge classique (1140–1378).* Histoire de droit et des institutions de l'Église en Occident. Vol. 7. Paris: Sirey, 1965.

Lecler, Joseph. "L'argument des deux glaives dans les controverses politiques du moyen-âge," *Recherches de Science religieuse,* 21 (1931), 299-339.

———. "Pars corporis papae . . . Le Sacré College dans l'ecclésiologie médiévale." *L'homme devant Dieu. Mélanges offerts au Père Henri de Lubac.* Paris: Aubier, 1964. 2:183-198.

Leclercq, Jean. "Les études bernardines en 1963." *Bulletin de la Société Internationale pour l'Étude de la Philosophie Médiévale.* Paris, 1963. 5:121-138.

Lecuyer, Joseph. "Le sacrement de l'Épiscopat," *Divinitas,* 1 (1957), 221-251.

Lefebvre, Charles. "Gratien et les origines de la 'denonciation evangelique' de l' 'accusatio' à la 'denunciatio,'" *Studia Gratiana,* 4 (1956-1957), 231-250.

———. "Pouvoirs de l'Église," *Dictionnaire de droit canonique,* 7 (1959), 71-108.

Legendre, Pierre. *La pénétration du droit romain dans le droit canonique de Gratien à Innocent IV* (1140-1254). Paris: Jouve, 1964.

Leitmaier, Charlotte. "Das Privateigentum im Gratianischen Dekret," *Studia Gratiana,* 2 (1954), 363-373.

Lesage, Germain. "Le Décret de Gratian et la nature du droit canonique," *Revue de l'Université d'Ottawa,* 22 (1952), 207-227.

Liber Pontificalis. Ed. Louis Duchesne. 2 vols. Paris: E. Thorin, 1886-1892 (Bibliothèque des écoles francaises d'Athenes et de Rome. Ser. 2:3).

Liber Pontificalis prout exstat in codice manuscripto Dertusensi; textum genuinum complectens hactenus ex parte ineditum Pandulphi, scriptorii pontificii. Ed. I. M. March. Barcelona: "La educación," 1925.

Linder, D. *Die Lehre vom Privileg nach Gratian und die Glossatoren.* Regensburg: F. Schöningh, 1917.

Loewenfeld, S. *Epistolae Pontificum Romanorum Ineditae.* Leipzig: Viet, 1885.

Lottin, Odon. "Le droit naturel chez saint Thomas et ses predecesseurs," *Ephemerides theologicae Lovanienses,* 1 (1924), 369-388; 2 (1925), 32-53, 345-366; 3 (1926), 155-176.

———. "Le problème de l' 'ignorantia iuris' de Gratien à St. Thomas d'Aquin," *Recherches de Théologie ancienne et médiévale,* 5 (1933), 345-368.

———. "Nouveaux fragments théologiques de l'école d'Anselme de Laon," *Recherches de Théologie ancienne et médiévale,* 14 (1947), 5-31.

Lubac, Henri de. "Le pouvoir de l'église en matière temporelle," *Revue des sciences religieuses,* 12 (1932), 329-354.

———. *Corpus Mysticum.* Paris: Aubier, Editions Montaigne, 1949.

Luccari [Lukarevic], G. *Copioso ristretto degli Annali di Rausa.* Venice, 1605.

Lulvès, J. "Die Machtsbestrebungen des Kardinal-collegiums gegenüber dem Papsttum," *Mitteilungen des Instituts für oesterreichische Geschichte,* 35 (1914), 455-483.

Luscombe, D. E. *The School of Abelard.* Cambridge: Cambridge University Press, 1969.

McIlwain, Charles H. *The High Court of Parliament, and its Supremacy: An historical essay on the boundaries between legislation and adjudication in England.* New Haven: Yale University Press, 1910.

——. *The Growth of Political Thought in the West, from the Greeks to the End of the Middle Ages.* New York: Macmillan, 1932.

——. *Constitutionalism: Ancient and Modern.* Ithaca: Cornell University Press, 1940.

Maitland, Frederick W. *Roman Canon Law in the Church of England.* London: Methuen, 1898.

——. "Introduction to *Memoranda de Parliamento, 1305,*" *Selected Historical Essays of F. W. Maitland.* Ed. H. Cam. Cambridge: Cambridge University Press, 1957. Pp. 56–92.

Manitius, Max. *Geschichte der lateinischen Literatur des Mittelalters.* 3 vols. Munich: C. H. Beck, 1911–1931.

Marchesi, Francesco. "De rationibus quae intercedunt inter Ecclesiasm et res publicas in Gratiani Decreto," *Studia Gratiana,* 3 (1955), 181–191.

Maurer, M. *Papst Calixt II.* 2 pts. Munich: Kaiser, 1886–1889.

Mélanges Saint Bernard. XXIVe Congrès de l'Association bourguignonne des Sociétés savantes (8e Centenaire de la mort de saint Bernard. Dijon, 1953). Dijon: Association des amis de saint Bernard, 1954.

Mercati, Angelo. *Raccolta di concordati su materia ecclesiastiche tra la Santa Sede e le auctorita civili.* Rome: Typografia poliglotta vaticana, 1919.

Merzbacher, Friedrich. "Das geschichtliche Bild des kirchlichen Richters," *Archiv für katholisches Kirchenrecht,* 129 (1960), 369–389.

Metz, René. "A propos des travaux de M. Adam Vetulani. La date et la composition du Décret de Gratien," *Revue de droit canonique,* 7 (1957), 62–85.

Michel, Anton. *Papstwahl und Königsrecht: oder Das Papstwahlkonkordat von 1059.* Munich: M. Heuber, 1936.

——. "Ordre." *Dictionnaire de Theologie catholique.* 11:1275–1298.

Mirbt, Carl. *Die Publizistik im Zeitalter Gregors VII.* Leipzig: J. C. Hinrichs' Verlag, 1894.

Mor, C. G. "La recezione del diritto romano nelle collezioni canoniche dei secoli IX–XI in Italia e oltr'Alpe." *Acta Congressus Iuridici Internationalis.* Rome, 1935. 2:281–302.

——. "Diritto romano e canonico pregraziano." *Europa e il diritto romano; studi in memoria di Paolo Koschaker.* Milan: Guiffré, 1954. 2:15–32.

Mörsdorf, Klaus. "Der Rechtscharakter der iuridictio fori interni," *Münchener theologische Zeitschrift,* 8 (1957), 161–173.

Mortimer, R. C. *Western Canon Law.* Berkeley and Los Angeles: University of California Press, 1953.

Moynihan, J.-M. *Papal Immunity and Liability in the Writings of the Medieval Canonists.* Rome: Gregorian University Press, 1961.

Mühlbacher, Emil. *Die streitige Papstwahl des Jahres 1130.* Aalen: Scientia Verlag,

1966 (reprint of Innsbruck: Universitätsverlag Wagner GmbH, 1876 edition).

Muldoon, James. "The Medieval Origins of the State." Ph.D. dissertation, Cornell University, 1965.

———. "Extra Ecclesia non est Imperium (The Canonists and the Legitimacy of Secular Power)," *Studia Gratiana,* 9 (1966), 553–580.

Müller, E. "Der Bericht des Abtes Hariulf von Oudenburg über seine Prozessverhandlungen an der römischen Kurie im Jahre 1141," *Neues Archiv,* 48 (1929), 97–115.

Müller, K. "Der Umschwung in der Lehre von der Büsse während des 12. Jahrhunderts." *Theologische Abhandlungen Carl von Weizäcker gewidmet.* Freiburg i. Br., 1892. Pp. 287–320.

Munier, Charles. *Sources patristiques du droit de l'Église du VIII au XIIIe siècles.* Mulhouse: Editions Salvator, 1957.

———. "Droit canonique et droit romain d'après Gratien et les Décrétistes." *Études Le Bras.* 2:943–954.

Naz, R. "Ordre en droit occidental." *Dictionnaire de droit canonique.* 6:1145–1150.

Nodilo, S., ed. *Chronica ragusina Junii Restii* (ab origine urbis usque ad annum 1451). *Monumenta spectantia historiam Slavorum Meridionalium.* Vol. 25. Zagreb, 1893.

Ochier, H. "Saint Bernard et la fin du schisme d'Occident," *Bulletin de la Société historique et archéologique, les amis des antiquités de Parathenay,* 1 (1952), 6–10.

Oesterle, G. "Graziano e l'opera sua giuridica," *Rivista camaldolese,* 1 (1926), 62–79.

Oliger, Paul Remy. *Les évèques reguliers.* Recherche sur leur condition juridique depuis les origines jusqu'à la fin du moyen-âge. Paris: Desclée de Brouwer, 1958.

Olsen, Glenn. "The Idea of the Ecclesia Primitiva in the Writings of the Twelfth Century Canonists," *Traditio,* 25 (1969), 61–86.

Omrčanin, I. *Graziano e la Croazia.* Chicago: Istituto storico Croato, 1958.

Onchin, Willem. "La contribution du Décret de Gratien et des Décrétistes à la solution des conflits de lois," *Studia Gratiana,* 2 (1954), 117–150.

Orsy, Ladislav. "Sacred Ordinations in Gratian's Decretum: The Conferring of the Order of Episcopate and of the Order of Presbyterate," *Heythrop Journal,* 3 (1962), 152–162.

———. "Bishops, Presbyters and Priesthood in Gratian's Decretum," *Gregorianum,* 44 (1963), 788–826.

———. "Irregular Ordinations in Gratian's Decretum," *Heythrop Journal,* 4 (1963), 163–173.

Ott, Irene. "Der Regalienbegriff im 12. Jahrhundert," *Zeitschrift der Savigny-Stiftung für Rechtsgeschichte,* Kan. Abt., 35 (1948), 234–304.

Ott, Ludwig. "Vivianus von Prémontré, der früheste Zenge für Benutzung der Summa Sententiarum," *Scholastik,* 14 (1939), 81–90.

Ottaviano, C. "Frammenti Abelardiani." *Rivista di Cultura,* 12 (1931), 425–445.

Pacaut, Marcel. "L'opposition des canonistes aux doctrines politiques de saint Bernard." *Mélanges Saint Bernard.* Pp. 187–193.

——. *Louis VII et les elections episcopales dans le royaume de France.* Paris: J. Vrin, 1957.

Palumbo, P. F. *Lo Scisma del MCXXX.* Miscellanea della R. Deputazione romana di storia patria. Rome, 1942.

——. "La cancelleria di Anacleto." *Scritti di paleografia e diplomatica in onore di Vincenzo Federici.* Florence, 1944.

——. "Nuovi Studi (1942–1962) sullo scisma di Anacleto II," *Bullettino dell'Istituto storico italiano per il medio evo e Archivio Muratoriano,* 75 (1963), 71–103.

Parsons, Anscar. *Canonical Election: An Historical Synopsis and Commentary.* Washington, D.C.: Catholic University of America Press, 1939.

Petrus Abelardus. *Opera Omnia.* PL 178.

Petrus Lombardus. *Libri IV Sententiarum.* 2 vols.. Quaracche, 1916.

Petrus Venerabilis. *Contra Petrobrusianos (Epistola sive Tractatus adversus Petrobrusianos haereticos).* PL 189, col. 719–850.

——. *The Letters of Peter the Venerable.* Ed. Giles Constable. 2 vols. Cambridge, Mass.: Harvard University Press, 1967.

Pflugk-Harttung, Julius von. *Acta pontificum Romanorum inedita.* 3 vols. Stuttgart-Tübingen: Kohlhammer, 1880–1886.

Pignot, J.-H. *Histoire de l'Ordre de Cluny.* Vol. 3. Paris: Durand, 1868.

Pinedo, P. "Decretum Gratiani, Dictum Gratiani," *Ius Canonicum,* 2 (1962), 149–166.

Pitsch, Wilhelm. *Das Bischofsideal des hl. Bernhard von Clairvaux.* Bottrop i. W.; Postberg, 1942.

Plochl, Willibald. *Das Eherecht des Magisters Gratian.* Leipzig: F. Deuticke, 1935 (Wiener Staatswissenschaftliche Studien N.F. 24).

Plucknett, T. F. T. *The Legislation of Edward I.* Cambridge: Cambridge University Press, 1949.

Pometti, F. *Il Decretum di Graziano nei suoi precedenti storici e nelle sue consequence storico-ecclesiastiche.* Corigliano Calabro: Popolano, 1910.

Poole, Reginald Lane. *Benedict IX and Gregory VI. Proceedings of the British Academy.* Vol. VIII. London, 1917.

Poppenberg, Everhard. *Die Christologie des Hugo von Sankt-Victor.* Hilgentrup: Herz Jesu-Missionshaus, 1937.

Post, Gaines. "A Romano-Canonical Maxim, Quod omnes tangit, in Bracton and in Early Pariaments." *Studies in Medieval Legal Thought.* Princeton: Princeton University Press, 1964. Pp. 163–240.

Proceedings of the Second International Congress of Medieval Canon Law. Boston College, 1963. Ed. S. Kuttner and J. J. Ryan. *Monumenta iuris canonici.* 1, ser. C. Vatican City: S. Congregatio de Seminariis et Studiorum Universitatibus, 1965.

Prosdocimi, Luigi. "Chierci e laici nella societa occidentale del secolo XI: A proposito di Decr. Grat. C. 12, q. 1, c. 7: 'Duo sunt genera Christianorum,'" *Proceedings of the Second International Congress of Medieval Canon Law.* Pp. 105–122.

Rambaud [-Buhot], Jacqueline. "Plan et methode de travail pour la redaction d'un catalogue des manuscrits du Décret de Gratien," *Revue d'histoire ecclesiastique,* 48 (1953), 211–223.

———. "Le 'Corpus Juris Civilis' dans le Décret de Gratien," *Bibliothèque de l'École des Chartes,* 111 (1953), 54–64.

———. "Les divers types d'abrégés du Décret de Gratien." *Recueil de travaux offerts à M. Clovis Brunel.* Paris: Société de l'École des Chartes, 1955. Pp. 397–411.

———. "Le Décret de Gratien et le droit romain," *Revue historique de droit français et étranger,* ser. IV, 35 (1957), 260–300.

———. "L'Étude des manuscrits du Decret de Gratien," *Congrès de Droit Canonique Médiéval.* Louvain-Brussels, 1958. *Bibliothèque de la Revue d'Histoire ecclesiastique,* 33 (1959), 25–48.

———. "Le legs de l'ancien droit: Gratien." *L'âge classique.* Ed. G. Le Bras. Pp. 52–129.

———. "Les Paleae dans le Décret de Gratien." *Proceedings of the Second International Congress of Medieval Canon Law.* Pp. 23–44.

Regesta Pontificum Romanorum. Ed. P. Jaffé. 2d ed. rev. Ed. W. Wattenbach, S. Loewenfeld, K. Kaltenbrunner, and P. Ewald. 2 vols. Leipzig: Veit, 1885–1888.

Reischle, Max. "Sohms Kirchenrecht und der Streit über das Verhältnis von Recht und Kirche," *Vorträge der theologischen Konferenz zu Giessen. VIII.* Giessen: J. Ricker, 1895.

Richardson, H. G., and George O. Sayles. *The Governance of Medieval England from the Conquest to Magna Carta.* Edinburgh: University Press, 1963.

Rivière, Jean. "Sur l'expression 'Papa Deus' au moyen-âge," *Miscellanea Fr. Ehrle,* 2:276–289. *Studi e Testi.* Vol. 38. Rome: Biblioteca apostolica vaticana, 1924.

———. "In partem sollicitudinis. Evolution d'une formule pontificale," *Revue des Sciences religieuses,* 5 (1925), 210–231.

———. *Le problème de l'Église et de l'Etat au temps de Philippe le Bel.* Louvain: Spicilegium Sacrum Lovaniense 8, 1926.

———. "Les 'capitula' d' Abélard condamnés au concile de Sens," *Recherches de Théologie ancienne et médiévale,* 5 (1933), 5–22.

Robert, U. *Histoire du pape Calixte II.* Paris: Alphonse Picard, 1891.

Rolandus Bandinelli [Alexander III]. *Die Sentenzen Rolands nachmals Papstes Alexander III.* Ed. A. Geitl. Freiburg i. Br: Herder, 1891.

Rufinus. *Summa decretorum.* Ed. H. Singer. Paderborn: F. Schöningh, 1902.

Russell, Jeffrey Burton. *Dissent and Reform in the Early Middle Ages.* Berkeley and Los Angeles: University of California Press, 1965.

Russo, R. "Pénitence et excommunication. Étude historique sur les rapports entre la théologie et le droit canonique dans les domaine pénitential du IXe au XIIIe siècle," *Recherches des Sciences religieuses,* 33 (1946), 257–279, 431–459.

Sägmüller, Johannes B. "Die Entstehung und Bedeutung der Formel 'salva Sedis apostolicae auctoritate' in dem päpstlichen Privilegien," *Theologische Quartalschrift,* 89 (1907), 93–117.

——. *Die Bischoffswahl bei Gratian.* Cologne: J. P. Bachem, 1908 (Görres Gesellschaft zur Pflege der Wissenschaft im Katholischen Deutschland, Bonn-Sektion für Rechts- und Sozial-Wissenschaft. Vol. 1).

——. *Zur Geschichte der Entwicklung des päpstlichen Gesetzgebungsrechtes.* Rottenburg: Bader'sche Verlagsbuchhandlung, 1937.

Saltet, L. *Les réordinations: Étude sur le sacrement de l'ordre.* Paris: Gabalda, 1907.

Saxer, Victor. "Chronique bernardine," *Revue thomiste,* 56 (1956), 741–778.

Sayles, George O. *The Medieval Foundations of England.* Cambridge: Cambridge University Press, 1950.

Schleber, A. *Die Reordinationen in der "altkatholischen" Kirche.* Bonn: L: Röhrscheld, 1936.

Schmale, Franz-Josef. "Die Bemühungen Innocenz II um seine Anerkennung in Deutschland," *Zeitschrift für Kirchengeschichte,* 65 (1954), 240–296.

——. "Papsttum und Kurie zwischen Gregor VII und Innocenz II," *Historische Zeitschrift,* 193 (1961), 265–285. (Revised in: *Probleme des 12. Jahrhunderts.* Vorträge und Forschungen xii. Stuttgart: Jan Thorbecke Verlag, 1968.)

——. *Studien zum Schisma des Jahres 1130.* Cologne: Böhlau Verlag, 1961 (Forschungen zur kirchlichen Rechtsgeschichte und zum Kirchenrecht 3).

Schmid, H. F. Review of Vetulani, 1955 (See *Studia Gratiana,* 7 [1959], *Zeitschrift der Savigny-Stiftung für Rechtsgeschichte,* Kan. Abt., 43 (1957), 365–373.

Schmid, Paul. *Der Begriff der kanonischen Wahl in den Anfängen des Investiturstreits.* Stuttgart: W. Kohlhammer Verlag, 1926.

Schmidlin, J. "Kirchenpolitische Ideen des 12. Jahrhunderts," *Archiv für katholisches Kirchenrecht,* 84 (1904), 39–55.

Schmoll, P. *Die Busslehre der Frühscholastik.* Munich: J. J. Lentner, 1909 (Veröffentlichungen aus dem Kirchenhistorischen Seminar München 5).

Schreiber, Georg. *Kurie und Kloster im 12. Jahrhundert.* 2 vols. Stuttgart: F. Enke, 1910 (Kirchenrechtliche Abhandlungen. Ed. U. Stutz. Vols. 65–68).

Schulte, J. F. von. "Zur Geschichte der Literatur über das Dekret Gratians,"

Sitzungsberichte der Wiener Akademie der Wissenschaften, Phil.-Hist. Cl. 63 (1869), 299–355; 64 (1870), 93–142; 65 (1871), 21–76.

————. *Die Geschichte der Quellen und Literatur des canonischen Rechts von Gratian bis auf die Gegenwart.* 3 vols. Stuttgart: F. Enke, 1875–1880.

Schützeichel, M. "Beiträge zur Geschichte des Sakularisationsgedanken im Mittelalter." Ph.D. dissertation, Münster, 1939.

Schweighoffer, Kolos. *Die Lehre des hl. Bernhard von Clairvaux über die Kirche.* Innsbruck, 1925.

Sententie Parisenses. Ed. A. M. Landgraf. *Écrits théologiques de l'école d'Abélard.* Pp. 3–60.

Smičiklas, T. *Codex Diplomaticus Regni Croatiae, Dalmatiae et Slavaniae.* Vol. 2. Zagreb, 1904.

Sohm, Rudolph. *Das altkatholische Kirchenrecht und das Dekret Gratians.* Festschrift der Leipziger Juristenfakultät für Adolf Wach. Munich-Leipzig: Duncker und Humblot, 1918.

Spitzig, J. *Sacramental Penance in the Twelfth and Thirteenth Centuries.* Washington, D.C.: Catholic University of America Press, 1947.

Stenger, Robert P. "The Development of a Theology of the Episcopacy from the Decretum." Ph.D. dissertation, Catholic University of America, 1963.

————. "The Episcopacy as an Ordo according to the Medieval Canonists," *Mediaeval Studies,* 29 (1967), 67–112.

Stickler, Alfons. "De ecclesiastica potestate coactiva materialis apud magistrum Gratianum," *Salesianum,* 4 (1942), 2–23, 96–119.

————. "De potestate gladii materialis ecclesiae secundum 'Quaestiones Bambergenses ineditas,'" *Salesianum,* 6 (1944), 113–140.

————. "Der Schwerterbegriff bei Huguccio," *Ephemerides iuris canonici,* 3 (1947), 201–242.

————. "Il 'gladius' nel Registro di Gregorio VII," *Studi Gregoriani,* 3 (1948), 89–103.

————. "Magistri Gratiani Sententia de potestate Ecclesiae in Statum," *Apollinaris,* 21 (1948), 36–111.

————. "Concerning the Political Theories of the Medieval Canonists," *Traditio,* 7 (1949–1951), 450–463.

————. *Historia Iuris Canonici Latini.* Turin: Libraria Pontificia Athenaei Salesiani, 1950.

————. "Il 'gladius' negli atti dei concili e dei RR. Pontefici sino a Graziano e Bernardo di Clairvaux," *Salesianum,* 13 (1951), 414–445.

————. "Alanus Anglicus als Verteidiger des monarchischen Papsttums," *Salesianum,* 21 (1959), 346–406.

Stoodt, Dieter. *Wort und Recht, Rudolf Sohm und das theologische Problem des Kirchenrechts.* Munich: Chr. Kaiser Verlag, 1962.

Sturzo, L. "Papacy and Empire: From St. Bernard to Dante," *Dublin Review*, 195 (1934), 25-45.

Stutz, Ulrich. "Gratian und die Eigenkirchen," *Zeitschrift der Savigny-Stiftung für Rechtsgeschichte*, Kan. Abt., 1 (1911), 1-32; 2 (1912), 343-343.

———. "Die Cistercienser wider Gratians Dekret," *Zeitschrift der Savigny-Stiftung für Rechtsgeschichte*, Kan. Abt., 9 (1919), 63-98.

Sydow, Juergen. "Il 'consistorium' dopo lo scisma del 1130," *Rivista di Storia della chiesa in Italia*, 9 (1955), 165-176.

Tangl, Michael. "Gregor VII, jüdischer Herkunft?" *Neues Archiv*, 30 (1905), 159-179.

Teetaert, Andrée. *La confession aux laiques dans l'Église latine depuis de VIIIe jusqu'au XIVe siècle, étude de theologie positive*. Wetteren: J. de Meester et fils, 1926 (Universitas Catholica Lovaniensis. Dissertationes ad gradum magistri in Facultate Theologica consequendum conscriptae. Ser. 2:17).

Tellenbach, Gerd. *Church, State, and Christrian Society at the Time of the Investiture Contest*. Trans. R. F. Bennet. Oxford: B. Blackwell, 1940.

———. "Der Sturz des Abtes Pontius von Cluny und seine geschichtliche Bedeutung," *Quellen und Forschungen aus italienischen Archiven und Bibliotheken*, 42/43 (1963), 13-55.

Thaner, Friedrich. "Über Entstehung und Bedeutung der Formel: Salva sedis apostolicae auctoritate in den päpstlichen Privilegien," *Sitzungsberichte der Wiener Akademie der Wissenschaften*, Phil.-Hist. Cl., 72 (1872), 809-851.

———. *Abälard und das kanonische Recht*. Graz: Leuschner & Lubensky's Universitäts-Buchhandlung, 1900.

Thomas Archidiaconus. *Historia Salonitana*. Ed. F. Rački. *Monumenta spectantia historiam Slavorum Meridionalium*. Vol. 26. Zagreb, 1894.

Thomas, Paul. *Le droit de propriété des laiques sur les églises et la patronage laique au moyen-âge*. Paris: E. Leroux, 1906.

Thouzellier, Christine. "Ecclesia militans." *Études Le Bras*. 2:1407-1423.

Tierney, Brian. *The Foundations of the Conciliar Theory*. Cambridge University Press, 1955.

———. *Medieval Poor Law*. Berkeley and Los Angeles: University of California Press, 1959.

———. " 'Tria Quippe Distinguit Iudicia.' A Note on Innocent III's Decretal Per Venerabilem," *Speculum*, 37 (1962), 48-59.

———. " 'The Prince Is Not Bound by the Laws.' Accursius and the Origins of the Modern State," *Comparative Studies in Society and History*, 5 (1962-1963), 378-400.

———. *The Crisis of Church and State*. Englewood Cliffs, N. J.: Prentice-Hall, 1964.

———. "The Continuity of Papal Political Theory in the Thirteenth Century.

Some Methodological Considerations," *Mediaeval Studies,* 27 (1965), 227–245.

Tirado, Victor. *De jurisdictionis acceptione in jure ecclesiastico.* Rome, 1940.

Turmel, J. *Histoire de la Theologie positive.* 3d ed. 2 vols. Paris: Beauchesne, 1904–1906.

Ullmann, Walter. *Medieval Papalism.* London: Methuen, 1949.

———. "The paleae in Cambridge Manuscripts of the Decretum," *Studia Gratiana,* 1 (1953), 156–216.

———. *The Growth of Papal Government in the Middle Ages.* London: Methuen, 1954.

———. "St. Bernard and the Nascent International Law," *Citeaux,* 10 (1959), 277–287.

———. *The Principles of Politics in the Middle Ages.* London: Methuen, 1961.

———. *The Individual and Society in the Middle Ages.* Baltimore: Johns Hopkins Press, 1965.

Vacandard, E. "Saint Bernard et le schisme d'Anaclet II en France," *Revue des questious historiques,* 43 (1888), 61–123.

———. *La vie de s. Bernard.* 2 vols. Paris: Lecoffre, 1897.

———. "Confession." *Dictionnaire de Theologie catholique.* 3:838–894.

Van den Baar, P. A. *Die kirchliche Lehre der Translatio Imperii Romani bis zum Mitte des 13. Jahrhunderts.* Rome: Analecta Gregoriana, 1956.

Van den Eynde, Damien. "La définition des sacrements pendant la première periode de la théologie scolastique (1050–1235)," *Antonianum,* 24 (1949), 183–488 (published under separate cover: Louvain: E. Nauwelaerts, 1950).

———. "Précisions chronologiques sur quelques ouvrages théologiques du XIIe siècle," *Antonianum,* 26 (1951), 223–246.

———. "Nouvelles précisions chronologiques sur quelques oeuvres théologiques du XIIe siècle," *Franciscan Studies,* 13 (1953), 71–118.

———. *L'oeuvre litteraire de Geroch de Reichersberg.* Rome: Apud Pontificium Athenaeum Antonianum, 1957.

———. *Essai sur la succession et la date des écrits de Hugues de Saint-Victor.* Rome: Apud Pontificium Athenaeum Antonianum, 1960.

———. "Les débuts litteraires de Saint Bernard," *Anaclecta sacris ordinis Cisterciensis,* 19 (1963), 189–198.

Van Hove, Alphons. "La territorialité et la personalité des lois en droit canonique depuis Gratien jusqu'à Jean Andreae," *Revue historique de droit français et étranger,* 3 (1922), 227–332.

———. *Prolegomena ad Codicem Juris Canonici.* 2d ed. Mechliniae: H. Dessain, 1945.

———. "Droit justinien et droit canonique depuis le Décret de Gratien jusqu'aux Decretales de Gregoire IX." *Miscellanea Historica in honorem L. Van der Essen.* Brussels-Paris: Editions universitaires, 1947.

————. "Quae Gratianus contulerit methodo scientiae canonicae," *Apollinaris*, 21 (1948), 12–24.

Vella, C. J. "Canon Law and the Mystical Body," *The Jurist*, 22 (1962), 412–432.

Vetulani, Adam. "Études sur la division en distinctions et sur les paleae dans le Décret de Gratien," *Bulletin international de l'Academie polonaise des sciences et des lettres*, Cl. philologie, hist., philosophie (1933), pp. 110–114.

————. "Über die Distinktioneneinteilung und die Paleae im Dekret Gratians," *Zeitschrift der Savigny-Stiftung für Rechtsgeschichte*, Kan. Abt., 33 (1933), 346–370.

————. "Une suite d'études pour servir à l'histoire du Décret de Gratien avec une preface de G. Le Bras. I. Les manuscrits du Décret de Gratien conservés dans les bibliothèques polonaises," *Revue historique de droit français et étranger*, 15 (1936), 343–358.

————. "Une suite d'études pour servir à l'histoire du Décret de Gratien. II. Les nouvelles de Justinien dans le Décret de Gratien," *Revue historique de droit français et étranger*, 16 (1937), 461–479, 674–692.

————. "Gratien et le Droit romain," *Revue historique de droit français et étranger*, 24 (1946–1947), 11–48.

————. "Encore un mot sur le droit romain dans le Décret de Gratien," *Apollinaris*, 21 (1948), 129–134.

————. "Nouvelles vues sur le Décret de Gratien," *Le Pologne au Xe Congrès international des sciences historiques à Rome*, 1955. Varsovie: Academie Polonaise des Sciences, Institute d'Histoire, 1955. Pp. 83–105.

————. "Le Décret de Gratien et les premiers Décrétistes à la lumière d'une source nouvelle," *Studia Gratiana*, 7 (1959), 273–353. (This work was published first in Polish in 1955.)

Viegas e Vales, E. *De philosophia juris apud Gratianum*. Lisbon: Escolas Professionais Salesianas-Oficinas de S. Jose- Lisboa, 1963.

Vilain, Noël. "Prescription et bonne foi, du Gratien à Jean d'Andreae," *Traditio*, 14 (1958), 121–189.

Villey, Michel. "Le Droit naturel chez Gratien," *Studia Gratiana*, 3 (1955), 85–99.

————. "L'idée de la croisade chez les juristes du moyen-âge," *X Congresso internazionale di scienze storiche*, 3:565–594.

Wallace-Hadrill, James M. "The *via regia* of the Carolingian Age," *Trends in Medieval Political Thought*. Ed. B. Smalley. Oxford: B. Blackwell, 1965. Pp. 22–41.

Wegner, Arthur. "Über positives göttliche Recht und naturliches göttliche Recht bei Gratian," *Studia Gratiana*, 1 (1953), 502–518.

Weigand, Rudolf. *Die Naturrechtslehre der Legisten und Dekretisten von Irnerius bis Accursius und von Gratian bis Johannes Teutonicus*. Münchener theologische Studien, Kan. Abt., 26. Munich: M. Hueber, 1967.

Weisweiler, Heinrich. *Die Wirksamkeit der Sakramente nach Hugo von St. Viktor*. Freiburg i. Br.: Herder, 1932.

―――. Review of Holböck, Rome, 1941. *Scholastik*, 18 (1943), 267–273.

―――. "Die Arbeitsmethode Hugos von St. Victor," *Scholastik*, 20–21 (1949), 59–87, 232–267.

Weitzel, J. *Begriff und Erscheinungsformen der Simonie bei Gratian und den Dekretisten*. Münchener theologische Studien, Kan. M. Abt., 25. Munich: M. Hueber, 1967.

White, Hayden V. "The Conflict of Papal Leadership Ideals from Gregory VII to Bernard of Clairvaux with Special Reference to the Schism of 1130." Ph.D. dissertation, University of Michigan, 1956.

―――. "Pontius of Cluny, the Curia Romana and the End of Gregorianism in Rome," *Church History*, 27 (1958), 195–219.

―――. "The Gregorian Ideal and S. Bernard of Clairvaux," *Journal of the History of Ideas*, 21 (1960), 321–348.

Wieruszowski, Helen. "Roger II of Sicily, Rex-Tyrannus, in Twelfth Century Political Thought," *Speculum*, 38 (1963), 46–78.

Wilks, Michael J. "Papa est nomen iurisdictionis," *Journal of Theological Studies*, vol. 8 (1957).

Williams, Watkin. *Saint Bernard of Clairvaux*. Manchester: Manchester University Press, 1935.

―――. "The Political Philosophy of St. Bernard of Clairvaux," *Blackfriars*, 24 (1944), 466–469.

Winandy, Jacques. "Les moines et le Sacerdoce," *La Vie Spirituelle*, 80 (1949), 23–36.

Wisser, Karl. "Individuum und Gemeinschaft in den Anschauungen des hl. Bernhard von Clairvaux," *Cistercienser Chronik*, 49 (1937), 257–263.

Wojtyla, Karol. "Le traité de 'Penitentia' de Gratien dans l'abrégé de Gdansk Mar. F. 275," *Studia Gratiana*, 7 (1959), 355–390.

Ysagoge in Theologiam. Ed. A. M. Landgraf. *Écrits théologiques de l'école d'Abélard*. Pp. 63–285.

Zazzera, F. *Della nobilità dell'Italia*. Naples, 1628.

Zema, Demetrius. "The House of Tuscany and of Pierleoni in the Crisis of Rome in the Eleventh Century," *Traditio*, 2 (1944), 155–175.

Zöpffel, Richard. *Die Papstwahlen und die mit ihnen im nächsten Zusammenhange stehenden Ceremonien in ihrer Entwicklung vom 11. bis zum 14. Jahrhundert*. Nebst eine Beilage: *Die Doppelwahl des Jahres 1130*. Göttingen: Vandenhoeck & Ruprecht, 1872.

Index

Scholars often want to know what has been said about specific passages in Gratian's Decretum; therefore, I have divided the index into two parts: one a general index and one listing all references to the Decretum. In the general index, I have not referred to comments in footnotes except where such comments are significant. In the index of the Decretum passages, I have referred to all mentions of the texts no matter where they occur.

General Index

Alexander III, pope. *See* Rolandus Bandinelli

Alger of Liège, 3 n. 3

Ambrose, Saint, 126

Anaclet II, antipope. *See* Petrus Pierleoni

Anastasius II, pope, 138–140

Anathema. *See* Excommunication

Anciaux, Paul, 124

Arnold of Brescia, 37, 58

Baptism, 77–82, 83, 85, 86–87, 92

Bede, Saint, 159

Benson, Robert L., 188–189, 202

Bernard of Clairvaux, Saint, 6, 24, 26, 36–37, 41, 42, 46–47, 64; attitude toward Roman Law, 61–62, 260–265; on bishops and *regalia,* 244; on Church and State, 58–59; on circumcision and baptism, 69–70, 143–144 n. 21; on judicial supremacy of pope, 182; on monk priests, 46 n. 41; on obedience, 114–116; on the ecclesiastical hierarchy, 53, 180; on the participation of monks in episcopal elections, 204, 205; on the Synagogue and Church, 68, 71, 73; on the two swords, 227–228, 245–246; on the types of law, 140 n. 14; view of the Church, 65, 67

Bernold of Constance, methodological suggestions, 2 n. 3

Blessing the Chrism, 175

Bride of Christ (Church), 65 (esp. n. 1), 67–68, 71–72

Calixtus II, pope, 23, 25–26, 30, 31–34, 35, 43

Canons regular, 42–44

Cathars, 41

Celestine I, pope, 199, 206–210

Chapel of Saint Nicholas of Bari in the Lateran Palace, 39 n. 33

Cistercians, 42; attitude toward law, 9 n. 12

Cluny, 22–26

Concordat of Worms, 22, 30, 31–32, 33, 58, 60

Concordia discordantium canonum. *See* Decretum

Confession, 113–114

Confirmation, 82–83, 85, 175

Congar, Yves, 205
Consecration of Churches, 175
Corpus Christi, 65, 75
Council of Dubrovnik (1151), 49

Dante, 48
Debil, A., 129–130, 131
Decretum (textual problems): divisions of, 10, 12 n. 19, 15–16; *paleae* in, 11–12; Roman law in, 14–15, 60–61; title of, 4–5
Dispensation (from law), 110
Draco Normanicus, poem by Stephen of Rouen, 47

Electoral decree of 1059, 19
Eucharist, 82, 83–85, 92–93
Eugene III, pope, 227
Excommunicated priests, 172–175
Excommunication, 87–91, 175; as result of sin, 88, 90

fas, 101–102, 108 n. 25
First Lateran Council (1123), 32, 33–34
Fons Decretorum. See *Draco Normanicus*
Frangipani (Roman family), 20, 27, 28–29, 32–33

Gaudemet, Jean, 53, 97
Gaudius, archbishop of Split (Spalato), 49–51
Gelasius II, pope, 31
Gerhoh of Reichersberg, 62–63 n. 64; attitude toward Roman law, 62; on bishops and *regalia,* 244
Gillmann, Franz, 15, 16
Glossa Ordinaria (to the Bible), 125
Grabmann, Martin, 100–101
Gregory, cardinal deacon of Sant' Angelo. See Innocent II, pope
Gregory I, pope, 117, 120, 240
Gregory VI, pope, 28 (esp. n. 16)
Gregory VII, pope, 149, 201, 204–205
Gregory VIII, antipope. See Mauritius, archbishop of Braga

Guigo, abbot of Chartreuse, 36
Guy, archbishop of Vienne. See Calixtus II, pope

Haimeric, chancellor of the Holy See, 20–21, 24, 25–26, 34–35, 36, 40, 42–43, 51–52, 59
Hariulf, abbot of Oudenburg, 52
Henry, archbishop of Sens, 41
Historia Salonitana. See Thomas the Archdeacon
Honorius II, pope, 21, 23, 25, 42, 43
Hugh of St. Victor, 18; on the ages of man, 104; on Church and State, 59; and the *Summa Sententiarum,* 167 n. 20; view of the Church, 65–66 n. 1
Hugueny, Étienne, 129–130, 131
Humbert of Silva-Candida, 27, 183

Image of the two swords. See chap. ix, *"The use of force by the Church,"* passim
Imposition of hands, 94
Innocent II, pope, 20, 25, 42, 43, 47, 227
Isidore of Seville: *Etymologies,* 102, 156, 237
ius, 101–102
ius naturale. See chap. iv, *passim*
Ivo of Chartres, methodological suggestions, 2 n. 3

John of Gaeta. See Gelasius II, pope
John VIII, pope, 226
Jordan Pierleoni, *patricius* of the Republic of Rome (1144), 37–38

Kempf, Friedrich, 213–214
Klewitz, Hans, 21

Lambert, cardinal bishop of Ostia. See Honorius II, pope
Landgraf, Artur, 87, 88–89
Laon, school of, 159, 162–163, 164, 171; and Gratian, 3 n. 3
Lenten Synod (March, 1112), 151–152
Leo I, pope, 199–200, 206–210

Leo Frangipani, 32–33, 34–35
Lukarević (Luccari), James, 49–50

Marriage: consanguinous, 74; treatise on in Decretum (cc. 26–36), 13–14 n. 21
Mauritius, archbishop of Braga, 31
Monk-priests, 163, 170–172
Montecassino, 25
mos, 101
Mühlbacher, Emil, 19, 20–21

Norbert of Xanten, archbishop of Magdeburg, 36

Origen, 191, 192–193
Orsy, Ladislav, 156, 157, 165, 172, 175–176

Papal election of 1124, 34–35
Papal election of 1130, 18–19; parties of cardinals, 19–20, 34, 35–37
Pascal II, pope, 21, 29
Penitence, 113–114, 169
Peter Abelard, 18; and Gratian, 2–3; on power of the keys, 157; school of, 160
Peter Lombard, 3, 124, 131–132
Peter the Venerable, abbot of Cluny, 6, 22–26, 36, 41, 42
Petrine doctrine, 186
Petrobrusians, 41
Petrus Pierleoni, 20, 30–31, 42
Pierleoni (Roman family), 20, 27, 28, 29, 30, 35, 37, 38
Placidus of Nonantula, 151–152
plenitudo potestatis, 178–179
Pontius, abbot of Cluny, 22–26
Post, Gaines, 205–206
Power of the keys, 113–114, 130, 132, 157, 187. *See* chap. vii, *passim*
primitiva ecclesia, 74
privilegium fori, 219–220

Quod omnes tangit, 206–210

Rastić (Resti), Junius, 49–50
Roger, King of Sicily, 40
Rolandus Bandinelli (Alexander III, pope), 1–2, 8–9
Rufinus (decretist), 57
Russo, F., 87

Sacrament of orders, 93
Sacraments: of necessity and dignity, 91–94; definition of, 9
Sägmüller, Johannes B., 188, 201–202
St. Victor, school of, 160–162, 163–164, 167, 170–171
Schmale, Franz-Joseph, 21, 30, 39
Second Lateran Council (1139), 38 n. 32
Silverius, pope, 234
Sohm, Rudolph, 7–10, 16, 155
Stephen of Rouen. See *Draco Normanicus*
Stickler, Alfons, 57, 59, 213–214, 224–228, 244–245
Summa Parisiensis, 106

Tellenbach, Gerd, 22–26
Third Lateran Council (1179), 8, 19
Thomas the Archdeacon (author of *Historia Salonitana*), 49
Tierney, Brian, 106, 186, 214
Tractatus de consecratione, 12 (esp. n. 19)
Tractatus de penitencia, 13 (esp. n. 20)
Tractatus ordinandorum (Dist. 21–101), 53, 64

Ullmann, Walter, 212–213, 214
Urban II, pope, 226

Vacandard, E., 128–129
Vetulani, Adam, 15, 255–259

Wjotyla, Karel, 13

Zöpffel, Richard, 19, 21, 39

Index of Decretum Passages

Tractatus de penitencia. See C. 33, q. 3

Dist. 1,
    dict. ante c. 1, 98, 101 n. 9, 102, 105
    c. 1, 101 n. 9, 108 n. 25
    dict. post c. 1, 99
    cc. 2–5, 101 n. 9
    c. 7, 100 n. 7, 105 n. 19
    cc. 6–12, 101 n. 9
Dist. 2, 101 n. 9
    dict. ante c. 1, 215, 263
Dist. 3,
    dict. ante c. 1, 110 n. 28, 215
    dict. post c. 1, 110 n. 28
    dict. post c. 2, 142 n. 16, 215
    dict. post c. 3, 263
Dist. 4,
    dict. post c. 1, 135–136
    dict. post c. 2, 136 n. 4, 251 n. 3
    c. 3, 251
    dict. post c. 3, 144
Dist. 5,
    dict. ante c. 1, 101 n. 9, 102 n. 11
Dist. 6,
    dict. post c. 3, 100 n. 7, 103 nn. 13–14, 104 n. 17, 109 n. 25
Dist. 7,
    dict. ante c. 1, 104 n. 17
Dist. 8,
    dict. ante c. 1, 105, 106 n. 20
    c. 1, 106 n. 20, 219 n. 15, 221
    dict. post c. 1, 106–108, 110 n. 26, 116 n. 4
    c. 5, 201 n. 26
Dist. 9,
    dict. ante c. 1, 110 n. 26
    dict. post c. 11, 108–109, 116, 140 n. 13
Dist. 10,
    dict. ante c. 1, 54 n. 53, 110 n. 26, 215
    c. 1, 54 n. 53
    c. 3, 54 n. 53

dict. post c. 6, 54 n. 53, 215
    c. 7, 54 n. 53, 215
Dist. 11,
    dict. ante c. 1, 110 n. 26
Dist. 13,
    dict. ante c. 1, 110 n. 26
Dist. 14,
    dict. ante c. 1, 110 n. 26
    dict. post c. 1, 110 n. 26
Dist. 15,
    dict. ante c. 1, 110 n. 27
Dist. 16,
    dict. ante c. 1, 137 n. 6
    dict. post c. 4, 137 n. 6
    c. 8, 137 n. 6
    c. 12, 144 n. 22
    dict. post c. 12, 144 n. 22
Dist. 17,
    dict. ante c. 1, 137
    dict. post c. 6, 137 n. 7, 175 n. 29, 182–183 n. 43
Dist. 18,
    dict. ante c. 1, 137
Dist. 19,
    dict. ante c. 1, 138
    c. 1, 138 n. 9
    dict. post c. 7, 138
    dict. post c. 8, 138–139
    c. 9, 139
Dist. 20,
    dict. ante c. 1, 165–168, 169
Dist. 21,
    dict. ante c. 1, 72 n. 5, 73 n. 6, 176–177, 180, 185
    c. 1, 156
Dist. 22,
    dict. ante c. 1, 182
    c. 1, 55 n. 54, 58 n. 57
Dist. 23,
    c. 1, 174 n. 27, 205 n. 32
    dict. post c. 6, 93 n. 36, 157–158 n. 7
Dist. 25,
    c. 1, 175

Dist. 28,
dict. post c. 13, 175 n. 29
Dist. 36,
dict. post c. 2, 181 n. 38
Dist. 40,
c. 6, 183, 184
c. 8, 189 n. 4
Dist. 45,
dict. post c. 4, 86 n. 25
c. 5, 86 n. 25
dict. post c. 13, 86 n. 25, 134, 230 n. 39, 233 n. 44
Dist. 50,
dict. post c. 32, 90 n. 31
Dist. 51,
dict. ante c. 1, 75 n. 10
Dist. 61,
dict. post c. 11, 207 n. 39
c. 12, 207 n. 39
c. 13, 200 n. 22, 206 n. 37, 207
Dist. 62,
dict. ante c. 1, 189 n. 4, 200
c. 1, 200 n. 24
dict. post c. 2, 200 n. 24
Dist. 63,
dict. post c. 25, 194, 201, 202 n. 26, 207–08
c. 26, 200 n. 22, 207–210
c. 27, 205 n. 33, 207–210
dict. post c. 27, 202 n. 26, 208–209, 217
dict. post c. 28, 75 n. 10, 140, 152 n. 33, 194, 201 n. 26, 209, 217
dict. post c. 34, 203, 205 n. 32
c. 35, 203, 204–205, 210 n. 45
Dist. 70,
dict. ante c. 1, 196, 197
c. 2, 196 n. 16
Dist. 71, 197
Dist. 79,
c. 9, 218 n. 13
c. 10, 190 n. 5
dict. post c. 10, 182
Dist. 86,
dict. post c. 5, 175 n. 29
Dist. 93,
c. 24, 264

Dist. 95,
c. 1, 176 n. 31
cc. 2–3, 175
dict. post c. 3, 175
Dist. 96,
dict. ante c. 1, 55 n. 55
c. 9, 55 n. 55, 201 n. 26, 217 n. 9
c. 10, 55 n. 55, 201 n. 26, 217 n. 9
Dist. 97,
dict. ante c. 55 n. 55
C. 1, q. 1,
dict. post c. 16, 75 n. 10
dict. post c. 24, 91 n. 33
dict. post c. 39, 91–92 n. 34
dict. post c. 42, 91–92 n. 34, 125 n. 17, 162 n. 15
dict. post c. 43, 91 n. 34, 93 n. 38, 194, 197–198
dict. post c. 45, 92 n. 35
dict. post c. 53, 92 n. 35
dict. post c. 57, 92 n. 35
c. 72, 93 n. 36
dict. post c. 73, 94 n. 39
c. 74, 94 n. 39
dict. post c. 74, 92 n. 35
dict. post c. 95, 93 n. 36, 157–158 n. 7
dict. post c. 97, 92 n. 35, 93 n. 36, 173 n. 27
C. 1, q. 3,
c. 1, 201 n. 26
C. 1, q. 7,
dict. post c. 23, 75 n. 10
C. 2, q. 6,
dict. ante c. 1, 181
dict. post c. 10, 181
dict. post c. 31, 256–258
dict. post c. 33, 60 n. 61
C. 2, q. 7,
dict. post c. 39, 184
dict. post c. 41, 56 n. 56
C. 3, q. 1,
dict. post c. 6, 89 n. 29, 123 n. 16, 183 n. 43, 218
C. 3, q. 4,
dict. post c. 12, 75 n. 10, 88 n. 26

C. 6, q. 4, 181
C. 7, q. 1,
  c. 11, 75 n. 10
  c. 17, 190 n. 5
  c. 39, 75 n. 10
C. 8, q. 1,
  dict. ante c. 1, 190
  c. 3, 190 n. 5
  dict. post c. 7, 190, 193, 194, 201 n. 26
  c. 16, 191
  dict. post c. 17, 174 n. 27, 191–193
  c. 18, 192–193
C. 9, q. 2,
  dict. ante c. 1, 178–179 n. 35
  dict post c. 9, 179 n. 35, 197
  c. 10, 197
C. 9, q. 3,
  dict. ante c. 1, 178 nn. 34–35
  c. 8, 179 n. 36
  dict. post c. 9, 179, 181, 183 n. 43
C. 11,
  dict. principium, 218
C. 11, q. 1,
  dict. post c. 26, 218–219, 222
  dict. post c. 30, 60 n. 61, 219
  dict. post c. 31, 219–220
  c. 42, 148 n. 27
  dict. post c. 47, 220–221, 243
C. 11, q. 2,
  148 n. 27
C. 11, q. 3,
  dict. ante c. 1, 89 n. 29, 116 n. 5
  c. 1, 117
  cc. 2–5, 88 n. 26
  c. 7, 88 n. 26
  c. 9, 88 n. 26, 90 n. 32
  cc. 16–19, 88 n. 26
  c. 21, 88 n. 26
  dict. post c. 21, 89 n. 29, 90 n. 31
  c. 24, 88 n. 26, 90 nn. 31–32
  dict. post c. 24, 88 n. 26
  c. 26, 89 n. 29
  dict. post c. 26, 89 n. 29
  c. 27, 117
  c. 32, 88 n. 26

c. 33, 90 n. 32
dict. post c. 40, 118, 123 n. 16
dict. post c. 43, 118 n. 9
dict. post c. 64, 89 n. 29, 90 n. 30, 117, 118, 123 n. 16
dict. post c. 65, 119
dict. post c. 72, 119
dict. post c. 73, 119
dict. post c. 77, 119–120
dict. post c. 90, 121–122 n. 15
c. 99, 121–122 n. 15
dict. post c. 101, 121
c. 106, 90 n. 32
C. 12, q. 1,
  c. 7, 203 n. 29
  dict. post c. 25, 54 n. 52
C. 13, q. 1, 148 n. 27
C. 15, q. 6,
  dict. post c. 2, 216
  c. 3, 56 n. 55, 201 n. 26, 216–217
C. 15, q. 8,
  c. 5, 93 n. 36, 157–158 n. 7
C. 16, q. 1,
  dict. post c. 19, 53 n. 52, 170–172, 177 n. 34, 196–197
C. 16, q. 2,
  dict. post c. 7, 173 n. 27
  c. 8, 174 n. 27
C. 16, q. 6,
  dict. ante c. 1, 89 n. 29, 123 n. 16
C. 17, q. 3, 148 n. 27
C. 22, q. 3,
  89 n. 29, 123 n. 16, 148 n. 27
C. 22, q. 4,
  dict. post c. 23, 146 n. 25
C. 22, q. 5,
  dict. post c. 17, 216
  c. 18, 216
C. 23,
  dict. principium, 228–229
C. 23, q. 1,
  dict. ante c. 1, 229–230
  dict. post c. 1, 230
  dict. post c. 7, 230
C. 23, q. 3,
  dict. ante c. 1, 230